Managing Information and Systems

The management of information systems continues to be a pressing strategic issue for business. With the speed of change in technologies increasing at an ever-faster pace, it is more important than ever for managers to be able to assess their information needs and then identify the technology which meets that need, rather than starting with the technology and 'making it fit'.

Managing Information and Systems focuses throughout on the integrated understanding of the role of systems within the business – organisationally and strategically. It clearly demonstrates theory in practice by including international case studies and analysing examples taken from the business world. Topics covered are:

- the nature of organisations
- management roles and functions
- information as a resource
- systems approaches
- different information systems and what they can achieve
- structural and cultural fit and IS
- change management and IS
- strategic business and IS management

Combining readability with theoretical concepts, *Managing Information and Systems* is suitable for both advanced undergraduate and Masters students.

Adrienne Curry is Senior Lecturer in Management Science at the University of Stirling.
Peter Flett is Lecturer in Management Science at the University of Stirling.
Ivan Hollingsworth is an Information Systems Consultant.

Managing Information and Systems

The business perspective

Adrienne Curry, Peter Flett and
Ivan Hollingsworth

Routledge
Taylor & Francis Group

LONDON AND NEW YORK

For David, Philip, Nikki, Joy, Ryan and Niamh

First published 2006
by Routledge
2 Park Square, Milton Park, Abingdon, Oxon OX14 4RN

Simultaneously published in the USA and Canada
by Routledge
270 Madison Ave, New York, NY 10016

Routledge is an imprint of the Taylor & Francis Group

© 2006 Adrienne Curry, Peter Flett and Ivan Hollingsworth

Typeset in Baskerville by
Florence Production Ltd, Stoodleigh, Devon

Printed and bound in Great Britain by
TJ International Ltd, Padstow, Cornwall

British Library Cataloguing in Publication Data
A catalogue record for this book is available from the British Library

Library of Congress Cataloging in Publication Data
Curry, Adrienne.
  Managing information and systems: the business perspective/Adrienne
Curry, Peter Flett, and Ivan Hollingsworth. – 1st ed.
      p. cm.
    Includes bibliographical references and index.
  Information technology – Management. 2. Management. 3. Information
  technology – Economic aspects – Case studies. I. Flett, Peter.
  II. Hollingsworth, Ivan   III. Title.
  HD30.2.C878 2005
  658.4′038′011–dc22   2004030871

ISBN10: 0–415–35586–9 (hbk)
ISBN10: 0–415–35587–7 (pbk)

ISBN13: 9–78–0–415–35586–5 (hbk)
ISBN13: 9–78–0–415–35587–2 (pbk)

Contents

Illustrations

···

Figures

Tables

Abbreviations

....

BPR	Business Process Re-engineering		FMS	Flexible Manufacturing Systems
CAD	Computer Aided Design		GDSS	Group Decision Support Systems
CAM	Computer Aided Manufacturing		GST	General Systems Theory
CBIS	Computer Based Information Systems		HRM	Human Resource Management
CIM	Computer Integrated Manufacturing		ICT	Information Communication Technologies
CIS	Customer Information System		IS	Information Systems
CMA	Cash Management Account		MIS	Management Information Systems
CNC	Computer Numerical Control		MRP	Materials Requirements Planning
CRM	Customer Relationship Management		MRS	Management Reporting Systems
			NAFTA	North American Free Trade Agreement
CSF	Critical Success Factors		NC	Numerical Control
DBMS	Database Management Systems		OS	Office Systems
DP	Data Processing		PCS	Process Control Systems
DSS	Decision Support Systems		PFI	Public Finance Initiatives
EDI	Electronic Data Interchange		SBU	Strategic Business Unit
EIS	Executive Information Systems		SIS	Strategic Information Systems
ERP	Enterprise Resource Planning		SSM	Soft Systems Methodology
ES	Expert Systems		TPS	Transaction Processing Systems
EU	European Union		TQM	Total Quality Management

Chapter 1

Introduction

....

Introduction

Business and the environment in which it is conducted have changed dramatically over time and will continue to evolve. These changes have engendered new pressures and challenges for the management of information, information systems and information technology, from which a variety of benefits are potentially to be realised. Trends in business have dictated new roles for information and information systems, creating opportunities but also complexities. As we are now in the 'information age' it is important to understand what that means and what has shaped the processes that exist today. Data and information (there is a difference that we will define later) and the Information Systems that manipulate them are in essence a tool; a powerful and complex tool but nonetheless they are in place primarily to enhance business and organisational effectiveness. Prior to examining how effective Information Systems can be we must first outline the environments in which they are used.

The nature of modern business

The world of business is dynamic and forever changing to meet new challenges and opportunities. This is nothing new. Since the Industrial Revolution over 200 years ago business organi-sations have had to change with circumstances. The main difference between then and now is that the speed of such change is now signifi-cantly quicker. Even in the last 50 years there have been major changes in the business environment. More recently the advent of the Internet and mobile phones has created a num-ber of opportunities and challenges. Typically these technologies have been grouped under the generic term of Information Communi-cation Technologies (ICT) which encompasses the increasingly convergent areas of information technology and telephone communications. While there is a lot of hyperbole associated with areas of ICT it does engender change, which in itself has to be managed to create positive outcomes for organisational effectiveness.

Trends in modern business

Increasing levels of competition

One change has been in the level of competi-tion faced by organisations today. This has resulted from increases in population, levels of automation and demand for products and services by an increasingly affluent society. This has made it possible for more and more organisations to seek opportunities to compete for greater market share.

Improvements in transport have also made it possible for organisations to compete beyond their local area. Indeed many organisations not only compete nationally but also internationally, pitting their skills against organisations from other countries, or even other continents.

The role of technology in levelling the playing field in terms of competitiveness is apparent in a number of areas.

The internationalisation of business

Business in general has become increasingly international in nature, with organisations competing in an international marketplace. Of course this means that, as well as competing in overseas markets, organisations have to cope with overseas competitors entering their own domestic markets. Organisations not only compete in overseas markets, they also source materials and labour from outside their own countries. Interfaces between nations are expanding, with trade, capital and goods flowing from one country into another with fewer restrictions. This situation has been aided by the increase in international trade groupings such as the European Union (EU) and North American Free Trade Agreement (NAFTA), and by the disparity between costs of material and especially labour in different countries.

The advent of globalisation has given organisations the opportunity to exploit such economic differentials between nations. For example, the garment and clothing industry moving operations to the Far East to take advantage of cheaper labour in what is still a labour-intensive industry. This trend is not limited to traditional products such as clothing. A number of Western European software companies have sub-contracted programming work to the Indian sub-continent. Similarly, more recently, the mobile communications and technologies industry has relocated its call centres to the Indian sub-continent.

Increasing cooperation

Despite the increased levels of competition, modern business organisations also cooperate more closely than in the past. This is sometimes to take advantage of economies of scale, or to avoid duplication of resources. For example, banks have cooperated to provide customer services, such as national and international automated-teller networks, which would be prohibitively expensive for banks to provide individually.

However, much of today's cooperation has resulted from the increasing diversity of business. Many organisations are now very specialised and rely on cooperation with organisations specialising in other related fields in order to function as a business. For example, many manufacturing organisations do not own their own means of delivering their product. Instead, they rely on specialist haulage or distribution firms to handle this for them. They may also rely on a variety of consultants to advise on or manage specialist functions such as advertising, recruitment and even product design. In the public sector quality initiatives like the Best Value agenda have promoted cooperation with the private sector and the voluntary sector to strive for more effective delivery of services. Public Private Partnerships (previously known as PFI – Public Finance Initiatives) have been employed to undertake high cost, high value construction projects, such as the Skye Bridge and the new Edinburgh Royal Infirmary. The denationalisation of the rail infrastructure in the UK has seen the wholesale transfer of rail networks and train companies to the private sector with mixed results.

The need to cut costs and rationalise on labour in addition to the joining of symbiotic businesses has led to increasing numbers of organisational mergers from large-scale international oil companies like BP and Amoco to charitable institutions. In the UK two charitable institutions, The Cancer Research Campaign and Imperial Cancer Research Fund, merged to form Cancer Research UK in 2002. The merger was driven by scientists who believed that the pooling of funds would increase the chance of finding a cure for cancer (Hill, 2001).

A turbulent environment

There is also an increasing trend towards customer/consumer orientation, the need to fulfil ever-spiralling expectations in terms of rapid response and value for money. In the face of rapid changes, organisations must defend themselves against threats and take maximum early advantage of innovative opportunities. On the one hand is the need to cope with deregulation, increased flexibility and greater opportunity for diversification (e.g. financial services), on the other stands increasing regulation in terms of legislation and statutory requirements (e.g. EU Directives, Environmental Protection Act), security for consumers and bureaucracy. Business and organisations have to cope with continuous change.

Changes in organisational structures

As the quantity and speed of information availability to managers increases, so the flow of information must become increasingly selective. The ability to collect, collate, filter and disseminate information is crucial, yet making sure it is relevant is even more important. Information overload can negate the effectiveness of communications applications such as email.

The rate at which information moves and decisions are made is speeding up, partly as a result of the need for a greater degree of responsiveness and partly because of increased flexibility in the way work is carried out. The last two decades have seen new structures emerging, often flatter and more decentralised, in response to greater devolution of responsibility

or empowerment. With flatter structures come more pressure and the imperative to harness any technology available to ease this load.

The way work is done

Production tasks have been increasingly automated and processes can be more accurately controlled. The advent of enterprise resource planning systems that support global enterprises has led to higher quality goods and services at lower cost.

Work can be coordinated by means of networking and communication systems that effectively eliminate time and distance restrictions. Teamwork is more widespread with organisational data, information and skills being more extensively shared and exchanged. Boundaries of organisations are becoming less clearly defined as to where work is done, when and by whom. Networks have enabled information to be available at any time, anywhere and lead times in supply and delivery to be significantly eroded.

As a result of automation, more information is yielded as a by-product. Often, new skills and new ways of thinking need to accompany the use of new information tools. Furthermore, a primary source of basic information may yield secondary information (e.g. sales figures revealing buying patterns and trend information on customer preferences, patient morbidity dependant on demographics and socioeconomic group).

The changing role of information

It is somewhat more difficult to quantify information as a resource, as opposed to other business resources such as money, machinery, time and people. Information is intangible and its value is subjective, yet it is essential to the successful running of organisations. In particular the move away from reactive recording to proactive planning to create enhanced products and services, which can be used to create a strategic advantage. The efficient and effective collection, storage, processing and communication of information all present important windows of opportunity. To achieve this managers need to be more efficiently and effectively informed to make the right kinds of decision to take their organisations forward.

As the business environment and the ways organisations operate constantly evolve, there is a consequent increase in information needs. At an executive level there is a constant need for real-time management information from both internal and external sources. Senior management has to be able to respond rapidly to tactical needs of the organisation and be in an informed position to undertake strategic planning, which is vital to future corporate success. Careful screening and reduction of information to senior management is essential to avoid information overload, which is a contributor to clouded and inadequate decision-making. The role of the 'executive summary' is as crucial as ever!

With the increasingly important role of information as a corporate resource, comes the need to maintain the security and integrity of information. Significant losses of information or information-processing capabilities can seriously damage the competitive or financial position of an organisation.

There is evidence to suggest that improved information centralises power and decision-making in the organisational hierarchy, thereby reducing considerably the discretion of middle managers needing to conform to standardised procedures. Furthermore, centralisation tends also to catalyse the merging of departments and bring about a simplification of the organisational structure.

Conversely, increasing information availability and communication can produce decentralised management decision-making. Devolved decision-making can be easily monitored by senior management, but organisations can also become more differentiated and therefore complex from a structural viewpoint.

Increased access to and availability of information by means of automation do not necessarily alter the distribution of organisational authority and control. CBIS (Computer-Based Information Systems) tend to reinforce organisational structures in existence, though centralisation is often more the resulting trend than decentralisation. Variables worthy of consideration include organisational size, type of industry, extent of task routinisation, organisational culture, the extent to which staff behave independently as professionals and the patterns of information usage and information flow.

The changing role of information affects social relationships within organisations and relationships between organisations and their external environment, particularly with the public at large who may well find themselves interacting more and more directly with information and information systems than through human intermediaries (e.g. automated teller machines in banks, automated check-in systems in airports, online educational material).

Information as a product

Information is now seen more as a product in its own right and companies compete on the basis of the quality of the information product that they offer. Marketing efforts have to go beyond merely offering 'junk mail' promotions in an ad hoc way. Information customers receive needs to be much more tailored to their individual needs. The filtering of appropriate information will elicit a more positive response, whether this information is electronic or in paper form. The gathering of data through a myriad of different channels, e.g. bank cards, store loyalty cards, bills, viewing habits, etc., all contribute to the formulation of strategies that aim to enhance competitiveness in the business environment. The role of Customer Relationship Management (CRM) can now be exploited as technology has made it possible to apply customisation to large mass markets. While the promise of the Internet has not been without a number of false dawns, the establishment of organisational websites is, of course, an ever-increasing example of information as a product and as a competitive weapon.

The changing role of information systems in organisations

Changes in information technology

One of the major factors (if not *the* major factor) for the increasing importance of information is the advances in technology available to process information quickly and effectively. The three strands of information technology – office equipment, computers and telecommunications – have all seen significant progress over the last 30–40 years. Not only have they progressed, but they have also converged; mobile phones with integrated cameras and personal organisers, intelligent fridges, dishwashers, the list is continually expanding. Whether this provides more effectiveness to the users is often debatable and the realisation of the effectiveness of technological innovation can take a considerable time to come to fruition. Typewriters and dedicated electronic word processors have been replaced by personal computers, while public and private telecommunications networks are increasingly based on digital technology. The digital revolution is actually starting to change markets, affect people's behaviour, work, social and cultural practices, and influence the way in which we live our lives.

The first practical computers were developed during the Second World War in the UK, America and Germany. Intended for military use, these computers were mainly used for ballistics calculations. Not long after this, in 1951, J. Lyons & Company in the UK implemented the first commercial application of computers. Since those early days computer technology has improved by leaps and bounds.

Since the advent of the modern computer there have been four consistent trends:

1 a reduction in the purchase price of computer systems, bringing them within the buying power of smaller organisations and individuals;
2 a reduction in the size of computers, requiring less space to be dedicated to storing them;
3 the increasing power and capacity for work provided by computers;
4 a reduction in the cost of ownership and use of computer systems.

These trends have been supported by several factors:

• the progress made by computer manufacturers in improving their products;
• the increasing availability of relatively cheap packaged software covering the needs of a wide variety of business functions;
• the increasing availability of skilled personnel, reducing the cost of staffing computer system operation and development.

The end result of all this progress is computer technology which has greater flexibility and increased user friendliness, with a decrease in the technical knowledge required to install and use the technology. Indeed, at the smaller end of the market, IT products have arguably reached the usability of 'white' consumer goods, i.e. fridges, televisions, etc., where the user simply has to plug them in and switch them on in order to be able to use them. Paradoxically, in the case of PC's, the increase in user friendliness can lead to reluctance to actually learn the full capabilities of the technology which hinders the gaining of efficiencies.

The three eras of information systems

The role that Information Technology, and more especially computer-based technology, has played in organisations has changed significantly with the changes in technology. Somogyi and Galliers (1987) place these developments in three eras.

Early commercial computing was used in the main to automate the routine clerical tasks of large administrative departments, using economies of scale in processing to reduce costs. Large centralised data processing (DP) installations operated remotely from their users and the business, resulting in user frustration and dissatisfaction as a result of too little flexibility and too much cumbersome formality. Data processing systems had the potential to change organisations, but their limitations were too great: remote, batch processing systems that were out of touch with the real-world business situation.

The advent of personal computers helped to reduce the scale of processing to more responsive, online systems, accompanied by the need to reduce processing complexity to manageable units. Management also needed to cross-relate and cross-reference data from operational processes in order to produce more coherent information and improve control, with the result that data management systems emerged to analyse and store data and provide better data accessibility.

Databases and data structuring reflect organisational interrelationships. It was necessary to consider the pertinence of certain data over others, which data would enhance organisational efficiency and who would need access to which data. Management needed information for planning, control and decision-making by aggregating and transforming data, i.e. via management information systems in automated form, providing reports and other structured information flows for middle managers. There had to then emerge the focus of meeting management information needs rather than data or information management alone.

The main task for IS (information systems) departments then moved in the 1980s to that of making information available in different forms and between different places via telecommunications. More systems were being developed by or in conjunction with users. DP professionals became advisers, supporters, facilitators. There was also the growing realisation that technology itself cannot solve problems, but the impact of technological change depends on how and why the technology is used. Technological choices needed evaluating in the business context using a planned approach. System strategy and strategic planning for IS became more familiar, as did the notion that systems could change the nature of business, the competition and the organisation's competitive position. The role of IS emerged as a strategic one with a corresponding need to connect the business strategy and the IS strategy to attain the best outcomes.

The three-era model

Although the model essentially plots the changing role and use of IS over time, it is perhaps more worthwhile in this context to concentrate on the different roles and their interdependence. Figure 1.1 shows the reasons for moving through the IS evolutionary model.

Data processing (DP) and management information systems (MIS) are basically subsets of strategic information systems (SIS) and each stage of the three-era model relies on the accuracy of information provided by the previous

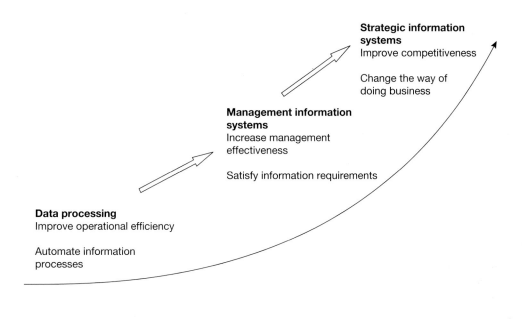

Strategic information systems
Improve competitiveness

Change the way of doing business

Management information systems
Increase management effectiveness

Satisfy information requirements

Data processing
Improve operational efficiency

Automate information processes

Figure 1.1 The IS evolutionary model

stage. In other words, good operational DP systems need to provide timely, accurate, up-to-date information to the MIS. Strategic IS may put a strain on DP and MIS, which may need to be redeveloped or more finely tuned to enable maximised benefits to the organisation as a result of strategic use of IS.

Early commercial computers were used mainly to automate the routine clerical work of large administrative departments, providing economies of scale for administrative processing. Typical systems developed in the early DP era were payroll and general ledger systems, which were essentially integrated versions of well-defined clerical processes. Such systems were often developed with little regard to other, possibly related, systems and there was consequent fragmentation with duplication of inter-related data. Most early development methods concentrated on perfecting the processes performed by the machine, putting less emphasis on data and giving little thought to the users of

the system. However, as more and more routine company operations became supported by computer systems, the need for a more flexible and coherent approach arose. The focus of attention shifted to the data itself and it became important to de-couple data from the basic processes so that it could then be used for management information. Independent data management systems were needed, as was accurate information for decision-making.

Corporate databases became the vehicle for the MIS era but a number of difficulties presented themselves in the form of data analysis and database design becoming rapidly obsolete in the face of the ever-changing business environment. Keen and Scott-Morton (1978) pointed out that the MIS function was more focused on information management than on management information. In other words, the concentration on data management precluded real preoccupation with meeting management information needs. Sprague and Carlson (1982) noted further that the MIS era contributed to a new level of information to serve management needs but was still focused and built upon information flows and data files. By the early 1980s computing had become much more distributed with personal computers existing alongside large data processing facilities. The major task was to make information available and maintain systems integrity. The problems of interconnecting and exchanging information in different forms and locations focused increased interest in telecommunications. Systems were being more closely controlled by users and data processing professionals began to assume the role of advisors, supporters and helpers.

As progression from one era to the next occurred there emerged the growing realisation that technology cannot solve problems and that technological choices have to be made in the context of business and organisational requirements. This necessitated a more planned approach in the form of strategic information systems planning. There ensued at the same time a realisation that technology could not only provide improved efficiency and effectiveness but also competitive advantage. By the mid-1980s this new strategic role of IS emerged. Systems had the potential to change the nature of business and the focus was on connecting the business strategy with the IS strategy.

Since these three eras of IS, extensive further developments have occurred in networking and data communications, image processing, multimedia applications and electronic commerce.

The changing view of IS/IT management

Information and IS/IT (information systems/information technology) management is changing and both IS/IT and business managers have to change with it. There have been problems in the past with IS/IT specialists having too much of an 'ivory tower' existence, behaving like a species apart and being singularly unable to understand the business of which they are supposed to be a part, to communicate with their business colleagues in other functions and deliver cost-effective systems. Investment in information systems frequently used to come about as an act of faith and still does if the proper rationale for their implementation is not created.

Many organisations have invested heavily in information systems where money has been spent and benefits have either not been forthcoming or been reaped. Senior managers have changed their attitude to IS/IT; investments in systems must be justifiable and information systems need to be profitable or potentially profitable. There immediately arises the issue of how to evaluate systems, particularly managerial applications where value to the business may well manifest itself indirectly (e.g. in the form of increased customer satisfaction), rather than in labour savings or capital productivity.

There still remains the danger of IS/IT management being interpreted in a 'cut and dried' sort of way. There are no infallible solutions, models or approaches, and approaches to strategic planning, such as those proposed in Chapter 8 of this book, are intended as guidelines only. Any theoretical model can merely assist, but ultimately cannot decide. What is an essential component of IS/IT management is the ability to think creatively and seek out innovative solutions to problems rather than remain constrained by techniques and technicalities. IS/IT has to be seen as an integrated part of business functioning, not as a specialised subsystem of the organisation which is far too remote and difficult to understand for the majority of staff. Business managers must comprehend and be involved in the IS/IT activities of the business and conversely IS/IT managers must be fully conversant with the complete spectrum of business requirements. In its approach and structure this book intends to address just this very central issue. Rather than concentrating on the minutiae of technological specifications, the focus is firmly on information and IS/IT management, which has to be wholeheartedly tackled and conquered if the future of it is to be anything other than bleak.

Skills required by IS/IT managers

MIS skills for the 1990s were identified by Leitheiser (1992) in a survey of MIS managers.

Feeny and Willcocks (1998) identified nine core IS capabilities required to underpin the pursuit of high-value-added IT applications and to capitalise on the external market's ability to deliver cost-effective IT services:

- *Integrating IS/IT effort with business purpose and activity* effective IS/IT leaders devise the organisational structures, processes and staffing to address each challenge area and to manage their interdependencies.
- *Envisioning the business process that technology makes possible* business systems thinking that understands connections and interdependencies in business activity with the potential for new organisational patterns.
- *Getting the business constructively engaged in IS/IT issues* relationship building, developing users' understanding of IT potential, helping users and IT specialists to work together and ensuring users' ownership and satisfaction.
- *Creating the coherent blueprint for a technical architecture that responds to current and future business needs* architecture planners develop the technical vision and formulate associated policies that ensure necessary integration and flexibility in IS services, the basis for shared IT services across the organisation.
- *Rapidly achieving technical progress* in the overlap between the challenges of architec-

ture design and delivery of IS services lies the core capability of making technology work, requiring planning insight, troubleshooting problems and dealing pragmatically with different complexities.
- *Managing the IS/IT sourcing strategy that meets the interests of the business* informed buying that involves analysing the external market for IS/IT services, selecting a sourcing strategy to meet business and technological requirements and leading the tendering, contracting and service management processes.
- *Ensuring the success of existing contracts for IS/IT services* prompt and fair conflict and problem resolution for users who receive services from multiple supply points within a framework of agreements and relationships.
- *Protecting the business's contractual position, current and future* effective contract monitoring means holding suppliers to account on both existing service contracts and the developing performance standards of the services market.
- *Identifying the potential added value of IS/IT service suppliers* IS/IT outsourcing requires considerable effort over time and the management of switching costs.

Skills required to achieve the core IS capabilities are a combination of technical, business and interpersonal skills.

In their guidelines for IS/IT managers who are trying to respond to business and technological changes, assume new roles and build relationships, Rockart *et al.* (1996) discuss the following eight imperatives for IS/IT management:

1 Align IS/IT strategy with the business strategy.
2 Develop effective relationships with line management.
3 Deliver and implement new systems.

4 Build and manage the IS/IT infrastructure.

5 Reskill staff beyond technological skills to business skills.

6 Manage vendor partnerships to compensate for skill shortages and relieve management of the need to oversee tasks that are not competitive strengths or core competencies.

7 Build high performance to meet increasingly demanding performance goals and improve the organisation's financial and operational track record.

8 Redesign and manage the positioning of the IS/IT resource, obtain the right balance of centralisation and decentralisation and the right distribution of managerial responsibilities. This should allow for significant autonomy at the local level in business organisations with sufficient capability for organisation-wide planning, resource allocation, centralised purchasing and technological research and development.

IS/IT managers of the future must address the dual demands of improving IS/IT services, while increasing the impact of those services on the organisation's bottom line. IS/IT resources will be aimed at the organisation's strategic needs and will be critical to the firm's operations, and IS/IT managers will need to possess greater expertise in both technology and business processes (Bassellier *et al.*, 2001).

To move on a step from here it is worthwhile examining the impacts of IS/IT both past and present and then to focus attention on benefits both real and potential which can and will make a significant difference.

Impacts of IS/IT

The impacts of IS/IT can be assessed at the societal, organisational and individual levels of activity. From the perspective of societal impacts, the issues of employment, quality of working life and increasing the nation's com-

petitive advantage need to be considered. From the organisational perspective, issues of restructuring, coping with increasing complexity, organisational change, resistance to change and job satisfaction are worthy of attention.

The transition from an industrial to an information society involves a restructuring of infrastructure and coping with a much more rapid transition pace than that involved in passing from an agricultural to an industrial society.

An issue at the forefront of societal considerations is that of employment. The two essential views are either that with the continued spread and penetration of IS/IT more and more jobs will be lost, or that in the longer term more new jobs will be created by IS/IT than were previously lost. The stimulation of economic demand will therefore counteract the tendency towards workforce shrinkage. The nature of work has also changed with remote working or networking being much more widespread, resulting in new configurations or patterns of working life. Communications have improved, productivity has increased and jobs have been enriched or altered.

Economic considerations revolve largely around the issue of competition and competitiveness, which rely upon innovation and the ability to innovate. Organisations have to be capable of managing the application of new technology in addition to introducing new products based on existing technology to respond adequately to market needs.

At the organisational level comes the clear requirement to match IS/IT with corporate/business unit needs. The reality is often one of political considerations influencing the choice of information systems, with resulting inconsistencies and inadequacies. The development of small, departmental systems may be able to evade the political agenda. Not so the development of large corporate systems spanning interfaces between a number of departments, which requires considerable negotiation skills on the part of IS/IT specialists. It is perhaps no surprise that there is a rise in the adoption of large-scale rationalised IT systems implemented by outside vendors that impose strictures on what departments can do on their own.

IS/IT has become much more the concern of senior management in the design and implementation of corporate strategies. Misalignment of IS/IT with corporate strategy can seriously damage a firm's ability to compete. Systems incompatibilities can result in production and service inflexibilities that can be a source of considerable managerial concern and frequent frustrations of different kinds.

Impacts of IS/IT have been felt in managerial structure, roles and processes, leading to organisational restructuring with the elimination of middle management and senior managers taking more of an active role in planning, controlling and business innovation. The organisation has in some cases become a 'collective entrepreneurship', encompassing teamwork and more ad hoc decision-making structures, with technology as the enabler, particularly from the perspective of electronic communications. Moving a step further, the impact that disintegrates the organisation, focusing not on how tasks are carried out, but on how the flows of goods and services are organised through value-added chains.

For managers has come the urgent need to manage interdependencies across functions and activities of various kinds, and the role of IS/IT as integrator is central. Changes in cross-functional integration, in the use of teams or integration within individual functions are compelling managers to manage increasing interdependence more efficiently and effectively than ever before. The manager's job is becoming more difficult as the rate of organisational change gathers pace and more complex with

the need to cope with less clear lines of authority and decision-making. More space- and time-spanning teamwork and problem-solving task teams all require new management skills and role definitions. New planning processes are emerging with IS/IT as organisations must identify key issues and react to them much more quickly than before. New measurement systems are evolving and are often out of step with organisational reality at the time. A clear example of this exists in the health care environment, where quantitative measures of performance do not lead to improved quality of services and where IT is far from being the integrative tool it could be. All in all, the creation of an effective IS/IT infrastructure involving accessible, well-defined data and clear networks is essential to effective integration in the future.

At the individual level IS/IT impacts upon user expectations and satisfaction, work attitudes, productivity and the organisational climate. Implementation of IS/IT can have considerable behavioural and psychological effects, which must not be underestimated. Resistance to changes of various kinds is a standard psychological response to negative perceptions at the onset, particularly if staff feel a threat of redundancy or devaluation of their job remit. Systems development has to be seen as part of a social process; productivity gains as a result of IS/IT implementation may otherwise be outweighed by loss of organisational well-being, of quality of working life. Deskilling is an impact of IS/IT that cannot be ignored, not only of clerical staff, but also of middle management.

The impacts of IS/IT have been both positive and negative at varying business levels, within and between organisations. The 1980s and 1990s have provided a number of opportunities for organisational learning, lessons which must be taken on board for future reference. The twenty-first century needs to witness a maximising of IS/IT benefits as a result of closer understanding and integration of IS/IT and other business functions.

Increasing the benefits of IS/IT

Whatever happens in the future, it will be necessary for information systems to deliver real business benefits in order to be seen to be commercially viable. Identifying, managing and measuring IS/IT benefits are, however, issues that tend to be avoided because of the perceived difficulties in measuring and assessing. Precise measures used will depend on the nature of the business, but generic benefits tend to be the following:

- efficiency systems that yield cost savings;
- effectiveness systems that provide a good return on assets/resources (e.g. people, materials);
- strategic systems that provide competitive advantage and contribute to increasing profitability.

The move from efficiency to strategic systems is an appropriate and essential development over time, but the capability of making sound financial estimates has decreased. Strategic benefits will inevitably be more varied, more complex and hence more difficult to measure than the hard benefits to be gained from efficiency systems. Efficiency systems, focusing on cost reduction, obtaining the same or more from fewer resources, can be relatively easily managed and the results measured. Effectiveness systems are aimed at providing better information for management decision-making, leading to improved performance and profitability. These systems embrace a wider variety of business issues, including personnel, production and marketing, and are therefore more difficult to measure. A detailed understanding of how the organisation works and

how it uses information is necessary to measure the performance of such systems, which are aimed at changing the way the company does business, at re-engineering or reconfiguring the business. At this point the role of information systems as strategic comes into focus. Considering the size of some IS/IT investments and their life spans, it is often necessary for management to take a long-range view of potential benefits to the company, rather than taking a short-range view of quarterly profit figures. All too often managers responsible for IS/IT have had difficulty in justifying the apparently high costs of IS/IT in comparison to other organisational costs.

Looking at cost reduction and the delivery of benefits is one part of the complex picture. The conditions for successful application and development of IS/IT must be carefully selected. Certain combinations of strategic positioning, organisational structure and IS/IT application appear to guarantee performance disasters. Appropriate actions need to be taken in the right sequence with the right amount of business judgement.

Reducing IS/IT costs and delivering benefits cannot be sustained in the longer term without positive relationships between IS/IT staff and the end users of the systems. Internal partnerships, supported and encouraged by senior management, need to be developed in organisations. Change of any kind is driven from the top so that risky consequences, obstacles and resistance can be controlled and overcome. IS/IT managers need to be more proactive in forging alliances with other business managers, who in turn must be more receptive to the development and implementation of new technologies. The importance of relationships between IS/IT specialists, users and organisational senior managers cannot be understated if IS/IT benefits are to be maximised in the future.

Without this type of cooperation and collaboration, misunderstandings are more likely to arise and the organisational culture will remain disunified. A common language relating to business and competitive advantage needs to emerge that is not confined to technological 'guruspeak'. The absence of organisational partnerships has all too often in past experience been at the root of the sub-optimisation of IS/IT (see Curry and Moore, 2003). When it comes to developing strategic systems in particular, the involvement of senior management is essential to ensure that the players in the game are not diverting their efforts away from strategic organisational goals and that business and IS/IT strategic alignment is maintained at all stages of development. Furthermore, senior management need to be involved in order to endorse what may be considerable investment of funds and other organisational resources.

Developing internal partnerships can, however, be extremely difficult in practice and three major challenges have to be faced:

1 Repositioning the IS/IT function from its traditional support role to one of playing a key part in the core business.
2 Creating a corporate-wide culture focusing on harmonising the diverse objectives of different parts of the organisation, as evidenced in the application of the organisation's IS/IT. Both the harmonisation and the changing of corporate culture are notoriously difficult to accomplish and need very careful handling.
3 Stimulating senior management to take a real interest in organisational IS/IT matters. Again there are considerable difficulties here to be overcome as senior managers often would prefer to ignore IS/IT or not become involved for fear of inadequate skills and know-how. Often the situation is opened up when senior managers perceive change to be absolutely essential and unavoidable.

A further issue worth considering is that of ownership. If systems are to improve efficiency, effectiveness or create a strategic advantage, they must be owned by individuals or departments attempting to bring about the benefits. There must also be clear responsibilities allocated to those driving the realisation of identified potential benefits. Information systems need to be evaluated, developed, maintained and audited by direct users rather than remote specialists with little in the way of vested interest in their success. Imposition of systems upon users has been identified as a clear reason for systems failure in the past. Motivation to use an information system as a business tool is crucial to success. Failure to use a system, abandoning a system or using it badly may all result in considerable financial losses.

Systems ownership starts early in the IS development life cycle when future users can make suggestions and be a valuable information source at the analysis and design stages of IS development. Likewise, users have to evaluate the success of systems and whether or not they warrant further development and hence additional funding.

Partnership and ownership issues with respect to IS/IT management are fundamental concerns if corporate financial performance is regarded as critical.

There has been growing dissatisfaction with IS/IT management in many organisations, but this must be considered in the context of leading models of excellent management which have performed well in the past, but have subsequently fallen from grace. Well-established business paradigms are not necessarily applicable to the twenty-first century, and there abounds a considerable lack of understanding as to what is required to produce sustainable corporate performance. Management and organisational functions can no longer be confined to their own specialist areas, but must be outward-looking and collaborative. Organisations must be constantly in touch with the marketplace and their competitors. The pace of change is phenomenal. The future role of people in information-based organisations is indeed that of everyone taking information responsibility (Drucker, 1993).

The development of CBIS (Computer-Based Information Systems) use in organisations

Looking at trends in technology and its potential use tells us about what is possible for organisations in general, but very little about individual organisations and how their use of CBIS evolves. There are three elements of CBIS use worth looking at here:

- the business areas targeted for CBIS use;
- the level of importance of CBIS in terms of the reliance of the organisation on CBIS and their spread throughout the organisation;
- the approach to managing CBIS within the organisation.

Targets for CBIS use

The success of CBIS in creating highly efficient supply chains in the fast-moving consumer goods sector has established an imperative for the use of IS/IT in creating operational advantage. With renewed attention needing to be focused on manufacturing as a competitive weapon and optimisation of available resources, the new challenge emerged of trying to make the best use possible of flexible automation systems.

Stages of manufacturing automation have led to the problem of how to integrate the relevant information systems to provide computer integrated manufacturing (CIM).

Mechanisation was the earliest stage of automation and focused principally on the replacement of human labour with machines, resulting sometimes in the optimisation of sub-systems at the expense of the system as a whole (see Chapter 4 for more detail on systems and subsystems).

Point automation was concerned with replacing human supervision, control and operation of machines with numerical control (NC) machines and later computer numerical control (CNC) machines. Consequently, the machinery could be programmed with the operator merely needing to feed in material and remove finished product.

Islands of automation saw the expansion of areas of point automation to encompass related or supporting functions, thereby producing islands of integrated automation (e.g. MRP – materials requirements planning systems; FMS – flexible manufacturing systems).

Computer integrated manufacturing (CIM) finally links the islands of automation to provide a company-wide integrated approach to manufacturing automation. Conditions under which CIM can be implemented are:

- definition of each product and its manufacturing process;
- definition of how all organisational processes interlink to support manufacturing;
- an appropriate manufacturing operation;
- organisational ability to cope with integrated automation;
- access to the appropriate automation technology in terms of function and cost.

There are indications that CIM systems can save time in product development and the production cycle, reduce consumption of raw materials, lower work-in-progress and finished goods inventory, generate less scrap and rework, create higher quality output and increased productivity. The real challenge, however, lies not so much in the design, but in the implementation of CIM systems, i.e. how best to integrate centralised and decentralised databases and linking communication to protect and strengthen the organisation's competitive advantage. What is more, computerised subsystems and databases can inevitably be integrated in a variety of different ways (e.g. accounting with order entry, purchasing and inventory). The integration of information systems in manufacturing and across organisational functions is of considerable importance. Intended integration could concern the following:

- internal administrative systems (e.g. accounting, human resources, purchasing, inventory);
- internal technical control systems (e.g. process control, shop floor control, quality control);
- market oriented administrative systems (e.g. sales forecasting, order entry, distribution);
- technical systems linking manufacturing to design, engineering and customers (e.g. CAD, CAM systems).

Enterprise Resource Planning (ERP) Systems aim to integrate all critical information into one single information database. The roots of ERP can be traced to MRP systems and were designed to include more of the supply chain rather than concentrating on the planning of internal resources alone. ERP systems are configurable information systems packages that integrate information and information-based processes within and across functional areas in an organisation (Tarn *et al.*, 2002). They serve to provide support for core organisational activities such as manufacturing and logistics, finance and accounting, sales and marketing and human resources. An ERP system helps the different parts of the organisation share data and knowledge, reduce costs and improve management of business processes. Practical and immediate concerns of the late 1990s, such as the Year 2000 problem and the introduction of the Euro, have further stimulated the market for ERP solutions and the last five years have seen an explosion of the implementation of ERP systems. Issues in ERP systems success and failure have been detailed by Markus *et al.* (2000) and Aladwani (2001).

As for service industries, there has been and still is a considerable amount of debate with respect to use of IS/IT and related impact upon productivity. It has been clear that service industries (e.g. banks) have invested heavily in IT and been unable to quantify subsequent benefits whether tangible or intangible. Furthermore, the development of high-cost IT infrastructures transferred the service sector's cost structure to one of less flexible fixed costs instead of variable labour costs.

However, what some service industries have done has been to transfer some operational costs to the customer by involving customers directly in those operations (e.g. ATMs in banks and self-service petrol stations). For the most part, customers are willing to use technology themselves as part of the service delivery process if there are positive benefits to be gained in the form of improved access and saving time.

The difficulty of looking at productivity in the service sector is that it may by no means be the sole priority. There is no doubt that financial services, for example, have had to rely on information technology to handle huge volumes of small detail much more quickly and thereby provide a more responsive service to customers. The concept of service value additionality is highly relevant with the increasing need to provide enriched services, encompassing greater quality, reliability, convenience, timeliness, safety, courtesy, sincerity, flexibility and variety. The central issue lies much more with understanding the capability of IS/IT to improve overall service performance to encourage greater customer loyalty, confidence and goodwill. After all, we are nowadays accustomed to making complex travel arrangements shortly prior to departure, being able to withdraw cash instantly from a variety of global locations and finding well-stocked supermarket shelves every day of the week!

Customer Relationship Management CRM Systems are a relatively new genre of computer-based applications, where the concern is to improve the selling and revenue generation processes of an organisation. The process of CRM is designed to collect data related to customers, analyse customer features and apply these qualities to specific marketing activities. CRM is fundamentally an integration of technologies and business processes used to satisfy the needs of a customer during any given interaction to create value for both the business and its customers. Although regarded by many as something new, CRM has existed continuously in the past as business orientations have over the last 150 years moved from being production-oriented in the nineteenth century to a more customer-centric focus in the current climate. CRM solutions in the late 1980s and early 1990s focused on automating and standardising internal processes to make customers an asset. The emergence of the Internet has revolutionised CRM and has resulted in the birth of e-CRM, the application of information and communication technology to increase the scale and scope of customer service.

The importance of CBIS in an organisation

The Sullivan matrix (Sullivan, 1985) provides a useful framework for discussing the importance of CBIS use and its spread across the organisa-

tion as a whole. The matrix represents the position of CBIS use along two dimensions – *infusion* and *diffusion* (see Figure 1.2). Infusion represents the extent to which CBIS have been employed in the fundamental operations of the organisation while diffusion represents the extent to which CBIS have been deployed in the organisation. The horizontal axis of the matrix indicates movement from low dependency on CBIS to a situation where CBIS are an integral part of the running of the organisation. The vertical axis of the matrix indicates movement from highly centralised use (typically by a specialist data processing unit) to decentralised departmental and personal use of CBIS.

Organisations with low infusion and diffusion of CBIS use are typical of the early years of commercial computing, though such organisations still exist. Typically they will have a CBIS for accounting and payroll, run by the accounts department, the failure of which will not prevent day-to-day operational activities. Organisations with high infusion and diffusion are heavily reliant on their CBIS, which are likely to cover all aspects of their operations.

Organisations in different industries show different characteristics in terms of infusion and diffusion. These depend on the nature of the work they do and the information content (see Robson, 1997) of their work and products/ services. Thus a national newspaper publisher will typically be highly infused and diffused in its CBIS use, while a small building contractor will show low infusion and diffusion.

The approach to CBIS management in an organisation

Although still unproven empirically, 'stages of growth' models provide useful conceptual models for considering the role of IS in organisational strategy and determining organisational maturity in terms of IS. A number of such

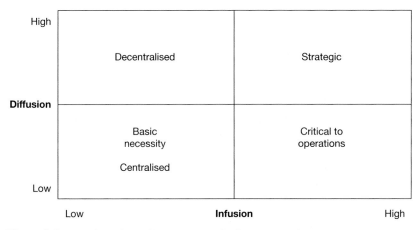

Figure 1.2 Based on the Sullivan matrix (Sullivan, 1985)
Source: Ward *et al.* (2002)

models have been described, of which perhaps the best known is Nolan's six-stage model (1979), developed from an earlier four-stage model (Gibson and Nolan, 1974).

Nolan (1979) finalised the six-stage model of the IS evolutionary process, focusing on use of and expenditure on IS from *initiation* to *maturity*, thus:

1 *initiation*, involving a purely operational systems focus;

2 *contagion*, moving to online systems and rapid growth with more users;

3 *control*, reflecting management beginning to evaluate costs versus benefits;

4 *integration*, using database management to provide users with a service rather than solving problems on an ad hoc basis;

5 *data administration*, involving information sharing, consideration of information needs and more of an appreciation of the value of information;

6 *maturity*, coordinating the planning and development of IS with business needs.

Table 1.1 Four-stage growth model

Element	Initiation	Expansion	Formalisation	Maturity
Applications	Cost reduction	Proliferation of applications	Emphasis on control	Database applications
Growth of personnel	Specialisation for computer efficiency	Specialisation to develop variety of programmes	Specialisation for control and effectiveness assurance	Specialisation for database technology and tele-processing
Management techniques applied	Lax management	Sales-oriented management	Control-oriented management	Resource-oriented planning and control

Source: Gibson and Nolan (1974)

Apart from viewing the progression along the six stages, Nolan's model is of particular value because it highlights a transition point between *control* and *integration* from DP or computer management to IS management. This transition reflects an important change in organisational attitude and behaviour with regard to computing. From the management of activities concerned more with operations, data collection and programming, the approach moves to one of managing a coordinated set of resources which are designed to meet future requirements.

Unlike Nolan's model, Earl's model (1989) concentrates on multiple learning curves which represent the stages through which organisations pass in planning their information systems. Earl argues that organisations begin by assessing the status quo with regard to IS coverage, moving on to management concern for closer links with business objectives and finally reaching a strategic focus. The learning curves tend to start at the DP stage, moving through database management and microcomputing to office automation and telecommunications.

The Hirschheim *et al.* model (1988) builds on the work of Nolan and makes reference to three evolutionary phases of IS management through which organisations pass once they have realised that IS are a vital business element for them. The three phases are:

1 The *delivery* phase where senior management have begun to critically assess the efficiency of the IS function and its capability to deliver what is needed. The aim of this phase is to restore credibility to the IS function.
2 The *reorientation* phase represents the change in focus of attention from basic IS delivery to the use of IS/IT for competitive advantage. IS/IT investment moves towards integration with the business strategy and the focus moves outward beyond the internal organisational boundaries to the external marketplace.

3 The *reorganisation* phase represents a concern with the management of interfaces between IS and the rest of the organisation. Some areas of the business will look to strategic dependence on IS while others will look more to IS for support. Whatever the case, the focus of this phase is internal to the organisation as opposed to external to the marketplace.

Galliers and Sutherland (1991) devised and revisited a further six-stage growth model based on application to the seven S's viewed at each of the six stages of the model. Strategy, structure, systems, staff, style, skills and superordinate goals are associated to the stages, as follows:

Stage 1   'Ad Hocracy'
Stage 2   Starting the Foundations
Stage 3   Centralised Dictatorship
Stage 4   Democratic Dialectic and Cooperation
Stage 5   Entrepreneurial Opportunity
Stage 6   Integrated Harmonious Relationships

Each of the S's constitutes an important aspect of how the IS function within an organisation might operate at different stages of growth.

'Ad Hocracy' describes the rather unstructured, uncontrolled approach to the use of IS at the beginning. Stage 2 marks the beginning of trying to assess user needs and meet them. At Stage 3 the need for planning is recognised and IS are centrally controlled. Stage 4 raises conflicts between user needs and centralised control. Integration and coordination are required at this stage. At Stage 5 the IS function can begin to provide some strategic benefit with the major operational systems up and running. Stage 6 heralds the new age of sophisticated IS use with the advent of integrated, harmonious working relationships between IS personnel and other staff in the organisation.

Chapter summary

Developments in IS/IT have made feasible many new applications of strategic importance. The importance of taking a strategic approach to IS has come much more to the fore as a result of reduced costs and increased functionality of IS applications. What is more, IS/IT has become so closely woven into the value-added chain of many organisations nowadays that developing an IS strategy has become a necessary foundation for building a corporate strategy. Banks, insurance companies and financial services organisations, for example, are now highly dependent on IS/IT to sustain their competitive advantage (Cash and McLeod, 1985). Information systems are pivotal to the success of the fast-moving consumer goods and retail sectors.

With the Industrial Revolution came the industrial economy with factory production systems bringing together money, machines, equipment, materials and people in order to produce goods. As the Industrial Revolution progressed, automation provided ever-closer links between the factors of production. The Age of Systems, born in the Second World War with the necessity for mass production on an unprecedented scale, had engendered national transportation and government systems of various kinds and more recently financial systems transgressing national political boundaries. Such systems require flows of information never before envisioned to manage increasing complexities. System components used communication networks to link them. Managers need information to guide and control systems and the cost of poor decision-making has become too high; decision-making relies on information. Information systems aid managers to solve problems and make better decisions. Information technology provides the enabling tools that supply those information systems. The industrial society has become an information society that is increasingly technology driven, which requires more than ever top-class management skills along with the ability to innovate and cope with a phenomenal rate of change.

This chapter explains first the changing nature of business and its corresponding information requirements to set the scene, followed by the changing role and management of IS/IT and the developing use of Computer Based Information Systems to fulfil business needs. It looks in particular at how things have gone wrong in the past and how they must be managed in the future if corporate benefits are to be maximised. After all, if businesses are not profitable, they will not survive in the medium- to long-term. Excellent service organisations have said quite clearly (e.g. Carl Sewell of Sewell Village Cadillac in Dallas, USA; Marks & Spencer, and John Lewis Partnership in the UK) that if they are not profitable they cannot reward and recognise staff, cannot provide a thriving working environment and ultimately cannot provide top-class service to their customers. Similarly, John Harvey Jones always spoke in terms of profitability as the main outcome of business success. He is open to suggestions as to which other measures he should use, but to date no-one seems to have been able to offer a better alternative. If business success depends to a large extent on the profitable use and management of information, information systems and information technology, so be it.

Improvements to system software and hardware rendered commercial systems more efficient and reliable, but the large DP departments that emerged were remote from users and inflexibility caused a number of frustrations. The advent of the minicomputer helped to solve this problem by providing 'online' services that were also cost-effective. Demand grew for more and better systems and a more systematic approach to system development. The focus of attention moved from collecting and processing to the data itself, which could be used for information and control in new types of independent data management systems. Complex data needs to be understood, organised and stored, resulting in the development of databases and database management systems (DBMS). Sophisticated new software started to appear to organise the complex data to be input into information systems.

There followed a more deliberate push to develop the integrated management information system to support management rather than clerical activity, to provide information to run the business by aggregating and transforming corporate data. Problems of interconnecting, exchanging and integrating information in different forms and in different places necessitated efforts to develop more integrated systems and telecommunications. More systems were being developed by users themselves or in conjunction with users as the need to bring CBIS and business issues closer together became more and more pressing. Technological options needed to be evaluated in the context of organisational and business options; the realisation was growing that technology in itself could not solve business problems but had to be used in an appropriate way.

References and further reading

Aladwani A. (2001) 'Change Management Strategies for Successful ERP Implementation', *Business Process Management*, 7(3): 266–275.

Bassellier G., Reich B.H. and Benbasat I. (2001) 'Information Technology Competence of Business Managers: a Definition and Research Model', *Journal of MIS*, 17(4), Spring: 159–182.

Cash J.I. and McLeod P.L. (1985) 'Managing the Introduction of Information Systems Technology in Strategically Dependent Companies', *Journal of MIS*, 1(4), Spring: 5–23.

Curry A.C. and Moore C. (2003) 'Assessing Information Culture – an Exploratory Model', *International Journal of Information Management*, 23: 91–110.

Drucker P.F. (1993) *Managing in Turbulent Times*, Butterworth-Heinemann: Oxford.

Earl M.J. (1989) *Management Strategies for IT*, Prentice Hall: New York.

Feeny D.F. and Willcocks L.P. (1998) 'Core IS Capabilities for Exploiting Information Technology', *Sloan Management Review*, Spring: 9–21.

Galliers R. and Sutherland A. (1991) 'Information Systems Management and Strategy Formulation: the Stages of Growth Model Revisited', *Journal of Information Systems*, 1(2): 89–114.

Gibson C.F. and Nolan R.L. (1974) 'Managing the Four Stages of EDP Growth', *Harvard Business Review*, Jan.–Feb.: 76–88.

Hill N. (2001) 'Let's Get Together' in Guardian Unlimited http://society.guardian.co.uk/fundraising/story/0.8150,443755,00.html.

Hirschheim R., Earl M.J., Feeny D. and Lockett M. (1988) 'An Exploration into the Management of the IS Function: Key Issues and an Evolving Model' in *Proceedings of the Joint International Symposium on IS: Information Technology Management for Productivity and Strategic Advantage*, IFIP TC-8, Open Conference, Singapore, March.

Keen, P.G.W. and Scott-Morton M.S. (1978) *Decision Support Systems: An Organizational Perspective*, Addison-Wesley: Reading, MA.

Leitheiser R.L. (1992) 'MIS Skills for the 1990s: a Survey of MIS Managers' Perceptions', *Journal of MIS*, 9(1), Summer: 69–91.

Markus M.L., Axline S., Petrie D. and Tanis S.C. (2000) 'Learning from Adopters' Experiences with ERP: Problems Encountered and Success Achieved', *Journal of Information Technology*, 15(4), December: 245–265.

Mukherji A. (2002) 'The Evolution of Information Systems: their Impact on Organisations and Structures', *Management Decision*, 40(5): 497–507.

Nolan R.L. (1979) 'Managing the Crises in Data Processing', *Harvard Business Review*, March–April: 115–126.

Robson W. (1997) *Strategic Management and Information Systems*, 2nd edn, Pitman: London.

Rockart J.F., Earl M.J. and Ross J.W. (1996) 'Eight Imperatives for the New IT Organisation', *Sloan Management Review*, Fall: 43–55.

Somogy, E.K. and Galliers R.D. (1987) 'Applied Information Technology: from Data Processing to Strategic Information Systems', *Journal of Information Technology*, 2(1): 30–41.

Sprague R.H. and Carlson E.D. (1982) *Building Effective Decision Support Systems*, Prentice Hall: New York.

Sullivan C.H. (1985) 'Systems Planning in the Information Age', *Sloan Management Review*, Winter: 3–11.

Tarn J., Yen D. and Beaumont M. (2002) 'Exploring the Rationales for ERP and SCM Integration', *Industrial Management and Data Systems*, 102(1): 26–34.

Ward J. and Peppard J. (2002) *Strategic Planning for Information Systems*, 3rd edn, Wiley: Chichester.

Chapter 2

Introducing organisations and information

....

Learning objectives

After reading this chapter you should be able to:

- compare different views and definitions of organisations;
- describe the different functions of organisations and relate them to each other;
- distinguish between the related concepts of knowledge, information and data;
- explain why quality information is necessary to support effective management decision-making.

Introduction

Before we can begin to understand how to apply information technology within an organisation we need to understand the fundamentals of both organisations and the information they use. These then form the basic background to our understanding of information systems and technology in an organisational setting.

Although in this chapter organisations are defined in a simple form, it is necessary to grasp this simplified model before becoming involved in the more complex issues. Knowing what information is, and how it differs from 'data', is the first step to appreciating the value and use of information in organisations. This chapter explores information in terms of *what* it tells us, *how* it is available, and *when*.

What is a business organisation?

Over the years researchers have struggled to develop a definition of exactly what constitutes a business organisation. This has resulted in many definitions based on the particular perspective of the researcher concerned (see Table 2.1). While each definition is true, it does not give a complete understanding of what a business organisation actually is. This is because all organisations, even small ones, are complex combinations of many different elements (see Figure 2.1).

Taking a simple, rational view of business organisations, they are in essence formal combinations of people, equipment and buildings brought together for some common purpose. Their three principal purposes (Clancy, 1989) are:

Table 2.1 Alternative definitions of organisations

Source of definition	Definition	Organisation view
Gerloff, 1985	A goal-oriented association of people which has identifiable plans, systems and structures that are designed to accomplish their intended purposes.	Rational
Miles, 1980	A collection of interest groups, sharing a common resource base, paying homage to a common mission and depending on a larger context for its legitimacy and development.	Social
Schein, 1980	The planned coordination of the activities of a number of people for the achievement of some common explicit purpose or goal, through division of labour and function and through a hierarchy of authority and responsibility.	Rational
Silverman, 1970	The outcome of the interactions of motivated people who are attempting to resolve their own problems and pursue their ends.	Social

1 to provide products or services;
2 to make a profit;
3 to continue to grow and survive as an organisation.

Alternatively, organisations can be defined (Galbraith, 1977) as:

• composed of people and groups of people;
• in order to achieve some shared purpose;
• through a division of labour;
• integrated by information-based decision processes;
• continuous through time.

To some extent all organisations share all three goals, as they are essentially interdependent. What differs is the balance of importance between the three.

Business organisations come in a surprisingly wide variety of forms. We often talk about the manufacturing sector and the service sector as though all organisations fall neatly into one or the other. In practice, many manufacturers also provide services, even if this is only in the form of warranty repairs and servicing. Equally, organisations in the service sector sometimes talk about the products they provide, for example the financial services industry has products such as personal pensions and life assurance. What separates manufacturing from services is that the manufacturing sector produces tangible products which the customer can take away as their main activity, whereas service organisations provide services over a period of time.

Another common distinction is that made between the public and private sectors. Most manufacturing organisations, whether publicly or privately owned, aim to make a profit. On the other hand, while privately owned service organisations usually aim to make a profit, public service organisations such as the Education, Prison and Health Services aim to provide services according to criteria governed by a different environment. The voluntary sector, consisting of charitable and voluntary

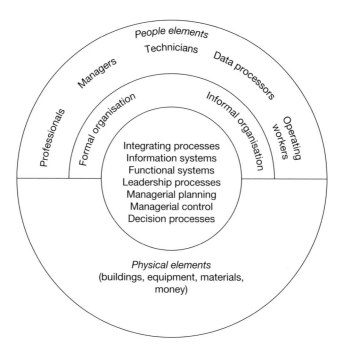

People elements
Technicians
Data processors
Managers
Professionals
Formal organisation
Informal organisation
Operating workers

Integrating processes
Information systems
Functional systems
Leadership processes
Managerial planning
Managerial control
Decision processes

Physical elements
(buildings, equipment, materials,
money)

Figure 2.1 Circular diagram of organisational components

organisations, has now more than ever taken an increasing role in the running of many types of public service either individually or in partnership with other public service organisations. The final broad category of organisation is in the voluntary sector. These organisations are run very much along the same lines as any other business, with profit being replaced by revenue generating from activities like grant funding and fundraising. Although this book is primarily concerned with business organisations, the concepts and ideas presented are also relevant to other types of organisation and the variety of chapter case studies reflects these different types.

The most well-known work on different ways of viewing organisations is Morgan's *Images of Organisations* (1986). This work examines the use of metaphors for organisations as a way of thinking about them and exploring how they work. The basic premise is that our theories and

explanations of organisational life are based on metaphors. They allow us to express very complex ideas and situations in relatively simple terms. Each metaphor gives a different view of an organisation, which is incomplete in itself, but which can contribute to our understanding. By using different metaphors, we can explore different aspects of the organisation, which, when combined, provide a more complete picture. The problem is that each metaphor is a simplified view of the complex reality of organisational behaviour, and, the more metaphors we use to explore an organisation, the more complex is the picture presented. Table 2.2 summarises Morgan's metaphors.

This still leaves us with the problem of how to examine the complex reality of organisations in a way which is both practical and not too simplistic. What is clear, looking at different views and definitions of organisations, is that there are two main aspects which need to be

Table 2.2 Morgan's organisational metaphors

Organisations as machines	Mechanistic, bureaucratic
Organisations as organisms	Focused on managing organisational needs and the environment
Organisations as brains	Importance of information processing, learning, intelligence
Organisations as cultures	Sustained by ideas, values, norms, beliefs
Organisations as political systems	Different interests, conflicts and power, shape organisational activities
Organisations as psychic prisons	People trapped in their thoughts, ideas, beliefs
Organisations as flux and transformation	Focus on logics of change shaping social life
Organisations as instruments of domination	Exploitation of employees, environment and economy to achieve own ends

considered. The first is the formal organisation – its structure, resources, processes and so on. These are the traditional considerations in organisational analysis and are based on a logical, rational view of organisations. The second is the informal organisation – its culture, power structures, personalities and so on. These represent a softer social view of organisations as collections of individual people, who don't always behave objectively or in the best interests of the organisation as a whole.

Neglecting either the rational or social view leads to a limited understanding of the organisation, with consequences for effective organisational problem-solving. The rational view shows organisations as a rational and objective set of processes and sub-processes structured to achieve organisational goals. It provides us with a definition that helps us get to grips with the complexity of an organisation by focusing on its tangible aspects, the things that give it shape and form. The social view focuses on more abstract and subjective aspects, in essence the character of the organisation, and is therefore more difficult to pin down. In the past, the social view has been overlooked in the study of information systems practice, largely because

of this difficulty. More recently, it has been recognised that the softer social aspects of an organisation can have a significant impact on the success or failure of its information systems. The development of soft systems methodology has also helped deal with more diverse and complex variables in organisations and management. The hard and soft systems perspectives are discussed in some detail in Chapter 4, while the impact of structure and culture on the relationship between information systems and organisations is covered in Chapter 6.

What do organisations do?

Marks & Spencer is one of the UK's leading retailers of clothing, foods, homeware and financial services, serving ten million customers a week in over 350 UK stores. The company also trades in 30 countries worldwide and has a group turnover in excess of £8 billion. Its long-standing tradition for service is based on focus on the customer, good quality products, an unconditional service guarantee and close links with its suppliers.

The British Telecom Group provides worldwide business solutions and services. It supplies

25

and services broadband and dial-up Internet access products as well as telecommunications for individual and business customers. It also provides networking solutions and engages in advanced technological research. BT's current share price stands at 180.5p (as at 20 May 2004).

Standard Life provides a variety of financial services including pensions, insurance and investment products. Standard Life Bank supplies mortgages and savings accounts, while Standard Life Healthcare provides health insurance for individuals and companies.

The Robert Taylor Group manufactures die castings for a variety of purposes, including components for computer hardware. It also has a traditional foundry business that manufactures large castings for lorry wheel hubs and many other uses. The Group has a long-standing reputation for good quality of both products and servicing. It has survived where other similar manufacturers have declined and gone out of business.

Hillcrest Housing Group is a not-for-profit voluntary organisation that is one of the largest housing providers in Scotland, offering over 5,000 homes for rent and low-cost ownership for families, couples and single-person households. It also provides a range of services from tenancy support services for people who are vulnerable to homelessness through tenancy breakdown, and to those who are experiencing difficulties and feel they are not coping well. Hillcrest also provides support services for people with learning difficulties, mental health problems and addiction issues.

An organisation's activities are often grouped into structural units, or business functions. This traditional, typically mechanistic, view of organisations is still prevalent and impacts on the organisation of businesses today. As illustrated in Figure 2.2 there are four main business functions in a typical organisation:

1 marketing and sales
2 operations
3 accounting and finance
4 human resource management

In addition, many organisations include administrative support services, which provide essential professional and non-professional support for the organisation's activities. This almost always includes secretarial services, and may also include legal, facilities management (i.e. buildings) and information systems services. In general, smaller organisations tend to use experts from outside the organisation to provide

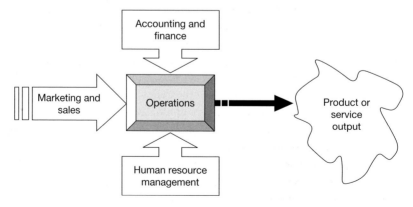

Figure 2.2 Main functions of a business organisation

all but secretarial services or have to rely on the available expertise at hand. In a small organisation the role of IT support may just be carried out on an ad hoc basis by someone who has a personal interest or by someone who has to make it work to allow them to complete their job function. At the other extreme, large national and multinational organisations may have hundreds of people working in these areas; for example BP has a range of contractors and sub-contractors working on its sites throughout the world. EDS (Electronic Data Systems) provide a range of services for BP at its site in Grangemouth in Scotland.

The precise nature of each of the four main business functions differs from organisation to organisation, but we will follow the classification used by other writers.

Marketing and sales

Marketing and sales serves two principal roles in an organisation. The first of these is promoting the products and services of the organisation. This involves the planning and management of the organisation's marketing and promotional channels. Marketing is essential to the continuing existence of the organisation. If customers do not know that the company exists or what it can provide by way of services and products, opportunities will be missed. Through advertising, direct mail promotions, press and public relations, exhibitions, and other means of end-user and industry promotions, awareness is created in the minds of potential customers.

This awareness then needs to be converted into a tangible revenue stream by selling to these potential customers. The management of sales is often a part of the marketing function. Sales people need to be managed and their activities coordinated to avoid unnecessary competition between the organisation's own resources. Orders generated by sales people

need to be processed and passed on to stock-control operations and distribution that will fulfil the orders. To assist other functions with their planning, a marketing and sales department will also forecast future trends in market behaviour, customer needs and current sales. This enables the organisation to be more proactive in its behaviour.

As well as promoting and selling existing products, marketing and sales may also plan and develop new products and services and identify new markets. This requires research to identify potential customer needs and desires. The results provide the future direction for the organisation's products and services and its position within the business environment. With the advent of increasingly sophisticated CRM systems organisations are capable of providing very accurate customer profiles, which in turn aids them in making the correct decisions in respect to sales and marketing. It is cheaper to retain customers than to gain new ones, therefore CRM systems can tailor promotional material to suit even large customer bases with the aim of keeping their custom.

Operations

Operations cover the basic productive activities of an organisation, designed to produce and deliver products and services to the customer. This is the function most likely to differ between organisations because it represents the core activity of the organisation.

In a typical manufacturing organisation operations would involve purchasing raw materials and components, managing the inventories of raw materials, work-in-progress and finished goods, managing and controlling the production process itself and shipping the finished goods to the customer. As well as the day-to-day activities of the organisation, the operations function is also responsible for planning and scheduling production resources (employees, materials, equipment) to ensure the meeting of all deadlines for delivery to customers. Depending on the nature of the product and the market, this can be a very complex process. Operations are also heavily involved in the development of new products based on market research done by the marketing and sales function.

In non-manufacturing organisations the operations function is much the same. The principal difference is in the levels of inventory management required. In retailing, all operations are focused around finished goods, with no production process being required and therefore no raw materials or work-in-progress inventories. In service industries, such as healthcare or education and training, the intangible nature of the service means that there is no finished goods inventory, but there are raw materials and equipment inventories, with the service delivery process replacing the production process (see Table 2.3).

Accounting and finance

Although accounting and finance are quite distinct functions, they are often grouped together in organisations. Finance is concerned with the management of the organisation's financial resources: cash, stocks, securities and other financial instruments. These activities are often focused on ensuring the availability of finances to support the main business activities of the organisation. However, in some larger organisations, they have actually grown to become a form of business in themselves by generating significant profits for the organisation.

The primary responsibility of the accounting function is to produce an authoritative set of accounts, which are summarised at the end of each financial year in the form of a balance sheet and profit and loss statement (see Figure 2.3). These statements, accounting for all flows of finance through the organisation, often have to be published. They will come under scrutiny by various interested parties outside the organisation: tax officials, auditors, customs and excise and shareholders. This means that there is great emphasis on ensuring the accuracy of the figures they contain, and the reliability of the financial records from which they are derived.

Table 2.3 Alternative operational transformations

Operation	Input resources	Transformation process	Outputs
Airline	Aircraft, pilots, crew, passengers, freight	Transport passengers and freight	Transported passengers and freight
Dentist	Dentists, equipment, nurses, patients	Check and treat teeth, give advice	Patients with healthy teeth and gums
Police	Police officers, IT systems, information, the public	Prevent and solve crime, apprehend criminals	Lawful society, public with feeling of security
Accountant	Accounting staff, information, IT systems	Prepare accounts, give advice	Certified and published accounts
Zoo	Zoo keepers, animals, stimulating environments, customers	Display animals, educate customers, breed animals	Entertained, informed customers, non-extinct species

Source: Slack *et al.* (1995)

XYZ plc

Profit and loss account for the year ended 31 December 2001

	£	£
Gross profit		94,650
Less: Sundry expenses	27,460	
Directors' fees and salaries	19,470	
Auditors' fees	1,800	
Debenture interest	2,000	
Provisions for depreciation:		
Equipment	4,600	
Motor vehicles	5,000	60,330
Net profit		34,320
Add: Retained earnings at 1 January 2001		22,450
Profit available for appropriation		56,770
Less: Transfer to general reserve		5,000
Preliminary expenses written off		2,300
Interim dividends paid:		
Preference (4%)	1,600	
Ordinary (5%)	10,000	11,600
Final dividends proposed:		
Preference (4%)	1,600	
Ordinary (9%)	18,000	19,600
Retained earnings at 31 December 2001		18,270
		56,770

Figure 2.3 A profit and loss statement

Accounting handles the receipt of payments from customers, the payment of suppliers' invoices and the processing of the organisation's payroll. All three are vital to the ongoing success of the organisation. In profit-based organisations customers who don't pay don't provide income, suppliers who don't get paid stop supplying, and employees who don't get paid stop working. Likewise in not-for-profit organisations, funds to pay for staff, materials and facilities are also needed to allow the 'business' to continue. It is also necessary to account for interest earned on financial assets, depreciation of fixed assets, debt repayments, financial traceability, etc. While having a less direct relationship with the organisation's main business activities, these are nonetheless important.

Human resource management

The role of human resource management (HRM) is to recruit, develop and maintain an effective workforce for the organisation. A large part of HRM involves record keeping. This primarily involves keeping records of all employees, including their position, their conditions of employment, their training and development needs and activities (see Figure 2.4), and any disciplinary matters. As part of the recruitment activities of the organisation, records also need to be kept on job applicants and current vacancies.

HRM also involves analysing the current workforce to identify skills gaps, requirements for more personnel, or opportunities to reduce the organisation's labour costs through redundancy and early retirement. This analysis is then followed up by appropriate action through the development of training programmes, recruitment drives or redundancy programmes.

An important activity within HRM is the management of salaries and benefits paid to employees. This is usually tied in with the defined status of individual jobs within the organisation, with each job typically having a salary range and maybe a package of other benefits, such as a pension, health insurance and possibly shares options. The value of such benefits can change over time due to government policy or changes in the stock market; the decreasing value of many pension schemes in the UK being seen as a case in point.

How are organisations structured?

Grouping of activities

Organisational activities at any level of the organisational hierarchy can be grouped in a number of ways:

- by functional specialisation, such as finance, marketing, production, distribution;
- by product group(s), such as plastics, resins, castings, moulded board, cardboard;
- by client group, such as wholesale accounts, company accounts, overseas clients;
- by geographical or territorial area, such as Southern, Northwestern Region, Far East, Europe;
- by process, such as assembly, finishing/packaging, testing, moulding, melting.

These groupings may also be combined, such as customer services, Southern Region.

Traditional function-based structures tend to have a manager related to a particular function and rely on specialisation of activity to determine structure. Information often flows vertically with some informal flow horizontally between

Figure 2.4 A training cycle based on an HRD (Human Resource Development) plan
Source: Beardwell and Holden (1994)

functions, such as from marketing to production and vice versa (see Figure 2.5). Information travelling too slowly and becoming distorted as more people become involved in the communication process often mars day-to-day problem-solving and coordination.

Product-based structures are well illustrated by the chemical and petrochemical industries, with products like polymers, ethylene, dyes and pharmaceuticals. Line managers in charge of individual products tend to coordinate with each other and provide information to one another. Such structures are also determined by grouping specialized activities that span the whole production process (see Figure 2.6). It is essential that information systems are implemented to enhance activity grouping to an optimum.

Client-based structures are common in service industries. Contract distribution to particular clients or client groups and computer services are examples of such structures. Servicing individual client needs goes hand in hand with the supply of the product to create value (see Figure 2.7).

Financial services and banking are also clear examples of such structures, geared to a high degree of differentiation of service provision for a whole variety of clients.

Geographic structures are determined by the areas in which the business operates, often involving branches or subsidiaries with a head office or holding company. The railway network is an example of such a structure, with FirstScotRail being a geographical division within the UK

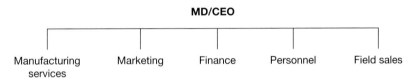

Figure 2.5 A traditional function-based structure

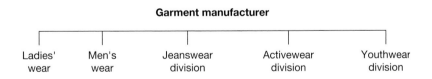

Figure 2.6 A product-based structure

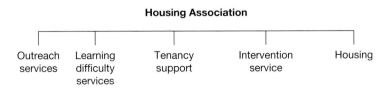

Figure 2.7 A client-based structure for a housing association

rail network. Multinationals have widespread geographic structures, often operating globally, and geographic divisions have a certain autonomy. Information systems are based in divisions and network with one another to a greater or lesser extent. Coats Ltd, a thread manufacturer with 22 per cent of the global market has divisions in the UK, Europe, the USA, the Far East and Japan, in total 67 countries.

Process-based structures tend to be associated with manufacturing or the provision of individual services (see Figure 2.8). Team working in the garment and clothing industry as a production method has involved structuring to produce discrete batches of finished garments with provision for rapid style changes in response to new market demands from major retailers such as Marks & Spencer. The whole Just in Time production approach is about structuring around managing processes from start to finish. A number of companies have redefined their processes and in some cases, such as banking and financial services, IS/IT have enabled such process redefinition, often aimed at completing tasks and hence processes in a much shorter time than previously. The theory of Business Process Re-engineering (BPR) attributed to Hammer and Champy (2001) identifies information technology and systems as the key enablers for organisations to alter their existing processes. Information about process characteristics, performance and outputs is critical for process management and even some of the most process-oriented firms in the USA have not fully developed infrastructures for providing process performance information to managers and workers (Davenport and Beers, 1995).

Matrix structures combine different structures and functions, often to respond to the need for change and increased business complexity. Such structures are multidimensional and may, for example, involve one group of managers managing functional activities and another group managing individual products requiring inputs from all the major functional specialist areas. Authority for products may be combined from technical and managerial areas of the business.

There are several combinations that potentially make up matrix structures, which are often structures within structures and offer a host of managerial challenges (see Figure 2.9). Project groups and task teams are used in the attempt to formalise horizontal communication and network information flows required to solve problems. Such groups and teams are often formed to tackle specific issues that span a number of areas of the organisation. Where formal authority and operating systems are not working in harmony with one another, task groups have to be set up to locate the main sources of problems, which would undoubtedly also have a potentially detrimental effect on information systems implementation. Examples of groupings in a matrix structure are as follows:

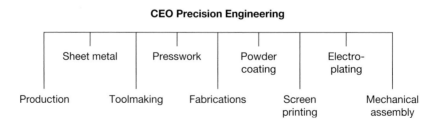

Figure 2.8 A process-based structure

- Regional groups, such as Europe, USA, SE Asia, each with product-based divisions, such as polymers, pharmaceuticals, dyes and pigments, which consist of process-based teams.
- Product-based divisions with regional offices which are based on functional specialisms within which are product-based teams.

As far as organisational structure in general is concerned, division of labour is largely achieved by grouping people with the same specialised skills in very small sub-systems, but as companies increase in size and complexity, sub-systems need to be managed beyond such groupings. Coordination of sub-systems becomes a much more significant problem and developing a for-mal management information system for such coordination may become essential. An example of a matrix structure for a university business school is shown in Figure 2.10.

The organisational value chain

It is useful when considering an organisation to recognise the distinction between primary and secondary activities carried out within the business functions. This distinction is embodied in the concept of the value chain (Porter, 1985). In the value chain primary activities form a linear flow from supplier to customer, adding the value to the organisation's products/services which allow it to make a profit. These value-adding

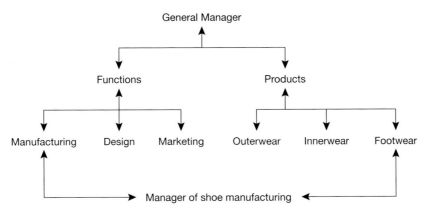

Figure 2.9 A matrix structure

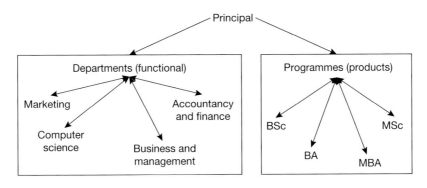

Figure 2.10 A matrix structure for a university business school

33

activities must be carried out effectively, both individually and as an integrated stream linking together appropriately to achieve optimum performance. The secondary activities of an organisation relate more to the organisation as a whole, adding value indirectly by providing essential support for primary activities in a cost-effective way. This distinction is important when considering the benefits expected from the application of information systems.

By examining an organisation's value chain, we can analyse:

- how effectively information flows along the primary processes and back again;
- how effectively information is used by each individual activity;
- how activities can be linked or integrated to minimise costs and maximise opportunities;
- how support activities can best serve the needs of value-adding processes, rather than being a potential hindrance.

Figure 2.11 illustrates an organisational value chain for a manufacturing organisation. The purpose of the value chain is to assess and improve the way a company operates by looking at its activities and the extent to which they contribute to the value-adding processes of the industry. The primary activities are those that add value directly and will to some extent be predetermined by the industry and the organisation's products, customers and suppliers. Not only must these activities be performed well, they must also link together effectively to optimise overall performance. The support activities are necessary to control and develop the business over time and thereby add value indirectly through the success of the primary activities.

The organisational environment

It is important to remember that no organisation exists in a vacuum. All have to function within the wider business environment, which is dynamic. They have to respond to competition, technological innovation and many other forces of change that may significantly impact upon their structure, activities and goals. A number of significant factors affect the environment in which organisations operate. These factors are summed up in Figure 2.12.

Support activities

| Infrastructure – Information systems, legal, accounting, financial management |
| Human resource management – personnel, pay, recruitment, training, manpower planning |
| Product and technology development – product and process design, market testing, R&D |
| Procurement – supplier management, resourcing, subcontracting |

Inbound logistics	Operations	Outbound logistics	Sales and marketing	Servicing	
Quality control	Manufacturing	Finished goods	Customer management and order taking	Warranty	Value added – cost = profit
Receiving	Packaging	Order handling	Promotion sales analysis	Maintenance	
Control of raw materials	Production control	Dispatch	Market research	Education and training	
	Maintenance	Delivery			
		Invoicing			

Primary activities

Figure 2.11 An organisational value chain

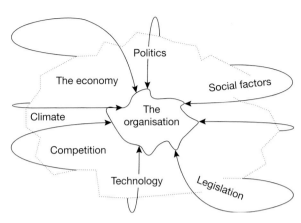

Figure 2.12 The organisational environment

Both the *national and global economies* influence organisational strategy and operations. In times of recession there is a tendency to shorter-term views and scaling down of operations, whereas in boom periods there is greater optimism, more gearing up to volume production and a willingness to consider more the medium and longer term.

Social influences on organisations might include a more pressing need to clean up the environment and reduce industrial and traffic pollution, or a more humane regard for animals, resulting in better conditions of transportation of livestock and more rigid restrictions on animal testing for medical research.

The *national political climate* has always been a major influence on organisations, in particular multinationals, in their decision to locate in or expand to different geographical areas. For example, the highly uncertain political climate in countries like Bangladesh has deterred companies in the oil and gas industry embarking on any potential exploration work there and those that have ventured there have experienced difficulties of various kinds.

Both *national and international legislation* impacts directly on the ways organisations operate or need to operate in the future. Health and Safety standards have tightened up over the years, as has environmental legislation.

Competition, both local and global, affects organisational performance, strategic planning and approach to change. Fierce competition creates many organisational pressures to which organisations may respond positively or negatively. Issues relating to the competitive environment are developed further in Chapters 7 and 8, which deal with organisational change and organisational strategy respectively.

The rate of *technological change and innovation* affects organisations, their customers and their suppliers. Speed of communication and information processing have increased customer expectations in terms of responsiveness and have enabled some proactive organisations to prosper while others have been left behind.

Organisations are also under the direct influence of two sets of forces, *pressure groups* and *stakeholders* (Ward and Peppard, 2002). Some of these overlap, implying that they can influence the organisation in more than one way.

Pressure groups make demands on the organisation, requiring acknowledgement of the pressure being exerted and expecting some form of rapid response from management. Such groups include the media, shareholders, competitors, suppliers, customers, governments, unions, the public, financial institutions and employees. Interfaces with such pressure groups must be constantly monitored, so that the organisation can establish a judicious balance between threats versus risks and optimise the opportunities that may lead to success.

Stakeholders, on the other hand, have a share in the organisation and all expect some form of material benefit from it. Shareholders are the first and foremost among these stakeholder groups if the organisation is publicly listed on the stock exchange. Other stakeholders include customers, suppliers, unions, employees, the government and the public. Organisations that have been most successful have passed on benefits not only to shareholders, but also to the community at large, to customers, suppliers and employees in the form of, for example, improved service, business partnerships and profit-sharing schemes respectively. The John Lewis Partnership is an example of this benefit sharing. Their business is set up in such a way that staff are partners and share in the profits and customers are entitled to purchase goods at the lowest prices. If a customer has seen the same product on sale more cheaply elsewhere,

John Lewis will honour their pledge of never knowingly being undersold.

The industry value system or value chain in which organisations exist brings together the value chains of the players in that system, i.e. customers, suppliers and competitors. Demand for end products and services depends on how much final consumers will pay for a given quantity less the costs incurred by the various organisations involved in the processes, from raw materials sourcing to final production. An individual organisation has to compete with suppliers and customers for available profit in the industry value system; additional profit can be generated and then shared by organisations which have developed strategic partnerships. Demand information flows from the final consumers back up the industry value chain with supply information flowing in the opposite direction, as shown in Figure 2.13. IS/IT can contribute significantly to capturing and transmitting this information more quickly and accurately, with a view to improving business performance by matching demand and supply.

Once an industry matures or enters its decline stage, it becomes more critical than ever to exploit all available strengths and potential.

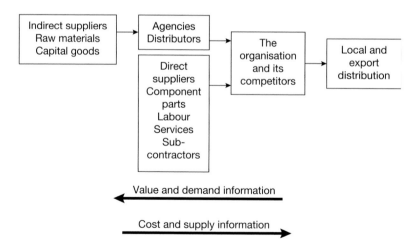

Figure 2.13 The industry value chain

Take, for example, the paper industry when it reached maturity; energy costs rose and environmental factors created stresses coupled with increased competitiveness. An industry survivor made the best of its experience and knowledge of the industry and used IS/IT to improve its distribution. The supermarket chain Sainsbury's have undergone a revamp of their supply-chain model with mixed results. For large retail outlets the efficiency of the supply chain is crucial to market success.

Environmental stability

In a *stable environment*, where products, services, customers, competitors and stakeholders have not changed to a large extent and where there is little technological innovation, senior management can keep a track on events and make strategic decisions. Products and production methods tend not to change dramatically and hence there is little impact on organisational structure. The brewing industry has responded to fluctuations in demand by developing distribution systems or changing the size of the workforce, rather than by a dramatic restructuring of the business as a whole. A stable organisational environment will impact upon the ability to automate and to what extent. Speed of innovation or information systems implementation may not, however, be rapid, as the pressure to respond quickly to change may not be significant.

In a *changing environment*, where stakeholder actions, products and services are rapidly fluctuating and major technological innovations are frequent, there is a constant pressure to adapt. Organisations in telecommunications, computer hardware and software, electronics and pharmaceuticals have revolutionised their products and production methods, resulting in major restructuring and network management systems. There

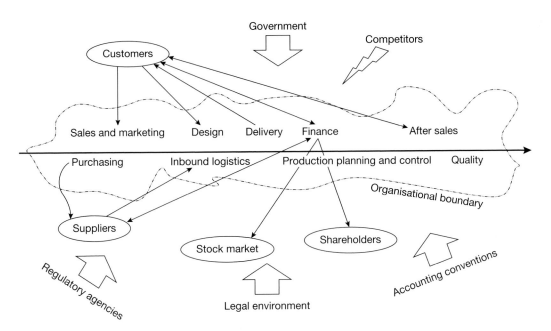

Figure 2.14 Information exchange with the environment
Source: adapted from Peppard (1993: 7)

is also a need to cope with a greater degree of organisational complexity, characterised by horizontal and vertical differentiation and spatial dispersion. Increased organisational complexity tends to introduce coordination, control and communication problems, which are a source of conflict. Such conflict is, however, positively related to effectiveness if it is resolved in an appropriate manner.

Figure 2.14 illustrates how information is exchanged between the organisation and its environment. There are the external influences of government, competitors, regulatory, accounting and legal bodies and there are the more direct information exchanges between the organisation and its customers in the form of orders, design information, delivery notes, invoices and payments; its suppliers in the form of orders, delivery notes, invoices and payments; and its shareholders and the Stock Exchange.

What is information?

Before considering issues relating to information and information systems, there is a need for some sort of definition as to what constitutes information. The two words, information and data are not synonymous. The use of information is a basis for learning and development, which in turn forms the basis for decision-making.

Galliers (1987) pointed out that our understanding of information technology has continued to outstrip our understanding of information, which has attracted a lot less interest. This is not especially helpful, given that the major goal of information systems is information provision. Ravault (1987) commented that the lack of scrupulous understanding of key concepts such as communications and information condemns the information age panacea to certain failure, as the information age is inevitably dependent on the dominant perspective of information.

Boland (1986) emphasised the need to include people in any perspective on information. While information and meaning are distinct from one another, both are dependent on the presence of a person. A popular scientism approach to explaining information is to invoke the communications theory image of transmission (Shannon and Weaver, 1949). The suggestion is that people give shape or form to a message, implying that people 'in-form' using the message.

Fox (1983) argues that information is not a process, rather the process is data generation and diffusion, and feels that confusion arises by not clearly distinguishing the process of informing from the information contained in the message. Blumenthal (1969) defines information using terms like 'recorded, classified, organised, related and interpreted' but this is more a definition of communication than information. Wersig and Neveling (1975) define information as a process occurring within the human mind when a problem and data useful for its solution are brought together productively, which once more implies the presence of people. Korn (2001) states that there is no agreed description of a concept of information, highlighting the task to be one of defining such a concept that makes it suitable to function as a product. Information is used to change the mental state of a receiver. Its effectiveness can be related to units, meaning, precision and number of pieces of information, all of which can be varied to affect effectiveness (Korn, 2001). One common definition of information is its reduction of uncertainty in that it alters confidence in decision-making. Whatever definition we wish to rely on, we must not confuse information with either meaning or data (Metcalfe and Powell, 1995).

The relationship between data, information and knowledge

Data

Data, as distinct from information, are raw facts and figures about events. Each datum represents some aspect of the event and must be processed along with other data in order to produce meaningful information. This information can then be used to furnish or enhance knowledge about a specific situation, thus contributing to decision-making. There are two fundamental issues associated with data: how the data is actually obtained and, now that you have the data, what you are going to do with it (Forte, 1994).

All too often data is collected in organisations and then discarded, abandoned or forgotten. This is simply because it was the wrong data. It may seem strange that organisations should waste effort collecting useless data. Often they are not aware that it needs to have explicit value before it is used. If the data is not recognised as useless until after it is collected, systems, both paper and computer-based, can be unproductively occupied with redundant data.

The principal reasons for unused data can be summarised in the following list:

- too much data has been collected for the resources available to process it;
- data that is collected is difficult to process into meaningful information;
- data is collected because it is more accessible and convenient to collect, rather than the data which is really required.

It is therefore important that decisions on which data to collect reflect the information which the data is meant to provide and the resources available to process them. The following boxed example highlights some of the problems in the NHS with collection of data and its transformation into information.

As previously mentioned, different types of data serve different purposes and each have their advantages and disadvantages. Formatted data provides a concise coded description of a situation or object, but cannot convey such a rich, full scenario as other types. Formatted data is the most common in computer-based information systems as it forms the basis for most data-processing activities. Video and audio can convey particular impressions and expressions in certain circumstances that the other data forms cannot. Fitness for purpose is essential when considering which data type to choose (see Table 2.4).

These different types of data can then be processed to produce information for managers. The form that the information takes does not necessarily have to match the type of data on which it is based. For example, a set of

The accuracy and timeliness of data collection and the information systems by which it is distributed either internally or interorganisationally is often badly out of step with rapidly changing information requirements. Responsibilities for gathering and using information are unclear. Staff at the local level tend to focus on the minutiae of data collection and validation, which can get in the way of constructive use of the data. Users are unable to identify their information needs or use relevant information when it is collected or set up systems to collect data. There are relatively few information specialists at the local level and information skills training is a low priority.

(Forte, 1994)

Table 2.4 Types of data

Data type	Description
Free text	Letters, numbers, characters that do not rely on specified meanings or definitions of items in the text, e.g. word processing systems.
Formatted data	Typically numerical or alphabetical material arranged in a specified format, e.g. date, time, product type, model number.
Images	Data in picture form, e.g. graphs, photographs, hand drawings which can be transmitted, modified and stored in the same way as free text.
Audio	Data in the form of sounds, e.g. voice messages, audio recordings.
Video	The combination of picture and sound to convey action, e.g. videoconferencing, video streaming.
Models	Data in the form of mathematical, geometric or rule-based models, e.g. engineering drawings, maps.

formatted data may be fed into a scheduling model, which presents the data as a graphical image, showing the best schedule that the model can produce.

Information

In all organisations, information fulfils two essential functions:

1 it facilitates *communication* between different parts of the organisation (its sub-systems), and between the organisation and its environment;
2 it provides a basis for informed *decision-making* at all levels of the organisation.

A purpose of information is to reduce uncertainty in a given situation. This means that the value of information is dependent on its context, both in terms of who receives it, and what it adds to their knowledge of the situation in question. Information which is useful to one person may be useless to someone else. For example, information on the organisation's business performance and that of major competitors will be of little value to a production

manager requiring delivery lead time information from key suppliers. It is perhaps worth noting at this point that the plethora of information available to most businesses due to the Internet, email and other media sources is such that it can increase uncertainty rather than reduce it: paralysis by analysis.

Knowledge

Knowledge, be it personal or organisational, is gained from the receiving of information. This information is combined with existing ideas and experience to form the basis for decision-making (see Table 2.5). These decisions then determine the actions to be taken at both an

Table 2.5 Data, information and knowledge

Term	Definition
Data	Raw facts and figures.
Information	Facts and figures taken in context, which convey meaning.
Knowledge	An accumulation of information, building on existing ideas and experience.

individual level and by the organisation as a whole. This accumulation of knowledge by an organisation (organisational learning) is an important factor in the organisation's continuing development.

Figure 2.15 illustrates the flows of data and information that need to take place in a generic manufacturing process to allow the accumulation of knowledge and experience needed to improve the process. In manufacturing processes the feedback loop of knowledge and experience is probably retained and accumulated better than in a project-type process where there can be a greater degree of unknown variables.

As stated earlier the capture of inappropriate data is always a danger with any information system, and the relevance of data is always fundamental to its worth. In project management the capture of mundane everyday activities is not particularly useful, as typically there is no learning that can take place. In contrast, by recording when an activity goes wrong or is carried out particularly well through the use of some form of innovative work practice then these events are worth recording as learning can take place. Figure 2.16 illustrates this concept.

To take advantage of such learning the organisation must be able to practice what is known as double loop or triple loop learning.

Converting data into information

If data is to be useful for a particular purpose it must be processed in some way to provide the relevant information. For data to be informative it has to be processed, given a useful context and acted upon (Forte, 1994). Exactly how it is processed will be determined by the purpose. There are a number of ways in which data can be converted into information.

Summarising The data may be summarised in order to give an overview of the situation, e.g. summarising all order data to provide a picture of the total orders for the month, or summarising all accounting data to provide a picture of the organisation's overall financial health.

Highlighting The data may be analysed to highlight any unusual events or circumstances which might require action to be taken, e.g. an unusually high level of scrap produced in a particular month, or a customer exceeding a credit limit.

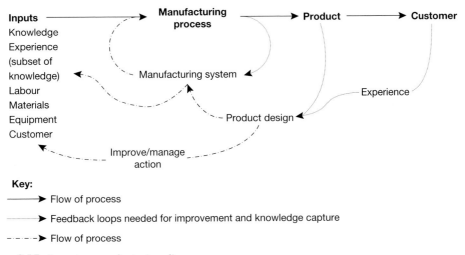

Figure 2.15 Generic manufacturing diagram

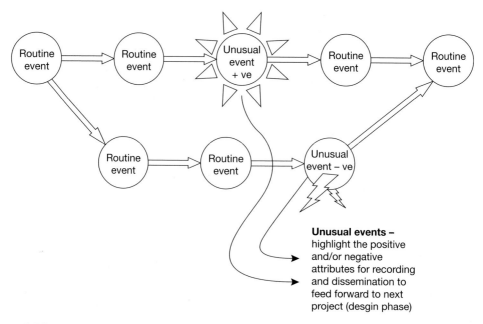

Figure 2.16 A schematic for a knowledge-based quality system for project management

Filtering The same data may constitute the basis for information to be used by different people, e.g. order data may be used to provide information to sales, production and accounts. To prevent irrelevant information being sent, the data must be filtered to ensure that, after processing, the right information goes to the right people.

Sorting Some data may simply need to be placed in a particular sequence, in order to make it into information, e.g. an alphabetic list of employees and their telephone extension numbers. Other data may need to be sorted into groups, in order to make it informative, e.g. production-rate statistics grouped by machine or production team. Of course, some data may need to be sorted into both groups and sequence.

Combining Some data may need to be combined with data from other sources, either internal or external to the organisation, in order to provide

a broad view of a situation, or to put a situation in context, e.g. combining internal performance data with industry norms to provide a comparison.

It is always essential to bear in mind the *aim* of converting the data to information, as this is the principal factor in determining which one (or combination) of the above processing methods will be required.

A systemic view of the interaction between data, information and knowledge is given in Figure 2.17.

How valuable is information?

The perceiver-concerns approach to valuing information is similar to that of the 'surprise' value approach, denoting the change in expectations triggered by the information (Metcalfe and Powell, 1995). The surprise value is determined by the amount of response evoked by a piece of information. A cognitive approach

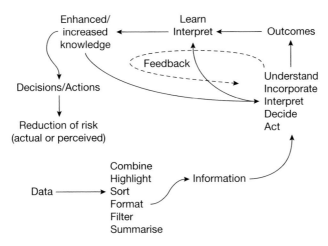

Figure 2.17 Interaction between data, information and knowledge

might well equate information to the degree of cognitive change caused by the message. Furthermore, the value of information content will vary as the perceiver's concerns change over time. Basic information tends only to be of value at the onset, after which more specific or detailed information will be of value.

Many managers feel the need to be able to pin a financial value on the availability of information. This allows information system investments to be justified on the basis of the added value they will bring in terms of information availability. Unfortunately, the value which can be placed on information is often difficult to define. While we can outline desirable characteristics for information in terms of accuracy, reliability, etc., it is more difficult to assess exactly how changes in the quality of information will actually affect the organisation's operations.

There are a number of reasons for this.

Information has no intrinsic value The value of information is wholly dependent on the context in which it is used. For example, seeing an advertisement for a concert is useless if the concert has already taken place. Time has robbed the infor-

mation of its value. Alternatively, information about the concert may have already been seen elsewhere, making the advertisement of value only as confirmation.

Information value is relative The value of information can only be judged on the basis of the presence or absence of the information when reaching a particular decision. If it is known how important the information is to support that decision, then, if a value can be placed on making the correct decision, some sort of value can be allocated to the information. However, this requires a detailed assessment of how the characteristics of the information might affect the decision: if it is available; is it clear, accurate, reliable, etc. and to what extent?

Information value is difficult to predict The contribution that information can make to decision-making can only really be judged with hindsight, as it depends on the results of the decisions made based upon it. This means that predicting in advance whether or not it is worthwhile to obtain the information before making the decision can be no more than a best estimate. Again this assumes that some

43

value can be placed on making the correct decision.

Information impact is difficult to identify Most decisions are based on a combination of information, often from different sources. Often information will only be valuable in combination with other information. The effect of an individual piece of information is difficult to isolate in the decision-making process, making the assessment of its impact practically impossible.

So, while it is possible to identify which data to collect in order to provide information, it is very difficult to assign a value to the process, even after the results of any decision are known. This is one of the reasons why information systems benefits can be so difficult to establish.

What sorts of information are there?

Having defined data and information, it is now possible to look at the different types of data and information which may be present in an organisation. It is important for anyone working in an organisation to understand the nature of the information they receive. It is this that determines how much they can rely on the information and what other factors they need to consider.

Dimensions of information

Sources of information used in organisations range from formal to informal, internal to external in varying degrees depending upon individual needs and preferences. Generally speaking, however, all types of information sought and needed by managers can be viewed along the following interdependent dimensions:

Content   the type of information
               conveyed and what it tells us

Presentation   how the information is actually
               presented to us

Timing   when the information is
               communicated to us

Scope   the part of the organisation to
               which the information relates.

It is important that managers understand the nature of the information they receive. By understanding its nature, it is possible to balance its importance and relevance to a specific situation. Without such an understanding, a manager might give undue weight to inaccurate or irrelevant information.

Content

Managers need to be aware of the type of information presented to them so that they can assess its value in the correct context. Land and Kennedy-McGregor (1987) outline five types of information, three of which provide a useful taxonomy of information content (see Table 2.6). These three types of information define what the information is actually telling us:

Descriptive information provides a one-to-one mapping of the world in information.

Probabilistic information provides a means of describing the world when a full description is unavailable.

Explanatory or evaluative information is subjective, and forms an addition to the two previous types.

Knowing whether information represents recorded fact, an estimate of the facts, or an opinion about the facts, affects how it is likely to be treated by the recipient. This is because estimates are by their nature less accurate than a true record, which means that they require more careful consideration, such as how accurate is the estimate and what allowance should be made for error. Equally, if information is subjective, in the form of an opinion, then

Table 2.6 Content dimensions of information

Informative content	Example
Descriptive	Describes actions to be taken, maybe in the form of a set of procedures to follow;
	describes the rules and constraints governing those actions;
	describes some aspect of the real world, as it was, or as it is now, e.g. current stock levels.
Probabilistic	Predictive information based on models of how some aspect of the world behaves, with its value very much affected by the validity of the model, e.g. weather forecasts;
	descriptive information based on inference from samples, e.g. quality control reports, or market research surveys.
Explanatory and evaluative	Explains why a particular described situation arose, in order to facilitate corrective action to be taken;
	defines norms of behaviour and understanding which are implicit, rather than explicitly described;
	provides judgements about a situation, e.g. someone's opinion;
	defines the values and attitudes held by people, both inside and outside the organisation.

Source: adapted from Land and Kennedy-McGregor (1987)

allowances have to be made for any bias (intentional or otherwise) which may be placed on the information by the person supplying it.

An important point to make is that without the context of descriptive or probabilistic information, over-use of explanatory or evaluative information can lead to poor decision-making.

Presentation

As well as the content of information, it is necessary to look at the forms it can take. These can vary widely depending on circumstances. The form information takes can have a significant impact on the way it can be handled by the recipient. The three main issues which need to be considered are whether it is:

1 qualitative or quantitative
2 formal or informal
3 structured or unstructured

Quantitative information is the easiest to define, in that it is simply information consisting of numbers, e.g. the quantity of all products produced in the last month. This makes it easy to summarise accurately. On the other hand, qualitative information is non-numeric in form, and includes opinions, instructions and descriptions. These are often difficult to summarise without compromising their accuracy.

It is important to distinguish between quantitative/qualitative data and quantitative/qualitative information. The nature of the data does not determine the nature of the information in this way. For example, a complaint is qualitative data, an analysis showing the most common complaints is quantitative information. Similarly, a survey questionnaire may be used to collect data using Likert scales for answers (as shown in Figure 2.18), which are then collated and presented as qualitative information about a particular topic.

Information can also be formal, in that it forms part of a recognised communication process, e.g. a report. On the other hand, organisations also use informal information,

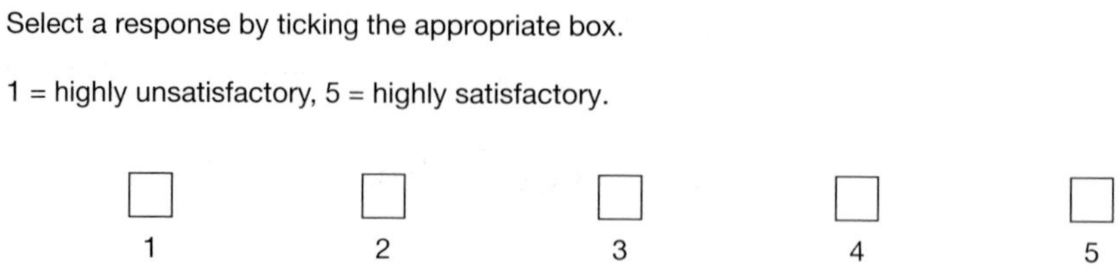

Select a response by ticking the appropriate box.

1 = highly unsatisfactory, 5 = highly satisfactory.

☐	☐	☐	☐	☐
1	2	3	4	5

Figure 2.18 A Likert scale

such as rumours and gossip. This leads to the need to consider the accuracy of information received. Generally speaking, informal information is less reliable than that produced by formal processes, though it must be remembered that even formal information can be used to mislead.

In terms of structure, organisations contain a wide variety of information. This can range from highly structured commercial information, such as invoices, through to relatively unstructured information in the form of conversations between colleagues. The issue of structure is central to the automation of information processing. Computers are good at handling structured information, but have difficulty with unstructured information. It must be remembered that the human brain is far more flexible than any electronic computer.

Timing

Having established the content and presentation of the information, we need to consider when it is available.

Information is produced and is required at different time intervals, some on a regular basis, and some as the necessity arises. It is important that managers understand what time period is covered by a piece of information, and whether or not it is directly comparable with similar information. Regular information can be used to monitor trends over time if based on a consistent time period. On the other hand, irregular information is unsuited to such a purpose.

Regular information

Regular information may be circulated on a daily, weekly, monthly, quarterly or yearly basis. It would be current information on the general state of the organisation, e.g. sales figures, production expenses, and the status of key customer accounts. Such information is intended to provide a consistent line of communication, with comparable information being available over a long period of time.

Irregular information

This would be provided on demand, or as the need arises, and may be in the form of exception reporting or warnings. Such information often needs to travel as quickly as possible, so that managerial action can be taken before further problems arise. Irregular information may come in the form of a sudden phone call, or arise as the result of a rapidly developing problem. Given the nature of irregular information, it is often inappropriate to use it as the basis for comparisons with previous events.

Scope

Finally, information can be viewed in terms of its scope. It is vital that managers know which part of the organisation is being described by the information they receive. If the question is asked 'How many people work here?', and the answer is 90, does this mean 90 in this office, this department, this country, or the whole organisation?

Within an organisation, the scope covered by information could be:

- an individual employee, e.g. training records;
- a subset of the product range, e.g. focused sales analysis;
- a team/task group, e.g. performance details;
- a business function, e.g. budgets;
- a cross-functional project, e.g. progress against schedule;
- the organisation as a whole, e.g. financial results;
- the business environment in which the organisation is operating, e.g. analysis of competitors' market share.

There is also a time factor involved in information scope, in that it is important to know if information is historical, current or about the future.

The above dimensions of information are useful when looking at the uses of information in organisations. However, it should be borne in mind that in reality the situation is very complex, and the classification of information, while aiding understanding, can only do so by taking a fairly simplistic view. In most cases, information will be found which fits into more than one category within each of the dimensions.

What about information quality?

Having looked at the types of information available in organisations, we need to consider what characteristics might be desirable in that information, and the data on which it is based. There are a number of issues which can be considered, the principal ones being:

- the accuracy of both the information and data;
- the timeliness of the information received;
- the reliability of both the information and data;

- the accessibility of the data and information;
- the appropriateness of the information.

All of these issues are important when deciding how to present information, both internally and externally to the organisation.

Accuracy

A helpful measure for accuracy is error rate and it is essential to keep errors to a minimum. Inaccuracy takes two forms: bias and error. Bias may well be a function of the way original data was generated, gathered, processed or presented. Random error is inaccuracy that arises from inherent variability, sometimes termed 'noise', while systemic (non-random) error may arise from selective collection of data, whereby greater emphasis is placed upon known data.

The more accurate the information, the more it contributes to the quality of decision-making. It normally also follows that the greater the accuracy of the information, the higher the cost of obtaining, verifying and maintaining the data on which it is based.

The degree of accuracy required will vary according to the needs of those who will use the information. Forecasts will, by their nature, be less accurate than reviews of historical data and information. Similarly, longer-term forecasts will be produced with and require less accuracy than, say, weekly sales projections. This is because information based on estimated data is less accurate that that based on actual data. The further into the future the data is projected, the less accurate the estimate will be. The level of accuracy needs to be sufficient for the task in hand.

Information that is inaccurate to the point of being misleading is clearly worse than no information at all. By the same token, spurious precision with figures to four or five decimal places may create unnecessary and unhelpful confusion. It is human nature to assume that very precise figures are also accurate. This is not necessarily so. Figures on bank statements and payslips need to display a high level of accuracy, whereas figures in company annual reports do not require that same level. Even if information is inaccurate, if this is known to the recipient, then he or she can make allowances for it. It should be borne in mind that spurious precision is not the same as accuracy, although it often lends an air of accuracy to data.

Finally, a word on the problem of cumulative inaccuracy. If data that is 90 per cent accurate goes through a number of processing stages, each with a processing accuracy of 90 per cent, then after just two processes, accuracy will have dropped to less than 73 per cent (90 per cent of 90 per cent of 90 per cent = 72.9 per cent).

Timeliness

Information must be available when needed; otherwise it may be considerably less useful or totally useless. This means that time must be allowed to gather and process the necessary information and data.

Another time-related factor is the time horizon over which information or data have been gathered. In most instances, resources will tend to be utilised to collect the most current information, unless historic trends are to be analysed.

Reliability

Reliability is often confused with accuracy. Accuracy is a measure of how good a description of events is given by the information. Reliability is a measure of the consistency of the information, i.e. how much it can be relied upon. Even if information is inaccurate, if this is known and the level of accuracy is consistent, we can still rely on the information. For example, if you ask a project manager whether or not his team will meet the deadline for a project he may say 'yes'. If you know that he is consistently realistic and usually correct in his estimates, you can accept

his answer. If, on the other hand, you know that he is always optimistic, you can make allowances for that when you make use of what he has told you, maybe by adding a month or two.

Reliability of information will vary according to the reliability of source data and the way(s) in which the data has been gathered, analysed and manipulated. Unreliable and misleading information is potentially highly problematic, especially if it is believed to be reliable. This makes reliability potentially more important than accuracy as a characteristic of data and information.

Accessibility

When deciding which data should be collected, the accessibility of the data needs to be considered. Some data can be very difficult to collect for a number of reasons. These include the remoteness of the source of the data, e.g. a long-distance lorry driver; the speed with which the data needs to be collected, e.g. in a fast-moving automated production line; and the physical environment of the data, e.g. monitoring the temperature in a kiln.

The information produced must also be accessible whenever it is needed and be presented in a useful, user-friendly format. For example, if large numbers of printouts are used to show columns of figures, instead of graphs, to depict important trends, understanding may be considerably diminished. What is more, different information users prefer different presentation formats according to what they respond to best in terms of clarity and what they feel most comfortable with. Morton Thiokol were criticised for the way they presented data to NASA prior to the failure of the space shuttle *Challenger*, yet the data presented was clear and according to the engineers unambiguous: the shuttle could suffer from a catastrophic failure if launched under a certain temperature.

Effective access to information is a frequent failing that can be overcome by designing and implementing the most appropriate information systems.

Appropriateness

Above all, information should be appropriate for its intended use. There are four main issues to consider:

1 the completeness of the information;
2 the level of detail required;
3 the level of summarisation required;
4 the relevance of the information to its recipient.

Completeness relates to the extent to which the information and data available are adequate for the task in hand. The main difficulty is deciding at which point information is complete. Unless the task is totally structured and clearly defined, it is frequently impossible to have totally complete information, as there will always remain other factors to be considered. Relevance has to be prioritised and cut-off limits established. In reality, it will often be necessary to work with incomplete information, otherwise decisions and actions will rarely be carried out on a timely basis.

[I]t is not the facts that decide: people have to choose between imperfect alternatives on the basis of uncertain knowledge and fragmentary understanding.

(Drucker, 1989)

A fine *level of detail* is appropriate in certain situations to a greater extent than in others. Financial statements need to be precise and clearly detailed, as do the results of crucial scientific experiments, but long-term estimates of sales figures cannot be stated precisely or in detail. Instead ballpark overview figures should be used. Spurious precision and detail in such situations lends an air of accuracy, which is misleading.

Care must be taken not to produce too high a level of detail where it is not required. As well as being unnecessarily costly, the details may swamp the essence of the information, leaving the reader confused. On the other hand, too much approximation too early, such as premature rounding of numbers, is also potentially dangerous.

Summarisation can help make information more readable and thereby more comprehensible, especially if the information is very detailed. While on the one hand a summary can provide clarity and highlight important issues, it can also hide and mask information, such as with averaging, which may hide significant outlying values.

Summaries are essential to busy senior managers and directors who do not have the time to review all the details of information contained in lengthy reports. However, summarisation has to be well done to be of any value, and the art of summary is by no means commonplace.

Relevance or pertinence depends upon factors already considered, such as timeliness and completeness, and can be measured by the extent to which the information directly assists in making decisions. Levels of precision and accuracy are also crucial and must match the particular needs.

Useful information should represent the minimum necessary to fulfil requirements for the decision or task to be undertaken. Information overload serves merely to confuse, distract and increase the costs of processing. For each situation there will be an optimal degree of summary and detail, e.g. the required detail in accounting statements will differ among diverse information users across the organisation. Auditors would require considerable detail, whereas shareholders would be quite content with a more concise summary.

It is worth considering the characteristics of good information relevant to different levels of management activity. Strategic planning involves a broader scope of information in the form of an overview, while operational control requires more detailed information from a narrow, specific perspective.

Finally, the issue of potential conflict is worth mentioning. Providing information which has more than one of the above attributes may result in conflict. For example, to provide information that is accurate and complete, but also concise may be difficult; likewise, to provide information that is complete and detailed may take too long, thereby being no longer timely, and may cost too much to produce. A suitable trade-off will be needed to arrive at an appropriate compromise between desirable attributes to produce the best outcome possible in a given circumstance. A different type of conflict arises between explicit and tacit knowledge, and the sharing of information can be problematic.

Knowledge

Knowledge management initiatives help organisations create and distribute internal knowledge and have become important aspects of organisational strategy. The knowledge-based theory of a firm suggests that knowledge is an organisational asset that enables sustainable competitive advantage in the face of ever-increasing levels of competition. Knowledge management systems are being implemented to increase the quality and speed of knowledge creation and distribution in organisations (Leidner, 1999). Corporate intranets are examples of such systems and their main aim is to provide easily accessible, accurate, relevant information to those who need it, irrespective of where they are in the organisation. BP's corporate intranet is a global resource for all parts of the organisation. In a recent roll out of PCs at a refinery in Scotland the subcontractor

was able to access software applications for installation from the BP portal where software from worldwide locations could be accessed. The financial services company, Standard Life, posts all relevant human resource information for its employees on the intranet, as well as using it to provide a 'single customer view', whereby anyone ringing in for information and advice can receive what they need from one phone call. Corporate intranets are private, web-based networks that connect employees and business partners to vital corporate information (Thyfault, 1996; Vidal et al., 1998).

Of considerable potential value from intranets is the provision of tools for knowledge management. Knowledge includes the understandings, insights and practical know-how that employees possess. Knowledge management is a method of systematically and actively managing ideas, information and knowledge of employees, and knowledge management systems are intended to help organise, interpret and make accessible the expertise of an organisation's human capital to help cope with numerous business challenges.

We need to make the distinction between explicit and tacit knowledge. The integration of explicit knowledge, such as details of training and development programmes, involves few problems because of its inherent communicability (Grant, 1996). Explicit knowledge is that knowledge that is transmitted in a formal, systematic way (Nonaka, 1994). It is externally documented tacit knowledge (Brown and Duguid, 1991). Technological advances have greatly facilitated the codification, communication, assimilation, storage and retrieval of explicit knowledge (Huber, 1991). However, it is the context-dependent knowledge held by professionals, referred to as tacit knowledge, that has to-date proved to be fairly elusive. The major challenge with tacit knowledge is less its creation than its communication and integration (Grant,

1996). Such knowledge is of limited organisational value if it is not shared. There is also the further interpretation of information as power that precludes such knowledge sharing. The first person with a piece of information may be able to obtain some form of financial advantage (Metcalfe and Powell, 1995). Boland (1986), meanwhile, disagrees with the concept of more messages formalised, captured and processed as equating to possession of more power, believing instead that it is not the capture of messages that is important but the ability to influence concerns. One problem with the schematic illustrated in Figure 2.16 is that to get organisations to share knowledge, they, or more accurately the people in them, will have to address the things that go wrong. Getting people to admit to their mistakes is not how most organisational cultures operate. What is clear is that issues of information sharing and information being associated with power are inextricably linked to issues relating to organisational culture, which is discussed in detail in Chapter 6.

Summary

Organisations can be defined and classified in a number of ways. It is important to understand what elements make up organisations, what functions are involved, what processes, what activities. Organisations can be structured differently and structure has to be considered prior to IS implementation to ensure a match between the two. Organisational structure will be dealt with in more detail in Chapter 6. Data, information and knowledge are extensively discussed and links between them underlined, the ways in which data can be processed to provide meaningful information are detailed, as are the value, perspectives and characteristics of information that increase its quality. The concept of knowledge management is briefly outlined, along with a number of the features of organisational learning.

Review questions

1   What are the different metaphors for organisations?
2   What are the main functions of a business organisation?
3   Explain the value chain.
4   How does an organisation relate to its environment?
5   Define data, information and knowledge.
6   What is the relationship between data, information and knowledge?
7   What types of data are there?
8   How can data be processed into information?
9   What is the value of information?
10   Explain the four dimensions of information.
11   Explain the three categories of information content.
12   Explain the three main elements of information presentation.
13   What characteristics are present in good quality information?
14   What do you understand by the terms 'knowledge management' and 'organizational learning'?

Case study

Information management in a Primary Care Trust

Current situation in the Trust

At present there are 8,000 staff and only 1,800 PC users, who are mainly administrative staff, and there is no consistency across the Trust with data and information input. Currently, senior management/clinicians have priority with access to the NHSnet; all other levels of staff will increasingly be given access where necessary. The gap between IS integration requirements and the current IS environment within the Trust has slowly improved over recent months. In the near future the Trust wants the majority of its systems to be used proactively to communicate and manage clinical tasks by all clinical disciplines. All data and information will be coded on user input and the collation of data sets will be aligned with national standards, such as the Scottish Intercollegiate Guidelines Network (SIGN). Additionally, the Trust wishes to have coordinated IS support for the new NHS24 helpline. At present, however, the Trust and associated hospital are at the basic level of usage of patient data.

The hospital operates on mainly a paper-based system and communication throughout the Trust is dominated by use of the telephone. Within the different departments there are inadequate levels of modern equipment, and investment in technology has been too slow and patchy through lack of government funding. The implementation of new systems such as the Patient Information Management System (PIMS), Paragon and CIS2000 have been implemented on a priority or ad hoc basis to replace legacy systems. Implementation of the Paragon system has caused both financial and future integration problems; it was implemented on the demands and preferences of senior consultants who refused to accept the PIMS system three weeks before the implementation date.

Currently, a small percentage of staff can communicate by email but this is limited to certain areas within the Trust. The introduction of email has caused operational problems for staff, many of whom do not understand how to use it and find it confusing, even after training has been provided. Further training has been offered to some staff but it must nevertheless be borne in mind that by 2004, 50 per cent of primary and community Trusts must have implemented the network infrastructure to support an integrated electronic patient-record system.

Current problems with data capture and encoding

The IM&T manager explained that realistically many of the benefits to be gained through information would only be achieved through the implementation and efficient use of computers throughout the Trust. However, data must then be organised, structured and encoded by staff and not simply be captured and stored as free text. The following data and information are used or needed by staff on a daily basis:

- clinical data
- demographic data
- financial data

- published literature
- research data
- epidemiological data

The main source of health care data is contained within patients' medical records. Problems arise with unreadable handwriting and complex or disorganised notes; more specifically, free text including abbreviations has hindered the transfer from paper files to computerised records. Currently there are two approaches to capturing data to facilitate decision-making:

1 Clinicians fill out medical forms or administrative staff at a later date extract data from the patient's records and fill out the same forms. While clinicians find it a laborious task to fill out the relevant forms, it is harder for the administrative staff to search through incomplete and inaccurate data. As a result, the extraction of data becomes costly and time consuming for each department.
2 At present, PIMS allows the clinical staff to use computers directly on certain wards during patient care. This ensures that key data items are suitably coded and entered on to the system after consultation with the patient. This approach is in line with the Audit Commission's vision that hospital IS/IT should focus on this type of system that records patient data at source. It is assumed that in the long term all staff will recognise the tangible benefits of data being collected electronically. However, at present, on wards with PIMS access doctors have expressed concerns about the time required to input all the data. Therefore data input has been passed down to the staff nurse, who in turn has refused to input the data for the same reasons and responsibility is then devolved to lower grade nurses. Consequently, the majority of nursing staff have returned to the old paper system or, in some instances, partial information is entered on both systems. Information is therefore lost and work time increased to retrieve data. Currently there is no solution to this problem as neither medical records nor the network manager can force staff to use these new systems. Change will only occur when access to paper systems has been withdrawn and that would be unlikely as the patient's life would potentially be put at risk.

Fear of technology

A senior clinician explained that fear of technology was a factor in IS introduction. A lack of keyboard skills among senior clinicians is viewed as 'being shown up in front of juniors'. Cultural issues, such as personal attitudes and staff training were also problematic. Training was never long enough or in depth and technical support was viewed as inefficient and poor. When asked about plans to enhance and change the hospital's information procedures, both clinicians and administrative staff were not happy, first, about the disruption of change and the inevitable teething problems and, second, about management being able to monitor and measure their work performance.

Nursing informatics in a GP surgery

Currently, data input has been via palmtop hardware, shortly to be replaced by the new Community Information System (CIS) 2000. The introduction of data input through a PC within the health centre will allow better time management and ensure a more efficient and effective service that can be integrated with the GPASS system and the NHSnet. However, the health centre is independently owned by the GPs through a business partnership and run as a small business. As a consequence, the Trust cannot implement or force new IS change if the practice does not wish to do so.

The CIS 2000 is a computerised database that allows the district nurse to input very precise and consistent information about the care and support of patients and is discipline specific. The system was introduced to support business processes, provide a data input facility and relevant, timely information and communication links for district nurses in their operational activities. Additionally, audit and management information was to be drawn from aggregate data. District nurses have experienced both advantages and disadvantages after the system became operational, as follows.

Advantages:

- Enhanced communication flows between nursing staff, with more legible, accessible electronic records.
- Improved confidentiality – records are password protected in the system.
- Better safety – paper records can be destroyed by fire, while electronic records are regularly backed up and can be restored/operationalised within 24 hours.
- Better security – if a file is accidentally deleted it still remains on the system back-up.
- Access to Word and Power Point.
- Improved speed of request – time spent on data entry is less and direct desktop access removes the previous need to upload data from palmtops.
- email will allow nursing staff to keep a record of correspondence and will encourage a focus on information needed from the internal/external environment.
- Improved presentation and organisation of information.

Disadvantages:

- Security – although a password is needed, it is sometimes pinned up on the wall for all to see – in future there will be restricted access.
- There is no connection of this system with any other system in the practice, it is not connected to the NHSnet and there are not enough terminals within the health centre.
- A lack of feedback from senior managers on the benefits of the new care plan report information.
- Data is duplicated – district nurses still have to enter data into a hand-held diary that must be kept for five years under current statute law. These records are also on paper and a further copy is held by patients in their home.
- Audit has become evidence-based. The system categories all district nurse visits as the same irrespective of individual patients' needs. This adds to problems of how to measure quality.
- There is no file provision for the input of equipment needed by patients and therefore the procurement budget is high.
- Increased data entry by clinicians may have significant effects on their time management.
- The medical problem with discharge details of a care package has a limited choice of medical diagnosis with consequent inaccuracies in reports that often upset patients.
- The system does not flag-up when a care package has expired and needs to be reviewed.

- Patient referral details do not indicate why in some cases a patient's treatment has been for long periods of time. Information is not stored on the report to help and advise the district nurse, especially if one district nurse is covering someone else's patients.
- The care aim may be 'achieved' or 'partially achieved' and this is difficult to differentiate. No guidance procedures have been given with the system to make a unified choice.
- The district nurse housekeeping report is a duplicate of the health visitor's report and therefore unnecessary duplication of visits may occur with consequent loss of labour and cost efficiency.
- The system does not deliver the information requirements for senior management decisions on budgets. The district nurse has to collate the information from relevant paper documents and files.
- The system has not delivered what the design team originally promised and no information requirements were elicited from the district nurses at the design stage.
- The system is supposed to be owned by all staff but the majority of the nurses are still returning to paper-based file entry as it is quicker. Time management is a problem and the new system has arguably increased the working day by at least one hour per day.
- The data set was rationalised to increase the reliability of the data items for use in clinical audit, practice and clinical governance, but rationalisation has taken place without consultation with the health centres by the working group.

The CIS 2000 system should have improved the communication and consistency of advice to patients, shared and integrated clinical information and improved the professional relationship between the district nurse and the GP. However, this has not happened and a senior manager explained that within the health centre the GPs are not enthused about nurses having access to patients' medical records at the touch of a button. Currently the GPs have access to the NHSnet and use a very basic Torex Meditel system to store patient information. Therefore the new CIS 2000 system cannot be integrated with Torex and no future plans have been made to upgrade to the favoured GPASS system, funded by the government at no financial cost to the health centre and already used by 84 per cent of all other health centres in the area.

The district nurse argued that to improve the efficiency of the community service provided, access to both the patient's clinical history and all current information held on record needs to be through integration of all practice IS. The creation of a longitudinal record was specified as necessary to support day-to-day work and would enhance the quality of care received by the patient.

Senior management decision support

It was assumed that senior management would provide greater input with the identification of information that would be required from the CIS 2000 system in order to support decision-making. However, when asked why summary data and reports from this system had not provided improved information analysis for monthly budgeting, the senior manager replied defensively, 'This system does not provide any type of information I can use. If I require specific information, I will phone the district nurse and ask her in person.' In contrast to this, the district nurse explained that, following training and briefings on the system, they were led to believe that this system was supposed to improve the quality of information to support senior management decision-making.

What it would mean to be paperless

To move away from a paper-based system in the health centre would entail the appointments system being completely computerised, which would allow audit of consultations and waiting times. The appointments would have to be backed up on a floppy disk at the end of the day. This would provide a copy in case of a systems failure that could easily be run on a standalone PC. During the consultation period the GP would have to work on a computerised patient-record file and consequently the receptionist would not need to file or retrieve patients' medical records.

The GP would Read code everything important, including the patient's diagnosis during the consultation. Additionally, blood pressure, weight, family history and smoking habits would also need to be coded. Items of service claims such as immunisation and minor surgeries would also have to be detailed and stored. This would reduce staff workload and ensure the claim is made within the given time period. The patient's history and examination would be entered in free text and medication entered into the prescribing module.

The advantage of changing to a computerised IS would benefit the users (the GPs) with possible prompts to guide them through the consultation process. Additionally, the business process could be enhanced through further protocols and templates. For example, when a diagnosis is entered, such as a high body mass index (BMI), an automatic prompt for referral would be highlighted to the practice dietician. To reduce the drug budget in the practice the system could suggest a cheaper alternative, thereby keeping the drug budget in line with any prescribing incentive scheme being encouraged.

Online help for GPs can be accessed as well as an electronic formulary for prescribing, which could be chosen as part of a package on the procured system. Access to the NHSnet and the Internet also provides access to information services, such as the National Electronic Library for Health, SIGN guidelines and eGuidelines.

Communication with other organisations outside the practice could be enhanced. Downloading hospital pathology results and X-ray reports would save both time and money and improved service delivery. As a result, the GP would be able to check all results online, make any further comments and store all the information on the patient's electronic record. The receptionist would then access this information when the patient enquired about their test results and relay any further comments made by their GP. Hospital letters could be scanned into the clinical system and the staff would be able to Read code the diagnosis made by the consultant and highlight in the electronic patient record any further action required. The letter would then be passed on to the GP to read and, when satisfied, the letter would be destroyed. All staff would have access to all relevant data and therefore security measures provided by an ID code would be imperative to indicate who entered the patient's information.

If the above measures were adopted by this health centre and health centres in general, practices would be able to deliver the government's vision of an integrated primary and community electronic patient record. However, at the same time, every hospital would have to become computerised for the whole system to work efficiently and effectively. A New Zealand example illustrates what could be achieved.

A benchmark: the New Zealand experience

In 1996 New Zealand's new coalition government changed direction and removed the health service from the private sector's competitive marketplace. As a result, greater emphasis was placed on collaboration than competition. The benefits gained through the unpopular reforms of 1993 had created Primary Care Groups and Trusts with newly developed IS/IT infrastructures and by 1996 these organisations were mature enough to be integrated with secondary care organisations.

In the largest primary care hospital in the South Island priority was given to the implementation of an appointment system. Only when this system achieved the required performance levels and benefits of staff members receiving information at the correct time, in the correct place and format was attention directed towards the management of outpatient referrals. Hospital consultants initiated most of the work needed to reduce patient waiting lists and inappropriate/inadequate GP referrals. Joint referral protocols and guidelines were developed to clarify when a patient should or should not be referred. Mandatory electronic referrals must be completed and sent to the consultant with the degree of urgency stated. GPs and consultants thereby engage in the prioritisation process, sharing resources and information to provide a better service. GP fax lines within outpatient departments permitted a 72-hour rapid response service, which reduced the volume of outpatient referrals.

There have been also national integrated-care pilot schemes to develop a seamless health service for the elderly. The executive team included stakeholders from the primary, secondary, community and residential organisations. Follow-up consultations were removed from the normal secondary care setting to primary care. An expert system was developed jointly by consultants and GPs to carry out post-discharge assessments through an agreed checklist. The information gathered was then shared with the consultant through electronic transferral. As a result, the waiting list for follow-up consultations was reduced by 80 per cent and the availability of outpatient appointments was greater.

Case questions

1 What are the main problems of data and information management in the Trust?
2 How do organisation cultural issues relate to these problems and to system development issues?
3 What sort of future developments are needed in the longer term to improve data and information management?
4 Which initial steps could be taken to begin the process of change for the better?

References and further reading

Ahituv N. and Neumann S. (1987) 'Decision Making and the Value of Information', in Galliers R. (ed.) *Information Analysis. Selected Readings*, Addison-Wesley: Reading, MA.

Ahituv N., Igbaria M. and Sella A. (1998) 'The Effects of Time Pressure and Completeness of Information on Decision Making', *Journal of MIS*, 15(2), Fall: 153–172.

Alter S. (1996) *Information Systems. A Management Perspective*, Benjamin/Cummings: Menlo Park, CA.

Anderson R. (1986) *Management, Information Systems and Computers*, Macmillan: Houndsmills, Basingstoke, Hampshire and London.

Barnes S.J. (2002) 'The Mobile Commerce Value Chain: Analysis and Future Developments', *International Journal of Information Management*, 22: 91–108.

Beardwell I. and Holden L. (eds) (1994) *Human Resource Management: A Contemporary Perspective*, Pitman: London.

Blumenthal S.C. (1969) *Management Information Systems*, Prentice-Hall: Englewood Cliffs, NJ.

Boland R. (1986) 'The Fantasies of Information', *Advances in Public Interest Accounting*, 1: 49–65.

Brown J.S. and Duguid P. (1991) 'Organisational Learning and Communities-of-Practice: Toward a Unified View of Working, Learning and Innovation', *Organisation Science*, 2(1): 40–57.

Ciborra C.U. and Andreu R. (2001) 'Sharing Knowledge Across Boundaries', *Journal of Information Technology*, 16(2), June: 73–81.

Clancy J.J. (1989) *The Invisible Powers: The Language of Business*. Lexington, MA: Lexington Books.

Davenport T.H. and Beers M.C. (1995) 'Managing Information About Processes', *Journal of MIS*, 12(1), Summer: 57–80.

Davis W.S. (1995) *Management, Information and Systems: an Introduction to Business Information Systems*, West Publishing: New York.

Drucker P. (1989), *The Practice of Management*, Heinemann: London.

Edmunds A. and Moris A. (2000) 'The Problem of Information Overload in Business Organisations: a Review of the Literature', *International Journal of Information Management*, 20: 17–28.

Forte P. (1994) 'Data Rich, Information Poor: Data, Information and Decision Support in the NHS', *European Journal of Information Systems*, 3(2): 148–154.

Fox C.J. (1983) *Information and Misinformation*, Greenwood Press: Westport, CT.

Friedenberger W.B., Lipp A. and Watson H.J. (1997) 'Information Requirements of Turnaround Managers at the Beginning of Engagements', *Journal of MIS*, 13(4), Spring: 167–192.

Frishammar J. (2002) 'Characteristics in Information Processing Approaches', *International Journal of Information Management*, 22: 143–156.

Galbraith J.R. (1977) *Organisation Design*, Addison-Wesley: Reading, MA.

Galliers R.D. (1987) *Information Analysis*, Addison-Wesley: Reading, MA.

Galliers R.D. (ed.) (1990) *Information Analysis. Selected Readings*, Addison-Wesley: Reading, MA.

Gerloff E.A. (1985) *Organisational Theory and Design. A Strategic Approach for Management*, McGraw-Hill: New York.

Grant R.M. (1996) 'Prospering in Dynamically-Competitive Environments: Organisational Capability as Knowledge Integration', *Organisation Science*, 7(4): 375–387.

Grise M-L. and Gallupe R.B. (1999–2000) 'Information Overload: Addressing the Productivity Paradox in Face-to-Face Electronic Meetings', *Journal of MIS*, 16(3), Winter: 157–185.

Hall R. (1991) *Organisations. Structures, Processes and Outcomes*, 5th edn, Prentice Hall International: Englewood Cliffs, NJ.

Hammer M. and Champy J. (2001) *Reengineering the Corporation: a Manifesto for Business Revolution*, HarperBusiness: London.

Hicks B.J., Culley S.J., Allen R.D. and Mullineux G. (2002) 'A Framework for the Requirements of Capturing, Storing and Reusing Information and Knowledge in Engineering Design', *International Journal of Information Management*, 22: 263–280.

Hislop D. (2002) 'Mission Impossible? Communicating and Sharing Knowledge via Information Technology', *Journal of Information Technology*, 17(3), September: 165–177.

Huber G. (1991) 'Organisational Learning: the Contributing Processes and the Literatures', *Organisation Science*, 2(1): 88–115.

Isakowitz T. and Bieber M. (1995) 'Navigation in Information-intensive Environments', *Journal of MIS*, 11(4), Spring: 5–8.

Johnson J.D. (1996) *Information Seeking. An Organisational Dilemma*, Quorum Books: London

Korn J. (2001) 'Design and Delivery of Information', *European Journal of Information Systems*, 10: 41–54.

Lambert R. and Peppard J. (1999) 'The Information Technology–Organisational Design Relationship', in Galliers R.D., Leidner D. and Baker B. (eds) *Strategic Information Management*, 2nd edn, Butterworth Heinemann: Oxford.

Land F.F. and Kennedy-McGregor M. (1987) 'Information and Information Systems: Concepts and Perspectives', in Galliers R.D. (ed.) *Information Analysis. Selected Readings*, Addison-Wesley: Reading, MA.

Lee S. and Leifer R.P. (1992) 'A Framework for Linking the Structure of Information Systems with Organisational Requirements for Information Sharing', *Journal of MIS*, 8(4), Spring: 27–44.

Leidner D.E. (1999) 'Information Technology and Organisational Culture', in Galliers R.D. and Baker, B. (eds) *Strategic Information Management*, Butterworth-Heinemann: Oxford, pp. 523–550.

Leonidas G. (2000) 'Information Design: the Missing Link in Information Management?', *International Journal of Information Management*, 20: 73–76.

Levitin A.V. and Redman T.C. (1998) 'Data as a Resource: Properties, Implications and Prescriptions', *Sloan Management Review*, Fall: 89–101.

Liebenau J. and Backhouse J. (1990) *Understanding Information. An Introduction*, Macmillan: London.

Martin C. and Powell P. (1992) *Information Systems. A Management Perspective*, McGraw-Hill: Maidenhead.

Metcalfe M. and Powell P. (1995) 'Information: a Perceiver-Concerns Perspective', *European Journal of Information Systems*, 4: 121–129.

Miles R. (1980) *Macro Organisational Behaviour*, Good Year: Santa Monica, CA.

Morgan G. (1986) *Images of Organisations*, Sage: London.

Murdick R.G. and Munson J.C. (1986) *MIS Concepts and Design*, 2nd edn, Prentice-Hall: Englewood Cliffs, NJ.

Nonaka I. (1994) 'A Dynamic Theory of Organisational Knowledge Creation', *Organisation Science*, 5(1): 14–37.

Peppard J. (ed.) (1993) *IT Strategy for Business*, Pitman: London.

Porter M.E. (1985) *Competitive Advantage*, New York: Free Press.

Ravault R.J. (1987) 'The Ideology of the Information Age in a Senseless World', in Slack J.D. and Fejes F. (eds) *The Ideology of the Information Age*, Ablex: Norwood, NJ.

Robbins S.P. (1996) *Organisational Behaviour: Concepts, Controversies, Applications*, Prentice-Hall: London.

Salaun Y. and Flores K. (2001) 'Information Quality: Meeting the Needs of the Consumer', *International Journal of Information Management*, 21: 21–37.

Schein E.H. (1980) *Organisational Psychology*, 3rd edn, Prentice-Hall: Englewood Cliffs, NJ.

Shannon C. and Weaver W. (1949) *The Mathematical Theory of Communications*, University of Illinois Press: Urbana, IL.

Silverman D. (1970) *The Theory of Organisations*, Heinemann: London.

Slack N.G.C., Chambers S.H., Johnston R., Harrison A. and Harland C. (1995) *Operations Management*, Pitman: London.

Swanson E.B. (1985–1986) 'A Note on Information Attributes', *Journal of MIS*, 11(3), Winter: 87.

Taylor A. and Farrell S. (1994) *Information Management for Business*, Aslib: London.

Thyfault M.E. (1996) 'The Intranet Rolls In', *Information Week*, 564(15): 76–78.

Tuomi I. (1999–2000) 'Data is More than Knowledge: Implications of the Reversed Knowledge Hierarchy for Knowledge Management and Organisational Memory', *Journal of MIS*, 16(3), Winter: 103–117.

Vidal F., Saintoyant P.Y. and Meilhaud J. (1998) *Objectif Intranet: Enjeux et Applications*, Les Editions d'Organisation: Paris.

Wang R.Y. and Strong D.M. (1996) 'Beyond Accuracy: What Data Quality Means to Data Consumers', *Journal of MIS*, 12(4), Spring: 5–34.

Ward J. and Peppard J. (2002) *Strategic Planning for Information Systems*, Wiley: Chichester.

Wersig G. and Neveling U. (1975) 'The Phenomena of Interest to Information Science', *Information Scientist*, 9: 127–140.

Yadav S.B. (1985) 'Classifying an Organisation to Identify Its Information Requirements: a Comprehensive Framework', *Journal of MIS*, 2(1): 39–60.

Information on Coats plc http://www.coatsplc.co.uk/co/aboutus/ accessed January 2005.

Chapter 3

Management, information and decision-making

··

Learning objectives

After reading this chapter you should be able to:

- describe what business managers do;
- describe how managers use information;
- discuss the relationships between different levels of organisational management;
- compare the characteristics of different management decision-making processes;
- understand information systems planning, control and decision-making.

Introduction

Having looked at what organisations are and considered some main characteristics of the information that flows around organisations, we now need to examine who managers are and what they do. Managers have a variety of roles and carry out a number of different activities in organisations for which they produce and use information.

Managerial roles are discussed and related to the different information needs of managers depending on what they are trying to do. The functions of planning, controlling and making decisions are also explained in some detail, highlighting the need to support these activities with good, relevant information. Different types of decision-making are examined as is the decision-making process to highlight different information needs at different managerial levels and pave the way for issues of decision support in Chapter 5.

Who are managers?

Managers set and monitor organisational objectives by allocating human and material resources and directing operations. They bring together the individuals in an organisation with its goals and needs, establishing individual and collective responsibilities to achieve what is necessary for the business. Managers have a variety of organisational roles and perform a number of functions, but essentially they are all decision-makers.

The importance of good management cannot be over-emphasised; it frequently determines business success or failure. Good management has two criteria, which must be carefully balanced to ensure optimisation of available resources. Managers have to be efficient, i.e. accomplish tasks in the best possible way, and effective, i.e. make sure the tasks they are performing are the right ones. A manufacturer of furniture could produce much more elaborate and attractive items by disregarding materials and labour costs, but this would be inefficient management. Similarly, service organisations which spend a great deal of time and money perfecting aspects of their service that are relatively unimportant to their customers are managing in a highly ineffective way. Poor management is often manifested in both inefficiency and ineffectiveness or ineffectiveness obtained through inefficiency.

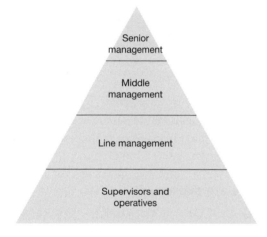

Figure 3.1 Levels in the organisation

Organisational members can be divided into the two principal categories of operatives and managers. Operatives work directly on tasks with little if any responsibility for overseeing the work of others. Managers, on the other hand, tend to direct the activities of other people and can be considered on three broad levels, outlined in the following list, with operatives making up the fourth level, as shown in Figure 3.1:

1 senior managers/directors, who formulate policy and strategy, set objectives and determine the direction in which the organisation should go;
2 middle managers/executives, who carry out existing policy within the corporate functions such as production or personnel;
3 line managers/supervisors, who coordinate and control operational processes and are in direct contact with the workforce/operatives.

Senior managers

Senior managers, such as the Chief Executive Officer, the Director of Research and Development, the Procurement Division Manager, are responsible for the overall direction and operations of the organisation. They establish objectives, policies and strategies for the organisation as a whole, for a single major business unit or for a major functional area. They frequently represent their organisations within the broader business environment. To a lesser extent they communicate with middle and line managers within the organisation.

Middle managers

Middle managers take the broad overall strategies and policies from senior management and translate them into specific objectives and plans for line management to implement at the operational level. Middle managers focus on solving business problems, such as providing a better, more responsive service to customers, and coordinating staff activities to improve efficiency and effectiveness. Most of their time tends to be spent on the telephone, attending various meetings and preparing reports. Middle managers may be departmental heads, district or divisional managers.

Line managers

Line managers have direct responsibility for specific activities within the organisation. They may be unit managers or project leaders. They provide an essential link between senior/middle management and the operatives who actually perform the work, and with whom most of their time is spent. Such managers usually lead hectic lives, solving problems and communicating on a daily basis within their own work areas to ensure that 'the job gets done!' They work in the 'firing line', at the sharp end where the action is and frequently have to 'fight fires' to avoid complete chaos.

Operatives

This may not at first glance seem to be a level of management. Almost by definition operatives are not managers, but organisations frequently rely on non-management grade staff to manage their basic business activities. Such people are often known as supervisors or foremen, i.e. those directly responsible for the production of goods and services. Operatives and their supervisors report directly to line managers.

It is worth noting that this is a traditional type of representation of management structure. There are many organisations that have eschewed the services of their middle management, preferring a flatter management structure in order to be more responsive to changes in the operating environment. Additionally, there can be cross-over between these levels depending on the industrial sector.

What do managers do?

A framework for managerial activities

The framework for managerial activities devised by R.N. Anthony (1965) is useful in helping us to understand what managers do. Table 3.1 shows three strands of managerial activity: strategic planning, management control and operational control, giving organisational systems examples of each.

Organisations need to plan for the future at the strategic level. Strategic planning is the process of deciding what are the mission, objectives and main priorities of the organisation. Resources required to achieve these objectives need to be allocated and appropriate corporate policies formulated to guide the strategic planning process. Management control ensures these resources are obtained and then used both efficiently and effectively to achieve the organisational objectives. The specific operational

Table 3.1 Planning and control systems

Strategic planning	Managerial control	Operational control
Sales forecasting	Budgetary control	Order entry processing
Financial modelling	Inventory management	Scheduling production
Capacity planning	Supplier evaluation	Stock control
Manpower planning	Market research	Cost accounting
Product range planning	Expense reporting	Word processing
Mergers/acquisitions planning	Work-in-progress control	Employee records
		Invoicing

Source: based on Anthony (1965)

tasks required to ensure the smooth running of the organisation and achieve efficiency and effectiveness constitute the process of operational control.

Examples of strategic planning, management control and operational control are given in the box below.

As far as evolutionary development of organisational systems goes, a solid foundation of operational systems is built first on a function-by-function basis. On this foundation, control systems are built by gathering operational information and analysing it with a view to facilitating coordination, communication and

Strategic planning

A major Healthcare Trust decided that a priority business objective was to establish a more comprehensive networked system of information for more accurate capacity planning and resource allocation. An early requirement was for a corporate-wide audit of all hardware and software, followed by an analysis of information flows from other parts of the Healthcare Trust, such as GP practices, into the Contracts and Planning Department, which was regarded as the organisational information hub. Also required was a thorough data collection with respect to demographics and geographical location of the different areas covered by the Trust so as to allocate available resources more equitably.

Management control

A medium-sized manufacturer of medical equipment wished to enhance its reputation for good service to its customers and trim manufacturing wastage costs. The customer services manager obtained the go-ahead and resources to implement an appropriate customer service training programme for all relevant staff. Prior to the programme, information was collected from operations on rework and scrap rates and from packaging and distribution on breakages and customer returns. Late deliveries and product unreliability, the two major sources of customer complaints, became the main themes for improvement in the training workshop sessions.

Operational control

A small curtain-manufacturer has procedures in place to monitor carefully the quantities of fabric delivered to incoming goods and check the fabric for faults prior to its release on to the shop floor. Once in the shop floor area, there is a large whiteboard on one wall, which details operational activities according to the urgency of different customer orders. This production schedule is altered frequently so as to reflect work completed or held up for any reason. Work in progress is monitored to optimise the use of staff time in the various tasks of cutting, machining and finishing and to prevent the build up of unproductive bottlenecks in the system. Quality control takes the form of sample in-process inspection and 100 per cent final inspection of finished curtains prior to folding and packaging.

control between different functions. Finally, the information is further transformed to develop strategic planning systems for senior managers to define the future direction of the organisation.

IS applications develop and spread up through the organisation hierarchy from the operational level to the senior management level. Different rates of evolutionary progress in different areas of the business can hamper the integration of control and planning systems, which are cross-functional. Nevertheless an upward evolutionary trend is the norm and incremental systems development can be viewed from the perspective of Anthony's framework for managerial activities.

Management roles

Management roles in organisations vary according to the levels of management. Senior managers are responsible for providing strategic direction, middle managers have tactical roles which tend to be functionally specific and line managers are responsible for keeping day-to-day operations of the organisation on track. Mintzberg (1989) identifies ten roles that can be grouped under the following three headings. These roles and their groupings help clarify how managers behave and help focus on the issues of communication and consequent information requirements.

Interpersonal roles

These roles comprise *figurehead*, *leadership* and *liaison* roles. The manager as *figurehead* represents the organisation or performs ceremonial and symbolic functions, such as attending a trade fair or taking a customer to lunch.

The *leadership* role falls to all managers to a greater or lesser extent and includes hiring, promoting, training, motivating and disciplining staff.

All managers should be keenly aware of needing to perform a *liaison role*. They seek support from people who can affect the success of the organisation, such as board members, customers, suppliers, or government representatives. Having a *project champion* from such organisations can make a huge difference to the success of any venture pursued by the organisation. Such liaisons may be internal to the organisation or externally oriented.

Bryan Upton of Richardson Steel, Sheffield is a high profile Chief Executive who has clearly stamped his authority on a manufacturing company of kitchen knives, making it an example to be admired in terms of innovation, product development and commitment to customer service. He has encouraged staff promotion to management positions from shop floor, fostered good staff interrelations, with the result that people in the organisation are generally willing to do whatever is asked of them, and has made sure that at all times his visible leadership commitment provides a clear example to the company as a whole. Good suppliers have been consistently rewarded with repeat business and international customers are always dealt with in their own language. Communication with suppliers and customers is highly responsive and whatever has been promised for a certain date has been delivered on that date.

A high level of interpersonal skills is more often than not the key to a very successful leader.

Informational roles

These roles of *monitor*, *disseminator* and *spokesperson* are highly relevant, given the increasing importance of information as an organisational resource. Managers as *monitors* receive and collect information from outwith the organisational boundary, such as informal gossip with contacts or formal meetings in other organisations. Such information then has to be filtered and evaluated and a decision made as to the extent of its usefulness.

The manager as *disseminator* passes and shares information with subordinates. This information may not otherwise be accessible to them and might need to remain confidential. Such passing on of information is time consuming and managers must therefore use careful judgement as to what is important and relevant and what is not.

The *spokesperson* role involves managers representing their organisation to outsiders, such as representatives of major oil companies giving TV interviews to put over environmentally friendly policies.

Effective managers develop networks of contacts to obtain and share information. Many contacts made while carrying out figurehead and liaison roles may provide managers with a great deal of important information which then serves them in their roles as monitor, disseminator and spokesperson.

Decisional roles

These management roles are arguably the most important of the three categories and involve managers behaving as entrepreneurs, handlers of problems, allocators of resources and negotiators.

The *entrepreneurial* manager is largely concerned with innovation and change, designing and instigating planned change to improve the organisation's position. Managers perform this role when initiating new projects or entering a new business market.

Managers are often problem solvers. The role of *disturbance-handler* involves taking corrective action in response to problems previously unforeseen. Broken contracts by suppliers or customers and strikes or crises arising from poor management of a situation over time are examples of circumstances in need of a disturbance handler.

As *resource-allocators* managers must choose between competing demands for human, physical and financial resources. Decisions may involve, for example, the amount of budget to be allocated to advertising or how many staff are required for different shifts.

Managers frequently need to be judicious *negotiators*, discussing and bargaining with individuals or groups to reach agreement. Negotiations may occur between functions or departments within the same organisation or with external groups such as government agencies or suppliers.

Alan Sugar of Amstrad is an example of the entrepreneurial manager, displaying both the advantages and disadvantages of that type of management. He has never been afraid of taking risks and being innovative, prepared to challenge the giants of the computing industry. On the other hand, the desire to make all the important decisions himself and a tendency to obstinacy led to the making of a number of errors resulting in Amstrad having a rollercoaster lifecycle.

Although these ten managerial roles have been considered separately in the context of their three groupings, it is important to remember that they are all interdependent. Managers, regardless of type of organisation or level in the organisation, perform similar roles, though the balance and mix of those roles will vary. Emphasis on certain roles tends to change with hierarchical level. The roles of figurehead, negotiator, spokesperson and disseminator, for example, tend to be more important at the higher than at the lower organisational levels.

Managers carrying out their roles all have to communicate, make decisions and solve problems to a greater or lesser extent. They all require information in differing formats and at different time intervals.

Management roles and information

The main users of information in an organisation are its managers. Different managerial roles and responsibilities require different types of information. Interpersonal management roles involve communicating within and outwith the organisation. The information needed is often for communication and presentation purposes. Informational roles require organisational information that is clear, understandable and available at the appropriate time. Managers in the decisional role require information often in the form of control and planning reports to make their decisions.

Mintzberg's managerial roles are useful for establishing information needs across the organisation. Most managers perform most of these roles to some extent. Table 3.2 matches information requirements with management roles.

Management functions

Considering the input/output model of a business, resources are the inputs that need to be converted into products, services, productivity and profits. Managers perform various activities (see pp. 63–65 for Anthony's framework for managerial activities) in order to achieve objectives and produce results, so management represents the conversion process in the business input/output model.

Anthony's structuring of managerial activities is a useful initial framework, but it does not

Table 3.2 Management roles and information needs

Management roles	Information needs

Interpersonal:
  figurehead
  leader
  liaison
	Personal and organisational communication (email, conferencing, presentation charts and graphs).

Informational:
  monitor
  disseminator
  spokesperson
	Information access, clarity, availability, analysis, such as spreadsheets, models, charts.
	Communication of organisational aims and objectives.

Decisional:
  entrepreneur
  disturbance handler
  resource allocator
  negotiator
	Information for decision making and to explain decisions, exception and regular reports, investment appraisal and resource availability.

Source: adapted from Alter (1992)

go far enough. Planning and control are carried out at all levels of the organisation and thereby affect decision-making at all levels of the organisation. Strategic planning is very important, but so is operational planning, such as production scheduling, in order to prioritise activities. The following structure is therefore more appropriate to the discussion of what all organisational managers do:

- planning
- control
  both of which are based on managerial
- decision-making

Management functions and IS

It is important to show all the components of managerial work as a reminder that these components cannot necessarily be separated. A manager who thinks creatively, for example, but does not take action will be removed from the realities of managing. Effective management requires a balance of functions, a form of thinking and leading by doing. A manager who believes his/her job to be merely one of control will soon become detached from the organisation, from its need to improve, to plan for the future and ultimately to survive.

This does not imply that all managers do everything with equal emphasis. The functions managers perform vary according to the needs of a particular task and the approach of the particular individual. Different managers emphasise different things in different ways. A systematic framework of what they all do in common is given in Figure 3.2. These functions are combined with the three essential roles of IS, i.e. communicating, structuring and coordinating, which will be developed more fully in Chapter 5. It is merely important at this stage to establish a link between what managers do and what IS can do to facilitate their activities.

The importance of planning and control

Planning is important because it defines organisational objectives or goals, establishes a strategy to achieve these goals and develops a framework of plans to integrate and coordinate appropriate business activities. Planning is concerned with both the ends and the means, i.e. what is to be done and how. Managers need to plan to give direction, reduce the impact of change, minimise repetition and waste and to set standards to be controlled.

The value of control lies in relation to planning. It is the final link in the functional chain of management before a decision is made. Activities have to be monitored to ensure that they are going as planned and, if not, that necessary corrective and preventative action is

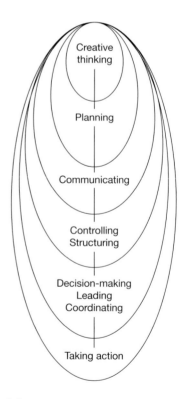

Figure 3.2 Managerial functions and IS roles
Source: adapted from Mintzberg (1994)

taken. Organisational objectives, once set and accepted, need to be accomplished.

Planning

Planning is a dynamic process whereby decisions must be made in the present about action in the future. Organisations tend to plan for the following reasons:

- to identify and commit resources to achieve specified corporate objectives;
- to manage and coordinate the efforts and activities of organisational staff;
- to match activities to specified objectives, minimising waste and duplication;
- to set standards to facilitate control;
- to measure and monitor progress towards objectives, taking corrective actions as appropriate;
- to reduce uncertainty by anticipating change.

Planning provides the guidelines for decision-making, which culminates in action being taken. Successes and failures in planning can make a significant difference in the performance of an organisation. Planning is used to offset uncertainty and change, to focus attention on objectives, to optimise operations and to facilitate control.

Planning may be either *formal* or *informal*. In the latter case nothing may be written down with little or no sharing of objectives with others in the organisation. The owner/manager of a small business may well have a vision of where the business should be and how to get there, but this vision may not be known or shared by other staff in the company. Formal planning, on the other hand, tends to involve specific objectives covering set periods of time that are written down and communicated to others in the organisation.

Types of planning

Plans may be strategic, tactical or operational. Different types of planning will be undertaken by different management levels in the hierarchy, cascading from strategic to operational plans.

Kwik Save, the discount supermarkets group, is planning to introduce its own label as part of a corporate shake-up, which will involve a number of store closures and considerable restructuring costs. Kwik Save does not plan to abandon its niche as a discounter of branded products, but it can add value by launching an own-label brand, which would be cheaper than those on offer from the other leading supermarket chains, such as Tesco and Safeway.

Own labels tend to produce profit margins about 5 per cent higher than on branded goods and the food retail sector relies very heavily on the money it makes from own-label products. The plan will no doubt trigger a price war among the supermarket giants and allow Kwik Save to regain ground lost to competitors as a result of not having its own brand.

Furthermore, Kwik Save plans to offer a wider range of convenience food, such as ready-made dinners, identified as a growing market, while still remaining first and foremost a discounter.

Strategic planning starts at the top of the organisation, seeking the overall direction of the organisation. It tends to cover a more extensive time period, which may be anything from two to ten years. Strategic plans cover a broad area which includes the formulation of objectives. They provide focus and general guidelines without locking into objectives or specific actions.

Information for strategic planning will come from internal sources relating to skills, capabilities, finance, plant and equipment and external sources such as the state of the economy, exchange rates, political trends and patterns of technological innovation. Techniques such as forecasting using time series analysis, regression, trend analysis and economic indicators analysis are helpful in generating information for strategic planning.

Management planning tends to be medium term and translates strategic plans into operational plans. Such plans are more specific, having clearly defined objectives with little in the way of ambiguity or potential for misunderstandings. Such specific planning is clear and helpful, providing that the percentage targets and time frames are realistic and achievable.

Operational planning concentrates much more on techniques to help middle- and line-managers do a better job.

Scheduling helps lower-level managers plan more effectively, listing necessary activities, the order in which they are to be done, by whom and within which time periods.

Operational plans are usually monthly, weekly or daily, emphasising the short term and assuming the existence of objectives.

Information for planning

Individuals in organisations set objectives and then determine resources and courses of action to meet those objectives. Both predictive and historical information will be important to extrapolate from past experience and plan for the future.

Descriptive or evaluative information may relate to previous experience, which is useful in

---

Examples of types of planning

Strategic planning	A company wishing to improve productivity between 5 per cent −10 per cent over the next year.
Management planning	A company may seek to increase on-time deliveries by 5 per cent and reduce scrap or rework by 3 per cent over a set period of time.
Operational planning	Budgets of various types such as expense budgets, fixed or variable budgets, programme budgets and zero-base budgets are used to improve time, space and material resources use. Gantt charts (as shown in Figure 3.3), work or load schedules, flow charts and critical path or network diagrams are widely used examples of operational planning tools. Other operational planning tools are break-even analysis, linear programming, queuing theory, simulation and time management.

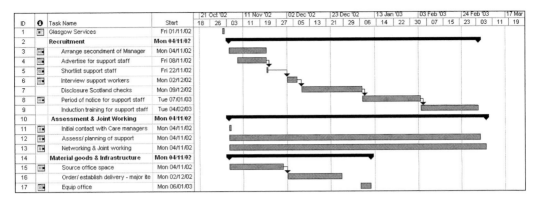

ID	❶	Task Name	Start	21 Oct '02		11 Nov '02		02 Dec '02		23 Dec '02		13 Jan '03		03 Feb '03		24 Feb '03		17 Mar
				18	26	03	11	19	27	05	13	21	29	06	14	22	30	07	15	23	03	11	19
1	🗎	Glasgow Services	Fri 01/11/02																				
2		Recruitment	Mon 04/11/02																				
3	▥	Arrange secondment of Manager	Mon 04/11/02																				
4	▥	Advertise for support staff	Fri 08/11/02																				
5	▥	Shortlist support staff	Fri 22/11/02																				
6	▥	Interview support workers	Mon 02/12/02																				
7		Disclosure Scotland checks	Mon 09/12/02																				
8	▥	Period of notice for support staff	Tue 07/01/03																				
9		Induction training for support staff	Tue 04/02/03																				
10		Assessment & Joint Working	Mon 04/11/02																				
11	▥	Initial contact with Care managers	Mon 04/11/02																				
12	▥	Assess/ planning of support	Mon 04/11/02																				
13	▥	Networking & Joint working	Mon 04/11/02																				
14	▥	Material goods & Infrastructure	Mon 04/11/02																				
15	▥	Source office space	Mon 04/11/02																				
16		Order/ establish delivery - major ite	Mon 02/12/02																				
17	▥	Equip office	Mon 06/01/03																				

Figure 3.3 Example of Gantt chart for the commissioning of a new support service

planning ahead. Similarly, probabilistic information is needed to make forecasts for planning purposes. Information for planning may be qualitative or quantitative or a combination of both. It is more or less structured and is often a mix of formal and informal information from various sources, internal to the organisation and external, depending on the particular planning horizon concerned. Information for planning comes from both regular and on-demand reporting.

Planning is closely linked to control. Information on control mechanisms and performance indicators will help plan, as will sensitivity analysis and forecasting of probabilities. Information on ratios, such as productivity and profitability and comparing projected and actual outcomes are also highly relevant. Uncertainty and speed of change complicate the planning process, so the importance of relevant, accurate, up-to-date, timely information cannot be overemphasised.

There must be a commitment to diligent information gathering, i.e. the right information in the required form, accompanied by clear communication of requirements to others. Information requirements change as situations develop and information gathering must be a shared responsibility. People at different levels of the organisation need to be recording the same information, or ambiguities will arise. This is one reason why procedures for recording and storing information are very useful.

Identifying the means of achieving desired targets will involve gathering information on a variety of alternatives and engaging in cost benefit analyses.

Information systems project planning

Planning effectively is not straightforward. Any plan is subject to change and replanning is an inherent part of coping with the changes that occur during the life cycle of a systems development project. Reflecting such continual changes in a practical plan is a difficult task. A common problem in project planning is for senior users or information systems managers to set targets and deadlines that might have been motivated practically or politically. Planning to dates which reflect important business, legislative or competitive deadlines might prove infeasible. This type of planning creates cynicism and demotivation as staff are not consulted and involved in the process. The aim here is to show how good project planning can bring greater benefits and fewer risks to information systems development.

The planning process

First of all, the whole project team must understand the background to the project and its relevance to the business. It is also useful to know who will be the main innovators and supporters of the new system so that a meaningful relationship can be built with key users, since good communication between the project team and the users is an essential prerequisite of system success.

As much data as possible should then be collected from similar projects carried out before in the organisation so as to learn any valuable lessons from experience. Similarly, projects undertaken by competitors might prove useful benchmarks. Research of this type is often overlooked and can be highly beneficial. A decision then needs to be taken about the development methodology and its applicability to the needs of the particular system to be developed.

Finally, it should be borne in mind that planning is both iterative and dynamic, whereby a certain amount of reworking will be necessary until a final workable plan has been produced.

Planning criteria

Planning needs to involve an understanding of the framework and constraints within which the plan has to be accomplished. The following eight points need to be addressed:

1 the overall budget available for the project development;
2 the timescale in which the system is to be developed;
3 the expected implementation date;
4 staff availability for the project;

5 necessary hardware and software to run the live system;
6 existing hardware and software to develop the applications software and how close the existing configuration is to that to be used for the live system;
7 maintenance organisation to support the system after its implementation;
8 commitment from the user department in terms of its staff availability to assist in project development.

Planning tools and techniques

It is important in project planning to make lists of activities, set deadlines and formulate quality plans, but they will be of little use unless they are documented in a structured way which allows for easy comprehension and rapid updating. Tools and techniques vary in their currency and complexity and their applicability will depend on attributes of the project being developed. Simple projects need simple planning tools, otherwise more time can be spent controlling the tool than the project. Complex projects with many interacting activities and dependencies will require the more advanced techniques, which themselves will require commitment of people and computing resources. This in turn will have an impact on the overall project cost.

Bar charts

While these are the simplest form of planning tool, they can be used for many projects irrespective of application or even type of business. Their limitations lie in the number of activities that can be plotted, along with the number of interactions, or dependencies, of activities. Once all activities have been plotted with their respective time lines, it is possible to see the overall length of the project or of one phase of the project. One major limitation of bar charts is the difficulty of scheduling effort to activities to ensure logical sequencing without over-staffing. Actual progress can be compared with projected progress to check for slippage or make any necessary adjustments.

PERT

The limitations of bar charts become evident when they are used for large projects. One such large military project, the Polaris Weapons System, led to Programme Evaluation and Review Techniques (PERT). Prior to embarking on this project, research had been carried out into previous military projects, which revealed the need for a more sophisticated tool to deal with time and cost overruns. PERT arose from a distillation of bar charts, milestone reporting systems and line-of-balance management techniques. It focuses especially on controlling the time element and employs statistical analysis to evaluate the probability of meeting target dates throughout the life of the project. PERT systems also produce valuable progress reports.

Planning with PRINCE (Projects IN a Controlled Environment)

PRINCE is a project management methodology created to increase the success of UK government IT projects. It has now developed into PRINCE 2, which is aimed at all types of project. PRINCE 2 is recommended, by the UK Government, as a project management methodology for public sector IT projects. The Cabinet Office paper, *Successful IT: Modernising Government in Action* (2001: 5) identified that:

In the past, Government IT projects have too often missed delivery dates, run over budget or have failed to fulfil requirements.

Planning with PRINCE focuses on production and delivery of products within an agreed timescale, to an agreed cost and by meeting stipulated quality criteria. PRINCE includes three levels of plan, each one relating to a corresponding level in the project organisation and to the tasks for controlling the activities at that level. At the top level is the *Project Plan*, which shows the main activities of the whole project, scheduling and identifying necessary resources. It covers the whole life of the project and is a fixed reference point against which progress can be measured. The Project Plan has a Technical Plan and a Resource Plan.

The *Project Technical Plan* shows the breakdown of the project into stages, referred to as 'work packages'. It defines what will be produced at each stage along with target completion date. It also shows all assessment points and management processes.

The *Project Resource Plan* estimates the amount of each type of resource that will be used, enabling calculation of associated costs. This plan is the master business or financial plan for the project and is used for ongoing review of project viability.

The next level down in the hierarchy involves the *Stage Plan*, made up of the *Stage Technical* and *Resource Plans*, which show all the products and activities of the Stage and the resources required to complete them.

At the next level is the *Detailed Plan*, which is only required when it is necessary to show a stage activity in greater detail. At the lowest level is the *Individual Work Plan*, which schedules the activities of each individual member of the project.

Outside this hierarchical structure is the *Exception Plan*, produced in circumstances where there will be or has been a cost or time overrun.

The process of planning with PRINCE begins with the identification of the major technical products to be developed, which in turn usually leads to the identification of the main stages of the project. Such technical products might, for example, be:

- an analysis of the present system;
- a specification of the requirement for the new system;
- a description of the logical design of the new system;
- the physical design of the new system;
- a developed and tested system;
- an installed system.

Each of these high-level products would then be broken down further so that within each product lower-level products are specified. This is often referred to as a classical thinking approach as illustrated in Figure 4.1 in Chapter 4.

Project planning steps

Although planning steps can be outlined, in practice other factors may influence the sequence and there will almost certainly be a number of iterations, compromises and trade-offs before an optimum plan is achieved. The purpose of the project needs to be defined, along with beneficial changes and key objectives. The feasibility study then develops the project proposal and the project scope is defined. The 'make or buy' decision relates to whether the system is to be developed in-house or purchased off the shelf. The project scope is then divided into manageable work packages and a responsibility matrix is drawn up. The critical path represents the logical sequence of activities, the schedule bar chart communicates relevant information and the procurement schedule relates to the supply of all bought-in items. A resource histogram shows over- or under-loading of resources; budgets and project cash flows show use of financial resources; and the communication plan relates to the collection and dissemination of appropriate information. Plans relating to quality and risk management are important as is the baseline plan, which is a portfolio of documents outlining how to achieve the project's objectives.

Control

Managers monitor organisational performance by comparing actual outcomes to previously planned goals and taking corrective action. Relevant information needs to be collected from available data and results analysed so that standards can be set and deviations from the standards dealt with promptly. Auditing is a widely used mechanism in the managerial control function.

All managers should be involved in the process of control even if their sections are performing as planned because it is always essential to compare actual performance against the set standards. An effective control system provides a measure of the extent to which organisational goals are being achieved.

The control process

An effective control system provides immediate evidence if any mismatch exists between what staff are doing and what they should be doing. It is then up to appropriate managers to seek out reasons for any mismatch and implement corrective action (see Figure 3.4). An effective control system permits managers to spend less time firefighting, so that delegation of certain tasks allows them more time to seek out root causes and solve the problems for which they will ultimately be held responsible.

The control process consists of three basic steps:

1 measuring actual performance;
2 comparing actual performance against desired performance, i.e. a standard;

Siebe, one of Britain's largest engineering groups, is about to embark on the use of a quality control system already being used by Motorola and General Electric. The Six Sigma system will entail a rise in annual profits, possibly by about 15 per cent. The manufacturing processes at more than 140 of the group's factories will be reassessed at the cost of some £20m.

The control system, once implemented, will enhance Siebe's competitive edge by reducing product defects from around 5,000-per-million units produced to almost zero. The costs related to such defects amount to about four per cent of annual sales, i.e. costs equivalent to some £104m per annum.

Texas Instruments have described the Six Sigma system as a very powerful tool for quality control, while General Electric committed around £120m in costs to reduce defects from 35,000-per-million units to about four-per-million with consequent positive effects on the profit margin.

3 taking managerial corrective action to eliminate deviations or correct inadequacies.

It is, of course, essential to any effective control process that appropriate, relevant performance standards, goals, and targets have been adequately developed at the planning stage.

Measuring

It is necessary to consider both *how* and *what* to measure. In terms of *how* to measure, the following are common sources of information:

- Personal observation, which yields first-hand intimate knowledge of an activity. It is, however, time consuming and subject to bias.

- Statistical reports, such as graphs, bar charts and computer printouts, measure actual performance, but tend to be limited to certain key areas of activity only, such as customer returns. They do, however, provide good visual information showing relationships where they exist.

- Oral reports are also a good source of information such as meetings, telephone conversations and conferences. Technological innovations like videoconferencing and fax messages have reduced the time-consuming disadvantage of transmitting such information, but with personal observation there still remains the potential for bias and subjective filtering.

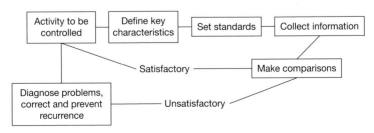

Figure 3.4 The control process
Source: adapted from Robbins (1988)

- Written reports also measure actual performance with the advantage of greater formality and are perhaps more complete and concise.

Because all four information sources have their advantages and disadvantages, it is better for managers to use a variety of them in combination.

In terms of *what* to measure there is more potential for problems and it is a critical issue for managers to deal with. The whole question of having the correct criteria or standards is central and has proved contentious in a number of situations involving, for example, school league tables and hospital mortality rates, which have been publicised on a national basis, creating perceptions of substandard service provision where it may not have been justifiable or fully substantiated by all relevant information.

Some control criteria are more widely used, such as turnover or absenteeism rates, budgets and staff job satisfaction; others will be relatively easy to measure, such as customer complaints, production units per day; compared to others which are more difficult to quantify, such as street cleanliness or teacher effectiveness. If performance indicators cannot be easily quantified, managers should still seek subjective measures,

though some of these do have significant limitations. To have no standards at all does cause problems. Managers cannot control what they cannot measure.

Comparing

Managers have to expect some degree of variation between performance and the standard in all activities; they must therefore determine an acceptable *range of variation*. Quality control charts are a clear illustration of just this issue. As a process is tracked over time, so warning and action limits are set on the chart. Once the warning limits are reached, a wary eye needs to be maintained on the process; once the action limits are reached, the process is running or has run out of control and immediate corrective action of some sort needs to be taken. Such warning and action limits sit on either side of the standard or norm. Both over- and under-variation need managerial attention. The example in Figure 3.5 charts the average exam results of a student cohort as they carried out their undergraduate degree.

Managerial action

Managers can choose between doing nothing, correcting the actual performance or amending

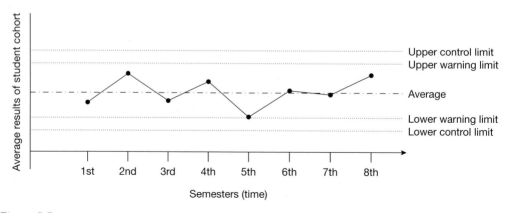

Figure 3.5 A quality control chart

the process or standard in some way. Different managerial actions lead to different outcomes. Sometimes, for example, only corrective action is taken where preventive or remedial action is also necessary. The immediate problem may be solved, but the root cause not tackled, so that the same or a related problem recurs on an ongoing basis without being definitively eradicated. Correcting actual performance may involve changing the strategy, arranging a training programme, redesigning the job or replacing a member of staff.

Furthermore, managers have to decide on whether corrective action is sufficient or whether preventive action needs to be taken. Effective managers analyse in some depth, seeking to discover root causes and thereby avoid the perpetual 'firefighting' and repetitive solving of the same problems, which seem to be the hallmark of managerial activity in a 'coping' rather than a 'controlled' organisational culture.

As to altering standards, it depends on whether a standard is unreasonable or unattainable, whether it may be perceived as irrelevant or inappropriate. Care is needed in revising standards down, because that may render even more difficult the process of continuous improvement. It is best if standards are on the whole realistic but challenging.

Focus of control

Managerial control efforts are directed at one or a combination of business areas, namely people, operations, finance, information and organisational performance.

People

Systematic performance appraisals are a formal mechanism of control, but informal control also exists in the form of letting an employee know, for example, that he or she is regularly arriving late or wasting time or maybe taking unnecessary risks. Reward and recognition reinforce good feedback control.

Operations

Efficiency and effectiveness in producing goods and services are essential. Production must be scheduled, equipment must be maintained, quality control must be undertaken and various costs must be managed by optimising, for example, inventory and work-in-progress. Operations management involves a whole variety of feedforward, concurrent and feedback controls.

Finance

Budgets provide the basis for financial controls. Ratio analysis and cost-benefit analysis help ensure that a company remains profitable in the longer term by minimising expenditure and wastage. Similarly, debt must be balanced against equity to ensure ongoing financial viability of an organisation.

Information

Inaccurate, incomplete or delayed information will impede corporate performance. It is vital that the right information reaches the right people at the right time. Managers must control both the quantity and quality of information so that it can be optimised as a vital organisational resource.

Just as control tends to be focused on certain areas of the business, so it must be carried out in an efficient and effective way. The following box illustrates the factors relating to control that are most likely to enhance its effectiveness.

Information for control

Performance measures are being increasingly used in business to some good effect. They must be sensible and achievable. Working towards

Characteristics of effective control

Control systems that work well tend to have certain common characteristics:

Accuracy	a control system needs to generate reliable, valid data to provide accurate information.
Timeliness	control must provide timely information by minimising the measurement time lag, so that any necessary action can be taken as quickly as possible.
Economy	a control system must be reasonable to operate and must provide added value to the business.
Flexibility	effective controls must adjust to conditions as necessary and be able to take advantage of new opportunities.
Comprehensibility	controls that cannot be understood have no value, may give rise to errors or frustrations and may lead to the eventual abandoning of the control system.
Reasonable standards	control standards that are unreasonable or unattainable may demotivate or encourage people to try and cheat the system.
Critical standards	controls should concentrate on organisational critical success factors rather than trivia, focusing on potential variations from the norm that could do the most damage.
Emphasis on exception	an exception control system ensures that managers concentrate on important information first and foremost rather than be overwhelmed by too much information, resulting in managers becoming confused and unfocused.

(Adapted from: Robbins, 1988)

The ABC Chemical Company, which produces dyes and pigments for paints, plastics, paper, textiles and printing inks, became aware of the need to implement a quality system along the lines of ISO9002 largely as a result of pressure from customers in the plastics and automotive industries.

The company's systems were not as good as they thought they were and a documented quality manual and documented procedures were required. A nasty shock came to a number of ABCs managers on the occasion of a preliminary audit by external consultants who discovered that operations relied too heavily on informal procedures and technical expertise.

After approximately 18 months' hard work, registration to ISO9002 was gained by ABC, which then had a fully documented, implemented quality management system. Such a system enabled the rapid and accurate transfer of information for reference, measurement, corrective action, training and continuous improvement. Procedures and work instructions had been reviewed, updated and improved to produce a higher level of operational efficiency with appropriate performance standards.

As a result of increased formalisation the ABC company was in a better position to meet the specific requirements of customers rather than merely selling a standard product. The company can now control the large number of customer specifications with consequent improvement in their strategic relationships with their customers. It should be noted that not all companies benefit from the implementation of industry standards like ISO9002 (now ISO9000/2000).

objectives involves managers acting as controllers. Mintzberg's roles of 'monitor', 'entrepreneur', 'disturbance handler' and 'resource allocator' involve control.

A common element of all control systems is information, and the systems for processing information are instrumental in organisational control. Three significant aspects of control are:

1 centralisation/delegation
2 formalisation/informalisation
3 degree of personal supervision

These issues have implications for the type of information required and by whom. Formalisation ensures information availability on a consistent basis to people, such as regular circulation of requests for approval signatures. Close supervision can replace formalisation to some extent. Rules and procedures can be used to control activities or supervisors can control activities directly.

Information must be available to staff and management according to the type of control that prevails. Information needs will change as control systems change and information systems can enable change in the nature of control to take place.

Information systems project control

The project leader must be careful to choose a system that provides the correct level of control.

Too much detail entails too many resources being used just to control the project and too little detail provides insufficient data to exercise effective control. Each project should be assessed in its own right and simple control tools used for simple projects, reserving the more complex, resource-consuming tools for larger projects. Project size and duration should dictate the level of reporting formality and the extent of monitoring frequency. Any automated control mechanism must be operative from the beginning and the organisation must exist to support the collection, entry and processing of data, followed by its distribution to project team members.

Reporting structure

Simple projects with teams of less than six staff at times of maximum activity require a simple, uncomplicated structure where each team member is allocated tasks by, and reports directly back to, the project leader. The frequency of such feedback can be every two to three weeks and at every significant project milestone.

When the project size increases to between six and twenty team members it becomes impossible for the project leader to control each individual personally so the team is broken down into logical units, each headed by a team leader. The units may reflect different sections of the application being developed and team functions differ during the phases of the project with analysis and design completed by one team, implementation by another and integration by a further team.

Reporting methods and techniques

Reporting project progress can be done verbally or in writing, informally or formally, frequently or infrequently, according to the type and size of the project. Regular written reports are probably the most effective reporting mechanism and should focus on comparison with predetermined plans and deadlines. One would expect reports from the team leader to the project leader, from the project leader to the line manager, from the project leader to user management, the user committee and to the quality manager.

Reports are useful but serve only a limited purpose without regular progress meetings. At the beginning of the project a series of such meetings should be planned to take place throughout the development process. Meetings should be planned to achieve maximum results in a minimum of time, as any time spent in meetings implies time lost developing software. Team members need to feel involved and able to make a contribution to overall progress. The allocation of tasks should be through team meetings and the project leader needs to liaise with team leaders and user management on a regular basis.

Control systems

Controlling a project is about comparing actual figures and values against planned figures and values determined at the start of the project. The planning tools mentioned on p. 72 can also be used for the purpose of control.

Bar charts

Bar charts are most commonly used for project monitoring, except with large projects. At each review stage the actual status of each activity is compared with the planned status. For more complicated projects subordinate bar charts can be produced for different sections or phases of the project to be reviewed independently and to provide appropriate detail where it is needed.

If computing resources are available and the project is sufficiently large, the bar chart reviewing procedure can be automated for the formal data collection from team members. In this way it is easy to retain historical data on such measures as coding rates, individual programmer productivity and the amount of code generated. This sort of information is useful for benchmarking purposes in subsequent projects.

The use of spreadsheets, although not specifically bar charts, allows the updating of an original plan with actual performance in order to generate a revised plan with timescales and costings.

PERT-based control techniques

For simple projects the manipulation of a PERT network can be done manually but a computer-based system is recommended even in simple networks where a lot of data analysis is required. Like all control systems, the output is only as good as the data input. Team leaders and their staff need to provide progress estimates that are as accurate as possible. A less accurate critical path produced from approximate values will not be as helpful.

The output from a computerised PERT system will list all activities on the critical path and their float, and highlight those activities so that the project leader can adjust resources and team tasks as necessary to improve the overall end date and utilise the floats. Some PERT systems will also help with resource allocation as a result of comparisons made.

Controlling projects with PRINCE

The aim of PRINCE is to ensure that a project retains its business and technical integrity. In other words, the work is being carried out to schedule and in accordance with resource and cost plans, and the development system meets its goals in terms of quality, reliability, security and maintainability. Project control is achieved using a structure that matches the planning and organising structure of the project. There is a hierarchy of controls, with approval being given for work to be carried out and criteria established against which progress and satisfactory completion can be compared. Control criteria include tolerance, checkpoints and reporting mechanisms. The control loop is completed through the identification of the need for corrective action and the actions themselves that follow. Project control procedures aim to detect deviations early on before the cost of rectification escalates. The implementation of a control procedure can be triggered by an event or a time. Typical control points are the following:

- The *project initiation control point*, which represents the first formal meeting of the project board. The output from this meeting is the project initiation document.
- The *end-stage assessment control point*, which is a mandatory control point at the end of each project stage and involves formal organisation and procedures.
- The *mid-stage assessment control point*, an optional control point. Such an assessment can be called at any time during a project stage, such as when tolerances are being exceeded, whereby the consequential exception plan needs approval by the project board.
- *Checkpoint controls and highlight reports*. Checkpoints are internal progress meetings to gather detailed information about progress, problems and resource usage. Highlight reports are a summary of the checkpoint meetings that review progress to date and highlight any actual or potential problems.

- The *project closure control point* comes at the end of the development phase and provides a formal controlled transition from development to system operation and maintenance. At this point the system must be in an acceptable state with complete and appropriate documentation. Complete acceptance by everyone who has to use, operate or maintain the system is then confirmed through a series of acceptance letters.

Managers and the decision-making process

Managers plan and control so that decisions can be made. Decision-making is central to a business and making the best decision is of vital importance to every facet of a manager's job. Decision-making and managing are almost synonymous. Managers strive to integrate the efforts of organisational members to achieve organisational goals and this involves making decisions. The 'social system' school of thought was based on Barnard's (1938) view of managers maintaining a set of cooperative, interdependent social relationships working towards a common goal. The 'decision theory' school focused on the analysis of choice processes available to managers seeking to make rational decisions within organisations (March and Simon, 1958). From these two conceptual schools emerged the 'information processing' school postulating that a key organisational function was to process information (Galbraith, 1973). The focus of the information processing school is to provide relevant information that enables managers to make better decisions in the face of uncertainty. Galbraith (1973) maintained that the greater the task uncertainty, the greater the amount of information that must be processed among decision-makers so as to achieve a given level of performance. The degree of task uncertainty involves a combination of variables and as their complexity increases, there is an increasing need to provide pertinent information to decision-makers.

The decision gap

As decision-making relies upon the availability of information within a certain time frame, managers have to appreciate that on a number of occasions there will be a shortfall in that information (see Figure 3.6).

Most decisions must be made in a timely way or opportunities may be missed. Hasty or reckless decisions are rarely effective, as are decisions not based on facts. The best decisions tend to rely on a combination of reliable experience or 'gut feel' and reliable, relevant supporting information. More often than not, such information will be incomplete either because it is not available or too costly to obtain within the desired time frame. A gap remains, which has to be filled by the skill of the decision-maker. This skill will tend to be a combination of requisite knowledge and previous experience. The relative importance of a decision will influence managerial behaviour, but managers should wherever possible take a rational approach which is neither too hesitant, nor too hasty.

The decision-making process

There is more than one way of regarding the decision-making process. One approach concentrates on information gathering and problem identification, followed by the analysis of the consequences of action before reaching a decision. This process involves asking a number of pertinent questions to obtain the broadest spread of alternatives and evaluating, selecting and monitoring the best solution. The final optimal course of action chosen will depend upon factors such as cost, effort required, potential impact and degree of associated risk.

A variation on this approach which is somewhat simpler involves five basic steps as follows:

1 *Intelligence*, which implies a seeking out of problems or opportunities which require decisions to be made. By processing different information from a variety of sources problems are formulated or defined.
2 *Design* of possible solutions to the problems or opportunities identified, developing decision criteria and their appropriate weightings.

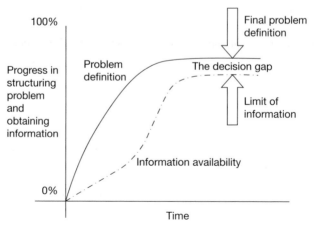

Figure 3.6 The decision gap

Cellnet (now BT Cellnet), the UK mobile phone operator, had decided to spend an extra £1bn on its digital network over five years to extend its geographical coverage to 80 per cent of the UK.

Having considered a number of options as to the company's way forward, Cellnet's technology director confirmed that higher geographic coverage and better quality levels were the main objectives to pursue. From research undertaken by Cellnet, quality came out by far and away top of customers' priority list.

The decision to invest in this way has meant building 1,700 radio sites or base stations, adding to more than 1,000 sites already in use. Upgrading the network from 70 to 80 per cent of the country and improving the quality of the service were strategic decisions aimed at securing an advantage over Cellnet's competitors Vodafone, the UK's largest operator, and the smaller players, Orange and One-2-One. Today, BT Cellnet has over six million customers. The company has already invested $3.1bn in building its UK mobile phone network, which handles over 20 million calls every day and covers 99 per cent of the UK population.

3 *Choice* implies selecting among known alternatives and solutions to achieve an optimum outcome. Methods for achieving this choice include decision trees, linear programming, queuing theory, break-even analysis and many others.

4 *Implementation* of the selected solution by planning and organising actions, taking account of the individuals who will be involved and the particular requirements of the situation.

5 *Review/evaluation* to check that the solution works at first and then continues to work in the future. This is an essential part of the process since it adds to managerial knowledge and experience which may be very useful in the making of future decisions.

Figure 3.7 illustrates the iterative nature of this process.

Levels of decision-making

Different decisions are made by different levels of management and are supported by different levels and types of information system:

- *Long-term/strategic decisions* involve managers assessing alternatives, often focusing on the organisation's relationship with its external environment. Examples of such decisions are the takeover of another company, diversification into international markets or implementing a new IS/IT strategy. Such decisions are

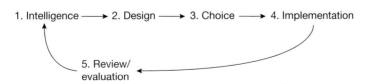

Figure 3.7 The decision-making process

frequently non-repeatable and have considerable cost/revenue implications.

- *Medium-term/tactical decisions* are rarely directly repeatable, have cost/revenue implications and enable policy to be put into effect. Decisions to increase production capacity or introduce new customer-research techniques are examples of this level of decision-making.
- *Short-term/operational decisions* are frequently repetitive, show results quite promptly and are covered by procedures formulated at the tactical level. Supervisory management make operational decisions about day-to-day activities, such as production output levels, stock control and distribution of numbers of staff to different activities.

Organisational models of decision-making

Decisions are often not taken by a single individual but by a group or by the organisation as a whole. Organisational models of decision-making take into account the structural and political characteristics of an organisation. Bureaucratic, political and 'garbage can' models have been proposed to describe how decisions are made in organisations.

Bureaucratic models are characteristic of organisations whose most important goal is the preservation of the organisation itself and who also wish to reduce uncertainty to a minimum. Policy tends to evolve incrementally because radical policy departures represent too much uncertainty. These models depict organisations governed by rules and operating procedures that have been developed and refined over years of active use. Changing the procedures and staff represents a potential risk and so these organisations tend to remain prisoner of their own standard solutions. Change may occur but it will take a long time. Decisions are made according to policy and procedures and tend to

be made in the same way over time, regardless of whether they were effective or not.

Political models of decision-making imply that whatever an organisation does occurs as a result of political bargains struck between key power brokers and interest groups. Such an organisation does not come up with a chosen solution to a particular problem but with compromises that reflect the conflicts, major stakeholders, diverse interests and different levels of power in the organisation. The confusion that often ensues is characteristic of this model.

The garbage can model reflects a more recent theory of decision-making, which states that organisations are not rational. Decision-making is largely accidental and the product of a stream of solutions, problems and situations that are randomly associated.

Types of decision-making structures

There are three basic types of decision-making structures:

1 *Independent, decentralised decision makers* have relatively low needs for communication and make decisions on what can be seen and heard from the immediate environment. Local store managers set prices using local information, and independent, local banks do not need to communicate with national headquarters before approving a loan. These independent decision-makers do not need nationwide information systems or long-distance communications but the very simplicity of such decisions implies that they are relatively uninformed. These decision-makers do not take account of what is happening elsewhere, do not learn from the experiences of people in other places and cannot pool resources or take advantage of economies of scale.

2 *Centralised decision-makers*, on the other hand, have significantly higher communication needs. They need information from a variety of sources to make informed decisions. National retail stores or banks need detailed information on pricing, policies and consumer preferences. An advantage of centralised decision-making is that, with more information, people can often make better decisions. They can also share best practice and capture economies of scale.

3 *Connected, decentralised decision-makers* generally require even more communication than centralised ones. They make autonomous decisions but based on potentially vast amounts of remote information available through electronic or other networks. These decentralised decision-makers sometimes cooperate with each other and on other occasions they compete. Examples of connected, decentralised decision-making occur all the time in the interactions among buyers and sellers in a market, in supplier relationships. In many cases, such market-based structures are cheaper, faster or more flexible than internal production.

Overall, the use of IS makes distance less important in determining where decisions should be made by bringing information to decision-makers wherever they are. There are also three factors that affect where decisions are made: decision information, trust and motivation. Factors affecting how decision-making power is distributed in organisations include government regulations, national cultures, organisational traditions and individual personalities, to name but a few.

Types of decisions and decision-making

All decisions fall somewhere within the range from programmable to non-programmable. The box below shows the characteristics of decisions within this range.

Programmable decisions are routine and have clear definition, such as invoicing, basic accounting and inventory control. Non-programmable decisions are more difficult to define completely; the method of making the decision may be unclear or unknown because such a decision may have only been made infrequently in the past or maybe not at all. Such decisions include strategic issues, ethical considerations or mergers and acquisitions.

Of course, many decisions do not fall neatly into one category. Information may be only partially complete and a situation may not be entirely new, though may by no means be routine.

When considering the potential for automation, there is a need to move decisions from the

---

The programmable/non-programmable decision spectrum

Programmable	Non-programmable
Routine	Unique
Repetitive	Non-recurring
Structured	Unstructured
Procedure involved	Uncertain
Regulated by rule or policy	Requiring judgement or creative thinking
Complete or near complete information	Requiring a custom-made solution

non-programmable to the programmable end of the spectrum. The reality is that some decisions can be readily undertaken by computers while others are non-programmable and always need the input of creative managers.

Human versus machine decision-making

While computer systems possess particular facilities and capabilities for information processing that human beings just do not have, such as accurate storage and rapid retrieval of large volumes of information, and the ability to perform complex calculations in a very short time, humans have distinctive capabilities that cannot be automated. Humans can think creatively, have the ability to work with incomplete information and can use intuition. Human decision-making can, however, involve a variety of errors of judgement, and judgements that are made may be unconsciously biased in a variety of ways.

Group decision-making

In practice, many management decisions are not made by individuals, and important ones in particular will tend to be made by groups. Committees, task groups and review panels are all examples of group decision-making within organisations.

There is a tendency to find solutions to problems that are satisfactory, but may not be optimum. A series of small, limited steps forward is often preferable to making decisions which involve a quantum leap or a dramatic change of direction. This approach is perfectly justifiable in view of the consistent need to achieve organisational stability.

Furthermore, company politics will tend to influence the making of certain decisions. Corporate objectives will arouse different interests and conflicts will arise among different groupings. Although a model of the decision-making process can be articulated in theory, there are 'real world' issues that will always bear upon the making of decisions in practice.

There are advantages and disadvantages of group decisions over individual decisions. Group decisions are more democratic, but often more time-consuming. Individual decisions are more timely, but more subject to bias. Table 3.3 provides a summary of the advantages and disadvantages of group decision-making.

Groupthink

Another aspect of group decision-making is the phenomenon of 'groupthink', which refers to a process of group dynamics formulated by Irving Janis. He argues that there are crucial situations

Table 3.3 Advantages and disadvantages of group decision-making

Advantages	Disadvantages
They provide more complete information.	They are often too time-consuming and hence inefficient.
They generate more varied alternatives.	A certain minority in the group will tend to dominate.
Group participation helps increase the acceptance of a solution.	There is often too great a social pressure to conform.
They are perceived as more democratic.	Final responsibility for the decision choice and outcome may remain unclear.

Source: adapted from Martin and Powell (1992)

where executive groups have made poor and unsound policy decisions (particularly in a critical situation), which are symptomatic of reaching conclusions in a group. Symptoms of this type of behaviour can be:

Major omissions in surveying alternatives. The group fails to explore all possible alternatives. Maybe one idea only is focused on with scant attention to other ideas. There are omissions in surveying group objectives. The group fails to consider all possible objectives available to choose from. The best objectives may not be chosen.

Costs and risks of preferred options are insufficiently explored. Assumptions are made and possible negative outcomes readily discounted or overlooked.

Information searches are superficial and lack penetration. There is a failure to obtain all possible data needed for decisional effectiveness. Information searches are incomplete, with poor techniques and often selective filtering of the results when communicated to others.

There is bias and selectivity in processing available information. The group tends to choose certain information, excluding valuable items that 'do not fit their picture'. Rejected alternatives are seldom and objectively re-examined. Alternatives, which may be rich in potential, are left discarded and unheeded.

The 'groupthink' group fails to work out implementation, monitoring, and contingency plans in sufficient detail, considering worst case scenarios and over-assuming what is/is not possible. Possible consequences and future problems are ignored or glossed over.

Classic examples of 'groupthink' include the London Ambulance Service IS failure and the *Challenger* space shuttle disaster.

Limitations of human information processing

Decisions are reliant on the availability of the right information at the right time in the required format. Having too little or too much information is a very common problem. The hazard of information overload has become a much more frequent occurrence with the increased use of computers, mobile phones and photocopiers. As technology can process such large volumes of data, managers have to be increasingly selective as to what is most relevant and most important. What is more, care must be taken not to give preference to more explicit, tangible, readily available data merely because it is easier to gather. Managers must consult representative data collected over time, rather than sticking slavishly to more recent or more familiar data.

Human information processing is also subject to bias and inconsistency. Past preferences and differing priorities among managers affect objective judgement, while unpopular and difficult decisions will tend to be shelved. Risk and time pressures cause confusion and uncertainty. Often it is difficult for managers to integrate information from a variety of sources or to handle probabilistic information. Decision-making of critical importance to an organisation demands courage and is often a test of real leadership.

Information for decision-making

Decisions are made at different levels of the organisation and information needs are determined by those decisions, which in turn are determined by objectives. Information systems exist at various levels of the organisation to provide information and support decision-making (see Chapter 5).

Strategic decisions concern the future and are associated with a considerable amount of uncertainty. Strategic decision-making involves establishing organisational objectives and long-term plans for achieving those objectives. Examples of such decisions are changes to product range, deciding which marketing strategy is required and the identification of sources of capital financing.

Tactical decision-making involves implementing strategic decisions and the more specific allocation of resources to meet organisational objectives. Production scheduling, budget allocation and shop floor layout decisions are all tactical or medium-term decisions.

Operational decisions are made by lower level managers and supervisors to keep the operation in line with predetermined standards; deciding how to allocate specific operators to tasks and maintaining inventory levels are day-to-day, short-term decisions of this type (see Figure 3.8.).

Decision-making and empowerment

IS can enable employees to access the necessary data and information required to make decisions and may even lead to the delegation of decision-making. These decisions can range from everyday operational ones to more complex and significant ones depending on the task at hand. Access to all necessary information is critical for empowerment and relates to enhancing employee understanding and involvement in the business. Empowerment will be dealt with in further detail in Chapter 6.

Critical information systems decisions

According to existing research (Proudlock *et al.*, 1998), IS decision-making in small organisations tends to focus on three areas in particular and these are to some extent indicative of IS decision priorities in organisations as a whole. In small firms these decisions are arguably more important because they lack the resources of larger organisations.

IS planning

IS planning has been consistently shown to be one of the top priorities of IS and business managers (Galliers *et al.*, 1994). While it is acknowledged that the formal planning techniques of large organisations are not necessarily appropriate for small firms, those smaller organisations adopting more formal planning systems were encountering fewer IS problems. The value of planning is also emphasised by Angéle *et al.* (1993), who regards IS planning as critical to success. Doukidis *et al.* (1997) found that even if planning does take place it is undertaken on an ad hoc, problem basis, is not undertaken by someone with specific responsibility for it, is informal and sporadic and is

Managerial levels	Decision	Information
Strategic	Long term	Summary/overview
Tactical	Medium term	Updates/regular
Operational	Short term	Detailed/day-to-day

Figure 3.8 Information and decision-making levels
Source: adapted from Martin and Powell (1992)

often influenced by people from outside with insufficient expertise and company insight.

IS risk management

Information systems risk management includes the 'make' or 'buy' decision. Purchase of off-the-shelf software provides scale economies and reduces risk during and following implementation. A top priority, particularly among small business managers, in selecting hardware and software is the popularity of the product being evaluated, with managers being far more likely to purchase industry-standard and market-leading technology.

The engaging of external expertise is also an important factor in risk mitigation. External professional support can overcome knowledge gaps, as can consultation with neighbouring organisations, training companies and support or advisory firms. Obtaining advice from informal sources, such as family and friends (the brother-in-law syndrome), who may have little if any knowledge of the business, might increase potential risks, particularly in terms of organisational fit and systems integrity.

Financial constraints, lack of in-house expertise, and short-term management imposed by an unstable environment result in smaller firms being exposed to greater risk in IS implementation than their larger counterparts. The lack of understanding of computers and internal IS expertise is a problem in itself and the costs of implementing inappropriate technology may prove fatal for an organisation which lacks adequate financial and productive cushioning (Doukidis *et al.*, 1997).

Product selection decision-making

How do organisations select IS products? Some firms use cost/benefit evaluation, competitive

pressure or client expectations, while others might purchase systems because of their popularity or the perception that they are a management prerequisite (Malone, 1997). Benefits are often anticipated that fail to be realised. Huff and Munro (1985) identified six phases of a rational IS/IT product selection process as the following:

1 *Awareness*, whereby the technology is brought to the organisation's attention but there is an information gap.
2 *Interest*, whereby the missing information is obtained.
3 *Evaluation*, whereby the use of the technology is mooted and a decision is made whether or not to try it.
4 *Trial*, which involves testing the technology to assess its appropriateness for current and future needs.
5 *Implementation*, whereby the trial is extended to full use of the technology within selected areas of the organisation.
6 *Diffusion*, which involves extending the innovation to other areas in the organisation.

Small firms, however, would tend to adopt the opportunistic model for selection, whereby no formal planning takes place and the identification of technology is seemingly unsystematic. Fewer resources are needed in terms of expenditure or specialist planning and IS skills. It would appear that only a small minority of small firms employ a full information requirements evaluation, preferring the opportunistic selection model (Doukidis *et al.*, 1997).

Chapter summary

Managers are crucial to organisations. They fulfil a variety of roles and perform a number of functions. It is important to understand the different levels of management and the different information requirements of each level.

Managers perform a number of roles; interpersonal, informational and decisional. They carry out three important functions, namely, planning, controlling and decision-making. Each of these functions is discussed in some detail with reference to their importance, the different types of planning, controlling and decision-making, how they are structured as processes and what information is required for each function.

This chapter concentrates on what managers do, how they do it and what information they need at different time intervals. Chapter 5 introduces the types of information system that support managerial work and provides more detail on the types of report that furnish managerial information.

Information systems project planning and control are also discussed to demonstrate how these managerial activities influence the development of information systems.

Review questions

1   Describe the levels of management in organisations. How do they differ from one another?
2   What are Mintzberg's management roles? How do information needs vary between the different roles?
3   Why is planning important?
4   What are the main types of plans in organisations?
5   What sort of information is needed for planning?
6   Explain the IS project planning process.
7   Why is control important?
8   Describe the control process.
9   Which types of control work well and why?
10   Explain the IS project control process.
11   Describe the decision-making process.
12   What is 'groupthink'?
13   What is the decision gap?
14   How does decision-making change with level of management?
15   What is the difference between programmable and non-programmable decisions?

Case study

The London Ambulance Service (LAS)

The LAS covers a geographical area of 600 square miles, making it the largest ambulance service in the world. The service covers 6.8 million residents, a number that increases with the influx of commuting workers during the day, and carries over 5,000 patients daily. It receives between 2,000 and 2,500 calls daily, including 1,300 to 1,600 emergency 999 calls that the computer-aided despatch system has to cope with.

The impetus for change

In the late 1980s the LAS was under huge pressure to increase its performance. The service was not reaching the nationally agreed performance standards. The specified time for the ambulance crew to receive the instructions triggered by an emergency call was three minutes. The crew was then required to arrive at the scene of the incident within 14 minutes. The LAS was not reaching these targets.

The existing system

The despatch system at this time was entirely manual, though attempts at computerisation had been made in the early 1980s. A change in specification had led to the project being abandoned in October 1990 at a cost of £7.5m. Despite this, parts of the system were later upgraded and integrated into the new CAD (Computer Aided Design) project.

The manual system was slow and relied on the physical movement of instructions; manual checking of maps, manual checking of ambulance availability and voice communication with the ambulance, which created bottlenecks in the system. It also relied on the efficiency of staff, who like all human beings can be prone to making mistakes. The new CAD system had to achieve the following objectives to fulfil the 'command and control' functions required:

- receive the call, confirm details and locate the incident;
- identify which ambulance to send;
- communicate the details of the incident to the ambulance;
- position suitably equipped and staffed vehicles to minimise response times;
- supply management information to assess performance and assist in future planning and resource scheduling.

The hidden agenda

The CAD system was perceived as a panacea to other problems that had beset the service in recent history, including poor industrial relations, outmoded work practices (as perceived by management) and no reliable information on resource utilisation. The introduction of the CAD system was seen as a catalyst that could justify the changes to work practices required by the management team. By removing decision-making from the control-room staff, the system would reduce any power they had, thereby allowing for further change. Throughout the entire project there was little or no consultation with the prospective users of the system – the ambulance and despatch staff.

Project problems

Problems tend to surface when an organisation's management does not have the requisite knowledge of the project objectives and obligations, which correlates to an unwillingness to listen to or communicate with the people who carry out the project work. Traditionally, authority relating to contractual links between client and supplier is as follows:

- contractual links between client and supplier are made at the senior management level;
- the authority to communicate from the client to the supplier and vice versa is then delegated at least two levels downward.

This is seen as common behaviour in most industries. Committing to a contract is seen as much riskier than carrying out the obligations of the contract. Therefore, it is a task left to top management, whether a group or an individual. This is understandable, as the senior management in an organisation would be expected to possess a global strategic view of the organisation's objectives. With the CAD project, the LAS appeared to follow this template: 'the logical hierarchy of decisions has corresponded to the classical hierarchy of management'.

Once the decision had been made to use the Apricot, System Options, Datatrack consortium, the actual successful execution of the project appeared to be of secondary importance to the management board. By accepting the lowest bid, they had achieved their objective and their responsibility had in effect ended. The ad hoc project team that evolved with the CAD project was then unwittingly left to implement a project that was doomed at conception.

In the LAS there was an assumption that the management were always capable of determining the best use of personnel resources, often despite not having any direct experience of the work themselves or without consultation with the personnel involved. Communication and feedback were not sought, therefore any decision taken on the alteration of working practices had a higher chance of leading to failure. Project success requires the downstream parties to be involved in deciding how to achieve the objectives of projects and sometimes in the setting of the objectives themselves. Human systems do not work well if the people who make the initial decisions do not involve those who will be affected later.

Why the project failed

Rather than any one specific area attributable as the prime cause of the failure, there was more of a chain reaction culminating in the operational failure of the CAD system as a mission-critical application. The culture, the procurement process, the inexperience of the contractors, the lack of involvement of the end-users, the absence of any project management are just a few of the factors that in themselves could have contributed to project failure. The CAD project did not just exhibit one or two of these problems; it encompassed them all.

With the advent of massive management cuts and a change of leadership, it is perhaps not surprising that there was a culture of fear among the remaining management staff at LAS. Admission of failure did not take place, which exacerbated the inherent flaws in the project procurement process. If at least there had been a project manager in overall charge of the project there would have been some recognition that the project would not attain its goals. As it was, the timetable was impossible and the lack of real world awareness was reflected in the naive implementation of the CAD system. Furthermore, the presence of a blame culture tends to lead to a reluctance in making or being responsible for decisions, in case there are any negative repercussions.

The procurement decision and the theory of groupthink

Systems Options, the reluctant contractor, had been told about the earlier abandonment of a previous project due to the earlier software house underestimating the complexity of the software needed. Bearing this in mind, it is surprising that the LAS committee did not have any doubts regarding the winning consortium's price or ability to carry out the work. At £973,463 it was £700,000 cheaper than the next nearest bid. There seems to have been some evidence of the phenomenon of 'group think', which refers to a process of group dynamics. There are crucial

Table 3.4 Identifying symptoms of groupthink in LAS

Symptoms	Case examples
The group fails to explore all the possible alternatives or consider all possible objectives available from which to choose.	LAS's focus on cost was a major criterion for the senior management team. There was no documented evidence of any discussion as to discrepancies between the bids and the external assessors' comments. No alternatives examined to the 'quantum leap' approach in implementing the CAD system.
Costs and risks of preferred options insufficiently explored. Assumptions are made and possible negative outcomes readily discounted or overlooked.	Legal redress after a previous IT project failure for LAS could have provoked a belief that similar action could be taken again to avoid any major financial loss. A previous review of the LAS mobile communications identified which technical and procurement options would minimise risk and recommended having a documented quality system to help reduce risk.
Information searches are superficial and there is a failure to obtain all possible data for decisional effectiveness. Information searches are incomplete, using poor techniques and often selective filtering of the results when communicated to others.	Two supplier references for System Options lead contractor to supply the LAS CAD system referred to the company's resources being heavily committed on other projects. Although an external assessor (the Scottish Ambulance Service) approved the selection process, it did make an important proviso regarding the management's need to ensure that a bespoke system was justifiable.
There is bias and selectivity in processing available information. The group tends to choose certain information excluding valuable items that 'do not fit their picture'.	LAS senior management clearly ignored or filtered out important warning signs about the CAD project.
Rejected alternatives, which may be rich in potential, are seldom and objectively re-examined and therefore are left discarded and unheeded.	LAS rejected the idea of having an independent quality assurance system implemented on the project consortium by another company, which might have given some warning of forthcoming problems.
The 'groupthink' group fails to work out implementation, monitoring and contingency plans in sufficient detail, thereby not considering worst case scenarios and over-assuming what is/is not possible. Potential consequences and future problems are ignored or glossed over.	In the LAS decisions and recommendations were passed between teams and committees with no real project driver appearing to be present at any stage. There was an air of detachment, with the assumption that at each stage of the procurement process someone else would take responsibility for the project.

Source: adapted from Robbins (1988)

situations where executive groups have made poor or unsound decisions (particularly in a critical situation), which are symptomatic of reaching conclusions in a group. Table 3.4 summarises the symptoms of defective decision-making attributed to group think.

Conclusion

Following the extensive enquiries into the system crash, the LAS took a radically different approach to their technological requirements and the consequences of their implementation, the main lessons learned being:

- to reduce complexity of operations;
- to concentrate upon key deliverables;
- to pay attention to staff and their needs;
- to establish a workable but acceptable pace for delivery and implementation;
- to build upon a number of infrastructure changes (a combination of new hardware systems and re-engineered control procedures).

In 1996 an interim system was implemented. Unlike its predecessor, this system was proto-typed with the users, who also had an input to the process. The business needs were also con-tinually reviewed to guarantee LAS's requirements were being met. The spectacular and high-profile failure of the project resulted in the LAS re-evaluating their approach to both oper-ations and project management. Failure can generate 'double loop' learning, in which people question the assumptions behind their failures as well as the failures themselves.

Case questions

1 What were the principal reasons for the failure of the LAS CAD system?
2 What does this case study tell us about management decision-making?
3 Explain the importance of fully understanding operations and project management issues before proceeding to system implementation?
4 What lessons were learned by the LAS as a result of the project failure and why are these important lessons to learn?

··

References and further reading

Alter S. (1992) *Information Systems. A Management Perspective*, Addison-Wesley: Reading, MA.

Angéle L., Cavaye M. and Cragg P.B. (1993) 'Strategic Information Systems Research: A Review and Research Framework', *Journal of Strategic Information Systems*, 2(2): 125–138.

Anthony R.N. (1965) *Planning and Control Systems. A Framework for Analysis*, Graduate School of Business Administration, Harvard University: Boston, MA.

Barnard C. (1938) *The Functions of the Executive*, Harvard University Press: Cambridge, MA.

Basi R.S. (1998) 'Administrative Decision Making: a Contextual Analysis', *Management Decision*, 36(4): 232–240.

Bennett R.H. (1998) 'The Importance of Tacit Knowledge in Strategic Deliberations and Decisions', *Management Decision*, 36(9): 589–597.

Burke R. (2003) *Project Management. Planning and Control Techniques*, 4th edn, Wiley: Chichester.

Butcher D. and Clarke M. (2003) 'Redefining Managerial Work: Smart Politics', *Management Decision*, 41(5): 477–487.

Chidambaram L., Bostrom R.P. and Wynne B.E. (1990–1991) 'A Longitudinal Study of the Impact of Group Decision Support Systems on Group Development', *Journal of MIS*, 7(3), Winter: 7–25.

Craft R.C. and Leake C. (2002) 'The Pareto Principle in Organisational Decision Making', *Management Decision*, 40(8): 729–733.

Daft R.L. (1991) *Management*, Dryden Press International: Orlando, FL.

Dibrell C.C. and Miller T.R. (2002) 'Organisation Design: the Continuing Influence of Information Technology', *Management Decision*, 40(6): 620–627.

Dixon R. (1991) *Management Theory and Practice*, Butterworth-Heinemann: Oxford.

Doukidis G.I., Pramataris K.C. And Paul R.J. (1997) 'Exploring Information Systems Potential in the ECR Context', in R. Galliers, C. Murphy, H.R. Hansen, R. O'Callaghen, S. Carlsson and C. Loebbecke (eds) *Proceedings of the 5th European Conference on Information Systems*, June 19–21.

Edmunds A. and Morris A. (2000) 'The Problem of Information Overload in Business Organisations: a Review of the Literature', *International Journal of Information Management*, 20: 17–28.

Euske K.J. (1984) *Management Control: Planning, Control, Measurement and Evaluation*, Addison-Wesley: Reading, MA.

Finkelstein A. and Dawell J. (1996) 'A Comedy of Errors: The London Ambulance Service Case Study', in *8th International Workshop on Software Specification & Design*, IWSSD-8, IEEE CS Press: 2–4.

Frishammar J. (2003) 'Information Use in Strategic Decision Making', *Management Decision*, 41(4): 318–326.

Galbraith J.R. (1973) *Designing Complex Organisations*, Addison-Wesley: Reading, MA.

Galliers R.D., Patterson E.M. and Reponen T. (1994) 'Strategic Information Systems Workshop: Lessons from Three Cases', *International Journal of Information Management*, 14: 51–66.

Gorry A. and Scott-Morton M. (1989) 'Retrospective Commentary on the Gorry and Scott-Morton Framework', *Harvard Business Review*, Spring: 58–60.

Hannagan T. (1995) *Management Concepts and Practices*, Pitman: London.

Harrison E.F. and Pelletier M.A. (1998) 'Foundations of Strategic Decision Effectiveness', *Management Decision*, 36(3): 147–159.

Harrison E.F. and Pelletier M.A. (2000) 'The Essence of Management Decision', *Management Decision*, 38(7): 462–470.

Harrison E.F. and Pelletier M.A. (2001) 'Revisiting Strategic Decision Success', *Management Decision*, 39(3): 169–180.

Hellriegel D. and Slocum J.W. (1996) *Management*, 7th edn, South-Western College: Cincinnati, OH.

Higgins J.C. (1976) *Information Systems for Planning and Control: Concepts and Cases*, Arnold: London.

Higgins J.C. (1980) *Strategic and Operational Planning Systems. Principles and Practice*, Prentice-Hall: Englewood Cliffs, NJ.

Hougham, M. (1996) 'London Ambulance Service Computer-aided Despatch System', *International Journal of Project Management*, 14(2): 103–110.

Huang W.W. and Wei K.K. (2000) 'An Empirical Investigation of the Effects of Group Support Systems (GSS) and Task Type on Group Interactions From an Influence Perspective', *Journal of MIS*, 17(2), Fall: 181–206.

Huff S.L and Munro M.C. (1985) 'Information Technology Assessment and Adoption: A Field Study', *MIS Quarterly* 9(4).

Janis I. (1982) *Groupthink: Psychological Studies of Policy Decision and Fiascos*, Houghton Mifflin: New York.

Koontz H. (1961) 'The Management Theory Jungle', *Academy of Management Journal*, 4(3): 174–188.

Koontz H. (1980) 'The Management Theory Jungle Revisited', *Academy of Management Journal*, 5(2): 175–187.

Laudon K.C. and Laudon J.P. (2001) *Essentials of MIS. Organisation and Technology in the Networked Enterprise*, 4th edn, Prentice Hall International: Upper Saddle River, NJ.

Malone T.W. (1997) 'Is Empowerment Just a Fad? Control, Decision-Making and IT', *Sloan Management Review*, Winter: 23–35.

March J.G. and Simon H.A. (1958) *Organisations*, John Wiley & Sons: New York.

March J.G. (1988) *Decisions and Organisations*, Blackwell: Oxford.

Martin C. and Powell P. (1992) *Information Systems. A Management Perspective*, McGraw-Hill: Maidenhead.

Mennecke B.E. and Valacich J.S. (1998) 'Information is What You Make of It: the Influence of Group History and Computer Support on Information Sharing, Decision Quality and Member Perceptions', *Journal of MIS*, 15(2), Fall: 173–197.

Mintzberg H. (1989) *Mintzberg on Management*, Free Press: New York.

Mintzberg H. (1994) 'Rounding out the Manager's Job', *Sloan Management Review*, Fall: 11–26.

Pinsonneault A. and Rivard S. (1998) 'Information Technology and the Nature of Managerial Work: From the Productivity Paradox to the Icarus Paradox?', *MIS Quarterly*, September: 287–311.

Proudlock M.J., Phelps B. and Gamble P.R. (1998) 'IS Decision-Making: a Study in Information-Intensive Firms', *Journal of Information Technology*, 13(1), March: 55–66.

Psoinos A., Kern T. and Smithson S. (2000) 'An Exploratory Study of Information Systems in Support of Employee Empowerment', *Journal of Information Technology*, 15: 211–230.

Reinig B.A. and Shin B. (2002) 'The Dynamic Effects of Group Support Systems on Group Meetings', *Journal of MIS*, 19(2), Fall: 303–325.

Robbins S.P. (1988) *Management Concepts and Applications*, Prentice-Hall: Englewood Cliffs, NJ.

Roberto M.A. (2003) 'The Stable Core and Dynamic Periphery in Top Management Teams', *Management Decision*, 41(2): 120–131.

Sashittal H.C. and Jassawalla A.R. (1998) 'Why Managers Do What They Do', *Management Decision*, 36(8): 533–542.

Scarnati J.T. (2002) 'The Godfather Theory of Management: an Exercise in Power and Control', *Management Decision*, 40(9): 834–841.

Successful IT: Modernising Government in Action (2001) http://www.archive.cabinet office.gov.uk/e-envoy/index-content.htm (18.07.02).

Simon H.A. (1977) *The New Science of Management Decision*, Prentice-Hall: Englewood Cliffs, NJ.

Wysocki R. and Young J. (1990) *Information Systems: Management Principles in Action*, Wiley: New York.

Yates D. (ed.) (1991) *Project Management for Information Systems*, Pitman: London.

Chapter 4

The systems approach to organisational problem-solving

Learning objectives

After reading this chapter, you should be able to:

- define what is meant by a system;
- discuss the basic principles underlying general systems theory;
- describe organisations in systems terms;
- apply appropriate systems thinking techniques to define problem situations and identify solutions.

Introduction

The principal aims of this chapter are to show how organisations and their information systems can be viewed using the systems approach. Systems thinking provides a very powerful tool for modelling large complex problems in a way that is both logical and practical. While it does not guarantee quality solutions to problems, it at least allows for the possibility that such solutions can be found. Given its common role in the analysis of the processes within an organisation, and as the basis for information systems design, it is an important topic for students studying organisational information systems at any level.

Origins of the systems approach

In order to understand the principles underlying the systems approach it is useful to look at how and why it was developed.

The complexity of modern business organisations creates a fundamental problem for anyone attempting to analyse them. It is very easy to be overwhelmed by the amount of information available when looking at organisational problems. This makes it difficult to focus on the main issues – a case of 'not being able to see the wood for the trees'. In order to cope with the problem of complexity, analysts must have some way of structuring the various pieces of information they acquire. Organisations are not unique in this respect; many other fields of study have encountered the same problem. Over the years, a common approach has been found which helps deal with large complex problems, namely breaking them down into several smaller simpler ones. We all learn this technique as children as we try to master skills such as reading, writing and arithmetic.

This approach to understanding the complexity of the world around us is embodied in scientific thinking. By understanding increasingly smaller bits of the world scientists seek to increase our overall understanding. However, this reductionist approach has its limitations. While we know more and more about the structure of the world around us, we are still relatively ignorant about its behaviour. Therefore, while scientists have developed laws for the behaviour of sub-atomic particles they still cannot reliably predict the behaviour of living organisms, which are simply lots of atoms, put together in certain patterns. By analysing small parts of the world they learn how they work in isolation but lose sight of how these parts interact with each other to create objects that are more complex. As illustrated by Flood and Jackson (1991), prior to alternative ways of thinking, mechanistic approaches were the 'classical or rational' views of organisations. To increase the performance of an organisation it was believed that reductionism and optimisation of the constituent parts would lead to better performance as a whole, as conceptualised in Figure 4.1. An analogy of this is frequently seen

in team sports, when some teams despite having individually brilliant players do not perform well as a whole. When the players do become a team there is a synergy produced that increases the performance of the team beyond its individual capabilities.

When analysing situations in which interactions are an important element of our understanding, such as living organisms or organisations, a different approach is required.

It was biologists who were the first to advocate an alternative non-reductionist approach, which would still have the ability to aid the analysis of complex problems such as the behaviour of living organisms. Ludwig von Bertalanffy's (1968) work in the 1940s on the generalisation of, what was then called, organismic thinking led in 1954 to the founding of the Society for the Advancement of General Systems Theory. A group of scientists from different disciplines founded the Society at the annual meeting of the American Association for the Advancement of Science. Its intended purpose was as a vehicle for the development of a universal theory – General Systems Theory (GST) – which could be applied to any problem. It is from these early beginnings that the systems approach, or systems thinking has developed.

Peter Checkland's paper 'The Origins and Nature of "Hard" Systems Thinking' (1978) highlights the different influences on the devel-

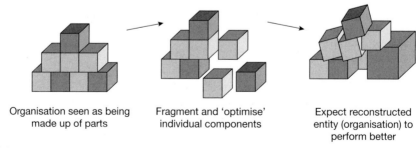

Organisation seen as being made up of parts   Fragment and 'optimise' individual components   Expect reconstructed entity (organisation) to perform better

Figure 4.1 The classical view – reductionist approach

opment of these early ideas into what is now understood as systems thinking. While the origins of systems thinking lie in biological and other sciences, the development of its practical application owes more to a different tradition, namely that of the engineer. While scientists were interested in increasing knowledge and developing scientific theory to describe the world around them, engineers were more interested in problem-solving in a specific context. Less a case of 'what have we learnt?', more 'will it work?'.

As well as recognising the distinct traditions of systems thinking, Checkland also distinguishes between its two separate applications – systems analysis and systems engineering. Systems analysis is defined as 'the systematic appraisal of the costs and other implications of meeting a defined requirement in various ways'. Its origins and uses in post-war America highlight its close links with operations research as a technique for analysing complex problems. Systems analysis is still widely used as an aid to decision-making, though now it is more commonly known as decision support. Systems engineering is defined as 'the set of activities which together lead to the creation of a complex man-made entity and/or the procedures and information flows associated with its operation'. This is essentially the carrying out of an engineering project, i.e. the conception, design, evaluation and implementation of a system to meet a defined need, and is the origin of the traditional techniques used for designing organisations and their information systems. Both applications have one major factor in common – the pursuit of a practical solution to a well-defined problem. This is a distinguishing characteristic of what is known as 'hard' systems thinking, where problems are formulated in terms of a current state and a desired state, and solutions are aimed at reducing the gap between them. As we will see later in this book this 'hard' systems approach has had a significant impact on how organisations approach their information systems.

What is a system?

Having established the origins of systems thinking, it is now possible to look in more detail at the ideas and principles at the heart of this view of the world. As with any field in which many researchers have been working over a long period of time, there are many different published definitions of what constitutes 'a system'. This has been compounded by the fact that the word 'system' is now in common usage to describe all sorts of things. We have the solar system, political systems, economic systems, sound systems, and of course, computer systems. Although this widespread use of the term 'system' to describe everyday ideas and products suggests a nebulous concept which can mean anything you want it to, there are common concepts that are usually implied by it. These concepts also underlie more formal definitions used by systems thinkers.

A definition of systems

The most basic definition of a system is that it is a coherent whole with a boundary, which separates it from everything else. What this means is that it is not just a collection of unrelated objects. The objects within a system are inter-related in an organised way. These could be the sun and planets along with their orbits within the solar system, or the cells which go together to make up the human body. Or they could be the various elements which go to make up an organisation.

There are three distinct types of object we need to consider: inputs, processes and outputs. Processes receive inputs, which they combine and transform into outputs, as shown in Figure 4.2.

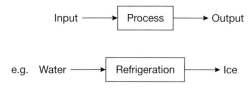

Figure 4.2 Input, process, output

The boundary of the system separates it from its environment, and defines the inputs and outputs of the system as a whole. If the system requires something from the environment, then that is an input, and if it provides something to the environment, what it provides is an output (see Figure 4.3). In organisational terms, these inputs may be materials, people, money or information, which the organisation transforms into outputs, such as finished goods, services, information and money.

In theory, the system's environment contains everything that is not in the system itself. However, this is not a very practical definition as the environment contains many objects, which have no relationship to the system at all. Therefore, the environment of a system is more

usually regarded as containing everything that is outside the system's control, but which affects its behaviour or performance in some way. This will of course include other systems. Deciding where the boundary of the system lies, i.e. the dividing line between the system and its environment is sometimes difficult. Often, analysts, to suit their own purposes, define the boundary in a purely arbitrary way. The key to making a sensible decision lies in remembering two things: if the system controls it, it is part of the system, otherwise it is part of the environment, unless it neither affects the system nor is affected by it, in which case it isn't part of either the system or its environment. Flood and Jackson conceive systems to exist in a hierarchy, consisting of other subsystems with the same characteristics as shown in Figure 4.4. Additionally they have created metaphoric classifications for systems and their attributes. The rationale behind this approach is to make the recognition of problems in a systemic environment easier and more coherent thus leading to the choice of an appropriate systems methodology to solve the problem.

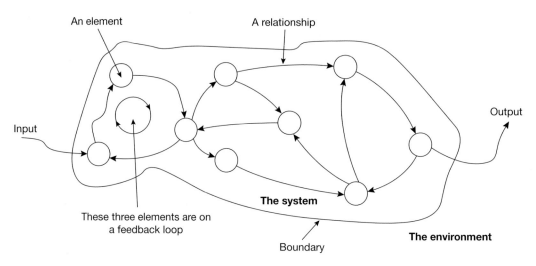

Figure 4.3 A representation of a system
Source: adapted from Flood and Jackson (1991)

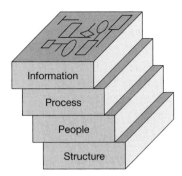

Figure 4.4 A multi-perspective model of an organisation

Systems thinking is a ...
Paradigm
    Vantage point
    Set of thinking skills
Learning method
    Process
    Language
    Technology

Figure 4.5 Richmond's operational definition of systems thinking

Some authors (Martin and Powell, 1992) talk about the system's interface as something distinct from the boundary. The boundary of a system simply denotes its limits. The term 'interface' also implies an exchange, and is therefore a more appropriate term for describing the point at which one system passes on its outputs to, or receives inputs from, another system.

Therefore, to summarise, we can define a system as: a set of interrelated objects, organised to form a coherent whole, with a perceived boundary which separates it from its wider environment.

Systems thinking and types of system

An alternative or complementary methodology to the analytical-based models is systems thinking that attempts to cover the areas the reductionist models cannot explain. The following personal definition of 'systems thinking' by Richmond (1994) although esoteric, does capture the essence of what systems thinking is, and in conjunction with his operational definition (illustrated in Figure 4.5), plots a route for newcomers to the field to follow:

systems thinking is the art and science of making reliable inferences about behaviour by developing an increasingly deep understanding of the underlying structure.

There is a wide range of ideas, opinions and techniques allied to systems thinking; gestalt therapy, cybernetics, chaos theory, general systems theory, soft systems methodology to name a few, but they all have a common thread: systems behave in a generic manner and this behaviour can be identified and articulated. It is pointed out by Balle (1994) that systems thinking is not 'holistic' in the sense that there is any connection between remote far-flung objects (his examples include trying to connect a crab, the ozone layer and capital life cycle together). Rather, it is in the 'understanding' that what is causing our immediate problem may not be in the immediate vicinity, and therefore the solution may not be in the immediate vicinity.

Over the years that systems thinking has developed there have been a number of attempts at developing a typology of systems to help understand how different classes of system behave. One of the most well known of these typologies was suggested by Peter Checkland (1981). Checkland divides systems into five broad categories:

1   Natural systems, such as the solar system and the human body, which have evolved and are simply as they are.
2   Designed physical systems, such as machines, which have been designed and constructed by human beings to fulfil some purpose, and are physically identifiable.

3 Designed abstract systems, such as mathematical and philosophical systems, which
   have been designed and constructed by
   human beings to fulfil some purpose, but
   which are less tangible than physical systems.
4 Human activity systems, such as organisations, in which human beings interact in performing activities to meet some purpose.
5 Social systems, such as the family which
   consist of human social relationships, and
   which span the boundary between natural
   and human activity systems.

A slightly different set of classes is presented
by Wilson (1984). The differences are subtle,
with the most obvious being the linking of all
designed systems, both physical and abstract,
under the same heading. What Wilson does add
is the idea that a human activity system, such as
an organisation, consists of a social system of
human relationships as well as a system of activities. If this idea is followed further, it can be
argued that human activity systems also include
designed systems, such as an organisational
structure, machinery including computers and
systems for processing information. These are
not separate systems, but different perspectives
on the same complex system, which can be combined to help understand its behaviour more
fully, with each highlighting different aspects.

There is no universally accepted model of
system classification, though the Checkland/
Wilson model is probably the most cited in
organisational and information systems literature. There are however, a number of characteristics that can be used to describe a particular
system more precisely.

System characteristics

There are a few key characteristics of any system,
which can help in understanding its fundamental behaviour. The level of interaction it has with
its environment indicates the importance of
understanding the environment. The level of
predictability is of obvious interest when looking
at what the future may hold. The rate of change
of the system is a factor in understanding its
behaviour. Last, the system's ability to regulate
itself will indicate its chances of survival in a
changing world. These characteristics are often
represented in terms of opposites (see Figure 4.6),
but in reality most systems lie somewhere
between the two extremes illustrated below.

Degrees of openness

Systems can be classified as *open* or *closed*.
Systems which interact with their environment,
exchanging materials, information, money or
energy, are called open. Closed systems have no
interaction with their environment at all. In
practice a totally closed physical system is difficult to envisage, and in most cases the concept
of a closed system is not particularly useful in
the practical application of systems thinking.
Thus, most systems of interest to us are open,
though the degree of openness can vary dramatically. A system would be classed as open if
it received a single input from its environment,
as would a system which has many very
complex interactions with its environment. It is
obvious from this that the term 'open system'
covers a wide range of systems.

Degree of determinism

Systems also vary in the predictability of their
behaviour. Systems which have well-defined

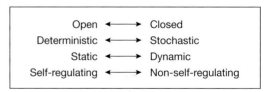

Figure 4.6 Key system characteristics

rules of behaviour, and whose behaviour is therefore predictable, are called *deterministic* systems. For example, the laws of mathematics mean that the results of equations are always predictable. Equally, the position of the stars in the sky is so predictable it can be used for navigation, if the rules are known. Deterministic systems tend to have relatively simple interactions between their component objects, or to be relatively closed and thus less susceptible to environmental influences.

Most complex systems, and systems with a relatively high degree of openness, have patterns of behaviour that are very difficult to predict. This is because the interactions are so complex that it is not possible to define a full set of behavioural rules, for example the economy, or the weather system. To analyse such systems requires the use of the laws of probability and statistics to fill the gaps in the behavioural rules. Such systems are therefore known as probabilistic or *stochastic* systems. As they contain human beings, human activity systems tend to be stochastic in nature. On the other hand, designed systems tend to be more deterministic as the rules are largely built into the design.

Degree of dynamism

Some systems never really change between being created and ceasing to exist, for example a structure such as an electricity pylon, or a model such as a map. These are known as *static* systems. However, most systems are *dynamic*, i.e. they perform some sort of activity.

Degree of self-regulation

Finally, systems vary in the degree to which they control their own activities. In order to survive, a system must be able to regulate itself. Systems that cannot regulate their behaviour well enough to counteract changes in circumstances become subject to entropy, and ultimately cease to exist.

Basic systems ideas

There are a number of basic ideas that underpin all systems irrespective of their type or characteristics. It is these ideas that make systems thinking the powerful problem-solving tool that it is.

Emergent properties

The definition of a system as an organised coherent group of objects suggests that this group has its own patterns of behaviour. The way the system as a whole behaves cannot be predicted by looking at the individual objects involved. This holistic view is key to the whole systems approach. It recognises that a group of interrelated objects has properties as a group, which are not present in any of the individual objects. In systems terms, the properties emerge when the objects are combined as a system. A classic example of this is living organisms. Individual cells have limited patterns of behaviour, depending on the type of cell they are. By bringing such cells together in an organised way we get living creatures with far more complex behaviour, which only emerges by examining the creature as a whole. This is also true of organisations that exhibit behaviour as a whole, which is not predictable by examining their constituent parts in isolation.

Hierarchy

The processes within a system are themselves systems in their own right (called *sub-systems*), with their own inputs, processes and outputs. Similarly, the whole system itself is part of a wider system (called a *supra-system*). Thus, any system being studied is a sub-system of a wider system, and contains its own set of interrelated sub-systems.

This idea of a hierarchy of systems is very useful in helping the analyst to handle the complexity of a problem. Each level in the hierarchy has a different degree of complexity – the lower down the hierarchy the simpler the system (see Figure 4.7). As was said earlier, the idea that smaller problems are simpler is not restricted to systems thinking. What makes the idea of hierarchy powerful is that by defining each sub-system in systems terms we can be certain that any changes we make to it that do not change the sub-system's interface will not require any further changes to the system as a whole. This means that the analyst can focus on a sub-system at any level of the hierarchy, within the context of the system as a whole, but without having to deal with all its complexities.

Looking at this from the other direction, it becomes clear that if we can define a sub-system's interfaces, we do not need to know the details of its inner workings to be able to understand its place within the system as a whole. In systems terms we can treat the sub-system as a black box. This is an idea borrowed from engineering, where knowing the internal detail of a ready-made mechanism is less important than knowing which combination of outputs will be produced by which combination of inputs. For example, it is unnecessary to know how a television actually works for you to be able to watch it, change channels and adjust the volume. The concept of the black box allows the analyst to ignore unnecessary detail. A sub-system's internal detail only needs to be analysed if it is relevant to the problem being investigated. The opposite of this concept is the white-box testing used in software engineering, which looks at code in high levels of detail to resolve output problems.

Communication

In order to function as a coherent whole the objects within a system need to be able to communicate with each other (and the system with its environment): the outputs of one sub-system becoming the inputs of others. It is often the breakdown of this communication that leads to the breakdown of the system as a whole. The closeness of the various sub-systems is known as *coupling*. With tightly coupled sub-systems, the output of one is immediately used as the input of the other. On the other hand, with loosely coupled sub-systems the outputs are not immediately required as inputs (see Figure 4.8). De-coupling of sub-systems can often be used to make the system as a whole work more effectively. A common example of this in organisations is the de-coupling of the purchasing and production functions. To ensure that sufficient raw material is available for production a pre-determined level of stock is held as a buffer, to compensate for the lead-time of purchasing more materials.

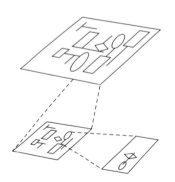

Figure 4.7 Hierarchy of organisational systems

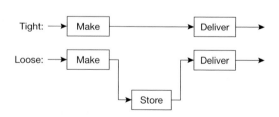

Figure 4.8 Coupling of sub-systems

Control

In order to survive as a whole, a system needs to regulate its behaviour. It needs to react to changes in its environment to ensure that it can cope with any threats or opportunities that present themselves. This requires some form of control mechanism. There are varieties of control mechanisms that can be applied to systems, and these are discussed in more detail in the next section of this chapter.

> Try to think of some of the systems in the world around you. What type of systems are they? What characteristics do they have? Can you identify their sub-systems?

Control mechanisms in organisations

In order to be successfully self-regulatory a system requires mechanisms to control its activities.

Different types of system require different levels of control in order to maintain their existence. A common framework for discussing the relative complexity of different types of system is that developed by Kenneth Boulding (Skyttner, 1996). Boulding's Hierarchy of Systems Complexity ranks system types on nine levels (see Figure 4.9). The lowest level (frameworks) contains static systems. The second (clockworks) contains simple dynamic systems with predetermined behaviour, such as simple machines like engines. The third level introduces the idea of uncertainty and the need for control mechanisms (cybernetic systems) to change system behaviour to suit changing circumstances, for example a thermostat regulating room temperature. These first three levels are concerned with physical and mechanical systems. The next three levels are concerned with the increasing complexity of living organisms, from single cells through plants and up to animals. The seventh level adds the complexity of abstract thought in viewing a human being as a system, with level eight adding the complexity of human social

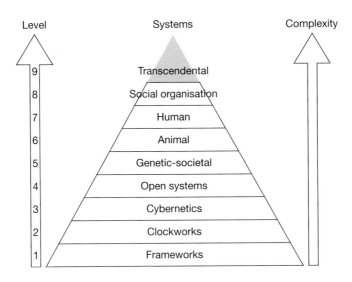

Figure 4.9 Boulding's Hierarchy of Systems Complexity
Source: Skyttner (1996)

interactions. The final level is by definition speculative – transcendental systems being beyond human comprehension.

Basic elements of control

All control is exercised by means of *control loops*. The purpose of a control loop is to monitor the outputs of a system, compare these with the desired output and make any changes to the system that may be required to make actual output match desired output. To do this requires four separate elements (Schoderbek *et al.*, 1985):

1 a control object, or variable;
2 a detector, or sensor, to monitor output;
3 a comparator, to compare actual and desired performance;
4 an effector, or actuator, to take any necessary action.

Open and closed loops

Many control mechanisms rely on using the effector to change a system's inputs based on the state of its own outputs (as shown in Figure 4.10). One of the simplest examples of this is in central heating systems. The heat output of the heating system warms the room until it reaches the desired temperature. The heating system then shuts down and relies on the heat already in the system to continue heating the room. When the heat output is no longer enough to maintain the desired room temperature the

heating system switches back on. Such a system is known as a *closed loop* control system, because the outputs of the system itself determine the changes made to its inputs.

However, there are also *open loop* control systems, where the outputs are not coupled to inputs. In such systems a change in output is still prompted by a change in input, but is not then linked back (see Figure 4.11). Examples include washing machines and lights. Once started by some input, e.g. being switched on, they work until they reach the end of their allotted time, or until there is a change in input, e.g. being switched off. In an organisation an open loop system might be a production process where raw materials are fed in and a certain number of finished products expected as a result. Control is based on the assumption that a certain level of input always produces a certain level of output and therefore no checks are made. When the materials are used up, the products must be ready. In practice this is unrealistic as there could be variations in the material, the process, or other unknown factors. Many open loop control systems use time as a means of limiting outputs. According to Schoderbek *et al.* (1985) organisations are basically open loop systems which use human beings to close the loop by comparing actual and planned performance. In the production example, this would be the role of a production controller or supervisor, who would check the outputs and either increase or reduce the materials input as required to meet the production target.

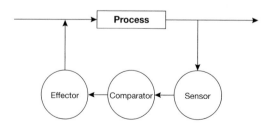

Figure 4.10 A control loop in an open system

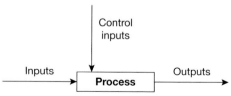

Figure 4.11 An open loop system

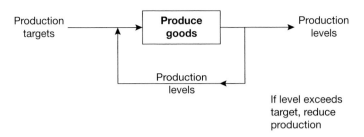

Figure 4.12 Negative feedback

Types of control

Having established the fundamentals of control we can now look at the different types of control mechanism, and how they behave. There are two basic types – feedback control and feed-forward control.

Feedback control

Where a system uses outputs to directly influence inputs (as in Figure 4.10) this is known as a *feedback* control mechanism. Most control is aimed at maintaining stability. This may be based on a product specification or activity target. The aim of the control mechanism is to correct any deviation from the specification or target by applying a counteraction. This is known as *negative feedback*, as shown in Figure 4.12. A good illustration of this is the heating system example mentioned earlier, where the thermostat switches the heating system on and off as the temperature varies. If the temperature is too high, the heating is switched off to allow the room to cool. If the temperature is too low the heating remains on until the target temperature is reached. Similar examples include using a combination of accelerator and brakes in a car to maintain the correct speed, slowing down when the speed is too high, and speeding up when it is too slow.

Positive feedback occurs when an increase (or decrease) in outputs prompts a further increase (or decrease) in inputs, which in turn leads to more (or fewer) outputs, and so on, as shown in Figure 4.13. Obviously, this is not a recipe for stability; on the contrary, it is usually a recipe for disaster. If outputs continue to increase, the system will inevitably reach the point at which it can no longer sustain the necessary level of activity. If they continue to decrease, the point will be reached when they cease altogether. The most widely recognised form of this is probably the feedback heard on public address systems. If a microphone is placed too close to a

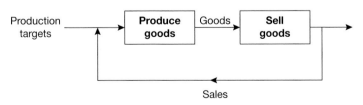

Figure 4.13 Positive feedback

loudspeaker, the microphone picks up the sound of the voice of the person speaking or singing from both its original source and from the loudspeaker. This creates a loop where the sound picked up by the microphone is broadcast through the loudspeaker which is itself picked up by the microphone, which is therefore broadcast a little louder, then picked up, and broadcast a little louder, and so on. This all happens very quickly, and the result is a deafening howl as the system fails to cope with the increasing volume of sound it is being asked to handle.

In a commercial setting positive feedback can be equally disastrous. A good example is the stock market crash of 1987, contributed to by automated trading systems, which were programmed to sell when share prices fell to a certain level. Unfortunately, if large numbers of a particular share become available for sale the price tends to fall, thus leading to more selling and more price falls. This positive feedback loop continued until someone intervened and pulled the plug.

Positive feedback increases the instability in a system, and usually requires outside intervention to halt the process.

System oscillation

Time is an important factor in control. Feedback controlled systems have an inherent tendency to *oscillate* around the target values of the system. This is because the control mechanism cannot act instantaneously to correct any deviation, so when the control is applied it may no longer be appropriate. This can take the form of time delays (where there is a time gap before control is applied), or lags (where control is applied but takes time to take full effect), or a combination of both (Skyttner, 1996).

The relative magnitude of feedback is also a factor. If feedback leads to a change in input that is the same in magnitude as the error it is correcting, the tendency is for the system to oscillate in a stable way. If the magnitude of the change in input is greater than the error, the level of instability in the system increases through overcompensation. If the magnitude of input change is less than the error, then this will tend to dampen down the oscillations, eventually returning the system to stability and its output back to its target.

Feedforward control

Feedforward control attempts to address the problem of oscillation by anticipating any deviations from target. The control mechanism can then be ready to counteract the problem as it happens, removing any time delays or lags. As Figure 4.14 shows, a feedforward control differs from feedback in that it incorporates a predictive model of the system's behaviour (a predictor) as well as the other components. This means that some prior knowledge is required about the system's behaviour so that it can be

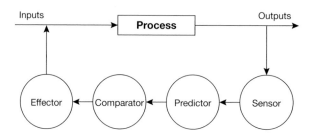

Figure 4.14 Feedforward control

predicted. The use of a predictive model helps smooth out some of the fluctuations in the system.

The use of feedforward is less common than feedback, partly at least because of the difficulty in developing reasonably accurate predictive models for the many different systems found in organisations. One area where its use is common is in inventory management, using demand forecasts along with current stock and demand levels to decide on the desirable stock levels for the future. Then any action taken to adjust stock levels, such as reducing production, is based not just on current levels of stock and demand but also on likely future demand. This allows the level of input, i.e. new stock, to be varied based on a long-term view rather than on short-term peaks and troughs. Reducing unnecessary variation in the level of an activity is a key element in maintaining organisational stability.

Continuous and discontinuous control

A final issue to consider when looking at control is whether it is applied continuously. This is determined by the type of variable being controlled, and by the nature of the control mechanism. In some cases a control mechanism can be designed to continuously make small adjustments to the system to minimise any deviation from target values, such as might be required by an airliner's autopilot, or by a process controller in a chemical plant. The more frequently the outputs are checked the less the scope for variation. In situations where small variations are of little importance, especially if they average out, then the frequency can be lowered. For example, organisations cannot realistically monitor the impact on cash flow of every individual financial transaction as it is made. Instead, they use budgeting periods to monitor transactions en bloc at fixed intervals. The more important cash flow becomes, the tighter it will

be controlled and therefore the more frequently it will be monitored.

However, in many cases the complexity and resource requirements of continuous control are unnecessary and discontinuous control inputs are used. In discontinuous mechanisms inputs are either present or not. While the overall level of small deviations from target is likely to be higher with discontinuous control mechanisms, this is compensated for by their relative simplicity. A good example is the thermostat of a heating system already mentioned in this chapter. The thermostat does not attempt to continuously maintain a fixed temperature by making small adjustments, it simply switches the heating on and off at discrete intervals to achieve the same result.

Applying control in organisations

Given the complexity of organisations, each one will use a variety of different control mechanisms, for both the organisation as a whole and for individual sub-systems. Over-reliance on too limited a set of controls can lead to an imbalance in the way the organisation operates, making it difficult for it to meet its goals. The number of different controls also has an impact on how flexibly the organisation can deal with changes in its environment. If the organisation's control mechanisms are not flexible enough to deal with environmental changes, the organisation will not be able to respond appropriately to change. The potential consequences of this are loss of efficiency and effectiveness, and in extreme cases failure of the organisation to survive. This idea is embodied in Ashby's law of requisite variety (Ashby, 1956), which implies that in order to achieve effective control a control system must be capable of the same level of variety as the system which it is controlling.

One of the most significant impacts this issue can have is on the ability to automate business processes. If automation cannot provide the necessary level of flexibility then human intervention will be necessary, and this must be allowed for. Typically, this is done by providing manual override facilities in case of circumstances which do not conform to the normal operating procedures. The person monitoring the system's activity can then intervene if necessary. Failure to provide this flexibility can result in exceptional cases being inappropriately handled.

Applying systems thinking to organisations

There are a number of reasons why the systems approach to problems is useful in helping to understand how organisations work in the real world. There is no need to know in detail about General Systems Theory in order to use its central properties and to understand the behaviour of organisations in systems terms. Many of the ideas presented below are common sense, but as is often the case with ideas that seem obvious when you know of them they would be difficult to establish from first principles.

Organisations as systems

We have already established that organisations are human activity systems, which can be viewed in different ways depending on the analyst's intentions (see Figure 4.4). However, it is useful to look at the idea of an organisation as a system in more detail in terms of the possible characteristics of a system.

All organisations exist within an environment with which they interact, acquiring resources and providing products and/or services. Therefore, all organisations are open systems. All organisations perform some sort of activity and are therefore dynamic systems. If they are to survive and prosper within a chang-

ing environment, they too must be able to adapt and change. This requires them to be able to regulate their own activities towards achieving their goals. Finally, given the unpredictability of their environment, and the fact that human behaviour within the organisation itself is unpredictable, we can also see that the behaviour of organisations is stochastic in nature.

Thus, we can define organisations in systems terms as:

open, dynamic, self-regulating, stochastic, human activity systems.

As we have already seen, organisations are part of a hierarchy of systems. Each organisation is made up of sub-systems such as the various business processes, departments or divisions. Each organisation is in turn part of a series of wider supra-systems such as an industry, a value chain, and the national and global economies. Each level in this systems hierarchy displays its own behaviour and properties, which emerge only when looking at that level.

Applying the systems approach

There is no one definitive method for applying the systems approach to a problem. This is a consequence of the general nature of systems theory. However, the following methodology contains the set of steps generally regarded as providing a suitable framework. The type of problem being solved will determine the details of the methodology used.

The problem-solving process

Step 1: Defining the problem

The starting point in the process is to identify and define the problem to be solved. All too often managers expend resources tackling the symptoms of a problem without ever really identifying the underlying cause. By defining the problem in systems terms all the relevant elements can be brought together, increasing the likelihood of separating the problem from the symptoms. Systems thinking can then be used to analyse the problem in more detail, establishing requirements and objectives in depth. This involves the development of one or more (often quantitative) models of the problem.

Step 2: Developing alternative solutions

The definition of objectives and requirements obtained from Step 1 forms the basis for identifying alternative ways of solving the problem. In some cases, the models of the problem will indicate that only one solution is possible, but usually there is more than one. Each solution represents a means of moving from the present state to a desired state in which the problem no longer exists. As well as identifying alternatives, criteria need to be established for evaluating them. At this stage of the process the solutions are not usually presented as fully designed solutions, as this would be very costly. More typically, they outline the various ways of achieving a solution, which when selected will allow the chosen option to be designed in detail.

Step 3: Selecting a solution

The next step is to compare the various alternative solutions and select the option which best addresses the requirements and objectives. The evaluation criteria established in Step 2 should be used as the basis for the comparison of the solutions. The same criteria must be applied systematically to all the alternatives to ensure a fair and objective choice.

Step 4: Designing the solution

Having selected a single solution to the problem, work can begin on its design. This involves specifying in detail how things should be. This specification will then provide a blueprint for change, which the organisation can follow. It is important that, as the design progresses, it is checked against the requirements and objectives identified earlier. Failing to do this could result in a design that does not provide a workable solution.

Step 5: Implementing the solution

The next step in the process is to implement the designed solution. Care must be taken to ensure that what is implemented is what was actually specified. This sounds like an obvious point, but is a crucial one to bear in mind.

Step 6: Reviewing the situation

The final step in the process is to review the impact of the changes, to see if they have achieved the desired results. If not, then this new problem needs to be investigated to see why. Maybe the situation had changed between the solution being designed and its implementation, or maybe there were errors in the way the original problem was tackled.

Fact gathering techniques

There are many different techniques that analysts can employ to gather facts about a problem. The principal techniques used in investigating organisational problems, especially those relating to information systems, are:

- questionnaires
- document analysis
- interviews
- observation
- special purpose records.

Some of these techniques will not always be appropriate, but most investigations include a mixture of interviews, document analysis and observation as a minimum. These techniques need to be applied in a planned and systematic way to ensure that the gathering of facts is as effective and efficient as possible. Having a strategy for your analysis makes it easier to optimise the process.

Questionnaires

Questionnaires are a very useful tool for obtaining information from a large number of people in a short space of time. However, they are limited in terms of the scope of information they can provide. The lack of dialogue between the analyst and the respondent means that there is little chance for answers to be expanded upon. To counter this the analyst must design the questionnaires with great care to ensure that the resulting information is useful. The limitations of questionnaires mean that they are best suited to the initial stages of fact gathering to obtain a general overview of the situation, or to establish who could be most profitably interviewed later.

Document analysis

All organisations have documentation of some kind. This may be restricted to statutory reports and scribbled notes, or since the rise of quality management systems it may include full procedures manuals and operational documentation for the whole organisation. A lot can be learned about an organisation's activities by analysing its use of documentation, especially when investigating information handling. The principal limitation of document analysis is the fact that the analyst may not understand how the documents are meant to be used, or how they are used in practice. To address this problem the best solution is to use the results of document analysis as the basis for interviews with relevant personnel who can explain.

Interviews

Interviews are often the single most useful technique available to the analyst. Talking to the people involved in a problem is a very rich source of information. It allows a great variety and depth of information to be obtained. It also allows you to assess their attitudes to what is happening through both what they say and their body language. By interviewing different people it is also possible to highlight differences of opinion between the participants.

Observation

An obvious technique which is sometimes underrated is to simply observe what happens in an organisation. This technique is most commonly associated with traditional time and motion studies, but is much more widely applicable. It is very difficult to reach conclusions about any organisational situation if you have not actually seen what happens there. Participant observation as a fact gathering technique is particularly useful in attaining high-quality data if approached in the correct manner.

Special purpose records

Finally, there are sometimes circumstances when the information required is simply not available via any existing source. To obtain such information it is necessary to use special purpose records. For example, if investigating the need for a new system for handling telephone sales queries, crucial pieces of information are call volumes, durations and patterns. It is unlikely that this information is routinely collected and so a special form will need to be designed to allow the information to be collected as part of the investigation.

Advantages and disadvantages of the systems approach

There are many advantages in using the systems approach to analyse organisational problems. Primarily, it provides a consistent theoretical framework for the analysis of many of the different elements that go into making an organisation, including its structure, processes and information systems. It also emphasises the fact that when looking at a problem, the context of the problem (its environment) is a crucial consideration. Through the idea of hierarchy it allows the analyst to control the level of detail at each point in the analysis, enabling the often large quantity of information to be effectively analysed. This has the added benefit that it also makes it easier for the analyst to communicate with the other people involved.

The systems approach also brings more implicit benefits. By focusing on the interfaces between sub-systems it highlights issues in what is often a weak area, namely communication between different employees, functions, departments and organisations. In addition, through the idea of emergent properties, it underlines the idea of synergy between the various elements of an organisation – the whole being

greater than the sum of the parts. This is a key issue when analysing organisations as it is all too easy to make improvements in one area which result in the overall organisation performing more poorly.

However, the systems approach is by no means perfect. The principal problem with the approach is that it is goal directed, with a starting point, which is a known problem and an identified set of objectives. In many organisational problem situations, this is in itself a problem as often all that is 'known' is that there is some sort of problem requiring some sort of solution, but no one is sure what either is. Trying to apply the hard systems approach to such 'soft' problems can lead the analyst to seek a solution to what is in effect the wrong question.

A second issue, which is seen by some as a drawback, is the potential for every different analyst involved in looking at a problem coming up with different models and subsequent solutions. Viewing this as a problem assumes that there is a single best solution, but in reality there are frequently several equally valid solutions to any given problem. This is known as equifinality, i.e. it is possible to take different routes to reach the same end. Indeed, it is possible to reach the same end without even starting from the same place.

The general nature of the approach also means that it is not possible to state a definitive method for applying it in detail. To a large extent this will be determined by the particular situation being investigated, and by the prejudices and preferences of the analyst concerned. Some prefer to look at inputs and outputs before identifying transformation processes, while others prefer to identify processes first. In reality, it is an iterative activity, and the analyst will look at all elements more than once.

The final problem is the fact that in the real world some parts of a system may also be part of another 'separate' system. For example, if an organisation subcontracts out its delivery process, the process is still part of the organisation's activities but is also part of the subcontractor's activities. Each will see the process in a different way. Such cases are increasingly common with organisations stripping down to core activities, and it is a real issue. Given the often arbitrary definition of system boundaries, great care has to be taken in including all relevant elements. However, as long as the analyst is aware of the fact that a particular resource (e.g. equipment or personnel) or a particular process is shared with other systems, it is not a significant drawback, as it can be taken into consideration.

Softer approaches to analysis

The fundamental flaw in the traditional hard systems approach is the need for an identified problem and objectives at the beginning of the process. While such approaches are suitable where a problem has been identified, e.g. we need a bridge here, or we need some way of reducing our stationery bill, they are not suited to less well-defined problems, e.g. what do we do about unemployment? This flaw was recog-

nised in the 1970s, and new softer approaches were developed. The most well-known of these is that developed by Peter Checkland and others at Lancaster University. This Soft Systems Methodology attempts to address the issue of problem identification by using systems thinking to model a problem situation so that individual problems can be identified. As Checkland (1981) says it is 'a systems-based means of structuring a debate' about the nature of a problem situation. Once identified, these problems can then be tackled using the more traditional approaches.

Applying Soft Systems Methodology (SSM)

The seven stages of SSM

The methodology falls into seven stages: stages 1 and 2, and 5, 6, and 7 belong to the 'real world' in which the system operates, stages 3 and 4 are conceptual and belong to the abstract world of systems thinking as shown in Figure 4.15. Although set out as a logical sequence, the stages do not necessarily have to be followed in that sequence. Depending on the context of the analysis, the methodology could start with any stage from 1 to 4. There is also likely to be a lot of iteration, and moving back and forth between the different stages.

Stage 1 Identifying the problem situation

The first stage of the Soft Systems Methodology equates to the first step in problem-solving using a more traditional hard systems approach. The major difference is that, whereas the traditional approach starts off with a specific problem, SSM's starting point is a general *problem situation*, in which there are thought to be one or more as yet unidentified problems.

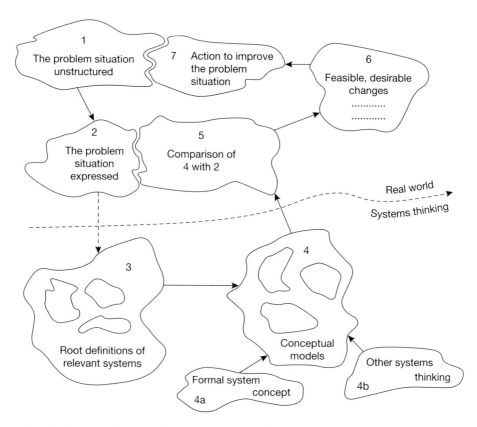

Figure 4.15 The seven stages of Soft Systems Methodology
Source: Checkland (1981)

Stage 2 Expressing the problem situation

In order to be able to identify possible problems the problem situation as a whole needs to be expressed in a structured way, using systems thinking. The aim is to build as rich a picture as possible of the situation. This should include:

- elements of structure within the situation, such as reporting hierarchies, geographic locations and departmental structures;
- elements of process within the situation, i.e. relevant activities;
- a view as to how structural and process elements are related to each other.

Expressing and structuring the problem is a major step towards identification of the specific problems within the situation. The idea of a rich picture of the situation is not just conceptual, it is also literally a technique for expressing the problem situation. At this early stage those involved in the situation (whether analyst, participant or both) may only have a very vague idea of what is involved or even of what they are trying to achieve. Physically drawing or illustrating the system as they see it is a very useful technique in that it can show what the system under consideration is all about. This not only provides a starting point but also brings home to all concerned where the problem situation lies in relation to other parts of the organisation.

The resulting 'rich' picture offers a number of advantages:

- important issues can be identified and attention is drawn to problems;
- those involved have a tool which helps them visualise the system under investigation;
- boundaries and interfaces between subsystems can be identified;
- issues such as conflict, or concerns from participants can be illustrated and brought out into the open (without identifying the source);
- the pictures can be developed and changed relatively easily as more data is gathered.

Visualisation of the system aids understanding of the system by the analyst and helps to 'slot-in' the roles and involvement of all the participants. Thus important activities can be analysed further as the picture develops. There are no rules for how to draw rich pictures, and wide variations exist in practice, as shown in Figure 4.16.

The rich picture is then used to select a viewpoint (or viewpoints) from which to study the situation further. This may involve different emphasis on the various aspects of the organisation (see Figure 4.4) depending upon the situation. Selecting a viewpoint identifies one or more systems as being relevant to the problem-solving process. This selection is not necessarily final, and may be reconsidered if the original selection proves unfruitful as analysis progresses. Therefore, by the end of this stage of the problem-solving process we have named a lot of notional systems which from our analysis seem relevant to the problem. We have not yet identified the problem itself.

Stage 3 Defining the relevant system(s)

In order to understand the situation in more depth it is necessary to define in more detail the systems identified as relevant. What is required is a *root definition* of what each is, as opposed to what it does. Each definition should be 'a concise description of a human activity system which captures a particular view of it'

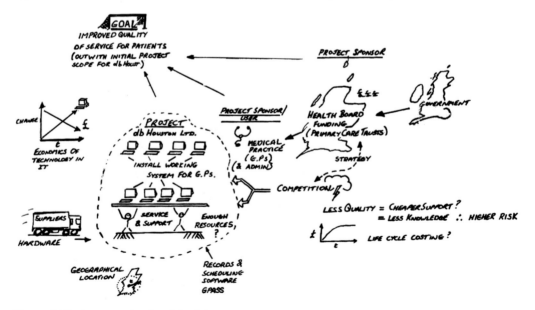

Figure 4.16 An example of a rich picture

(Checkland, 1981). Given the fact that root definitions are at the crux of SSM, it is important to ensure that the root definition of each system is formulated with great care. An idea of what constitutes an adequate root definition is embodied in the mnemonic CATWOE. Each element must be explicitly contained (or excluded as irrelevant) in the definition. Even though in many cases the W is implicit, it must always be stated in order to make the definition as a whole meaningful.

C The **C**ustomers who are, generally speaking, those who will be the beneficiaries or victims of the system's activities.

A The **A**ctors who are the agents within the system who carry out its main activities.

T The **T**ransformation process which is the main overall activity of the system by which defined inputs are transformed into defined outputs.

W The **W**eltanschauung (or world view) which embodies the implicit viewpoint that provides the meaning behind the system's existence.

O The **O**wners of the system who are the agency with a prime concern for the system, and the power to cause it to cease to exist.

E The **E**nvironment in which the system exists, and which constrains its behaviour.

The root definition below shows students as customers of a system owned by a Court or Senate. The actors in the system are academic and administrative support staff. The transformation is the education of students, in an environment whose main element is Government education policy. The Weltanschauung is that the education provided should be academic, based on research by the academic staff, and be delivered in a way which makes good use of resources. Of course this is not the only possible root definition. Any element of CATWOE could be interpreted in a different way.

Stage 4 Conceptual modelling of the defined systems

Having defined the relevant system the next stage is to create a conceptual systems model of the minimum necessary activities required to fulfil the system's root definition. Again, the idea here is to look at what the system must do to

---

Possible Weltanschauung for a university

- Universities exist to provide academic education for a minority of society.
- Universities exist to provide training for a significant proportion of school leavers.
- Universities exist as focal points for academic research.
- Universities exist as sources of highly trained staff for industry and commerce.
- Universities exist as a means of reducing the number of school leavers registering as unemployed.

Possible root definition for a university

A system owned by the University Court/Senate and operated by academic and administrative support staff, to deliver a higher academic education to students of the university, based on sound academic research, and making efficient and effective use of available resources within the constraints of the government's current education policy.

---

fulfil its definition unconstrained by any real world considerations. Having defined what each system is, we are now looking at what it must do to be that system, but are not yet concerned with how it will do it. This separation of what from how is central to the ability to identify potentially radical changes to an organisation.

Stage 5 *Comparing the models and the real world*

Having derived conceptual models of the systems we can use them as a basis for the discussion of potential change to the real world problem situation expressed in Stage 2. The comparison allows examination of differences between the current real world situation and the conceptual models of the relevant systems, and facilitates debate as to why these differences exist. The aim of the comparison is to highlight possible better ways of carrying out activities (new 'hows') or to identify new activities (new 'whats').

If the problem situation is a 'greenfield situation' with no systems in existence, then the conceptual model should be compared with participants' expectations of what the new system will do. This is usually less demanding than having to debate changes to an existing real world system.

Stage 6 *Identifying desirable and feasible changes*

The debate in the previous stage is used as a means of identifying possible changes to the real world problem situation. Not all possible changes identified are necessarily implemented. To be worth implementing a change has to be desirable in terms of its effect on the system involved. It also has to be feasible given the context of the problem situation under investigation.

In the more traditional hard systems approach the change is usually the creation and implementation of a new system. While this is also sometimes the case in softer problems, more often the change is less drastic, e.g. a change in structure, procedures or, what is often more difficult, in attitudes.

Stage 7 *Taking action to improve the problem situation*

The final stage is to implement actions designed to fulfil the changes identified as both desirable and feasible. This is itself a new problem situation, requiring the (re)design of the relevant systems. Having identified what is to be done, it is now a hard systems problem, which can be tackled using the traditional engineering-based approach.

Summary

As we have seen, the systems approach provides a useful framework for the solving of organisational problems. The traditional hard systems approach enables a better understanding of control elements that are important in organisational management situations. Soft Systems Methods provide a way of identifying problems in softer, more complex, less clearly defined situations, such as those often found in organisations. By adopting a systematic approach and taking a systemic view of organisational problems, it is possible to identify them more accurately, and therefore determine effective solutions.

Review questions

1 What is meant by the term 'system'.
2 List the different types of system.
3 Name the key characteristics of systems.
4 Describe the four basic ideas central to systems thinking.
5 What is the key difference between open and closed control loops?
6 Describe the different types of control mechanism available.
7 What are the steps in applying the systems approach to problem-solving?
8 What are the advantages and disadvantages of the systems approach?
9 What is the key difference between hard and soft systems approaches?
10 What are the stages in applying Soft Systems Methodology?

Case study

Balfour Kilpatrick Ltd

Company background

Balfour Kilpatrick is part of a multinational organisation which primarily carries out electrical and construction projects for large corporate customers. Typical projects include high-voltage and low-voltage cabling, undersea cabling projects, overhead line cabling and electrical wiring of large buildings. Balfour Kilpatrick is part of the BICC Group, a global conglomerate. The BICC Group is an international engineering business which serves the world's markets for infrastructure development in power, communications, transport and building. It has two principal businesses: firstly, Balfour Beatty, a leading UK-based construction and engineering company, and secondly a company representing one of the world's largest cable-making businesses. The Group's primary objective is to provide long-term value for its shareholders through the exploitation of its core competencies. It is dedicated to total quality, technical excellence and satisfaction of customer need. BICC was formed in 1945 through the merger of two of the UK's leading electrical cable companies. For the next 25 years the company developed its international interests, largely in the Commonwealth, and in 1969 acquired Balfour Beatty, at that time predominantly a power construction and power engineering company.

The relationship between the different companies in the group was not always apparent, even to those in the companies. Balfour Kilpatrick's quality manager based in Derby suggested having the organisational chart on a sheet of Velcro due to the frequent in-house reorganisations of the group structure and subsequent name changes. A recent example was the amalgamation of the overhead line part of Balfour Kilpatrick and its underground cabling business, leading to a reorganisation of both companies, with common overheads and costs being merged, such as wages and accounting. An extra layer of management was introduced into a relatively flat management structure. It was too early to determine whether or not this created any significant changes in the operational abilities of either business but it did cause a degree of uncertainty with existing admin-istrative staff with respect to security of employment.

The Walpole project

Although not technically unique, the Walpole project did have its unique circumstances, which could have provided useful lessons and feedback for the future. It was the intention to find a practical way of capturing this information to enhance the carrying out of future projects.

Project stakeholders

The primary customer and project sponsor was National Grid Co. Projects Division. This depart-ment in National Grid was in overall charge of the extension to the Walpole substation. Balfour Kilpatrick therefore had two direct customers: the National Grid Company and BICC Supertension Cables Ltd. BICC manufactured and supplied the cable with Balfour Kilpatrick as their recognised installers.

The National Grid Company (NGC) is responsible for the distribution of power throughout England. It is responsible for the development, construction, operation and maintenance of the National Grid transmission system, which encompasses the provision of any connections to the system by power generating companies. A network of 7,000km of overhead lines and 600km of underground cables, including substations, distribute power between power generators like PowerGen and Enron to regional electricity companies.

The purpose of the Walpole substation extension

Construction had commenced on a combined gas-cycle power station at Long Sutton, which when completed would supply electricity into the electricity network through National Grid's 400kV substation at Walpole. In order to accommodate this extra input, National Grid were obliged to build a new generator bay and upgrade the plant and equipment at the substation.

This obligation stemmed from the privatisation of the electricity industry. In England and Wales the industry was divided into three:

1   the generating companies, PowerGen and National Power;
2   the National Grid, responsible for the distribution network;
3   the Regional Electricity Companies (RECs), such as East Midlands Electricity.

The work involved extending the substation, undergrounding existing overhead pylons, build-ing new pylons and adding new switchgear. This is a considerable amount of civil, mechanical and electrical work, the costs of which were being met by both NGC and Enron (the power gen-erator). Other contractors involved in the project were May Gurney, GEC Alstom, NGC and Reyrolles, including the subcontractors employed by these companies.

The quality management system at Balfour Kilpatrick

Balfour Kilpatrick used an industry-based quality system, British Standard BS EN ISO 9002 (1994) *Quality Systems Specification for Production and Installation*. The ISO 9000 series of Standards are primarily geared towards improving the economic performance of a company by implementing a quality system. The system concerns itself with the monitoring, measuring and auditing of all aspects of the organisation that affect directly or indirectly the quality of the product or service supplied. Approval to ISO standards is achieved by certification granted by independent approved bodies and paid for by the organisation seeking approval.

The rationale behind the process of quality system certification is to provide assurance to the customer that the company is committed to quality and is able to supply products and services that conform to customer requirements. The quality system itself is determined by the individual company and can hence be either simple or complex, as deemed necessary. In any event, it must be specifically tailored to the organisation.

Balfour Kilpatrick's certification to ISO 9002 was, in theory, meant to indicate to its customers that its quality management system had been independently assessed as effective. To achieve this, an extensive documentation system, consisting of a Quality Manual, Quality Control Procedures and Work Instructions, had to be put in place.

System metaphors

Organisational metaphors were discussed in Chapter 2. System metaphors are similar and can be related to this case study. The machine metaphor closely resembles the quality system that had been used as a 'quality veneer' at Balfour Kilpatrick, concentrating on the bureaucracy and efficiency of individual parts. The political metaphor is also in evidence because of the subterfuge adopted to circumnavigate the quality system. Conflicts of interest had arisen as a result of the need to remain certified to ISO 9002 and in practice alternative 'underground' solutions were often found. Finally, the culture metaphor was also apparent at Balfour Kilpatrick. The unspoken, but familiar, ways of thinking and acting are difficult to quantify and elaborate on but can be regarded as the following:

- the underlying desire to finish the project despite any difficulties, which can lead to risk-taking;
- the ability to adapt to a changing environment;
- an adversarial approach in some circumstances, contributing to performance breakdown;
- project ownership can produce autocratic behaviour unless dissipated by other project team members;
- a risk culture akin to 'heroism'.

Figure 4.17 is a systemic representation of contributors to risk in the project environment. The diagram is incomplete in that the increased risks will feed back to create more pressure; a 'positive reinforcing loop'.

System dynamics

Figure 4.18 is an adaptation of the system dynamics template Administrative Main Chain (Richmond *et al.* 1993), which in its generic form is used to depict the sequence of events in an administrative process. The model attempts to illustrate the quality system administrative process at Balfour Kilpatrick. It emphasises the complexity of the order and way in which tasks are carried out and the interdependencies that exist. The benefit of this type of model is its dynamic ability;

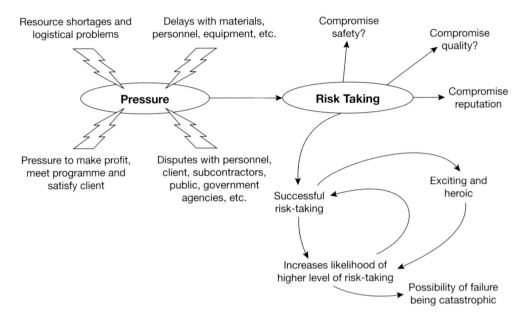

Figure 4.17 Contributors to risk in a project environment

the process is triggered by a completed activity. In the case of Balfour Kilpatrick a large volume of administration caused by the quality system coincided with the most important activities of the Walpole project (such as the cable installation), which had to take priority.

The main chain infrastructure of particular interest is the sequential work flow main chain, which involves a generic representation of a sequential work completion process. This simulates the project management issues involved at Balfour Kilpatrick. Figure 4.19 represents the work flow main chain infrastructure for the cable installation project and Figure 4.20 expands the install process.

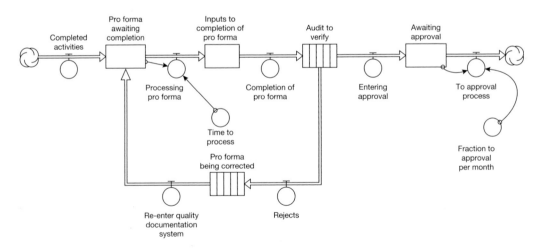

Figure 4.18 The quality system administrative process at Balfour Kilpatrick

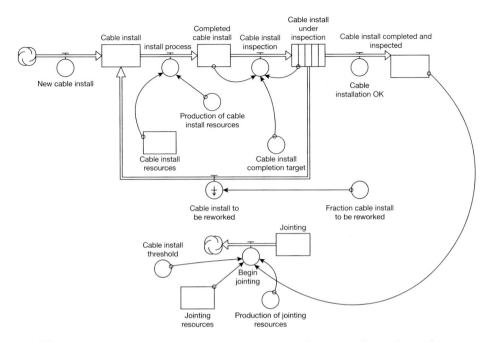

Figure 4.19 Workflow main chain infrastructure template applied to Balfour Kilpatrick

The model illustrates the installation of a cable followed by the jointing of a cable. Parts of the organisation can be modelled in isolation and then used to contribute to the larger picture. There are a number of system boundaries in this case. The reason for the project was the need by National Grid to extend a substation to cater for the input of energy from a new power station being built nearby. The reasons for building the power station did not directly affect the cable project other than its conception. A higher-level model could be constructed to take account of factors like government policy, finance and technological advances.

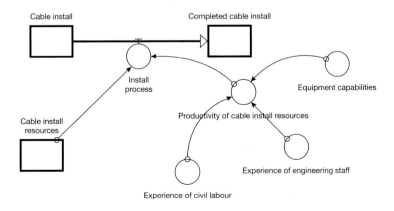

Figure 4.20 Expanding the install process

Case questions

1 Explain why you think the Balfour Kilpatrick project lends itself to a systemic approach.

2 Why is Figure 4.17 useful and what important issues does it help us to understand?

3 Figure 4.18 could be used to illustrate any quality system administrative process – in what ways could such a model help organisations in general?

4 Identify the system elements in Figures 4.19 and 4.20 and comment on what they are showing about the cable installation process at Balfour Kilpatrick.

···

References and further reading

Ashby W.R. (1956) *An Introduction to Cybernetics*, Chapman & Hall: London.

Balle M. (1994) *Managing with Systems Thinking*, McGraw-Hill: London, p. 36.

Checkland P.B. (1978) 'The Origins and Nature of "Hard" Systems Thinking', *Journal of Applied Systems Analysis*, 5(2): 99–110.

Checkland P.B. (1981) *Systems Thinking, Systems Practice*, John Wiley & Sons: Chichester.

Checkland P.B. (1982) 'Soft Systems Methodology As Process: a Reply to M.C. Jackson', *Journal of Applied Systems Analysis*, 9: 32–39.

Checkland P.B. and Scholes J. (1990) *Soft Systems Methodology in Action*, John Wiley & Sons: Chicester.

Checkland P. (1991) 'Towards a Coherent Expansion of Systems Ideas', *Journal of Applied Systems Analysis*, 18: 25–28.

Flood R. and Jackson M. (1991) *Creative Problem Solving Total Systems Intervention*, John Wiley & Sons: Chicester, pp. 3–6.

Flynn D.J. (1992) *Information Systems Requirements: Determination and Analysis*, McGraw-Hill: New York.

Jackson M.C. (1982) 'The Nature of 'Soft' Systems Thinking: The Work of Churchman, Ackoff and Checkland', *Journal of Applied Systems Analysis*, 9: 17–29.

Martin C. and Powell P. (1992) *Informational Systems. A Management Perspective*, McGraw-Hill: Maidenhead.

Patching D. (1990) *Practical Soft Systems Analysis*, Pitman: London.

Richmond B. (1994) *System Dynamics Review*, 10: 2–3, Summer–Fall: 135.

Richmond, B., Peterson, S. and Charyk, C. (1993) *Introduction to Systems Thinking and Ithink*, High Performance Systems Inc.: Lyme, NH.

Schoderbek P.P., Schoderbek C.G. and Kefalas A.G. (1985) *Management Systems, Conceptual Considerations*, 3rd edn, Business Publications: Boston, MA.

Skyttner L. (1996) *General Systems Theory. An Introduction*, Macmillan: Basingstoke.

Von Bertalanffy L. (1968) *General System Theory: Foundations, Development Applications*, Braziller: New York.

Waring A. (1996) *Practical Systems Thinking*, International Thomson Business Press: London.

Wilson B. (1984) *Systems: Concepts, Methodologies, and Applications*, John Wiley & Sons: Chichester.

Chapter 5

Information systems and their uses

....

Learning objectives

After reading this chapter you should be able to:

- define what is meant by an 'information system';
- appreciate the different types of information systems;
- understand the levels and scopes of information systems;
- understand the roles information systems play in organisations;
- assess the potential impact of different information systems or business process management.

What is an information system?

The system that monitors and retrieves data from the environment, captures data from transactions and operations within an organisation, filters, organises and selects data and presents them as information to managers and provides the means for managers to generate information as required is called the *management information system* (Murdick and Munson, 1986: 6). Managers have always required and used information but all too often in the past the sources they had to rely on were haphazard and miscellaneous. Information was often processed on a personal basis, with the result that different managers operated on different perceptions about their environment.

Information systems can be formal or informal, computer-based or not. Information can be provided in a variety of ways (see Chapter 3) through a variety of channels. It is important for organisations of the future to gather the most reliable, relevant information in the most efficient and effective ways possible. This often entails using the right balance of formal and informal information systems, computer-based, structured systems and verbal, ad hoc systems.

What types of information systems do organisations use?

Information systems can be used to fulfil many different functions within organisations. To help our understanding of these functions it is useful

125

to group them into distinct categories. Over the years the categorisation of information systems into taxonomies has been an ever-present feature of information systems research. There are different views but Table 5.1 provides one of the most common overarching classifications of information systems. Using this classification as a basis, the sections that follow will develop the taxonomy in such a way as to show different interpretations and hence the diverse nature of information systems.

As new uses have been found for computer-based IS, so new categories have been developed. Another potential classification is shown in Table 5.2.

Many of these have been too closely linked to particular technological views and so are of limited use as long-term models of information system typologies. To help understand the organisational use of information systems it is necessary to remain focused on business use of the systems, not their underlying technology. Another taxonomy of business relevance is Farbey *et al.*'s (1995) Benefits Evaluation Ladder (see Table 5.3), which relates to change and IS and provides a means of deciding what benefits have resulted or might result from different IS applications.

The bottom rung represents forced and mandatory changes, whereby the organisation may have to change to survive or be forced by an external agent to change. The second rung represents applications designed to replace existing methods in order to reduce costs by automating certain standard routines. The third rung involves applications that not only reduce costs but add value directly, often by doing things that were not done before. MIS and DSS applications provide information for planning, control and decision-making and are often

Table 5.1 An information systems classification

Type of information system	Transferable features	Examples
Transaction processing system	Control, procedures and rules, repetition	Processing credit card payments
Management information system	Emphasis on measurement and performance monitoring	Sales/production reports, receivables report showing invoices and payments
Decision support system	User control, models, semi-structured tasks	Production data models, insurance policy alternatives, current specification for machine operator
Executive information system	User-friendly interface and methods for data analysis	Flexible access to regional sales/corporate financial/ production data
Expert system	Use of inference in problem-solving, 'what if' scenarios, user-driven	Diagnosis of machine failure, pricing competitive bids, identifying trend changes
Office automation system	Multiple forms of information, immediacy and interactivity of communication, avoidance of unproductive work	Spreadsheets, email, e-calendars, desktop publishing, voicemail, video conferencing

Table 5.2 Types of information systems

Information system type	Purpose
Office automation system	Provides effective processing of organisational and business data, creates documents.
Communication system	Helps people work together by interacting and sharing information in many forms.
Transaction processing system	Collects and stores information about and controls some aspects of transactions.
Management information system and executive information system	Converts TPS data into information for monitoring and managing performance; provides easily accessible, interactive information.
Decision support system	Helps people make decisions by providing information, models or analytical tools.
Enterprise system	Creates and maintains consistent data-processing methods and an integrated database across multiple business functions.

Source: Alter (2002)

Table 5.3 The Benefits Evaluation Ladder

Rung No.	Description
8	Business transformation
7	Strategic systems
6	Inter-organisational systems
5	Infrastructure
4	MIS and DSS
3	Direct value added systems
2	Automation
1	Mandatory changes

gic use of systems and technology and the top rung involves applications which enable changes to take place that transform an enterprise. Such business transformation is always strategic in intent and may involve business process re-engineering (see also Chapters 7 and 8).

Taking Table 5.1 as a basic template, the following types of system are discussed in more detail, highlighting in particular their business purposes and their relationship with different organisational levels.

directed at the higher levels of management. The fifth rung is represented by investments which provide a general capability but may not be targeted at any specific application. They provide the foundation upon which subsequent value-adding applications can be built. The sixth rung involves systems which cross organisational boundaries, systems which are shared by two or more organisations, chiefly trading partners. The seventh rung represents the strate-

Transaction Processing Systems (TPS)

TPS are the oldest type of information system, developed soon after the Second World War in the accounting departments of major corporations. They are highly structured and detailed, involving the collection of specific data in specific formats. TPS check transactions for errors, such as inconsistent or missing data. An example of this type of system is the processing of cheques and direct debits by banks.

Online systems involve a direct connection between the operator and the TPS programme. The transaction is processed simultaneously as the data is collected, followed by confirmation that the transaction has been completed. Examples of online TPS are frequently to be found in financial services, such as the validation of credit and cash cards and payment of invoices. Consulting an inventory database to check if a customer's requirements can be met is another example.

Batch TPS involve the grouping of transactions and their processing as a unit, rather than individually. Batched data are then sorted according to particular criteria, such as by account number. Batch processing has the advantage over online processing in that the processing is more controllable, but in certain situations can be an unwieldy mechanism in comparison to online systems. Processing cheques and credit card slips, or generating pay slips, are common examples of situations using a batch-processing approach.

In some organisations not all basic business transactions are simple. For example, automatic underwriting systems in insurance companies need to handle complex combinations of factors to determine the risk involved, and therefore the premium required, in issuing an insurance policy. In the past this required an expert underwriter to perform the calculations and reach a decision. Automatic underwriting replaces the human expert with a computer system known as an expert system (ES). Such systems rely on established rules and norms built into the computer application to handle the complexity. This means that the user of the system only needs to enter the required data to generate an appropriate answer. From the user perspective this makes the operation of such systems little different from more traditional transaction processing.

Expert Systems are not true 'experts' in the human sense of the word as they lack common sense and 'gut feel', but expert knowledge has been captured in the form of facts and reasoning so that it can be made available to those with less knowledge or experience. The system encodes knowledge that it can take a human several years to learn, so that the knowledge of senior, seasoned, experienced employees need not be lost and new employees can become productive more quickly. The rationale for developing expert systems can be summed up as:

- to preserve the knowledge of experts;
- to improve the performance of less experienced people carrying out similar tasks;
- to assure a degree of consistency in the way particular types of tasks are accomplished.

Office Systems (OS)

Office Systems (OS) are a specialised form of TPS designed to facilitate day-to-day office operations in terms of communication and information processing. These information systems generate, store, modify, display and transmit business communications in a variety of formats. Unlike other types of TPS, OS are often used across the whole organisation. While operatives, mainly secretaries and administrators, are the main users, managers in many organisations also use them to prepare reports.

Management Reporting Systems (MRS)

Managers use the structured, summarised reports produced on a regular basis by MRS to review business performance indicators and act upon relevant feedback. MRS effectively take forward the output from TPS and other internal information sources with a view to providing information for management. A typical example would be the classification and analysis of sales data processed on a day-to-day basis. It is essential to summarise and focus on such data to highlight where performance has been strong and weak, for example in terms of product line and sales agents, so that appropriate action can be taken to effect improvements.

MRS applications aggregate and reformat TPS data for direct reading or process an extract selected from TPS data, as well as storing data of their own. In the latter case the MRS application may include a simple static model for producing the same periodic report for a particular manager. An MRS programme may also produce exception reports, such as generating the names and dates of particular training courses with less than ten registered participants two weeks prior to course commencement dates.

The MRS reports information in a format relevant to the potential user, such as profit and loss statements and spreadsheet sales summaries. It does not indicate how decisions are to be made or actions taken.

Management reports

Having looked at information requirements for decision-making, it is necessary to consider in what form this information is produced. Information needs to be supplied on a regular basis or made available as required. Reports of different types are issued or requested. They vary in terms of detail and specificity and may be forecasting things to come or evaluating what has already occurred. Five main types of report are used in organisations.

Scheduled reports

These are generated at regular intervals, such as daily, weekly or monthly and are widely distributed to users. Monthly sales figures and product range information, for example, would require regular reporting.

They often contain large volumes of information, only some of which is immediately relevant or useful. As machine readability increases in usage and accessibility, there will be a corresponding decrease in the need for scheduled reports, as users will be able to access directly and very specifically the particular information they require at the time. One must bear in mind, however, that some managers will always prefer hard copy of reports, unless speed is crucial.

On-demand reports

Such reports as these are unscheduled and produced on request. A requirement for a report of this type might arise when responding to a need for information about a particular customer's complaint. These reports fulfil irregular needs for information and can nowadays be produced very speedily. In the past, unanticipated demands for information were problematic and fraught with delay.

Exception reports

Management by exception entails an immediate focus on situations that are out of control. Activities progressing according to plan do not need managerial attention. Exception reports are part of the control function in an organisation, signalling the need for corrective action, such as outstanding late deliveries from suppliers and overdue accounts. Error reporting, such as the sudden rise in scrap being produced from a particular process, would constitute the content of an exception report.

Predictive reports

Predicting the future is difficult at the best of times, but techniques such as time series analysis, correlation and regression and simulation exercises can be most valuable. Such reporting effectively fulfils the need for sensitivity, or 'what if' analysis, and is very important for planning. Reports analysing potential profit increase or decrease with an increase in sales volume or increase in fixed or variable costs would be a typical business example of sensitivity analysis. Since predictive reports frequently rely on historical data, such data must be readily accessible and the data sources valid or the predictive models and reports produced will be of little value to management.

Summary reports

These reports summarise information from a variety of sources. They range from executive summaries or projects undertaken, to summary reports on specific operational issues, such as productivity rates and monitoring of special processes. Summary reports are exchanged between the various organisational levels, and play a crucial role in the communication process.

Decision Support Systems (DSS)

Decision Support Systems (DSS) provide an interactive system to aid the decision-making process in situations where no one is exactly sure how decisions should be made or tasks carried out. DSS provide tools, models or information to support or facilitate making decisions in unstructured or semi-structured sit-uations. They manipulate and present data for managers to use in conjunction with their experience and judgement to find solutions to problems by focusing more quickly and efficiently upon the real business issues.

Unlike both TPS and MRS, which support regular ongoing processes, DSS are frequently used on an ad hoc processing basis. Where TPS and MRS are better designed to facilitate the resolution of more structured problems, DSS are designed to be effective in less-structured situations, so their capability to be flexible and adaptable is crucial.

DSS are not structured, finished systems, but have a more facilitative quality to them, ranging from more general tools, such as statistical, word-processing or graphics packages and spreadsheets, to highly customised and often complex models. They have arisen from an ever-increasing need for information system support in non-routine, non-repetitive uncertain situations where success criteria are by no means clear. TPS focus very much on coordination, data collection and repetitive decision-making at lower levels of the organisation. MRS provide regular information for management, but are often inflexible and cannot produce the information in the most useful format. The

---

Characteristics of good management reports

All the reports discussed above relate to business performance, and the value of information presented in them can be enhanced in the following ways:

- if reports are presented as frequently as is cost effective;
- if they are provided as soon after the reporting period as possible;
- by giving credit to good performance and highlighting reasons for below average performance;
- by including only controllable items;
- if reports are accurate and full comparisons made;
- by emphasising exceptional items requiring management attention.

limitations of both TPS and MRS have given rise to the need for DSS.

DSS can be used in a number of different ways. An example of repetitive use of DSS would be in financial services where insurance agents need to structure sales situations and respond to clients' requests by choosing the best combinations from a set of options. Similarly, a financial broker would use DSS to help shape clients' best share portfolios.

An example of analytical use of DSS would be the consideration of product range, features, prices, sales, margins and amounts of advertising to help marketing management decide on future plans and market research and monitor results by consulting various models and databases.

Features of DSS

All decision support systems focus on making managers and professionals more productive and effective. Unlike data processing systems, the benefits of such systems are not measured in terms of outputs, such as credit and payment slips or man-hours saved, but in terms of better and faster decisions made by managers. These decisions ultimately aim to improve the overall productivity of the organisation.

DSS aim to improve the effectiveness of decision-making. They need therefore to be easy to use, flexible and adaptive over time. Management views of DSS have stressed above all the importance of their being user-friendly interactive systems. It is also highly desirable that such systems provide support for managers at all levels of the organisation, thereby assisting the integration between these levels wherever appropriate. A number of decisions rely on previous decisions or impinge on future ones. Ideally, DSS should be capable of supporting interdependent, shared, sequential decisions as well as independent ones. Moreover, it helps if DSS can support the different phases of the decision-making process from intelligence to final choice. If new demands emerge on any of these phases, the original DSS can be updated and refined to create an improved system.

Examples of DSS can be found in financial modelling, capacity planning and production scheduling.

Group Decision Support Systems (GDSS)

A GDSS is an interactive computer-based system that supports a group of decision-makers working together on unstructured or semi-structured problems. GDSS are involved in

---

The main characteristics and capabilities of DSS are:

- to provide support for decision-makers mainly in either unstructured or semi-structured situations by combining computerised information with human judgement;
- to increase the number of alternatives considered;
- to enhance different levels of managers' understanding of the business;
- to enable a more rapid response to unexpected situations;
- to enhance teamwork by providing support to both individuals and groups who are making decisions;
- to improve management control, while not controlling management. DSS support but do not replace the decision-maker who can at any stage override recommendations made by the computerised system.

face-to-face group meetings, remote site tele-conferencing and remote and local computer conferencing. GDSS contain conventional DSS, which involve the model base, database and human interface, but must also have a communications base, particularly if the GDSS are distributed in terms of time and space. The DSS model base has to be enhanced for GDSS to provide facilities for voting, ranking and rating so that consensus between decision-makers can be developed. GDSS also need to be more reliable than simple DSS in terms of uptime because more people are affected simultaneously if a GDSS goes down and financial costs are much greater. A GDSS requires capital investment in physical facilities and much more in the way of display and communications hardware.

GDSS are increasingly to be found in the larger financial institutions, computer service groups and in governmental agencies. Inter-faced conferencing predominates to support certain types of tasks, but decision-room GDSS are also used for different sets of tasks.

Process Control Systems/Automation

Process Control Systems (PCS) are specialised systems designed to control process machinery. Such systems are unique to the machinery they control. This might be a small machine tool, a jumbo jet or a nuclear reactor in a power station. Their primary objective is to replace human control of the machinery with automatic control, requiring limited human intervention. The need for such systems has arisen from improvements in machine performance, leading to the human operator being the limiting factor. Replacing the operator with direct computer control removes that limit in many cases.

Levels of information system

Managers now recognise that information systems can help to improve business performance. They need access to the right data, the right technology and the right communications environment. They also need to rely on information systems designed to improve day-to-day operations, to support decision-making and to establish links with suppliers and customers. Information systems are used at various levels of the business. At the operational level information systems are used to track day-to-day business activities, at the tactical level to help maximise the use of resources, and at the strategic level to provide information to support decision-making and help achieve organisational objectives. An information systems classification is shown in Table 5.4.

Each level of management in an organisation requires different types of information system to provide their information processing needs. Modern information technology means that computer-based information systems often transgress the boundaries between levels of management, with the needs of several levels being met by a single system. Even though this is the case, it is nonetheless useful in understanding managers' use of information to look at the relationship between the levels of management and the types of system they are likely to use, as shown in Table 5.5.

Operational Information Systems (OIS)

Operational information systems are the basic systems, which keep a business running on a day-to-day basis. Their principal users are the operatives responsible for carrying out the basic business activities of the organisation. This level of information system consists mainly of transaction processing systems (TPS) designed to support day-to-day operations by collecting and storing data relating to business transactions. In

Table 5.4 An information systems classification – a different perspective

Type of information system	Explanation
Transaction Processing System (TPS)	Input-intensive system designed to process basic business transactions.
Management Reporting System (MRS)	Query-intensive system designed to provide mainly predefined routine management information.
Decision Support System (DSS)	Query-intensive system designed to support mainly ad hoc problem-specific management decision-making.
Office System (OS)	System designed for general office work, such as document production, diary and appointments, person-to-person communication.
Process Control System (PCS)	System designed to control automated processes, such as production machinery.

Table 5.5 Matching IS and management

Level of IS	Type of IS	Level of management
Executive Information Systems	Decision support, office	Senior management
Management Information Systems	Management reporting, decision support, office	Middle and line management
Operational Information Systems	Transaction processing, low-level management reporting, office, process control	Operatives and supervisors

order to control and coordinate the activities of the operatives, supervisors also need access to management reporting systems.

Supervisory control

If supervisors are to supervise operatives effectively, they need access to both control information and short-term plans. Their line manager will usually have generated the latter, but it is the responsibility of the supervisor to control supervisees to ensure that the plans are met. This means that they need access to basic management reporting systems (MRS) to keep them informed of progress and work status. These MRS are entirely predefined, providing routine low-level control information derived from the TPS. A common example is problem reporting.

Management Information Systems (MIS)

MIS provide information for the effective management of an organisation by its line- and middle-managers. They generate regular performance monitoring information, maintain coordination and provide background information about organisational operations. This can take the form of routine management reporting (MRS) or ad hoc decision support (DSS). Three features of organisations of today are as follows:

1 *Management* has become system-oriented and more sophisticated in management techniques.
2 *Information* is planned for and made available to managers as needed.

3   A *system* of information ties planning and control by managers to operational systems of implementation.

The combined result of these concepts is the *management information system*. The purpose of an MIS is to raise the process of managing from the level of piecemeal information, intuitive guesswork and isolated problem-solving to the level of systems insights, systems information, sophisticated data-processing and systems problem-solving (Murdick and Munson, 1986).

Executive Information Systems (EIS)

Executive Information Systems (EIS), sometimes called Executive Support Systems (ESS) are highly interactive and take the basic concept behind DSS a stage further. EIS are designed for use by very senior executives and provide flexible access to information for monitoring results and business conditions, presented in a highly relevant, user-friendly format. Typically, there are a number of format options, which are clear and straightforward to produce. The aim is very much to overcome the limitations of DSS that have tended to provide tools requiring quite a high level of expertise to use them. Executives need *direct* access to information without the intermediary of systems and technical analysts.

The result is that EIS must be conceptually easy to use and demand as little knowledge or skill as possible on the part of the executive user. It is essential that such systems integrate many sources of data into a broad, aggregated perspective, often in graphical format.

An EIS interface would present a number of options to select from, such as reviews/evaluations, sales information over a large range of products, production reports on lead times, process control, scrap and rework and a summary of personnel and their training needs.

What are the roles played by IS?

Given the complex nature of organisations it is unsurprising that they employ several distinct types of information system. The following boxed example gives us some idea of the range of IS employed and the purposes they serve.

In spite of this diversity, all organisational information systems fulfil one or more of three distinct roles:

1   structuring the process
2   communicating between processes or people
3   coordinating processes or people

Comparing these roles with the functions performed by information itself (see Chapter 2, pp. 38-39) highlights the distinction between information and information systems. The roles played by information systems are more specific than the functions performed by information in general, though they obviously use information to communicate and inform decision-making.

IS for structuring

Structure is provided to a very limited extent when specific information is made available to help perform a decision or task. A greater degree of structure is imposed when an information system evaluates alternatives and still a greater degree when it determines a particular decision process or course of action. This gradation in degree of structuring can be categorised in three distinct ways:

Providing the user with access to information and information system tools, such as telecommunications, word-processing, spreadsheets, computer aided design (CAD) systems, simulation and optimisation models. These mechanisms help shape and structure to a varying extent, but do not restrict the final decision or action.

Boots the Chemists has developed its systems to quite a sophisticated extent compared to its retail competitors. Some of the systems used are the following:

- A database established by data mining on customers' needs and preferences – it is part of the CRM (Customer Relationship Management) system. The Advantage Card is very popular and provides added value for customers.
- The ERP (Enterprise Resource Planning) system ensures consistency and process integration across the organisation.
- The company intranet provides a valuable communication and management information system for staff and branches.
- The internet site is a user-friendly, easily navigable promotional tool for the company.
- The transaction processing bar-coding system is efficient and enables rapid service to customers, as well as feeding into the database, where customer details are analysed to provide management information.
- The personnel system is a staff database – it stores training and training needs data and includes a payroll system.
- The inventory and stock control system links to individual tills to provide up-to-date information to staff on availability of items and also links to warehousing and distribution for prompt restocking when required and to suppliers for quick response/Just in Time supply.
- Modelling and analytical tools provide information on cost, value, customer trends and financial predictions.
- Simulation models are used to examine peak loading and service queues to avoid unhappy customers and ensure optimum staff usage.

This list is by no means exhaustive. It merely serves to illustrate the diversity of systems in terms of types, location in the organisation and purpose served by each system.

Guiding the user by imposing procedures and rules, such as providing warnings and indications for corrective action, giving procedural guidelines and indicating the steps to a final decision or action.

Substituting people with technology. Typical examples of this degree of structuring would be data capture scanners, automated teller machines (ATMs) in banks, and robots used in manufacturing cars and computer hardware. These systems automate most or all of a task and therefore impose a high degree of structure. It is essential to evaluate such systems in the light of their being efficient or restrictive.

IS for communication

For communication to take place meaning must be conveyed and understood, information or ideas must be imparted. Communication is the transference and understanding of meaning. Perfect communication could be said to exist when a transmitted thought or idea is perceived by the receiver precisely as it is envisaged by the sender. Good communication is not to be equated with agreement, but with clarity of understanding. When analysing communications in a system, there are questions to raise as to how various messages are transmitted from one point in the system to another:

- Is information flowing and, if so, how much?
- How many different types of messages are being transmitted?
- What and how much meaning is conveyed to the recipient?
- How valuable are the messages?
- How often are messages sent and do they correlate with other messages passing through the system?

Methods of communication

There are a number of methods of communicating, all of which need to be considered in the context of organisations.

Oral communication includes speeches, formal or informal one-to-one talking, group discussions, rumour, and the company and industry grapevines. A verbal message can be quickly conveyed and a response received in a minimum amount of time. When a message has to be passed to a number of people, however, the potential for distortion is great as each individual interprets the message in his or her own way. Speeches can have a rousing effect, the one-to-one interchange is often vital but rumour can be inaccurate and hence damaging. Oral communication provides no abiding written record of what has been said and cannot therefore be verified later.

Written communications include memos, letters, newsletters and notice-board materials. Such communication provides a tangible record and can be both verified and stored. Generally speaking, more effort goes into preparing written messages, so that they are more likely to be well thought out, clear and logical. Though more precise, written communications

take time to produce and have no built-in feedback mechanism. It may take only 15 minutes to say something that it would take an hour to put in writing.

Nonverbal communications, such as a warning light, can be very effective in conveying information. Similarly, body language, such as facial expressions, often speaks louder than words. Experience shows that this may cause offence or misconceptions, which unfortunately cloud the communication process. Verbal intonations convey or can change meaning. Emphasis on certain words conveys their importance, for example. Every oral communication tends to be complemented by nonverbal accompaniments and the latter frequently convey much more of the meaning than the actual words used. Once more, however, as with rumour, there is a danger of inaccuracy or unintentional nonverbal messages that subsequently give rise to misunderstandings.

Electronic communications such as mobile phones, email, SMS (Short Message Service) texting videoconferencing are increasingly used in conjunction with speech or paper. PC's linked to a central computer make information readily available in words, numerical or graphical format and people communicate directly through computers, which provide fast accurate information that can be stored in very large volumes. A disadvantage of this type of communication is that it may be perceived as user-unfriendly, causing feelings of alienation or embarrassment.

As to the effectiveness of communications, the method(s) chosen will tend to reflect the circumstances and specific requirements. In terms of effective recall, however, this tends to result from an exposure to a combination of oral and written methods, with oral communication alone coming a close second. It is better to vary the form of communication to fit the particular occasion and perhaps avoid a preponderance of either formality or informality.

Formal and informal communication

People in organisations fulfil roles within an authority hierarchy, which makes the communication process more complex. As well as the more visible formal information systems, all organisations also have informal information systems. While formal communications tend to follow the organisational structure, informal communications tend to be less defined or restricted by the organisational structure.

Formal communications form part of the defined activities of the organisation, following the chain of command, or the value chain of business processes. Formal information systems are those which process and produce official information in the form of reports and commercial documents. Formal communication also takes place between organisations, providing the basis for commercial relationships between suppliers and their customers.

Informal communications tend to arise as a direct result of employee needs. They are often not approved by management, nor are they defined as part of the structural hierarchy of the organisation. Friendships, cliques and other social groupings generate informal communication in the form of facts, fiction and gossip, filling the communication gaps within the formal channels. Such informal information systems satisfy a need for social interaction among staff, which is an essential component of working life. What is more, it provides an alternative means of obtaining and passing information that is needed quickly. A quick telephone call to a friend in another part of the organisation may resolve a query or provide additional

important detail that it would have taken a lot more time and effort to obtain through the formal channels. Informal communication can act as a valuable support system to formal communication.

Informal IS are an important aspect of information processing in an organisation, and despite the emphasis placed on formal IS, some managers place more emphasis on informal information than official reports. More attention is usually focused on formal information systems when studying organisations simply because they are easier to identify and define, not necessarily because they are more useful or informative. The relative dependence on formal and informal IS varies from organisation to organisation, and from individual to individual. This is highlighted in organisations where trust has broken down between management and the workforce, with rumours taking over from suspect official reports as the primary source of information.

Although informal IS are more difficult to monitor and control, they are inherently more flexible than formal IS. This is because they are less bound by a fixed structure, and so are more adaptable to changes in information content or form. Unfortunately, they are also often less accurate, especially when the lines of communication are very long. Once started, a rumour can grow out of all proportion to the original communication, as there is often no means of checking it against the facts of the matter.

Every organisation needs to recognise the role played by informal information systems in supplementing the formal systems on which they rely to conduct business. Ignoring informal IS can mean missing out on very useful information. Equally, a modern organisation cannot really afford to rely solely on informal IS as a means of doing business. Table 5.6 compares formal and informal information.

Table 5.6 Comparison between formal and informal information

Formal	Informal
Often printed, such as reports	Often verbal, such as gossip
Conveyed by regular communication channels	Conveyed by the 'grapevine'
Largely inter-functional communication	Largely interpersonal communication
Quantitative and qualitative	Almost all qualitative
Communicated in an organised way	Communicated in an ad hoc, fragmentary way

Flows and networks

In order for communication to take place within an organisation, the information within the organisation has to flow from one place to another. Organisational communication flows in a number of directions:

- horizontally across the organisation's activities;
- vertically up and down the organisation's hierarchy;
- diagonally which combines the two.

Horizontal flows

These flows cross the organisation horizontally, moving between the different functions of the organisation. Such flows are usually along the value added chain, sending information up the chain with the product or service until final delivery to the customer, and sending information back down the chain to confirm that activities have taken place. Horizontal flows are not restricted to internal communication. They may also cross organisational boundaries, facilitating trade between suppliers and customers, or cooperation between organisational partnerships.

Vertical flows

There are also vertical flows between the different management levels of the organisation's hierarchy. These flows represent reports being sent up the hierarchy, and instructions being sent down.

Upward communication from employees to management is essential to highlight progress and problems, or to suggest improvements. The extent of upward communication will vary depending upon the corporate culture. A more open climate of trust and respect will tend to engender more upward communication than an authoritarian climate of strict managerial control, often evidenced in reporting problems.

Downward communication is used by managers to inform, direct and coordinate their subordinates. The way in which this is achieved will vary depending on the management style of the individual manager, and may be formal or informal. The pointing out of problems requiring attention may be perceived as the apportioning of blame, while recognition for a job well done will do wonders for employee morale. Information on policies and procedures in the form of memos, and personal letters to employees relating to terms and conditions of work, are examples of downward communication flow.

Diagonal flows

Diagonal communication cuts across both organisational functions and levels. For example, a supervisor in one area of the business may communicate directly with a senior manager in another area. This may be necessary to discuss a problem within the functional responsibility of the senior manager, but which has an impact on the supervisor's own work. A good illustration of this would be a production planner complaining to the sales manager that sales staff do not provide adequate information to production planning.

The difficulty with this type of communication is that it may bypass people in the command chain who only find out what has been going on after the event, and thus feel aggrieved. This may give rise to an unsatisfactory situation unless such people are also encompassed in the communication process. If, on the other hand, such people are merely being used as channels of communication between the sender and intended recipients of the information, such diagonal flows can be both efficient and effective.

Information flows

Information flows vertically between different management levels. Reports of various kinds are sent up the hierarchy and instructions flow in a downward direction. The level of detail in reports, information and instructions flowing up and down the organisational hierarchy varies considerably, from very detailed information provided and instructions received by the shop-floor operational level to the summarised overview information provided and received by senior management. Decision horizons also vary from long-term strategic at senior management level to short-term operational at shop-floor level. The filtration/distillation diagrams shown in Figures 5.1 and 5.2 illustrate these relative differences.

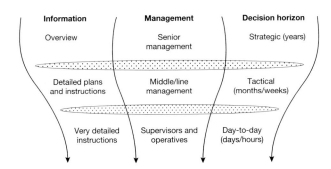

Figure 5.1 Filtration of information (downward flows)

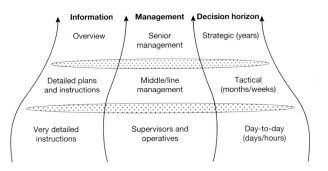

Figure 5.2 Distillation of information (upward flows)

It is also necessary to establish who is responsible for generating and communicating information. This will reflect the structure of the particular organisation. There may be a centralised specialist data processing or information services unit whose task is to gather data from across the organisation, and convert it into meaningful information for communication to the relevant people. At the other extreme, all information-processing activities could be integrated within the normal business processes of the organisation, making the people performing the business process responsible for providing any associated data and information to others.

Information also flows horizontally in organisations (see Chapter 2). It is essential that interconnecting functions 'dovetail' their procedures and operations if the value of products and services is to be maximised and costs of operations are to be minimised.

The level of detail of the information moving around the organisation remains fairly constant within each level of the hierarchy. People at the same level in the organisation tend to communicate at the same level. This contrasts with vertical flows of information up and down the management hierarchy (see Figure 5.3) with their consequent changes in level of detail and time horizon, as shown in Figures 5.1 and 5.2.

Information systems provide support for management at all levels of the organisational hierarchy. They supply information for planning and controlling, but their greatest con-

tribution is the enabling of more effective decision-making (see Chapter 3 for detail on these management functions).

Barriers to effective communication

There are two fundamental problems that affect communication. The first one relates to attenuation or distance; the further a message has to travel, the higher the probability of losing its clear definition and accuracy. The second problem relates to distortion and the passing on of inaccuracies, a form of 'Chinese whispers'.

Apart from general distortions that can occur at any stage of the communication process, there are other barriers to effective communication that need to be considered.

Filtering involves deliberately manipulating information so that it becomes more acceptable to the recipient, in other words 'telling someone what he/she wants to hear'. The more vertical levels in an organisation, the greater the opportunity for filtering. Communication between several layers of management can be curtailed or changed at each level, so that the cumulative filtering process results in major distortion of the original message. Furthermore, the nature of the organisational reward system will tend to encourage or discourage filtering.

Selective perception on the part of the communication recipient essentially involves seeing or hearing what he/she chooses depending on experience, background, personal agenda or needs. There may be an inability or unwillingness to understand the meaning conveyed by the communication. Perceptions are, or course, personal interpretations of reality. They are subjective and therefore open to bias and misinterpretation.

Emotions hinder effective communication by imposing subjectivity and inconsistency depending

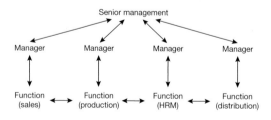

Figure 5.3 Organisational information flows

upon the mood of the moment which precludes clear, rational judgement.

Language is used differently by different people to convey different meanings. Employees come from a variety of backgrounds and some will use jargon and technical terms that are immediately incomprehensible to others. A strong corporate culture can help to establish a common organisational language, which may go some way to help break down this particular communication barrier. Jargon is frequently used in a variety of contexts. It is acceptable as long as those exposed to it are familiar with it. Otherwise it tends to have an instant alienation effect.

Nonverbal communications more often than not reinforce an oral communication of some sort, but on occasion there may be an inconsistency between them, resulting in the receiver of the message being confused as to the meaning of the message itself. For example, a boss telling a subordinate that he/she is sincerely interested in his/her problem, while being obviously preoccupied with something else.

Time Pressures can create communication problems, when channels are short-circuited in the haste to get things done and some people are left unaware of what has happened. Messages may also be unclear or incomplete as a result and a multiplicity of problems can arise.

IS for coordination

IS for coordination are in effect a specific subset of IS for communication. Communication in its simplest form is a one-way process. Coordination, on the other hand, requires two-way communication to ensure the coordination of the activities of more than one person, process or organisation. As well as responding in some way to information received to ensure that their actions fit in with those of the sender, recipients must also inform the sender what they are doing.

Different information systems support coordination in a variety of ways. They link individuals to one another, promoting coordination and teamwork between a workgroup or a group of individuals, who collaborate with one another. They link systems to one another, promoting coordination within an organisation. Consistency and standardisation help maintain coordination, interdependency and efficiency. The linking of the order entry system to the inventory management system and the accounting system will provide a more complete and coordinated IS when estimating potential delivery lead-time to a customer. They link organisations to one another, promoting coordination, such as is required for Just in Time manufacturing, government reporting systems and overseas subsidiaries passing and receiving information to and from the parent company or head office.

Information systems cover a variety of scopes.

Personal information systems

Personal IS are designed to serve the user's needs for analysis, tracking and monitoring. Personal IS add value by facilitating personal processes, enhancing personal productivity and improving personal 'quality'.

In terms of personal processes it is helpful to regard these at all levels from the strategic to the operational level. Personal strategic planning looks to set the aims and objectives of an individual's job. Management processes involve acquiring and making effective use of available resources to accomplish that job. Operations involve the actions taken on a day-to-day basis to accomplish that job. All personal processes can be supported, improved and facilitated by personal IS. Likewise the characteristics and speed of delivery of what someone produces on a daily basis can be considerably enhanced. The net result is a much higher probability of increased efficiency and effectiveness in tackling the tasks, activities and decisions of personal working life.

Workgroup information systems

The fundamental purpose of workgroup IS is to facilitate workgroup effectiveness. This involves producing high quality output, providing for the personal needs of individual group members and empowering the group to perform as a coherent team. The factors determining such effectiveness are the efforts made by the group, group knowledge and skills contributed, and the group strategic approach. Workgroup IS can facilitate in particular the last two of these factors by enhancing communications and by enabling the learning and application of new strategic approaches.

Workgroup systems, as opposed to personal IS, must support the *controlled sharing* of data, information and knowledge and other resources. The concept of *security* is important to note here, since it may not be necessary or desirable for every group member to have access to all the group's information resources.

Like personal IS, workgroup IS enhance the value of group strategic planning, group management and group operations, resulting in improved product output and delivery and more efficient and effective workgroup processes as a whole.

Functional or departmental information systems

Departmental IS go beyond the bounds of the workgroup to encompass whole organisational departments. These systems are designed to support the business operations of a particular department, such as accounts or sales. To facilitate interdepartmental communication,

departmental IS may be linked together into a corporate information system. A good example is a system that connects sales to production, so that sales people do not promise unrealistic delivery dates to their customers before having actually checked with production that such dates can be feasibly scheduled. A commonly experienced problem!

Corporate information systems

The term 'corporate' encompasses a whole range of organisations, both profit and non-profit making, public or private sector, limited companies or single owner/manager companies.

Naturally, the application of information systems to the organisation as a whole is very broad. It is useful here briefly to consider two possible types of application. *Localised applications* include personal and workgroup IS, while *departmental and interdepartmental systems* move a step beyond workgroup IS to provide integrated support across different departments with consequent integration of business processes. An order-entry system integrates, for example, the processes through which an order travels from sales, through production and operations to accounting and invoicing.

In neither of the two above applications are radical changes in business procedures and organisation necessary. This, however, is not the case with *business process re-engineering* (see Chapter 7) where the information systems are geared to effecting a fundamental change in the way business internal processes are carried out. For example, an information system could generate a collaborative selection of product lines, rather than a single decision being made by the marketing department alone. The various opinions could then be integrated from the different areas of the business to build a consensus.

Inter-organisational information systems

Inter-organisational IS refers to IS providing innovative ways of doing business with other organisations, such as the exchange of and access to inventory information for greater responsiveness. DIY stores are linked to their suppliers to provide rapid restocking of large volumes of product lines, which are particularly popular and in great demand, so that customers are not disappointed. More radical changes to business operations are implied by inter-organisational IS.

These systems can dramatically alter the balance of power in supplier/customer relationships, creating clear competitive advantage and building vital barriers to entry in some industry sectors. They can and do influence the way business is carried out and key competitive forces in a particular industry. Some inter-organisational systems have major social and public policy implications.

Some of the main trends impacting upon the increasing need to implement inter-organisational IS are the following:

- the increasing demand for faster information interchange between suppliers and purchasers of rapidly changing products and services;
- the increasing emergence of standards and regulations in certain industry sectors, such as the chemical industry now subjected to more rigorous environmental controls;
- the increasing capabilities and availability of innovative IS/IT, such as telecommunications and teleconferencing;
- the increasing drive by companies to add value via IS/IT to give them an edge in the creation of innovative products or the delivery of exceptional customer service.

What impact do CBIS have on business processes?

Process characteristics and IS

First, it is important to define the fundamental process characteristics of interest, which are:

- degree of structure
- range of involvement
- level of integration
- rhythm
- complexity
- degree of reliance on machines
- prominence of planning and control
- attention to errors and exceptions

Information systems to impose structure. Successful IS impose the amount of structure that is appropriate for the activity being supported. Imposing too much structure stifles creativity and demotivates participants, who feel as though they have no responsibility for the outcome. Imposing too little structure results in inefficiencies and errors.

Range of involvement. When the span of people involved in the business process is too narrow, decisions tend to be made at too local a level with little in the way of consideration of the organisation as a whole. When the range of involvement is too broad, business processes move at a very slow pace. An example of this would be the committee and permissions processes in local and national government. IS can serve to increase or decrease the range of involvement.

Level of integration. Relates to mutual responsiveness and collaboration between distinct activities or processes, in particular to the speed with which one process or activity responds to events in another. This speed depends on the immediacy of communication and the degree

143

to which the processes respond to the information communicated. IS can play roles in both aspects of integration, first, by supporting the communication and second, by making it easier for each business process to use information for an effective response.

Rhythm. This refers to the frequency and predictability with which a process occurs. Its rhythm may be periodic, event-driven or haphazard. From a production perspective, operating to a predictable, linear schedule usually permits the greatest efficiency. IS can support responsive business rhythms, either in terms of Just in Time or 24/7 operations, such as call centres that operate beyond normal office hours.

Complexity. Is the combination of how many types of elements the process contains and the number and nature of their interactions. As complexity increases, systems are more difficult to develop and manage and it is also more difficult to understand exactly what is going on and therefore to anticipate the consequences of changes throughout the system. IS can help eliminate variation by standardising processes with low value variation and highlighting more complex processes, whose variation cannot be dealt with in the same way each time.

Degree of reliance on machines. This involves getting the balance right in the division of labour between people and computers. Increased integration of computer and communications technologies into business processes brings both advantages and disadvantages. Too much reliance may be placed on automation to solve problems in need of human intervention. Services are a case in point. Users can be more in control of delivering their own service and receive services more speedily and flexibly, but they often would prefer a personalised service,

such as has been indicated in the banking sector (Curry and Penman, 2004).

Prominence of planning and control. Participants in a business process need to know what to do, when to do it and how to make sure the work is being done properly. Planning can be aided by creating a standard planning format and by the provision of computerised information for the automation of planning calculations. Execution can be improved by judicious use of interactive systems, and collection of control data can be made an automatic by-product of doing the work.

Attention to errors and exceptions. IS can be very useful in helping to eliminate errors and highlight exceptions. There is a trade-off between wasting time and resources by being unsystematic as opposed to diverting energy from the system's major goals through excessive formalisation of exception processing. A highly informal process might produce inconsistent responses to similar situations and would not gather useful information on causes. An overly formalised process might have too many categories and cross-checks and would become a process bottleneck.

Table 5.7 illustrates the consequences of redesigning processes using IS, where there is either an increase or decrease of each process characteristic. The balance has to be correct and appropriate for the situation.

Process performance and IS roles

There are key variables for the evaluation of process performance. Each variable involves genuine choices, with too much often as bad as too little along any of the dimensions. In some cases the variables are mutually reinforcing but in others an over-emphasis on one may entail negative consequences for others. For example,

Table 5.7 Impacts of excess or deficiency in process characteristics

Process characteristic	Problem if level too high	Problem if level too low
Degree of structure	System participants' judgement reduced/have too little autonomy.	Errors occur because rules applied inconsistently/outputs are inconsistent.
Range of involvement	Work slowed because too many people involved.	Too narrow personal considerations result in sub-optimal decisions.
Level of integration	Steps in process too intertwined/ too much interference, influence elsewhere.	Steps in process too independent/ more integration needed to produce better results.
Rhythm	Too inflexible and ability to respond impaired.	Rhythm undefined and process efficiency lost.
Complexity	Too difficult to understand how system operates or consequences of change.	System cannot distinguish between cases needing to be handled differently.
Degree of reliance on machines	People disengaged from work, skills decrease, mistakes occur.	Productivity and consistency decrease as bored people doing repetitive work.
Prominence of planning and control	Too much effort into planning and control with not enough going into execution.	Insufficient effort in planning and control leaves process inconsistent and unresponsive.
Attention to errors and exceptions	Process focuses on exceptions, becoming inconsistent and inefficient.	Process fails or handles exceptions incorrectly, resulting in poor quality.

Source: Alter (2002)

increasing consistency often increases productivity by reducing waste, while too much attention to consistency might slow down work and reduce productivity. Information systems can improve levels of process performance with respect to the different process variables but it is important that both business process participants and managers are involved in designing and evaluating information systems as they have the understanding of the advantages and disadvantages of different levels of process performance.

Table 5.8 illustrates these process performance variables and the roles that information systems can play. Looking at each variable in turn helps in understanding most information system applications.

Chapter summary

This chapter has built on material from previous chapters relating to information, organisations, managerial activities and systems concepts to provide useful insights into different IS typologies. These IS types are discussed in terms of what they do and where they are likely to fit in the levels of the organisation. The three main roles of IS are structuring, communicating and coordinating, and are developed in some detail, looking at different extents of

Table 5.8 Process performance variables and related IS roles

Process performance variable	Typical measures	Common IS role
Activity rate	Number of work steps completed per day.	Track rate of work step completion; decide order of steps to keep work flow steady and inventory balanced.
Output rate	Average units completed and peak load units per hour/week.	Increase output rate by automation; increase output rate by systematising the work.
Consistency	Defect, rework rates and percentage variation.	Systematise work to reduce variation; provide feedback to identify/correct errors and help find causes of defects.
Productivity	Output per hour; ratio of outputs to inputs; scrap rate; cost of rework.	Help produce more output with same effort; automate data processing; systematise work to reduce waste; schedule work to improve resource utilisation.
Cycle time	Time from start to finish; total work-in-process inventory divided by weekly output.	More rapid data processing; combine steps to reduce delays; perform steps in parallel; systematise work to reduce waste and rework.
Downtime	Time out of operation compared to length of time period or scheduled uptime.	Track process and equipment toidentify when going out of spec; back-up and recovery to reduce computer-related downtime.
Security	Number of process breaches in a time interval; seriousness of breaches.	Systematise record keeping about process, computer access and usage; track non-standard transactions.

Source: Alter (2002)

structuring, different types and directions of communication, barriers to communication and information flows. Coordination is related to the different scopes of IS from the personal information system to inter-organisational information systems. Finally, different IS are related to process management and the effect they can potentially have on different process characteristics and key process performance criteria is discussed.

Review questions

1 What do you understand by the term 'information system'?
2 Why are there different classifications of information systems?
3 What do you believe to be a useful IS classification and why?
4 Choose two types of IS and compare them in some detail.
5 What are the three main roles played by IS?
6 Choose one of these roles and show how IS serve a purpose.

7   Why do you think that the role of coordination has become more important in recent years?

8   What are the critical elements of process management?

9   Explain how IS can have an impact on process management.

10 Explain how IS can have an impact on process evaluation.

Case study

The Dunlop Recall Management system (DRM)

Background

A general practice in Scotland has taken an innovative approach to the management of its patients. The practice has a register of 4,958 patients, 3 GPs, 1 GP registrar, 1 pre-registration house officer, 1 full-time practice nurse and has recently recruited a new part-time practice nurse. The ancillary staff comprise the following:

- a practice manager
- a part-time secretary
- a phlebotomist
- five part-time receptionists

The practice uses the NHSScotland recommended GPASS and SPICE software packages for the recording of patient details and Dunlop Recall Management (DRM) for the recall and management of chronic disease patients.

Disease management

A holistic approach to the management of patients with chronic diseases is adopted by the practice. Working together as a primary care team by viewing the patients and their condition as a complete entity, the practice believe that they can deliver the most appropriate care for the patient. With the aid of DRM, suitably skilled staff are able to deliver the appropriate care, ensuring efficient resource usage and team management. In the course of a diabetes clinic it is possible to review other conditions, seeking to harmonise co-morbidity reviews so that the patient is visiting a 'one stop shop', allowing, for example, one blood sample to be taken and multiple tests to be undertaken, instead of multiple visits and blood samples. The practice nurse is responsible for the vast majority of chronic-disease management, becoming a manager or coach to each patient. The GPs are responsible for the complex cases, however, their general reviews are still nurse-managed.

Patient recall

During the implementation phase of DRM the recall of patients was led by the practice nurse, however this is scheduled to become an administrative task. A missed deadlines report, generated daily from DRM, highlights all patients who are due for or who have missed a review or sched-uled care component. As the system is still in its infancy, the practice nurse checks the details on DRM and then prints a letter from the system. A decline in the number of missed deadlines has been achieved as a result of patients having tailored care plans as the information is available to schedule an appointment when necessary.

When a patient telephones to make a review appointment, the administrative staff consult the DRM system to see who is the assigned team member and schedule an appropriate appointment. The review is carried out and the date of the next appointment is scheduled. DRM also has a deadline interval, which is modified to each case and allows the review deadline to be surpassed, allowing a 'grace period' before the patient appears on the missed deadlines report. A summary of the process is represented by the current physical data flow diagram shown in Figure 5.4.

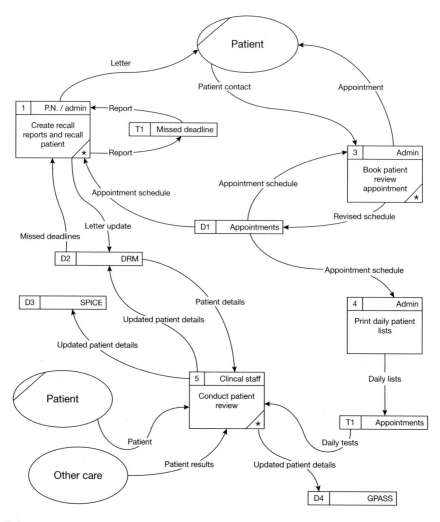

Figure 5.4 Current physical data flow diagram of the recall process

Practice management

The management of the practice appears to be balanced between the partners, the practice nurse and the practice manager. The practice is small, both from a patient register and staffing point of view, and this does serve the purpose of providing an advantage, whereby ideas and issues can be discussed in a more productive, less frenetic environment. There are undertones of slight power struggles between key members of the management team but these do not really surface and the logic of best practice has prevailed in any strategic or daily operational issues.

Culture

Communication channels are open and informal throughout the practice. Weekly structured practice meetings between clinical staff and the practice manager, and regular meetings between the practice manager and administration staff are vehicles for formal communication, welcomed by all, where discussions are open and encouraged.

The use of information systems and technology is seen as a fundamental part of patient care and practice life. The strategic development of a computerised information system (DRM) from a paper-based information system was designed and employed by members of the clinical team; a clear demonstration of commitment to IS/IT. Staff members, administration and clinical staff alike, have embraced DRM, which has tempered the criticisms of GPASS. Staff have become comfortable with the use of all information systems required for them to carry out their duties, although some do need further exposure to achieve a satisfactory familiarity and speed of use.

The practice appears to be open and welcoming of change and is proactive in bringing about necessary change if a process is not working or a bottleneck appears.

Practice strategy

Although there is no formal documentation that describes the practice strategy or its business objectives, there is an air of confidence among staff in general whenever they discuss where the practice is going and how it is going to get there. Strategic and business planning is included in the agenda for the weekly meetings of the partners and practice manager. Analysis is undertaken prior to these meetings, update reports are tabled on the implementation of DRM, latest GPASS releases and the move towards a paperless working environment. Although there is initial resistance to change (almost inevitable!), the strength of the practice is collective agreement and their ability to work together with a clear vision for the future.

Conclusion

DRM is a software tool that focuses on the recall of patients. It is a chronic-disease management system, not a clinical decision-making system. It was described by its developer as:

An innovative generic medical information management system which delivers patient specific medical information ... to allow the patient care process to be uniquely defined. Reporting of missed deadlines for patient recall is central.

In essence, DRM is a tool which attempts to provide patient-centred care through the efficient management of co-morbidity patients. It also promotes effective team management around the needs of the patient by enabling suitably skilled staff to be assigned various tasks associated with patient care, such as the assignment of a phlebotomist to carry out blood tests, thereby maximising the efficiency of the phlebotomist and reducing the amount of time wasted by the practice nurse, who is not required to perform the task. Each component of a chronic disease stands alone, defined by its Read Code, person responsible, assessed date, review date, review interval and priority.

Coordination of patient co-morbidity through DRM allows clinical staff to see instantly an on-screen holistic view of the patient, thereby negating the need for searching through multiple screens or paper files and promoting the paper-light concept currently being driven by NHSScotland.

Finally, DRM allows the production of a personalised care plan, devised through consultation between clinical staff and the patient. The patient is issued with the plan and can see at a glance when the next review is due and what it is for.

Case questions

1 How would you classify the DRM system in terms of IS typology/typologies?
2 To what extent do you believe the DRM system fulfils the IS roles of structuring, communicating and coordinating? Give your reasons.
3 What do you regard as the key business and organisational factors that have facilitated the implementation of the DRM system?
4 Why do you think such a system as DRM is particularly important in the NHS context, both from the perspective of clinical and administrative staff and patients?
5 In what ways does the physical data flow diagram in Figure 5.4 help define and understand the DRM system?

··

References and further reading

Ahituv N. and Neumann S. (1987) 'Decision Making and the Value of Information', in Galliers R. (ed.) *Information Analysis. Selected Readings*, Addison-Wesley: Reading, MA.

Ahn T. and Grudnitski G. (1985) 'Conceptual Perspectives on Key Factors in DSS Development: a Systems Approach', *Journal of MIS*, 2(1), Summer: 18–32.

Alter S. (2002) *Information Systems. The Foundations of E-Business*, Prentice-Hall International: Englewood Cliffs, NJ.

Anderson R. (1986) *Management, Information Systems and Computers*, Macmillan: Basingstoke.

Bensaou M. and Venkatranam N. (1996) 'Inter-Organisational Relationships and Information Technology: a Conceptual Synthesis and a Research Framework', *European Journal of Information Systems*, 5: 84–91.

Boddy D. (2000) 'Implementing Inter-Organisational IT Systems: Lessons from a Call Centre Project', *Journal of Information Technology*, 15(1), March: 29–37.

Burkan, W.C. (1991) *Executive Information Systems. From Proposal Through Implementation*. Van Nostrand Reinhold: New York.

Bussen W. and Myers M.D. (1997) 'Executive Information System Failure: a New Zealand Case Study', *Journal of Information Technology*, 12(2), June: 145–153.

Chen M. (1995) 'A Model-Driven Approach to Accessing Managerial Information: the Development of a Repository-Based Executive Information System', *Journal of MIS*, 11(4), Spring: 33–63.

Curry A.C. and Penman S. (2004) 'The Relative Importance of Technology in Enhancing Customer Relationships in Banking – a Scottish Perspective, *Managing Service Quality*, 14(4), April: 331–341.

Davis W.S. (1995) *Management, Information and Systems: an Introduction to Business Information Systems*, West Publishing: St Paul, MN.

Dennis A.R., Hayes G.S. and Daniels R.M. (1999) 'Business Process Modelling with Group Support Systems', *Journal of MIS*, 15(4), Spring: 115–142.

Dennis A.R., Wixom B.H. and Vandenberg R.J. (2001) 'Understanding Fit and Appropriation Effects in Group Support Systems via Meta-Analysis', *MIS Quarterly*, 25(2), June: 167–193.

Dhaliwal J.S. and Tung L.L. (2000) 'Using Group Support Systems for Developing and Knowledge-Based Explanation Facility', *International Journal of Information Management*, 20: 131–149.

Dolphin R.R. and Fan Y. (2000) 'Is Corporate Communications a Strategic Function?', *Management Decision*, 38(2): 99–107.

Drucker P. (1989) *The Practice of Management*, Heinemann: London.

Edwards J.S., Duan Y. and Robins P.C. (2000) 'An Analysis of Expert Systems for Business Decision Making at Different Levels and in Different Roles', *European Journal of Information Systems*, 9: 36–46.

Farbey B., Land F.F. and Targett D. (1995) 'A Taxonomy of Information Systems Applications: the Benefits Evaluation Ladder', *European Journal of Information Systems*, 4(1): 41–50.

Fazlollahi B. and Vahidov R. (2001) 'A Method for Generation of Alternatives by Decision Support Systems', *Journal of MIS*, 18(2), Fall: 229–250.

Ferioli C. and Migliarese P. (1996) 'Supporting Organisational Relations Through Information Technology in Innovative Organisational Forms', *European Journal of Information Systems*, 5: 196–207.

Galliers R.D. (ed.) (1990) *Information Analysis. Selected Readings*, Addison-Wesley: Reading, MA.

Gerloff E.A. (1985) *Organisational Theory and Design. A Strategic Approach for Management*, McGraw-Hill: New York.

Gremillion L.L. and Pyburn P.J. (1985) 'Justifying Decision Support and Office Automation Systems', *Journal of MIS*, 2(1), Summer: 5–17.

Hall R. (1991) *Organisations. Structures, Processes and Outcomes*, 5th edn, Prentice Hall International: Englewood Cliffs, NJ.

Johnston R.B. and Gregor S. (2000) 'A Theory of Industry-Level Activity for Understanding the Adoption of Inter-Organisational Systems', *European Journal of Information Systems*, 9: 243–251.

Klein S. (1996) 'The Configuration of Inter-Organisational Relations', *European Journal of Information Systems*, 5: 92–102.

Land F.F. and Kennedy-McGregor M. (1987) 'Information and Information Systems: Concepts and Perspectives', in Galliers R. (ed) *Information Analysis. Selected Readings*, Addison-Wesley: Reading, MA.

Laudon K.C. and Laudon J.P. (1995) *Essentials of Management Information Systems*, 3rd edn, Prentice-Hall International: Englewood Cliffs, NJ.

Leidner D.E. and Elam J.J. (1993–1994) 'Executive Information Systems: Their Impact on Executive Decision Making', *Journal of MIS*, 10(3), Winter: 139–155.

Liebenau J. and Backhouse J. (1990) *Understanding Information. An Introduction*, Macmillan: Basingstoke.

Martin C. and Powell P. (1992) *Information Systems. A Management Perspective*, McGraw-Hill: Maidenhead.

Miles R. (1980) *Macro Organisational Behaviour*, Good Year: Santa Monica, CA.

Murdick R.G. and Munson J.C. (1986) *MIS Concepts and Design*, 2nd edn, Prentice-Hall, Englewood Cliffs, NJ.

Nunamaker J.F. (1991–1992) 'Special Issue: Decision Support Systems for Teams, Groups and Organisations', *Journal of MIS*, 8(3), Winter: 3–5 (guest ed.).

Olkkonen R., Tikkanen H. and Alajoutsijarvi K. (2000) 'The Role of Communication in Business Relationships and Networks', *Management Decision*, 38(6): 403–409.

Reed Doke E. and Barrier T. (1994) 'An Assessment of Information Systems Taxonomies: Time to be Re-evaluated?', *Journal of Information Technology*, 9(2): 149–157.

Riggins F.J. and Mukhopadhyay T. (1994) 'Interdependent Benefits from Inter-Organisational Systems: Opportunities for Business Partner Reengineering', *Journal of MIS*, 11(2), Fall: 37–57.

Robinson M. (1994) 'Computer Support for Meetings: Formalisms for Local Control?' *European Journal of Information Systems*, 3(4): 259–267.

Robbins S.P. (1988) *Management. Concepts and Applications*, Prentice Hall International: Englewood Cliffs, NJ.

Satzinger J.W. and Olfman L. (1995) 'Computer Support for Group Work: Perceptions of the Usefulness of Support Scenarios and End-User Tools', *Journal of MIS*, 11(4), Spring: 115–148.

Schein E.H. (1980) *Organisational Psychology*, 3rd edn, Prentice-Hall: Englewood Cliffs, NJ.

Segars A.H. and Grover V. (1994) 'Communications Architecture: Towards a More Robust Understanding of Information Flows and Emergent Patterns of Communication in Organisations', *European Journal of Information Systems*, 3(2): 87–100.

Sprague R.H. and Watson H.J. (eds) (1989) *Decision Support Systems: Putting Theory into Practice*, 2nd edn, Prentice Hall: London.

Steiger D.M. (1998) 'Enhancing User Understanding in a Decision Support System: a Theoretical Basis and Framework', *Journal of MIS*, 15(2), Fall: 199–220.

Straub D.W. Jr and Beauclair R.A. (1988) 'A Current and Future Uses of Group Decision Support System Technology: Report on a Recent Empirical Study', *Journal of MIS*, 5(1), Summer: 101–116.

Taylor A. and Farrell S. (1994) *Information Management for Business*, Aslib: London.

Thornett A.M. (2001) 'Computer Decision Support Systems in General Practice', *International Journal of Information Management*, 21: 39–47.

Vandenbosch B. and Higgins C.A. (1995) 'Executive Support Systems and Learning: a Model and Empirical Test', *Journal of MIS*, 12(2), Fall: 99–130.

Ward J. and Peppard J. (2002) *Strategic Planning for Information Systems*, John Wiley & Sons: Chicester.

Waring T. and Wainwright D. (2000) 'Interpreting Integration with Respect to Information Systems in Organisations – Image, Theory and Reality', *Journal of Information Technology*, 15(2), June: 131–147.

Yadav S.B. (1985) 'Classifying an Organisation to Identify Its Information Requirements: a Comprehensive Framework', *Journal of MIS*, 2(1): 39–60.

Zmud R.W. (2003) 'Special Issue on Redefining the Organisational Roles of Information Technology in the Information Age', *MIS Quarterly*, 27(2): 195 (Foreword).

Chapter 6

Information systems and organisational 'fit'

··

Learning objectives

After reading this chapter you should be able to:

- understand an organisation's key structural elements that relate to IS implementation;
- relate an organisation's IS to its structure;
- understand the potential impact of IS on organisational design and performance;
- describe an organisation's basic culture and how it is likely to affect the use of CBIS;
- appreciate the relevance of leadership and motivation to IS implementation.

What is organisational fit?

The concept of organisational fit is especially relevant when considering IS development and implementation. It relates to the matching of organisational elements to ensure a consistent environment, one in which conflicts are minimised. Many difficulties experienced in organisations can be traced to the absence of organisational fit. An example of such a problem might well arise in a company wishing to implement team working in its production facility. This was a key trend in the clothing and garment industry in the 1990s, as customers like Marks & Spencer and Jaeger were no longer demanding large batches of mass-produced clothes; small batches of different styles were required to compete with the American clothing retailers such as Gap who were able to offer rapid style changes to the market and an immediate capability to supply more garments for popular designs. Team working was an ideal way to respond to this 'pull' rather than 'push' approach to manufacturing. The problem arose when the management style did not match the more open, informal team-working approach to operations. Management imposed a culture of strict control, whereby people in the teams were not expected to discuss among themselves and were regarded as 'wasting time' when in reality they were engaging in problem-solving on the shop floor.

What this example illustrates is the imperative to match elements of organisational structure, culture and management style. An informal, entrepreneurial company must be managed with more of a risk-taking, experimental, innovative style of management. Large bureaucracies are managed in more formal ways, with rules and procedures to maintain control. If such organisations were to be managed informally, they would rapidly decline into chaos. The main difficulty lies in detecting such organisational mismatches and deciding which elements need to be changed (see Chapter 7 for more detail on issues of change and IS). The structure, culture and management style must all complement one another to create the right environment for IS development.

There are a number of definitions of technology, structure and the fit between the two (Fry, 1982; Gerwin, 1981; Joyce *et al.*, 1982). Alexander (1982) identified three characteristics of structure: vertical participation, horizontal participation and formalisation. Vertical participation is the degree to which supervisors and subordinates consult together concerning job-related tasks and decisions that must be made. Horizontal participation is the degree to which individuals are involved with colleagues in making decisions and defining tasks. Formalisation is the extent to which rules, procedures and controls are in place and in use.

As technology becomes less routine, work units need to become increasingly organic to be effective. Conversely, as technology becomes more routine, work units need to become increasingly mechanistic to be effective. This suggests that fit between technology and organisational structure is an important predictor of performance (Dewar and Werbel, 1979; Joyce *et al.*, 1982).

Organisational and IS interdependence

What is often not fully appreciated in IS development and implementation is the organisational context into which IS are to be introduced. It is therefore a logical deduction that, if there are mismatches in the organisational context, the introduction of IS is more likely to be problematic. Organisations have to anticipate the potential for change and hence disruption with the introduction and development of IS. The problem is also compounded by the fact that some organisations use technology as the starting point for IS development, rather than beginning with the business justification for new or upgraded systems. Some companies imagine that using technology similar to that of their competitors will address their own business IS issues. This is a dangerous assumption to make.

It must also be remembered that there is a reciprocal relationship between IS and the business context. The structure, culture and management style may all impact upon IS development, either singly or in combination. Similarly, the introduction and development of IS may impact on structure, culture and management style. Any one or more of these three elements may need to alter to accommodate IS. Such change is likely to be difficult and it is therefore especially important to be able to anticipate any potential for organisational mismatch prior to the introduction and development of IS.

The levels of IS failure associated with problems of organisational fit are as follows:

Technical failure as a result of the technologies implemented not being appropriate for the organisation – the technology may be either too complex (sometimes the case when a small organisation implements a software application designed for a large organisation) or it may be insufficient in terms of capability and compatibility with existing systems.

Data failure resulting from an insufficient understanding that data entered onto systems needs to be both accurate and up-to-date. This is often the case when staff are used to paper systems and find computerised data entry more time consuming than useful.

User failure as a consequence of users not having been sufficiently prepared for the introduction and implementation of IS. More often than not, this does not mean that users themselves are at fault but that the training, support and advisory systems in place are not appropriate or sufficient.

Organisational failure results from the internal mismatches explained in the previous section. This is a serious issue because it relates to suboptimal organisational performance, the potential for loss of value, duplication and waste of resources.

Environmental failure arises when the organisation has not evaluated effectively the environment in which it operates. The organisation may, for example, not have gauged speed of industrial or technological change in its sector or may not have anticipated economic, legal or political pressures likely to provoke the need for IS introduction and development.

Characterising organisations

There have been different attempts made to characterise organisations, and the following are just two of the many examples. Mintzberg's (1979) structural classifications are provided in Table 6.1 below.

Linkage between organisation structure and information architecture

In a conceptual study by Leifer (1988) there were certain ideal matches between four information architectures and Mintzberg's typologies of organisational structure discussed earlier (see Table 6.1). Leifer suggests that certain organisational structures are more compatible with certain information architectures. A mismatch potentially results in inferior performance, unless a change is effected to either the architecture or the structure or both.

Table 6.1 Mintzberg's organisational structures (1979)

The simple structure	Coordinated by direct supervision	Centralised with an organic structure
The machine bureaucracy	Coordinated by standardisation of work processes	Formalised, specialised, functionally grouped
The professional bureaucracy	Coordinated by standardisation of skills	Professionalised, horizontal job specialisation, vertically and horizontally decentralised
The divisionalised form	Coordinated by standardisation of outputs	Market groupings, performance controlled, some vertical decentralisation
The adhocracy	Coordinated by mutual adjustment	Organically structured, selectively decentralised, horizontal job specialisation, functional and market groupings

Table 6.2 Linkage between organisation structure and information architecture

Type of organisation structure	Type of information architecture
Simple structure	Stand-alone PCs
Machine bureaucracy	Centralised systems
Professional bureaucracy	Centralised and distributed systems
Divisionalised form	Centralised, distributed and decentralised systems
Adhocracy	Decentralised systems

Source: Leifer (1988)

Bureaucracies are matched with centralised systems, while professional bureaucracies use both centralised and distributed systems. Divisionalised organisations use centralised, distributed and decentralised systems because such structures may take many forms and may be either tightly or loosely structured. Adhocracies, on the other hand, are small autonomous structures that are highly organic with project teams and therefore use decentralised systems. Table 6.2 illustrates these matches. Daft (1994) classifies structural and cultural organisational features, as summed up in Table 6.3.

There are aspects of organisations that are particularly relevant to CBIS, namely structure, size, culture and communication. This chapter looks at each of these aspects in turn, beginning with structure. The organisation's structure, systems, sub-systems and processes constitute its framework, its physical identity. Different structures are examined and their impact on CBIS. Conversely CBIS influence organisational structures and this influence is also examined. The structural issues of control, formalisation, integration and coordination are discussed with reference to CBIS. Finally, the influence of the external environment and organisational size is evaluated with reference to both structure and CBIS.

The organisation's culture is its personality, its social identity. Culture impacts upon the implementation and management of CBIS, which in turn may bring about cultural change. Issues of culture are dealt with in this chapter while issues of change are dealt with in Chapter 7.

Table 6.3 Structural and cultural features

Organising the vertical structure	Work specialisation; chain of command; authority, responsibility, delegation; span of management; tall versus flat structure; formalisation; centralisation/decentralisation; administrative overhead.
Departmentalisation	Functional approach; divisional approach; matrix approach; team approach; network approach.
Coordination	Collaboration across departments; task forces and teams; integrating managers.
Mechanistic/organic	Tight vertical structure versus loose, empowered horizontal structure.

Flowing around the organisation are communication and information. Both have to be well-managed and controlled if they are to be optimised as important organisational resources!

By looking at organisational structure, culture and communication, this chapter develops further the three main roles played by information systems, as detailed in Chapter 5, i.e.:

1 structuring
2 coordinating
3 communicating

It also relates the organisational issues of structure, culture, size, formalisation and the environment to the types and levels of CBIS. Figure 6.1 encapsulates the main organisational issues of this chapter.

Organisational structure and IS

Organisational structures differ for a variety of reasons. Managers have a variety of roles and functions to perform and the environment in which the organisation operates will impact significantly on management activity. The managerial tasks of controlling, coordinating, solving problems and making decisions may well be hindered by existing structures which need to be changed. Similarly the introduction of CBIS may create further mismatches that need to be managed. The concept of organisational 'fit' is crucial particularly if the implementation of CBIS is being considered. Structure, culture, management activity, and CBIS all need to blend together to produce an optimum entity.

Organisational structures emerge from groups of people with the same skills or objec-

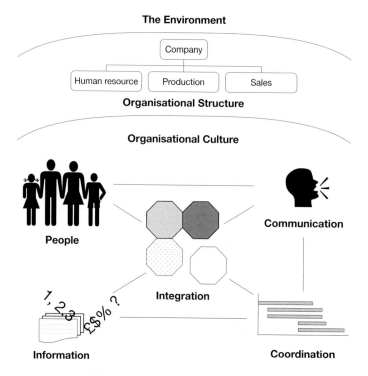

Figure 6.1 The organisation and its environment

tives, from delegation of responsibilities and authority and from integration of decision systems based on available information. Interpersonal relationships in an organisation are vitally affected by structural considerations, by changes in structure and often by the introduction of CBIS. Whatever structure prevails it must allow managers to perform their tasks to the best of their ability. CBIS have to fit with the structure and facilitate management activity. The interrelationships between organisational structure, management activity and CBIS are so often the cause of many organisational problems.

There are two important dimensions of tasks, variety and analysability that impact upon information processing requirements. Task variety refers to the degree of unanticipated or novel events arising in a process, while analysability refers to the breakdown of a process into discrete steps to reduce uncertainty. These dimensions of departmental activity are of structural relevance in classifying task complexity. A task with low variety and high analysability is routine, predictable, repetitive, well understood and consistent over time. A task with high variety and low analysability does not remain consistent over time. Task characteristics impact on structure and hence on IS/IT use.

Increasing environmental uncertainty and competition entail less routine tasks and increased demands for information. The matrix structure helps organisations to enhance their information processing capabilities. Instead of processing information exclusively in vertical form, the matrix structure allows for both vertical and lateral information processing. This structural innovation permitted organisations to share information across traditional functional areas.

The network structure is delayered, highly flexible and controlled by market forces rather than by internal procedures. Such structures are revolutionary in that most resources complementary to the organisation's core competencies are secured through strategic alliances and outsourcing. For these structures to operate effectively, Miles and Snow (1995) believed that they process high volumes of information and have information accessible by their employees and strategic alliance partners. A high value is placed on the availability of relevant information to all components of the networked organisation, as enabled by continual IS/IT developments.

According to Galbraith (1973, 1977), organisations exist to process information and an organisational structure should reflect the type of task environment surrounding it. As the external environment becomes more uncertain, organisations will move towards flatter structures and embrace IS/IT more effectively. The role of IS/IT will continue to evolve from a tool that supports organisational structure to a mechanism that acts as a replacement for organisational structure.

Centralisation

In 1958 Leavitt and Whisler predicted that IS/IT would lead to the elimination of middle managers and to greater centralisation of decision-making. Whisler (1970) further explained how IS/IT has impacted on organisational structure through increased vertical relations of information resulting in greater centralisation of information at the top of the hierarchy. He hypothesised that technology introduction would result in fewer employees, a narrower span of control and a reduction in organisational levels. IS/IT allows organisations to reorganize tasks through automation, resulting in a greater centralisation of information. Whisler argued for increased centralisation of decision-making to enable top management to make better

decisions under increasing environmental uncertainty and to control costs and other organisational resources more efficiently. IS/IT
therefore acts as a greater control mechanism.
Technology entails greater consolidation and
rigidity in decision-making, increased centralisation of authority and routinisation in the
content of lower-level jobs. Further, it creates
shifts in power towards departments with
CBIS, typically the accounting department.
Power devolves to those who gather, disseminate, process or possess information (Gotlieb
and Borodin, 1973). The increasing value of
information as a commodity brings the potential to change existing power bases and create
new ones.

Decentralisation

Evolving computer architectures and changing
organisational structures have moved from a
centralised to a decentralised design. In both
cases power is distributed from one central node
to a number of decentralised sources, a shift
characterised by a significant reduction in formality and increased exchange of data and
results (Leifer, 1988). Decentralised systems,
while still requiring some central control and
authority, produce higher levels of communication and task accomplishment among users
and a flexibility which gives the capability to
cope with a wide variety of information.

Argyres (1999) claimed that technology
replaces a defined vertical structure, with key
information systems enabling greater control
and coordination of activities. Information
systems aid coordination directly by making
information processing less costly and this
enhanced information processing enables
improved project management. Homburg
et al. (2000) noted that technology enables a
more decentralised organisational structure, as
employees are no longer geographically con-

strained in project involvement. Lal (1991)
found a positive relationship between decentralisation and technology and Hitt and
Brynjolfsson (1997) that more extensive user
involvement was associated with flatter, more
decentralised organisational structures. Furthermore, heavy investment in technology tends to
be linked to more decentralised organisational
structures. In this way organisations will be able
to adopt emerging organisational structural
forms with IS/IT as a core attribute, acting as
a flexible substitute for centralisation and formalisation.

Overall there is no clear indication of the
effect of IS/IT on centralisation and decentralisation. In some cases IS/IT appears to have
led to more centralisation, in others to more
decentralisation and in others has produced no
effect at all. What is clear is that decentralised
decision-making should predominate when
communication costs are high and when such
costs fall centralised decision-making becomes
more desirable.

Organisational complexity

Planning and control as management functions
have been dealt with in detail in Chapter 3. As
far as organisational structure is concerned,
planning and control reflect that structure and
accordingly can vary considerably. Costs and
budgets will tend to be associated with structural units. Cost centres for example are tied
into particular functions, clients or product
lines. Resource systems may well exist as sub-
systems to feed the planning and centralised
control of resources. Typical resource sub-
systems are capital assets, materials and work in
progress, human resources, plant and machinery and data.

Matrix structures are multidimensional and
as a consequence planning and control will be
conducted in a variety of ways. In a function-

based structure, for example, job costing will take place. Any mismatch between structure and the planning and control mechanisms will cause problems. As organisational complexity increases, so too will the potential for such a mismatch. Responsibilities need to be clearly defined and information flows developed to facilitate the planning and control of each dimension and sub-system. Management must not be insular, but more between the dimensions, functions and groupings within the organisation. It is crucial wherever organisational complexity exists that IS do not exacerbate complexity, but serve to simplify, focus and clarify.

IS/IT use can induce structural complexity, a more differentiated and specialised structure, by increasing the deployment of specialists required to carry out systems development, operation and control activities (Blau *et al.*, 1976; Robey, 1981). Organisations in which more management techniques, such as inventory control, quality control, project management and financial analysis, are applied, more sophisticated information support (Raymond, 1990) and information resource management (Olson and Chervany, 1980) are required. A complex structure implies more elaborate coordination, control and communication mechanisms, which in turn require an infrastructure that can be enabled or enhanced by IS/IT (Robey, 1981; Leifer, 1988). In other words, IS/IT sophistication and structural sophistication or complexity are positively and mutually related.

Formalisation

Highly formalised procedures exist on assembly lines to ensure consistent production. The processing of certain types of information follows a standard format, as the same information is always returned to the requester, such as

a computerised response to credit card bill enquiries regarding under- or overpayment. Care is needed, however with some computerised responses, particularly as nowadays customers tend to prefer more personalised replies to their enquiries. On the other hand, some pre-programming is necessary for routine replies if speed of response is to be achieved and this is indeed recognised as a key service dimension nowadays.

Non-formalised organisations deal constantly with new situations for which precedents do not exist, such as organisations involved in frontier areas of research. Where manufacturing industries have long been accustomed to formalisation, service industries are also now looking to measurement and standardisation much more to enhance consistent service delivery which can be very difficult to achieve. Standardising service tasks and systematising abstractions, such as human values, can help simplify the management activities of planning, organising and controlling.

Naturally there is a relationship between routinisation and formalisation. Organisations performing routine tasks are more likely to have greater formalisation of organisational roles. Issues of repetitiveness of tasks, predictability and consistent performance are characteristics of such organisations. Greater formalisation and routinisation can often permit automation of tasks with perhaps a consequent reduction in staff boredom with respective tasks. However, various applications of technology can lead to increased formalisation by requiring formal representations of the object systems and decision processes that are to be supported (Huber, 1984).

There is always the danger that rules are followed for the sake of it and that organisational goals become subjugated to those rules. Too much formalisation and rigidity may lead to diminished flexibility and adaptability to change. Formalisation is, however, necessary in organisations and necessary for the implementing and managing of IS. It is a variable that needs to be closely monitored at different levels of the organisation and which tends to decline in intensity as managers move up the organisational hierarchy.

Formalisation is manifested by the existence of more rules, procedures and documentation. It tends to increase as organisations increase in size. Other control mechanisms do, however, exist, such as professionalisation. Organisations with more professionalised staff, regardless of their size tend to exhibit less formalised structures. The need to be highly formalised is not deemed to be so imperative and a more informal social system tends to exist.

There is a tendency to associate informality and a greater ease of communication with small organisations, but it is dangerous to make generalisations. Barriers to communication come in various guises and informality may create problems of traceability and intangibility. What can, however, be said is that the more routine the product or service and the technology, the more standardised the structure and the greater the extent of formalisation with increasing size. If, on the other hand, organisational procedures are highly non-routine with many problems and

exceptions, a less formalised structure would tend to emerge with increasing size.

The influence of the environment on structure/environmental 'fit'

Organisational response in terms of structure varies according to environmental influences. The *mechanistic* structure is characterised by clear definition of tasks and roles, and reliance upon rules and procedures; strict control and monitoring tend to be more appropriate in a more stable environment. The *organic* structure is characterised by informality, staff initiative, networking, and interconnecting dynamic tasks, which are less predictable; laxer managerial control tends to be more suited to a dynamic environment. Table 6.4 summarises the essential differences between the two types of structure.

The external environment affects organisational design. Complexity of organisations is reflected in the extent to which they differentiate products and services and in the difference between structure, tasks and managerial orientation. Integration on the other hand is the extent to which departments and groupings across the organisation work together as a team to achieve organisational objectives. In both stable and dynamic environments high per-

Table 6.4 Mechanistic and organic structures

Mechanistic	Organic
Tasks highly specialised	Tasks interdependent
Tasks clearly defined	Tasks continually adjusted
Specific employee roles	Generalised employee roles
Control, authority, communication structured by hierarchy	Control, authority, communication structured by network
Communication vertical	Communication vertical and horizontal
Concentration on instructions and requests for information	Concentration on advice and information exchange

Source: Burns and Stalker (1961)

formance organisations tend to exhibit the right amount of integration (e.g. by using task teams) to maximise their effectiveness.

What is important is that an organisation's structure fits its environment and that there is an appropriate mix between mechanistic and organic elements. The production department may, for example, choose a mechanistic structure, while marketing and research and development need to be organic. A mechanistic structure tends to lend itself more to automation of tasks and activities, but ironically it is the organic structure that may benefit more from the implementation of IS to enhance networking, communication, integration and coordination.

Decentralisation and newer organisational structures, such as matrix, hybrid and network structures, have been found to be a more appropriate response to cope with increasing turbulence in the external environment. New structures to cope with new environmental realities have been facilitated in large part by the potential of information and control provided by CBIS.

IS/IT enables an organisation to be both more reactive and proactive in an environment. Ciborra (1997) explained how technology enabled a flexible response in highly uncertain environments by processing more information about the environment and facilitating better decisions about the environment. For highly unstable environments the traditional strategy–structure linkage fails to create flexibility for organisations that are centralised and formalised.

Organisational size

As far as size and IS implementation are concerned, it is difficult to generalise, as industry sector, competitor activity and organisational attitudes to IS will all play an important part.

All large organisations tend to implement IS to a certain extent. Small organisations may have virtually no IS or else be particularly innovative with IS. IS success may be less likely in smaller organisations (Ein-Dor and Segev, 1982) as they tend to be resource-poor and less developed in terms of structure and functions. Small firms are thought to be more prone to IS failure because they lack managerial and technical expertise with respect to the development and operation of CBIS. Furthermore, more mature organisations are more likely to implement IS successfully. However, the effect of size on IS is less clear overall.

The impact of organisational size must also be considered here and generally smaller organisations have:

- less complex structures
- less formal structures
- greater centralisation

There is evidence to suggest that organisational size affects its structure. An increase in size tends to be correlated with an increase in degree of complexity, which may well demand a different structure involving new functions and groupings. On the one hand, structural differentiation may be a consequence of increased size. Increasing the number of organisational activities gives rise to the need to add more staff and new functional groupings. Evidence to date does seem to indicate that increasing organisational size affects its structure at a decreasing rate, i.e. the impact of size becomes less pronounced as the organisation expands beyond a certain critical mass.

A larger scale of operational activities tends to lead to recurrent events and repeated decisions, which are reflected in the type of structure and which may become automated over time. A hierarchical structure with more rules and procedures may be appropriate, or a greater degree of decentralisation with clearly devolved control and decision-making. In either case the structure resulting from organisational growth may lend itself to progressive automation and IS implementation.

The overall size of an organisation is important in terms of the number of people needed to control, communicate and coordinate. There is always the danger that increasing size may lead to depersonalisation, poor communication and inadequate information flows. As organisational growth is a dynamic process, so responses to maintaining equilibrium and effectiveness need to be dynamic and innovative in terms of information systems for planning and control. Certain planning and control activities like finance and accounting may well remain centralised, while other functions are decentralised. It is important to appreciate above all that the ways in which planning and control activities are carried out will need to change as the organisation grows, and IS implementation and management will need to support and enhance those changes.

With the advent of the Internet, the greatest impact has been on the role and operations of small businesses (Mukherji, 2002). Studies have indicated that over 60 per cent of small businesses have a computer and modem, use online banking functions and have their own web pages (Friel, 1999). Another survey revealed that about 61 per cent of small businesses operate some kind of computer network, with nearly 40 per cent planning to update their network within a year (Pepe, 1999).

Location

Several small and medium-sized organisations are located in geographically isolated areas and have needed to develop their own IS to enable their managers to receive and transmit timely information and thereby be competitive in their

business environments. Advances in IS and IT development have enabled remote locations to process data locally and then link up with their head offices. Geographic dispersion of organisations has become more feasible as IS have given them the opportunities to be efficient even if they are not established in major industrial or commercial centres.

While IS permits a greater geographical structural flexibility for organisations, there is a reverse side of the coin to be examined, i.e. the effect of remote location on the management of IS. Four main points are of particular relevance:

1 Acquiring and retaining qualified staff is difficult in remote geographical locations.
2 Gaining hardware and software support is also difficult as vendors await a critical volume of business in a certain location before committing supporting personnel.
3 Providing professional development activities and opportunities is also difficult. Distances to be travelled to courses, meetings and conferences may be very great.
4 Data communications costs often escalate in remote locations to the point where information flows have to be rationalised. Being part of a distributed network can be overbearingly expensive.

It is clear that geographical location, particularly in remote areas, is a significant structural issue when related to IS, with both advantages and constraints.

Organisational performance

It is difficult to demonstrate fully the impact of IS/IT on bottom-line business performance and empirical evidence to date has tended to be largely inconclusive. Garsombke and Garsombke (1989), however, found computerisation to be a significant predictor of performance in small manufacturing firms, who stand to make significant gains in production, sales and profits at the expense of their unsophisticated competitors.

In terms of strategic information systems for competitive advantage (see also Chapter 8), IS/IT has been shown to improve performance by reducing operational and transaction costs, differentiating products and services and increasing market share (Peppard, 1993).

The concept of congruence, match or 'fit' between an information system and its organisational context has long been considered to play a determining role in information systems success (Wetherbe and Whitehead, 1977; Markus and Robey, 1983). High-performing organisational subunits match a decentralised and differentiated structure with non-routine operations technology. Matching structures must be defined if the resulting performance and productivity gains are to be high. For example, the attainment of benefits from new IT such as EDI (Electronic Data Interchange) and expert systems, is conditional on the establishment of specialised subunits, the hiring of expert staff and the creation of mechanisms to coordinate their efforts (Bergeron and Raymond, 1992).

Organisational culture and IS

Issues of organisational structure and IS have been highlighted more than issues of organisational culture and IS, much in the same way as traditional hard systems approaches have been more widely applied and understood than soft systems approaches. Nowadays cultural issues are being recognised as equally important as structural considerations.

The people in an organisation are essential for IS development and implementation. An atmosphere of confidence and cooperation will contribute positively. If, however, people lack self-esteem or feel undervalued and unrecognised, a negative impetus for IS is likely to result.

Similarly, a pro-technology innovative culture will propel forward the development of IS and IT, as opposed to a cynical, backward-looking culture. Attitude to change is also important, as is the level of senior management commitment to change and innovation. If the need for IS and IT is perceived to be real and beneficial, implementation is more likely to be successful and sustainable over time.

Organisational culture conveys assumptions and norms that govern activities, values and goals. Staff learn how things are to be accomplished and what the priorities are. A blame culture, for example, where staff are mistrusted and highly controlled will tend to be characterised by formality and an authoritarian management style.

Organisational culture refers to a system of shared meanings and shared values that shape organisational approaches to solving problems and responses to the external environment. The value of information as a resource may not be fully acknowledged in an organisation with the result that competitors are able to gain a market edge. The culture may be one of undemocratic management, functional possessiveness and the keeping of information to oneself. Formal corporate decision-making may become severely restricted. Culture change often becomes necessary to ensure organisational survival.

Elements of organisational culture

Organisational culture is often perceived and portrayed as something abstract and intangible. To aid the understanding of what constitutes organisational culture, it is important to pinpoint its visible signs, the tangible evidence of that culture, including the following:

Material objects, such as corporate documentation, advertising brochures, corporate logos, mission statements and products made.

Example: Carter Holdings is an organisation with some 50 employees with well-kept buildings and no reserved parking spaces. The sign at the front door with the company name and logo is discrete and tasteful. Inside there is an atmosphere of activity and one can hear the noise of printers and keyboards as people work. The office layout is functional and informal with no indication of status or hierarchy. People seem relaxed in their demeanour, call each other by first name and are neatly but informally dressed. Those in the sales office and marketing functions do however tend to wear a smart suit or jacket.

From the *language* people use one gets the impression the people know each other well. Nicknames like 'sunshine' and 'the king' are used and the jargon exists in the form of technical expressions, such as 'sweep up the rubbish from the disc' and 'byte switchers'. Sometimes the language becomes quite tough and aggressive, for example the use of 'bird brain' or 'amateur' if a mistake has been made.

Traditions in Carter Holdings mean celebrating company jubilees, a Christmas lunch, a summer party and an annual company trip with partners. When a major contract is signed, champagne is opened and there is a leaving ceremony for all who move on from the company.

Physical symbols, such as technology, office layout and dress code. The organisation may have open-plan offices where staff move freely around on a relatively informal basis or offices may be discrete self-contained closed units requiring that people always knock before entering. Style of dress for work may range from fairly casual to extremely smart and formal depending upon the type of business and prevailing attitudes in the organisation.

Language, such as jargon, phrases and nicknames. The language code may be more or less formal with a variable degree of courtesy and deference when approaching different staff members. There may well be specific vocabulary and phrases which are only meaningful to those working in a particular organisation.

Traditions, such as routines and ceremonies, may reflect much about the organisation's approach to staff which may for example be caring and paternalistic. Recognition systems may be manifested by elaborate award ceremonies for high-achieving individuals or teams.

Stories, such as jokes, myths, legends and anecdotes tend to be the most specific indications of organisational culture, often relating to the behaviour of particular individuals and may be indicative of staff attitudes to social, political or racial issues of the day.

Norms of behaviour, which dictate what are considered to be appropriate and inappropriate responses from employees in certain circumstances. They develop over time as individuals interact and negotiate with one another on how problems are to be solved. There are, for example, certain norms concerning the basis on which individuals command respect. In technically oriented organisations respect may be based on level of expertise, while in traditional manufacturing it may be based on experience and length of service.

Heroes, such as Bill Hewlett and Dave Packard at Hewlett-Packard, who were regarded as legends in their own time by company employees. Such individuals make success seem attainable, they provide role models, symbolise the organisation externally, lead by exemplifying corporate values and urge commitment through increased motivation.

Rules, systems, procedures and programmes, such as human resource systems dealing with appraisal and promotion, rules governing the frequency of committee meetings, quality assurance procedures and quality improvement initiatives.

Aspects of culture

Visible signs of culture reflect the cultural values of an organisation. Core values of organisational culture often reflect the work-related values of the society in which it operates. There are a number of different aspects to organisational culture, which are worth considering as the context for the use of information and information systems:

- the organisational metaphors used by the members of an organisation to describe their working environment;
- the leadership style of the organisation's management, and the degree of delegation;
- the organisation's approach to the motivation of its members;
- the nature of the workforce in terms of education, professional status, etc.;
- the level of formality within the organisation;
- the level of cooperative working;
- the adaptability of the workforce based on the combination of freedom, initiative,

responsibility and risk acceptance prevalent and accepted.

There are a number of basic assumptions that can be made about an organisation's culture by considering the visible signs and what they reflect about the above aspects. Such assumptions relate to human nature, human relationships, human activities and everyday experiences. They guide people's perceptions, feelings and emotions about things. Basic assumptions differ from ordinary beliefs in three ways. Beliefs are held consciously and are relatively easy to detect, whereas basic assumptions are held unconsciously and are not superficially identifiable. Beliefs are easier to debate and change, while basic assumptions are not. Basic assumptions are more complex than beliefs in that they involve not just beliefs but interpretations of those beliefs plus values and emotions. The interaction of levels of culture is shown in Figure 6.2.

Sources of culture

There is a good degree of consensus that three of the most important sources of organisational culture are the following:

1 the societal or national culture within which the organisation is situated;
2 the vision, management style and personality of an organisation's founder or other dominant leader;
3 the type of business the organisation is in and the nature of its business environment.

According to Drennan (1992), there are 12 key causal factors that shape the culture of an organisation, which are:

1 the influence of a dominant leader;
2 a company's history and its traditions;

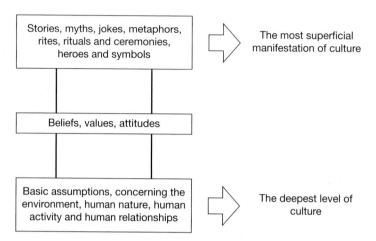

Figure 6.2 Interaction of levels of culture
Source: adapted from Schein (1985)

3 a company's technology, products and services;

4 the nature of an organisation's industry and competition;

5 an organisation's customers;

6 company expectations;

7 the information and control systems in place;

8 legislation and the company environment;

9 corporate procedures and policies;

10 reward systems and measurement;

11 the company's organisation and its resources;

12 corporate goals, values and beliefs.

While Drennan regards these twelve elements as shapers of organisational culture, others regard them as being integral parts of organisational culture. However we wish to interpret them, they are undoubtedly key considerations here.

Typologies of organisational culture

It is useful to look at a few typologies or classifications of organisational culture, if nothing else to be able to appreciate the sorts of variations that exist between cultures. Some of the best-known classification schemes are those of

Harrison (1972), modified by Handy (1978; 1985), Deal and Kennedy (1982), Quinn and McGrath (1985) and Scholz (1987).

The Harrison/Handy typology contains four types of organisational culture:

1 The *power* culture has a single source of power from which rays of influence spread throughout the organisation, connected by functions and specialist areas which facilitate coordinated action.

2 The *role* culture is a bureaucracy governed by logic and rationality with its strengths in its functions and specialities.

3 The *task* culture is based on expertise, on accomplishing the job or project in hand by bringing together the appropriate people and resources.

4 The *person* culture develops when a group of people decide to work collectively for their own best interests, such as lawyers, doctors or architects wishing to pool and share office costs, equipment and services.

The Deal and Kennedy typology also contains four types:

1 The *tough guy, macho* culture is composed of individuals who have to take high risks and receive rapid feedback on the quality of their actions, such as surgeons, police departments and management consultancy companies.

2 The *work hard/play hard* culture is a low risk, rapid feedback culture emphasising fun and action, such as real estate, computer companies and some manufacturing organisations.

3 The *bet-your-company* culture is high risk and feedback on actions and decisions takes a long time, such as large aircraft manufacturers and oil companies like Boeing and Shell.

4 The *process* culture is a low risk, slow feedback culture typified by banks, insurance companies and the civil service.

Quinn and McGrath identified four generic cultures:

1 The *market* – a rational culture designed to pursue objectives using productivity and efficiency as the key performance criteria.

2 The *adhocracy* – an ideological culture which can support broad purposes through external support, growth and resource acquisition.

3 The *clan* – a consensual culture which gauges performance on the basis of facilitation of group cohesion and morale.

4 The *hierarchy* – a culture that follows rules and regulations in order to remain stable and controlled.

Finally, the Scholz typology attempts to connect culture and strategy with its five types:

1 The *stable* culture is introvert, backward-looking, risk averse and does not accept change.

2 The *reactive* culture is also introvert, oriented to the present, accepts minimum risks and tolerates minimal change.

3 The *anticipating* culture is partially introvert/extrovert, oriented to the present, accepting of familiar risks and of incremental change.

4 The *exploring* culture is extrovert, oriented to the present and the future, operated on a risk/gain trade-off and accepts radical change.

5 The *creative* culture is extrovert, oriented to the future, prefers unfamiliar risks and seeks novel change.

National, organisational and occupational culture

National culture is based on strong, enduring values and beliefs, which are unlikely to change over a person's lifetime. Organisational culture is based on norms and shared practices learned in the workplace, which are considered valid within the boundaries of a particular organisation. Occupational culture involves shared practice and values regarding how things should be done in the context of a particular occupation or profession.

From the perspective of technology design and implementation, national culture can be an important issue in transferring technology across nations, designing systems with culturally diverse teams or deploying systems for users from different cultural environments. In terms of occupational culture, dysfunctional interactions among different professional groups involved in IT projects are often the cause of deficient implementation. Schein (1996), for example, witnessed different assumptions held by engineers, operators and top executives. While engineers saw networking technology as an opportunity to eliminate cumbersome hierarchy, executives saw hierarchy as a necessary mechanism for control and coordination. While engineers considered expert systems and management information systems as excellent aids for decision-making, executives felt unnecessarily constrained by them.

Unlike national and occupational cultures, organisational culture can, at least to some extent, be modified. Being aware of national and occupational culture can aid the management of technological innovation but they cannot be changed. On the other hand, there are a number of ways in which, given the need, time and resources, management can attempt to influence and shape an organisation's culture.

Organisational metaphors

Kendall and Kendall (1994) describe nine metaphors used by members of organisations to describe their working environment. This is a different use of metaphors to that based on the work of Morgan (1986) of which he sees culture as only one metaphor. Instead it is derived from the work of Clancy (1989), using metaphors as a component of organisational culture. Such metaphors tell us how the members of an organisation view it. The nine metaphors are:

The journey, which may take the form of a voyage on a ship, shared by a crew led by a captain. Along the journey the crew may meet many risks or dangers which may sink their ship. By pulling together the crew can reach their destination, led by their strong and possibly charismatic leader – the captain.

The game, in which teamwork is key to beating the opposition/competition, with the ever-present risk of losing. In this metaphor each member of the team has their allotted position to play, led by the team coach. The reputation for successful leadership that the coach has depends very much on the current form of the team as a whole.

The war, in which the enemy/competition are fought in the pursuit of a goal. The army is led by a general set apart from the foot soldiers.

Intelligence is gathered and used by the general to direct his/her troops. The rules of engagement and conduct of the war are clearly laid down, and are adhered to by the troops as they obey their general's orders.

The machine, which operates rationally and predictably. Members of the organisation are cogs in the machine, which can be replaced as necessary. The essence of the machine is in the predictable nature of the actions of its components, with any deviations from standard practice likely to upset the machine's delicate balance.

The organism, which is born, matures and grows nurtured by its leader. By innovating, the organism can prolong its life, adapting to changes in its environment.

The society, which like the wider society in which it operates must cater for the differing aims of its members. The balance between these different aims is achieved through negotiation, with a leader as head of state helping to focus on a general direction. Also, like society in general, it must have its rules to remain workable.

The family, in which different members pursue their own goals, with a leader as head of family who decides on the balance between the other members of the family. Despite any sibling rivalry the good of the family is still a consideration.

The zoo, which houses an odd assortment of people who do not logically belong together but have been collected for the purposes of the organisation. The leader in this case is the keeper who simply needs to keep them clean and fed. With no common goal to unite them the members of such an organisation seek improvement in their own conditions, even at the expense of others within the zoo.

The jungle, in which the members of the organisation are stranded. The law of the jungle operates with survival being each member's primary goal. 'Every man for himself' is the chief cry, as members keep a watchful eye on those around them and especially on their external environment. Each is hoping for a leader to guide them to safety.

Such organisational metaphors are not static. A single organisation can be described by different metaphors at different stages of its life. Each metaphor has four attributes which summarise their nature – organisational orientation, whether goal or alternative; the nature of the internal working environment, whether chaotic or ordered; the internal or external scope; and the type of leader needed. These are summarised in Table 6.5.

The likelihood of IS developmental success, given the presence of the various metaphors is given in Table 6.6.

Nature of the workforce

Schein (1981) has proposed the idea that a culture may be defined in terms of its basic assumptions, which relate to the implicit, deeply

Table 6.5 Nine metaphors and their attributes

Type	Orientation	Environment	Scope	Leader needed
Journey	Goal	Chaos	Internal	Captain
Game	Goal	Order	External	Coach
War	Goal	Chaos	External	General
Machine	Goal	Order	Internal	Designer
Organism	Both	Balanced	External	Innovator/nurturer
Society	Alternative	Order	Internal	Head of state
Family	Alternative	Order	Internal	Head
Zoo	Alternative	Chaos	Internal	Keeper
Jungle	Alternative	Chaos	External	Guide

Source: Kendall and Kendall (1994)

Table 6.6 Likelihood of developmental success

Type of information system	Success least likely (if these metaphors are present)	Success most likely (if these metaphors are present)
Cooperative	Society; Zoo	Journey; Game; Organism
Competitive	Zoo; Family; Society	War; Game; Organism
Traditional MIS	War; Jungle	Society; Machine; Family
Expert system/AI	Jungle; Zoo	Machine; Game; Organism
Decision support system	War; Journey	Family; Society; Organism
Executive information system	Journey; Zoo	Organism; Game

Source: Kendall and Kendall (1994)

rooted assumptions people share and which guide their perceptions, feelings and emotions about things. These assumptions will relate directly to the way in which people work and interpret their working environment. Employees may be proactive achievers who, through hard work and diligence, are able to achieve given objectives or they may be constrained by rules and procedures and become demotivated because they are unable to achieve objectives. Some may prefer to work on their own initiative, while others may favour team work, collective action and cooperation. Some people prefer to interact with work colleagues as friends, while others may wish to retain more distant, strictly professional relationships with colleagues. Some organisations consider work as the primary activity, whereas others foster a culture in which the private lives of employees are more valued, others might prefer a balanced and integrated combination of work and private life to be feasible and desirable. These different organisational attitudes will shape to some extent the nature of the workforce.

There are, of course, individual characteristics that define the nature of the workforce. Some people are by nature more ambitious, prepared to take risks and wish to be empowered. Others are more risk-averse and wish to be told by others what to do. Some people are natural leaders and have enthusiasm and a high level of interpersonal skills; others are more reticent and find interacting with others more difficult. Some employees are adaptable and reasonably receptive to change, while others are more set in their ways and wish to stick to tried and tested, established methods of operation.

Whatever the nature of the workforce, it is important that managers understand their workforce so as to be able to anticipate where problems might arise and identify training and education needs if the staff skill-mix is not as good as it should be. It is also vital to keep staff informed and prepared for any IS-related changes that involve them so that they can articulate concerns and potential problems. Inspired leaders know how to make the best of their people potential.

Certain aspects of working are particularly important to consider here with respect to IS introduction and development.

Extent of control

Organisations vary in the amount of control they exert over individuals. Tightly controlled cultures may observe strict rules and procedures regarding the way things are done, such as the holding of meetings, and may show a strong cost-saving consciousness, whereby even minor expenditures have to be sanctioned by a relatively senior manager. Loose control organisations are more permissive about individual preferences, such as accepting public jokes about the company.

Organisations may also vary in the extent to which they are controlled by and feel inclined to conform to institutional pressures. Pragmatic cultures are more market driven and are open to ad hoc solutions, while normative cultures are more concerned with following institutional rules, in adhering to the correct procedures as a way of obtaining legitimacy.

Level of cooperative working

Organisational units coordinate or operate independently from one another to a greater or lesser extent. This is tied into the degree to which staff identify with the organisation as a whole, which often implies a strong positive corporate culture. Staff may identify with one particular area of expertise, whereby that culture may tend still to be strong, but more fragmented across the organisation. Patterns of communication are also important and the

degree of formality or informality that charac-
terises them.

Adaptability of the workforce

The people in an organisation determine its
culture to some considerable extent. People
cannot be pre-programmed and estimated
absolutely; human variability can be extremely
difficult to manage.

Organisational culture is shaped as a result
of the following considerations:

- The extent to which people prefer to have
  rules and procedures to follow or act upon
  their own initiative.
- The extent to which people wish to be
  empowered, taking responsibility and making decisions themselves, or prefer more
  control and supervision, their tasks and
  responsibilities clearly delineated.
- The extent to which people work as a team
  or prefer to act independently. A team-
  working culture will only work if people
  enjoy and see the benefits of operating in
  teams. Such a culture must naturally be fostered by appropriate reward and recognition
  schemes.
- The extent to which people feel comfortable
  with and accept change or resist change and
  stand in the way of progress and innovation.
  Cynicism and scepticism or lack of commitment are serious obstacles to the change
  process.
- The extent to which people are skilled professionals or feel insufficiently trained or
  competent to fulfil their role in the organisation.
- The extent to which people fit with the
  organisational strategy, objectives, systems
  and structure. People are, after all, the essential cohesive force bringing together systems
  and culture to meet organisational goals.

People are a vital organisational resource
requiring inspired leadership and careful,
competent management. A repressive blame
culture will tend to stifle that resource, whereas
a trusting enlightened culture will frequently
enable that resource to be optimised to its fullest
potential.

People in organisations need to be fully
aware of what is feasible and permissible. This
may well not correlate with what they want. At
the same time there must be some room for
creativity, particularly with the development of
IS and IT without too much fear of reprisals
if mistakes are occasionally made.

The culture of an organisation defines the
kind of things that can and cannot be done. It
helps to predict the likelihood of certain changes
being accepted over others. Culture defines
potential and the people in that culture largely
control attainment or not of that potential.

The longer an organisational culture has
existed the longer people in that organisation
have been doing things in a certain way and the
more behaviour patterns and expectations
have become ingrained. Some companies,
for example, build in a respect for people in general, both within and outwith the organisation.
Others regard staff, customers and suppliers with
contempt and as victims.

Empowerment

Staff may be directly controlled and supervised
or be allowed autonomy and independence.
They may be more or less innovative as appropriate or may require management support.
Power may be centralised with decisions being
made by a relative minority of senior managers,
while staff have clearly delineated roles with
little in the way of discretion. Some traditional
industries, such as the garment and clothing
sector, have long been accustomed to a formalised approach and are now finding it very

difficult to relinquish tight management and supervisory control to make way for facilitation and team working.

Bowen and Lawler (1992) regarded the dissemination of performance-related information to the lower levels of the organisation as a key feature of empowerment. Jarvenpaa and Ives (1994) researched firms reporting daily performance indicators through sophisticated IS directly to employees. Such systems can help focus employee and team efforts on the problems and opportunities facing the organisation as a whole. Clement (1994) examined the use of desktop computers by secretaries, who were thereby able to assume greater power in their dealings with management. In reality, computerisation serves not so much as an empowering tool but as the catalyst to expand the possibilities for organisational realignment. Ryker and Nath (1995) noted a positive effect on the job satisfaction and motivation of end users, while Simons (1995) examined the ways interactive control systems focus attention on the strategic uncertainties that need to be monitored. It is the empowering organisation which decides how and for what purpose technology will be employed to support employees. Traditional hierarchical structures can be transformed into team structures with interactive control mechanisms and two-way information flows. The way in which information is used in an organisation is entirely a matter of management discretion (Wareham *et al.*, 1997) but is nonetheless critical to the realisation of the benefits of IS.

Empowerment is about unlocking the energy and creativity of people in an organisation, about devolving control, about more radical decentralisation. IS enables subsidiarity and the devolution of tasks to the smallest possible unit, which is increasingly viewed as desirable for business organisations. Instead of all legitimate power being derived from the top and delegated down, all legitimate power originates

at the bottom and can be delegated up whenever beneficial.

The organisational environment

The nature of an organisation's activities and the environment in which it operates have a profound effect upon its culture. According to Deal and Kennedy (1982), the business environment is the single greatest influence in shaping organisational culture. Typically, some of the more significant influences on organisational culture come from stakeholders, professional associations and strategic issues.

Stakeholders include customers, the government, the public and shareholders. Customers have demonstrated their substantial influence on organisational culture with the increasing number of companies that have sought to improve the quality of their products and services. The government has considerable regulatory powers over public bodies like the NHS and local authorities, and affects private companies through adjustments to the legal framework, rulings on monopolies and mergers, and management of the economy. The public has been able to exert influence on culture, as evidenced, for example, by an increasing awareness of the rights of women and ethnic minorities, with both public and private sector organisations building 'equal opportunities for all' into their cultures. Shareholders, on the other hand, have surprisingly little influence on organisational culture unless company ownership is closely held by an individual or family or when management is afraid of a takeover.

Professional associations tend to dominate in certain organisations, such as health care organisations, teaching institutions and accountancy practices. Professional associations like the British Medical Association and the Institute of

Chartered Accountants often impose training and experience requirements on their members and publish codes of practice. The difficulty comes when there is a conflict between loyalty to the professional culture and loyalty to the organisational culture, something perhaps particularly problematic in the health care environment.

Strategic issues relate, according to Deal and Kennedy (1982), to degree of risk and speed of feedback on decisions and actions. The degree of risk faced by an organisation depends on factors such as the number of potential suppliers and competitors, the relative scarcity of resources and the stability of the market. Many organisations face considerable uncertainty and cannot predict their market because of increased levels of competition, such as clothing retailers and supermarkets, while others have a far more predictable business environment, such as local authorities and electricity supply companies. Inevitably, organisations have to be innovative, imaginative and flexible to a greater or lesser degree depending on their business environment. Similarly, if feedback is rapid, decisions and actions can be validated or reviewed easily, whereas long-term projects, such as oil and gas exploration programmes and drugs trials for pharmaceutical companies, expose the companies undertaking them to higher levels of risk, which have to be incorporated into the organisational culture.

The impact of organisational culture

Organisational cultures vary and so does the influence they have on their respective employees. Strong cultures have a greater impact than do weak cultures. Organisations in which the core values are intensely held, widely shared, readily accepted and which enlist commitment have an identifiable and influential culture.

Weak cultures display none of these characteristics and often staff find it difficult to differentiate between what is important and what is not.

Managerial behaviour is shaped to a large extent by organisational culture and decisions are often made on the basis of the way things are done. A more confident approach allows for a greater degree of risk to be encompassed in the planning process, which may well be longer term rather than geared to imminent deadlines only. A stronger culture will often involve clear performance criteria and these will influence the planning process in an organised and prioritised way.

In a weaker culture there is less in the way of clear definition of rules and responsibilities, and information flow may well not be as efficient as it should be. Consequently there may be a need for tighter managerial control with less delegation and freedom for staff. It is difficult to be specific about issues of control and empowerment because strong cultures have differing management styles which are nonetheless effective.

Strong cultures have been shown to affect corporate performance in a number of ways:

- in *financial terms* they have produced increased profits and organisational growth;
- *work atmosphere* has shown distinct improvements, with staff feeling more motivated and committed to give of their best;
- on a *personal level* people across the organisation have experienced a greater degree of self-esteem, a greater willingness to be open and cooperative with one another and have consequently exhibited a reduction in stress symptoms.

Organisational cultures can differ considerably in terms of their relative strength. Hampden-Turner (1990) regards organisational culture as especially strong in situations where people need reassurance and certainty. The elements and impact of strong culture are shown in Table 6.7. Much of the interest in culture strength relates to organisational performance or to the fact that an organisation has undergone significant culture change over a long period of time. Organisations with strong cultures tend to be described as having a certain style, flair or atmosphere but these are rather intangible qualities and are therefore difficult to evaluate. Payne (1990) suggested that strength of an organisation's culture could be measured by plotting the *strength of consensus* among its members against their *intensity* of feeling. Strength of consensus refers to the degree to which there is agreement on core beliefs, values, attitudes and assumptions. The intensity variable is a little more complex and relates to both psychic depth and range. Psychic depth refers to how deeply felt and influential the culture is and range to the scope of assumptions, beliefs, values, attitudes and behaviours influenced by a culture. Examples of strong and weak cultures, evaluated in this way, are shown in Figure 6.3.

Whatever culture prevails, be it autocratic or democratic for example, there needs to be clear definition of what is important. Critical success factors play an important role in strategic planning for IS (see Chapter 8). The same is true when looking at the relationship between organisational culture and IS. Quantifying purpose, scope and expectations for IS and IT up front will enhance the likelihood of success with development and implementation.

Without people IS cannot be implemented or managed or provide benefits for the organisation over time. People must be willing to cooperate with one another and commit themselves to make IS work. The organisational culture can therefore positively impact upon the IS function in the following ways:

- there needs to be a positive, productive corporate attitude to IS and its potential benefits;
- staff at all levels of the organisation need to be involved before, during and after IS implementation;
- adequate training and support for IS must be committed by management;
- a cooperative and communicative approach has to reassure staff who are uncertain about IS implications and facilitate innovative IS experimentation wherever appropriate;
- staff must ultimately be 'kept on board' regardless of management style, which may be more or less autocratic and regardless of organisational structure, be it controlled or decentralised.

Conversely, IS implementation impacts on organisational culture, maybe imposing a greater degree of formalisation. Problems may well arise in relatively informal organisational cultures that do not lend themselves to extensive use of IS.

Professional corporate environments are, however, an exception. Professionalism is often combined with informality to produce a culture that is fertile ground for the development of IS and IT.

Table 6.7 Elements and impact of strong culture

Elements of strong culture	Impact of strong culture
Commitment	Enthusiasm
Clear responsibilities	Motivation
Clear rules	Confidence
Clear performance measures	Ability to cope with risk
Efficient information flows	Ability to cope with change

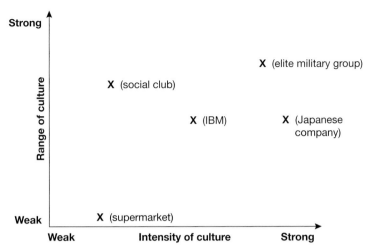

Figure 6.3 Examples of strong and weak cultures
Source: adapted from Payne (1990)

Care must be taken to ensure that the balance between formality and informality is not disturbed to an unacceptable extent.

Different technologies used by organisations play an important part in the development of culture. Whatever a company does, and how it does it, shape perceptions and behaviour for the future. Organisational activities may benefit from more or less automation and the consequences of technological plans need to be evaluated upfront. Traditional ways of doing things may give rise to more resistance to implementation of IS and IT than more modern approaches to work. Batch and process technologies have very different effects on business culture. The two-way influence between culture and IS must be carefully considered. A culture audit prior to IS and IT implementation is always a useful exercise.

Diagnosing organisational and information culture

Examining organisational culture normally involves the use of a combination of questionnaire, interview and direct observation techniques. Questionnaires have the advantage that they can be circulated to a large and representative sample of employees and thus provide the researcher with a good overall impression of the prevailing beliefs, values and attitudes within an organisation. An example of such a questionnaire asked respondents to assess the state of their organisation's culture by answering questions in 12 categories, as follows:

1 creativity and innovation orientation
2 power and conflict orientation
3 information and communication orientation
4 rules orientation
5 learning orientation
6 individuality orientation
7 cooperation orientation
8 trust orientation
9 conflict orientation
10 future orientation
11 loyalty and commitment orientation
12 work orientation

More specifically related to information culture, the following categories were used for

177

the basic structure of the questionnaire (Curry and Moore, 2003):

- strategy and objectives
- information
- environment
- professional associations
- information systems
- relationships
- communications

In the particular case organisation where the research was carried out, conclusions could be drawn about information culture, which is naturally closely aligned to organisational culture.

Leadership and motivation

The importance of leadership as a source of organisational culture was highlighted by Selznick as long ago as 1957 and more recently by Davis (1984). Edgar Schein (1985) has, however, been the most influential author in popularising the concept of the single influential individual, often the founder, creating organisational culture. Organisations do not originate spontaneously or by accident, but through the efforts of individuals or groups with specific aims in mind. Henry Ford at the Ford Motor Company and Ken Olsen at DEC (Digital Equipment Company) are well-cited examples of founders whose personality hugely shaped the culture of the organisation. Other leaders have then had the opportunity to mould an organisation's culture according to their theories of what constitutes good organisational practice, such as Lee Iaccoca at General Motors, Sir John Harvey-Jones at ICI and John Scully at Apple Computers.

The development and implementation of IS involves organisational change, which must be guided and supported by managers. Commitment to making change come about is often reflected in leadership style. At the same time staff need to be motivated to work in different ways, feeling confident that they can cope and will be supported by their managers as the need arises.

Some managers are more in the leadership role than others. One view about good business leadership is that it brings about good, sound economic performance, such as increased profitability. It is inappropriate to try and characterise the universal good leader, because, as in the case of organisational structure, leaders differ but still enjoy similar degrees of success. Requisite characteristics for good leaders could nonetheless be regarded as the following:

- an above-average intelligence with the capability to extrapolate and cope with abstractions;
- initiative, independence, inventiveness and the ability to identify the need for action;
- self-assurance, self-confidence;
- the capability to rise above a situation, separate the vital from the trivial and relate to the overall 'big picture', rather than view things purely in isolation.

Other qualities for measuring leadership are: imagination, courage in taking risks, decisiveness, persuasiveness, determination to see things through and energy/vitality. The reality is often such that a given situation occurs or is created and the best leader deals with it efficiently and effectively, influencing others and possessing appropriate managerial authority.

Leadership style

At the one extreme the leader makes the decision, tells subordinates and expects them to carry out that decision. At the other extreme, the leader fully shares decision-making authority, allowing each member of the group involved to carry an equal voice. The scale runs from auto-cratic to democratic leadership style.

An important question for leaders and managers remains that of how much participation should be allowed or encouraged in subordinates. Shared decision-making has often been viewed as crucial to the achievement of high employee productivity, but participation must not merely be regarded as a panacea for successful leadership. Similarly, empowerment works well in some situations and not in others. Some staff do not wish to be empowered, but prefer to be told precisely what to do.

Effective leadership is vital, particularly in the case of excellent service organisations. Examples of highly successful leaders who have stood the test of time are Fred Smith of Federal Express and Carl Sewell of Sewell Village Cadillac. Perhaps such leadership comes from inspiring a shared vision such as unremitting commitment to provision of faultless customer service or invoking enthusiasm for the achievement of organisational goals. Being an exemplary and visibly supporting the staff, being consistent, trustworthy and reliable also send out clear positive messages about a leader's style. Leadership can be regarded to some extent in isolation, but effective leadership can really only fully be evaluated in the whole context of the organisation and its people.

Motivation

From a behavioural viewpoint there can be no motivation without a goal. It is important to consider why people work, why they work in a particular way, why they change their jobs, why some are motivated to succeed while others are not. Managers must discover how they can motivate staff to achieve optimal performance, either as individuals or in groups. Adopting the right management style to achieve this motivational role is essential.

The issue of motivation is both complex and abstract. It is therefore helpful to devise models to simplify and clarify what is important and find the best way to manage motivation in a particular organisational situation. In any event, if people are not 'on board', the likelihood of introducing information systems successfully is significantly diminished. The subject of motivation has been tackled in many different ways. The main models are briefly discussed here.

Maslow (1943) studied human needs ranging from the most basic needs of the body to the need for self-fulfilment (self-actualisation), see Figure 6.4. A person's behaviour will be dominated by a certain need until it is fulfilled. Maslow's model is of value because it describes people's needs at work and the ways in which their motivation can be enhanced by managers.

McGregor's (1960) *X and Y Theory* consists of two sets of assumptions:

1 Workers are inherently lazy, need to be coerced and only value their security, i.e. the X model or the pursuit of self-interest.
2 Workers enjoy their work and if they are committed to the organisation's objectives, they will seek responsibility for themselves, i.e. the Y model or the self-actualizing person.

Herzberg's (1968) studies concentrated more on the issue of job satisfaction. Certain factors (*motivators*) relate to the *content* of work, such as achievement, recognition, while *hygiene* factors

Figure 6.4 Maslow's hierarchy of needs

	Motivators	**Hygiene Factors**	
Satisfaction		Working conditions Company policies	No dissatisfaction
	Challenge Responsibility Recognition Achievement Advancement	Supervision Co-workers Salary Job security	
No satisfaction			Dissatisfaction

Figure 6.5 Herzberg's motivators and hygiene factors

relate to the *context* of work such as supervision, job security or pay. Motivators create positive satisfaction, while hygiene factors serve only to prevent dissatisfaction, as shown in Figure 6.5.

Theories such as these have been used to a greater or lesser extent in organisations to describe management style and attitudes to employees. There is no doubt that people-management issues impinge considerably on the implementation and management of IS/IT in organisations and in creating a corporate culture that can cope with change. The issue of culture has been dealt with in this chapter and change is dealt with in some detail in Chapter 7.

Reward systems

Employees are sometimes rewarded on merit and sometimes on the basis of seniority. The objectives for reward and the performance measures used as the basis for decisions are of crucial importance. Adherence to merit-based procedures tends to entail highly qualified personnel operating at a decentralised level who are often entrusted with considerable power.

It is interesting to note that companies with diametrically opposed cultures can be equally successful and there is no one exemplary cultural configuration. Take the cases of Hewlett Packard and General Electric. The latter has

extensive rules and regulations for employees and specific objectives for them to achieve. Communication and information flow largely through formal channels and managerial control is tight. Effort, cost-effectiveness and avoidance of errors are highly prized. Hewlett Packard, on the other hand, is informal and more loosely structured. Employees are encouraged to solve their own problems, having recourse to managers when they need help and support. Departments are evaluated both individually and on the extent to which they coordinate their activities with those elsewhere in the organisation. It is a highly humanistic company.

Motivation and IT

The context of IT has made things more complex and there still remains the need to resolve the dichotomy between concern for people and concern for production. The effects of IT are still being investigated where usage impinges upon employee motivation, attitudes, ergonomics and social behaviour in general.

The knowledge gap between systems operators and users has caused immense problems for managers. Process analysis, information analysis and various matching models are increasingly attempting to address the issue of optimising human motivation and productivity alongside IT development.

Impact of CBIS on organisations

There is a two-way relationship between organisational structure and CBIS. In other words, organisational structure has an influence on CBIS choice, development and implementation, while in turn CBIS have an influence on the structure of an organisation, how it should be designed or changed over time. The impact of structure on CBIS has already been examined to some extent, but the three factors of organisational complexity, formalisation and centralisation/decentralisation need to be taken a step further.

Different types of organisational structure often reflect specific characteristics of the organisation, such as the following:

- degree of complexity or differentiation may well be matched by a matrix structure according to the variety of products or services;
- degree of reliance on rules and procedures will show itself in a more formalised or bureaucratic structure;
- degree of centralisation or decentralisation will be evidenced by autonomy of self-regulating business units or centralisation of all or most corporate controls.

CBIS have created changes in organisational structures which relate to hierarchy, centralisation and authority. As DSS have increased managerial productivity, so the levels of management have tended to decrease, hierarchies to flatten, and middle managers to disappear. As spans of control have widened with lower-level staff able to perform higher-level tasks, so flatter structures have emerged.

The issue of centralisation is somewhat less clear-cut. In some instances there has been an increase in the power of decentralised units which have become less dependent on corporate headquarters. In other cases highly centralised planning and control systems have emerged. CBIS can support either centralisation or decentralisation. Large DSS and ES allow senior management to centralise decision-making which was previously the remit of lower-level managers, while PCs and data communication networks allow senior management to devolve a greater degree of authority and responsibility to middle management, who can still provide senior managers with the information they require for planning and control.

Authority and power over CBIS and information resources cause conflict and affect perceived organisational structure. A power shift may occur from professionals to administrators and between different levels of management in the hierarchy. With the increasing importance of coordinating and networking organisational systems, authority and power could be seen to be shifting to IS/IT specialists, creating a new structural imbalance.

Organisational complexity comes in various guises and is associated with a variety of issues relating to structure, communication, functional or specialist divisions, managerial roles and styles and information flow. Taking a systemic view of organisations helps in the understanding of some of that complexity. Integration and coordination in organisations help to provide vital links to further reduce complexity. A central role of IS is to provide integration and coordination.

The formal functional or business activity groupings in an organisational system are always at risk of being isolated from one another, so that the system as a whole remains sub-optimised. The integrating processes should prevent this or at least help to reduce it to a minimum.

The three issues of complexity, formalisation and centralisation are directly linked to the roles of CBIS (see Chapter 5). Structural complexity is linked to coordination, structural formalisation is linked to structuring and structural centralisation is linked to communication. There needs to be a 'fit' between structural and cultural issues and CBIS, a concentration on the priorities as they arise and how they can best be tackled. Centralised CBIS are easier to control and can achieve cost-efficiencies through economies of scale. Distributed CBIS can be designed to fit an organisation's chosen operating and management structure without imposing too many technological constraints. There needs to be the right balance between formal and informal ways of working, between control and autonomy, an ability to adapt to the change brought about by IS implementation and the realisation of benefits to the quality of working life from IS.

IS can impact organisations in terms of enhancing opportunities for empowerment by enabling people at the lower levels to make decisions and by disseminating information on a democratic basis. People can thereby be more involved with and in control of their own performance and that of the organisation as a whole.

Chapter summary

This chapter has focused on organisational structure and culture with regard to CBIS. There is a two-way influential relationship in both cases. There has to be organisational fit between the structure or framework of the company and the chosen CBIS. Cultural issues are important, strong cultures giving rise to more positive benefits than weaker ones.

More specifically, the issues of centralisation, decentralisation, complexity, formalisation and organisational size and performance are discussed with respect to IS development and implementation. These structural factors are key themes and will remain so into the future.

On the cultural side, there are the issues of leadership, motivation and empowerment that are central in the IS context. Different types of culture have been explained along with subcultures, which may compete with one another when IS are introduced.

Communication, integration and coordination are important beneficial outcomes of having the right CBIS and managing information more efficiently and effectively. These themes underpin the discussions of structure and culture. The external environment also has an influential role to play in the organisation/CBIS relationship. It has been examined in this chapter and is further developed in chapter 8.

Review questions

1 What do you understand by the term 'organisational fit' in the context of IS?
2 What impact can organisational structure have on IS?
3 What impact can IS implementation have on organisational structure?
4 Which particular structural aspects have to be considered in conjunction with IS implementation?
5 How can organisational culture affect IS implementation?
6 How can different aspects of organisational culture help guide IS implementation?

7   How do Kendall and Kendall's organisational metaphors aid our understanding of the links between organisational culture and IS?

8   Which 'people aspects' shape organisational culture and why is it important to consider these in conjunction with IS implementation?

9   What are the key links between organisational culture and information culture?

10 How do leadership and motivation affect IS implementation?

Case study

Developing and implementing IS in social services

Introduction

The issues in this case study regarding the implementation of a comprehensive social services package go beyond the problems of introducing computers per se and touch upon questions of social work practice and how technology can be assimilated into an environment where professional autonomy is predominant. The project was concerned with the implementation of a system that would make a difference to the performance of the organisation. The timescales for the project are shown in Table 6.8.

The logistics of the project were daunting, as the authority had 2,000 staff working in 34 locations and needed to replace the existing system in a short time-frame (three months) to save on further leasing costs. A further 18 months would then be spent consolidating the initial implementation and introducing new functionality which would provide the real project benefits by transforming working methods. For the authority the most important objective for the new system was to integrate all the aspects of social work and cost packages of care. This would provide the capability to track an individual client moving through the system, analyse the performance of the various aspects of the service and control the budgets.

The new system had a modular design, used new technology and was intended as a proactive tool for practitioners to use in planning, case recording and managing their area of responsibility. It therefore scored well on the following criteria: functionality; usability; ease of maintenance; flexibility to accommodate future growth; confidence that it has been designed by people who understand social care. The cost, however, was relatively high.

The authority was moving from a simple computer system, predominantly used by clerical staff to record 'after the event', to a more sophisticated system requiring practitioners to interact with it as an integral part of their work. Some risks associated with such a move are the following:

- the stakes are high – large investment and potential benefits;
- the systems may be seen as intrusive by the professionals, influencing the way they work and demanding cognitive and technical skills they may not have or may not wish to acquire;
- there may be insufficient anticipation of resistance to change in ways of working and increased dependence on systems.

Table 6.8 Milestones in the project

Phase 1: replacement of current system

December 1995	Evaluation and choice of system.
January–February 1996	Explanations of the strategy throughout the department.
February–May 1996	Development of the system to meet the department's practices and processes.
	Start of procedural manual.
	Start of development of resource directory and personnel system.
March–April 1996	Major training initiative involving over 400 staff.
May 1996	Cross-over from old system, initially in 21 care management sites.

Phase 2: introduction of new functionality

May–September 1996	Intensive on-site support; preparation for care management and workload functionality. Introduction of registration and inspection module.
	Initial work on developing the personnel function.
September 1996–March 1997	Development of foster care. Development of care management and assessment and further work modules. Preparation for home care management module. Development of child protection module.
	Work started on financial strategy. Training courses expanded. Procedural guidelines developed. Support systems extended. Extensive work with children teams to accommodate children specialist functions.
November 1996	Implementation of care management and assessment and workload management modules.
March–September 1997	Revised finance strategy when decision to buy corporate finance system deferred. Links to corporate ledger built. Service packaging developed.
	Financial profiling developed.
September 1997–March 1998	Major training initiatives around service packaging. Procedural work in financial links and contracting process. Development of the resource directory to accommodate this. Completion of all planned work for the development stage; planning for the next stage.
April 1998	Implementation of internal commitment profiling.

Phase 3: consolidation (ongoing)

April 1998 onwards	Need to address technical performance and continue to address practice issues.

With these risks in mind, the authority appointed an assistant director to manage the information strategy, including the implementation of the new computer package. She had a practitioner background, the management overview and the authority to enlist cooperation from all parties. The authority also agreed to a participative approach to the implementation to maximise learning opportunities and focus on delivering the concept of a practitioner tool. The key elements of this approach were as follows:

- The launch involved awareness sessions for all staff, explaining the broad nature of the information strategy and its likely impact on working methods (rather than just talking about computers) and introducing the idea of managing change.
- The team had practitioners seconded to examine specifically how the processes and practice could be optimised with the use of the new system.
- As each new area of functionality was addressed, staff were involved to review the system component, agree any refinement and align practice.
- Regular audits were conducted to assess who was using the new system and with what results (such as improved data quality and trails of how practice was being reflected).

Phases of the project

Table 6.8 highlights certain pressure points in the project:

- The initial changeover from the old system involved transferring the data and training 400 staff in a three-month period. Pressure from staff who had 'ownership' of the old system led to the decision to transfer data that probably should have been scrapped. The consequences of this decision influenced data quality over the whole period of implementation.
- The 'holding action' for the next five months, during which there was no new functionality, involved intensive support for 400 staff 'thrown in at the deep end' and concurrent activity to prepare for the introduction of care management and the registration and inspection module.
- A further six months of dual activity – extending the training and dealing with the emerging challenge of an event-driven practitioner system, while trying to bring children's services 'on board'. At the same time, work was beginning on negotiating how the system would fit with the organisation's plans to acquire a new corporate finance system.
- A complicating factor at this time was that registration and inspection decided not to implement their module: the main project was too stretched to respond.
- The final stretch of phase two in which the deferred decision on corporate finance meant that the project plan had to be revised and substantial development effort put in to support financial management from within the system. This also involved changes to other parts of the system and extensive training for care managers in how to use commitment accounting.
- An additional stress, characterised by tension between the technical IT unit and the user-led project, resulted in the authority instigating a broad review of project conduct and results in late 1995.

Findings and analysis

The findings of the project confirmed the sort of obstacles arising from introducing sophisticated computer systems. In particular, the desired changes in working practice were very difficult to realise. The clear impression was that in relation to the planned approach, the technical tasks absorbed much of the team's time and attention but the challenge of 'institutionalizing' the system depended on the 'organisation preparation' tasks – particularly process mapping, practice alignment and training. The rapid transition from the old system (a business decision, based on saving leasing costs but with substantial technical implications) probably contributed to many of the 'people problems' that occurred later. In particular, the central IT unit felt their advice was being ignored, thus contributing to the complaints about the conduct of the project.

The success of the project was assessed against the following criteria:

- the need for efficient recording, collation, presentation and interpretation of data;
- the need for comprehensive case recording;
- the importance of informing people about policy, strategy and good practice through the provision of clear procedures;
- the recognition that organisational 'intelligence' consists of a combination of hard data and softer information, accumulated and shared through experience.

The project was successful in raising the profile of data management and case recording, and the increase in the user-base was phenomenal (from 15 to over 800). Some teams also benefited from the emphasis on a process-driven method of working to streamline their procedures. However, data and information used to create true organisational intelligence remain negligible.

Analysis of the stakeholders involved in the project yielded the following groups:

- Those who were involved in the project appreciated the challenge and were largely satisfied that they had achieved something innovative and valuable (the project leader and technical and practitioner members of the team).
- Those who felt outside the team had doubts about the project from the outset and declared that the basis of the project was unsound, the conduct unconventional, the exposure too great, but did not generally dispute that the results were good (such as trainers, social services finance and central IT).
- The users, who were varied in their response: each set (clerks, team managers and practitioners) had initial hopes or fears but those who believed in the possibility of systems as a tool for best practice and client benefit generally 'made it work', while others found reasons to object or avoid involvement.

Problems

Some aspects of the project did not go according to plan.

Confidentiality

The policy was for the system to be 'open' to all trained users, in the expectation that access would be self-regulated through applying the same professional standards as those relating to manual records. However, staff still felt that 'electronic access' represented more of a risk than someone 'borrowing' the manual file and this created anxieties for certain groups. During 1994 there were protests from foster parents about their records appearing on the system and this was likely to be even more problematic with more data and information being put on the system in the future.

Training

The intention was to integrate technical training and practice so that staff would be able to appreciate how the system would be able to change working practices. However, there was insufficient practitioner resource and the training was therefore largely technical. Project training was also not integrated with training sessions for other management initiatives.

Project management

A deliberate decision was made to set and achieve milestones, leaving a degree of latitude in how tasks and problems were approached. Milestone planning tends to subordinate the tasks to the goal, thereby underplaying some important risks or areas of uncertainty. Documentation and formality were sometimes sacrificed to move the obstacles faster. This contributed to the anxieties of some stakeholders who prefer a more regulated regime.

Practice issues

The project aimed to map the system to processes as it progressed but this was hindered by debate between teams who all worked differently. Where the project attempted to rule on methods of working, it was open to criticisms of 'technology-driving practice'. However, it was not possible to replicate the existing complex, variable processes without sacrificing consistency, costs and quality improvement.

Management support

Every attempt was made to involve senior management in the project and emphasise their role in setting the strategy, defining information requirements and leading change. However, they ended up largely as bystanders. There were real problems with the following through of initiatives and it was a difficult time for everyone.

Exposing business problems

In mapping the system to the way people worked, it became clear that the introduction of community care was creating pressures. The purchasing strategy was unclear as were the required controls and split of responsibilities between purchasers, commissioning officers, clerical staff and finance, which was causing duplication of work. Arrangements with consumers and suppliers varied from team to team and it was difficult to systematise this variation. Quite clearly, team managers had been left to get on with it in the past and had adopted a variety of approaches.

Furthermore, it was difficult to take an integrated approach to implementation and keep the children's division 'on board'. It appeared that the children's social workers saw themselves and their work as 'different'. It was hard to find 'project champions' in children's services in the way they were beginning to emerge for adult services.

There were problems of data quality arising from an historical indifference to data precision. Social work has been seen and to some extent still is seen as a creative process involving the worker and the consumer.

An independent analysis

Towards the end of the second year of the project an independent review was conducted and certain themes emerged. Insufficient training and hardware contributed to people's resistance to the system, whereas a pilot site with more resources had not experienced this problem. There were insufficient terminals and equitable access had to be assigned. Sharing was difficult, given the design of buildings, and clerical staff did not have sufficient access to word processing. Some participants refused to make any changes to their practice or style of work because they thought it affected their professional autonomy, while others welcomed the system because it 'profession-alised' their work.

The majority of people expressed concern about confidentiality and there were additional concerns about the sharing of sensitive information. However, the majority also felt that the system was potentially a better system because it provided integration and a consistent structure.

The review concluded that there was resistance to the introduction of new technology in relation to social work recording. Feelings were expressed about being given no choice, technology leading practice, no worker involvement, no benefit from training, not enough hardware and inconsistent use by individuals and teams. All of this could potentially lead to cynicism about technology and a return to paper records, gradually eroding progress made to date.

Concluding comments

Users learning to use the system were working in an environment where they were constantly being bombarded by demands for change. Many were seeing their roles transformed almost beyond recognition as the shift began from the traditional social work service to care management and the delivery of resources.

One of the most frustrating elements of the project was that there was so much to gain and yet there were so many obstacles in the short term. Stakeholder analysis revealed some of the conflicting pressures. It would have helped to qualify the goals by specific measures. Standards for case recording and targets for streamlining the client entry process would have been useful, as would questions for management on resourcing. Being able to demonstrate more specific improved capability in these areas might have provided a valuable incentive to 'stick with the vision'.

Social services is a difficult environment in which to introduce practitioner systems because of the required investment in infrastructure and training and the resistance against imposing greater control and accountability on previously autonomous individuals. Every attempt was made to use resistance as a clue to understanding power-bases and political forces at work within the organisation. The impression, however, remains that it is an anomaly for 'caring organisations' to appear to be so intractable in the face of introducing technology which would appear to benefit its consumers.

A key professional dilemma seems to reside in case recording, as evidenced by a reluctance to 'expose' what has been recorded, to record comprehensively and to do so in a managerial manner. Case recording is seen by social workers as a boring chore and as subsidiary to the main work of interacting with the client. However, social workers are increasingly required to communicate effectively with other agencies in complex cases and the absence of such communication has been highlighted as a problem in high-profile failures. They are, however, often under enormous pressure and are more likely to be scapegoats in contentious cases. It is not surprising that they become possessive of what they do. Sophisticated technology makes social work transparent and allows easy access to record-keeping, decision-making and money spent. There is then the further issue of practitioners and managers seeing things from different perspectives and having conflicting priorities.

A common theme is the fear of losing position and seeing one's role being downgraded in the name of 'progress'. This is closely associated with empowerment and control. Empowering can be seen as 'allowing things to get out of control' but the allocation of appropriate responsibility is also important so as not to demotivate people. Resistance to changing established roles and pecking orders is often couched in terms of warnings about loss of control. The nature of monitoring is also important, with the monitoring of conformance not being as effective as the monitoring of outcomes, which must be agreed from the outset.

Finally, there were a number of 'boundary issues'. There was a reluctance by the children's teams to 'lose their identity' by taking on a system which they perceived to be driven by community care. Other boundary issues occurred over the ownership of records between social workers and provider services managing day-to-day issues for the client. Similar struggles are emerging where social services and healthcare are trying to negotiate shared responsibilities.

Divisional rivalries are relatively common in social services. For instance, foster link workers may not communicate well with children's social workers. Similarly, specialist teams providing input to the joint care of a client may not share information. Such polarisations will only serve to exacerbate the difficulties inherent in trying to reframe methods of working.

Table 6.9 summarises the relationship between reactions and refusals, suggesting four types of defensive behaviour. Two (professional dilemma and behavioural defence) are about what an individual thinks they may lose if a change goes ahead and typically involves a 'reaction against' something. The other two (political distaste and boundary defence) are about the lack of gain (in political terms) perceived in a course of action and typically involve a 'refusal to tackle' something.

Case questions

1 What were the main problems associated with the introduction of a sophisticated computer system such as the one in this case?
2 What sort of groundwork do you think would have helped enhance the project outcome?
3 Which cultural and professional issues impinged on the project and to what extent were they detrimental?
4 To what extent do you think organisational fit was achieved in this case?

(Source: adapted from Riley L. and Smith G. (1997)
'Developing and Implementing IS: a Case Study Analysis in Social Services',
Journal of Information Technology, 12(4): 305–321)

Table 6.9 Reactions and refusals: an analysis of organisational defences

Reaction against challenge to traditional social work values	Refusal to tackle major change
Professional dilemma 'This undermines my values'	Political distaste 'I do not have the political will for this battle'
Reaction against challenge to traditional ways of working	Refusal to tackle (cross-organisational) business process issue
Behavioural defence 'This undermines my role'	Boundary defence 'This threatens our sense of who we are, our territory'

References and further reading

Adman P. and Warren L. (2000) 'Participatory Sociotechnical Design of Organisations and Information Systems – an Adaptation of ETHICS Methodology', *Journal of Information Technology*, 15(1), March: 39–51.

Alexander J.W. (1982) 'The Relationship of Technology and Structure to Quality of Care on Nursing Subunits', unpublished doctoral thesis, University of South Carolina: Columbia, SC.

Alexander J.W. and Randolph W.A. (1985) 'The Fit Between Technology and Structure as a Predictor of Performance in Nursing Subunits', *Academy of Management Journal*, 28(4): 844–859.

Angell I.O. and Smithson S. (1991) *Information Systems Management: Opportunities and Risks*, Macmillan: Basingstoke.

Argyres N.S. (1999) 'The Impact of Information Technology on Coordination: Evidence from the B-2 Stealth Bomber', *Organisation Science*, 10(2): 162–180.

Barki H. and Hartwick J. (2001) 'Interpersonal Conflict and Its Management in Information System Development', *MIS Quarterly*, 25(2), June: 195–228.

Barua A. and Ravindran S. (1996) 'Reengineering Information Sharing Behaviour in Organisations', *Journal of Information Technology*, 11(3), September: 261–272.

Baskerville R. and Smithson S. (1995) 'Information Technology and New Organisational Forms: Choosing Chaos Over Panaceas', *European Journal of Information Systems*, 4: 66–73.

Bergeron F. and Raymond L. (1992) 'The Advantages of Electronic Data Interchange', *Data Base*, 23(4), Fall: 19–31.

Blau P.M., Fable C.M., McKingley W. and Tracy P.K. (1976) 'Technology and Organisations in Manufacturing', *Administrative Science Quarterly*, 21: 20–40.

Bowen D.E. and Lawler E.E.I. (1992) 'The Empowerment of Service Workers: What, Why, How and When', *Sloan Management Review*, 33(3): 31–39.

Brown A. (1998) *Organisational Culture*, 2nd edn, Prentice-Hall: Harlow.

Burn J.M. (1996) 'IS Innovation and Organisational Alignment – a Professional Juggling Act', *Journal of Information Technology*, 11(1), March: 3–12.

Burns T. and Stalker G.M. (1961) *The Management of Innovation*, Routledge & Kegan Paul: London, pp. 119–122.

Cabrera A., Cabrera E.F. and Barajas S. (2001) 'The Key Role of Organisational Culture in a Multi-System View of Technology-Driven Change', *International Journal of Information Management*, 21: 245–261.

Ciborra C.U. (1997) 'Improvising in the Shapeless Organisation of the Future' in Sauer C. and Yetton P. (eds) *Steps to the Future: Fresh Thinking on the Management of IT-Based Organisational Transformation*, Jossey-Bass: San Francisco, CA, pp. 257–277.

Clancy J.J. (1989) *The Invisible Powers: the Language of Business*, Lexington Books: Lexington, MA.

Clement A. (1994) 'Computing at Work: Empowering Action by Low-Level Users', *Communications of the ACM*, 37(1): 53–63.

Curry A.C. and Moore C. (2003) 'Assessing Information Culture – an Exploratory Model', *International Journal of Information Management*, 23: 91–110.

Daft R. (1986) *Organisation Theory and Design*, 2nd edn, West Publishing: St Paul, MN.

Daft R. (1994) *Management*, 3rd edn, Dryden Press, Orlando, FL.

Daniel E.M. and Grimshaw D.J. (2002) 'An Exploratory Comparison of Electronic Commerce Adoption in Large and Small Enterprises', *Journal of Information Technology*, 17(3), September: 133–147.

Davis S.M. (1984) *Managing Corporate Culture*, Ballinger: Cambridge, MA.

Deal T.E. and Kennedy A.A. (1982) *Corporate Cultures: the Rites and Rituals of Corporate Life*, Addison-Wesley: Reading, MA.

Dewar R. and Werbel J. (1979) 'Universalistic and Contingency Predictions of Employee Satisfaction and Conflict', *Administrative Science Quarterly*, 24: 426–448.

Dibrell C.C. and Miller T.R. (2002) 'Organisation Design: the Continuing Influence of Information Technology', *Journal of Management History*, 40(6): 620–627.

Drennan D. (1992) *Transforming Company Culture*, McGraw-Hill: London.

Ein-Dor P. and Segev E. (1982) 'Organisational Context and MIS Structure: Some Empirical Evidence', *MIS Quarterly*, 6(3), September: 55–68.

Farbey B., Land F. and Targett D. (1993) ' IT Investment: a Study of Methods and Practice', *Management Today*.

Fiedler K.D., Grover V. and Teng J.T.C. (1996) 'An Empirically Derived Taxonomy of Information Technology Structure and Its Relationship to Organisational Structure', *Journal of MIS*, 13(1), Summer: 9–34.

Finnegan P. and Longaigh S.N. (2002) 'Examining the Effects of Information Technology on Control and Coordination Relationships: an Exploratory Study in Subsidiaries of Pan-National Corporations', *Journal of Information Technology*, 17(3), September: 149–163.

Friel D. (1999) 'Window on the Web', *Business Economics*, 34(1): 67–68.

Fry L.W. (1982) 'Technology-Structure Research: Three Critical Issues', *Academy of Management Journal*, 25: 532–552.

Galbraith J.R. (1973) *Designing Complex Organisations*, Addison-Wesley: Reading, MA.

Galbraith J.R. (1977) *Organisation Design*, Addison-Wesley: Reading, MA.

Gallupe R.B. (1982) 'The Management of Information Systems in Remote Centres', *ASAC Conference*, University of Ottawa, Canada.

Garsombke T.W. and Garsombke D.J. (1989) 'Strategic Implications Facing Small Manufacturers: the Linkage Between Robotization, Computerisation, Automation and Performance', *Journal of Small Business Management*, 27(4), October: 34–44.

Gerwin D. (1981) 'Relationships Between Structure and Technology' in Nystrom P. and Starbuck W. (eds) *Handbook of Organisational Design*, Oxford University Press: Clifton, NJ, pp. 3–39.

Gotlieb C.C. and Borodin A. (1973) *Social Issues in Computing*, Academic Press: New York.

Gremillion L.L. (1984) 'Organisation Size and Information System Use: an Empirical Study', *Journal of MIS*, 1(2), Fall, pp: 4–17.

Hall R.H. (1991) *Organisations, Structures, Processes and Outcomes*, 5th edn, Prentice Hall International: Englewood Cliffs, NJ.

Hampden-Turner C. (1990) *Corporate Culture: From Vicious to Virtuous Circles*, Economist Books: London.

Handy C.B. (1978) *The Gods of Management*, Penguin: Harmondsworth.

Handy C.B. (1985) *Understanding Organisations*, Penguin: Harmondsworth.

Harris M. (1996) 'Organisational Politics, Strategic Change and the Evaluation of CAD', *Journal of Information Technology*, 11(1), March: 51–58.

Harrison R. (1972) 'Understanding Your Organisation's Character', *Harvard Business Review*, 50, May–June: 119–128.

Herzberg F. (1968) 'One More Time: How Do You Motivate Employees?', *Harvard Business Review*, Jan.–Feb.: 53–62.

Hitt L.M. and Brynjolfsson E. (1997) 'Information Technology and Internal Firm Organisation: an Exploratory Analysis', *Journal of MIS*, 14(2): 81–101.

Homburg C., Workman J.P. and Jensen O. (2000) 'Fundamental Changes in Marketing Organisation: the Movement Toward a Customer-Focused Organisational Structure', *Journal of the Academy of Marketing Science*, 28(4): 459–478.

Huber G.P. (1984) 'The Nature and Design of the Post-Industrial Organisation', *Management Science*, 30(8): 928–951.

Jarvenpaa S.L. and Ives B. (1994) 'The Global Network Organisation of the Future: Information Management Opportunities and Challenges', *Journal of MIS*, 10(4): 25–57.

Joyce W., Slocum J.W. and Von Glinow M. (1982) 'Person-Situation Interaction: Competing Models of Fit', *Journal of Occupational Behaviour*, 3: 265–280.

Kambayashi N. and Scarbrough H. (2001) 'Cultural Influences on IT Use Amongst Factory Managers: a UK–Japanese Comparison', *Journal of Information Technology*, 16(4), December: 221–236.

Kanellis P., Lycett M. and Paul R.J. (1999) 'Evaluating Business Information Systems Fit: From Concept to Practical Application', *European Journal of Information Systems*, 8(1): 65–76.

Kendall J.E. and Kendall K.E. (1994) 'Metaphors and Their Meaning for Information Systems Development, *European Journal of Information Systems*, 3(1): 37–47.

Lal M. (1991) 'Organisational Size, Structuring of Activities and Control Information System Sophistication Levels: an Empirical Study', *Management International Review*, 31(2): 101–113.

Leavitt H.J. and Whisler T.L. (1958) 'Management in the 1980s', *Harvard Business Review*, 36, Nov.–Dec.: 41–48.

Lee S. (1991) 'The Impact of Office Information Systems on Potential Power and Influence', *Journal of MIS*, 8(2), Fall: 135–151.

Lehman J.A. (1985) 'Organisational Size and Information System Sophistication', *Journal of MIS*, 11(3), Winter: 78–86.

Leifer R. (1988) 'Matching Computer-Based Information Systems with Organisational Structures', *MIS Quarterly*, 12(1), March: 63–72.

Lucas H.C. and Baroudi J. (1994) 'The Role of Information Technology in Organisation Design', *Journal of MIS*, 10(4), Spring: 9–23.

McGregor D. (1960) *The Human Side of Enterprise*, McGraw-Hill: New York.

Malone T.W. (1997) 'Is Empowerment Just a Fad? Control, Decision Making and IT', *Sloan Management Review*, Winter: 23–35.

Markus M.L. (1983) 'Power, Politics and MIS Implementation', *Communications of the ACM*, 26(6), June: 430–444.

Markus M.L. and Robey D. (1983) 'The Organisational Validity of Management Information Systems', *Human Relations*, 36(3): 203–225.

Maslow A.H. (1943) 'A Theory of Human Motivation', *Psychological Review*, 50: 370–396.

Miles R.E. and Snow C.C. (1995) 'The New Network Firm: a Spherical Structure Built on a Human Investment Philosophy', *Organisational Dynamics*, 23(4): 5–18.

Mintzberg H. (1979) *The Structuring of Organisations*, Prentice-Hall: Englewood Cliffs, NJ.

Morgan G. (1986) *Images of Organisation*, Sage: Beverly Hills, CA.

Mukherji A. (2002) 'The Evolution of Information Systems: Their Impact on Organisations and Structures', *Management Decision*, 40(5): 497–507.

Nunamaker J.F. and Sprague R.H. (1994–1995) 'Special Section: Information Technology and IT Organisational Impact', *Journal of MIS*, 11(3), Winter: 3–6.

O'Donnell D. and Henriksen L.B. (2002) 'Philosophical Foundations for a Critical Evaluation of the Social Impact of ICT', *Journal of Information Technology*, 17(2), June: 89–99.

Olson M.H. and Chervany N.L. (1980) 'The Relationship Between Organisational Characteristics and the Structure of the Information Services Function', *MIS Quarterly*, 4(2), June: 57–68.

Payne R.L. (1990) *The Concepts of Culture and Climate*, Working Paper 202, Manchester Business School: Manchester.

Pedersen J.S. and Sorensen J.S. (1989) *Organisational Cultures in Theory and Practice*, Avebury: Aldershot.

Pepe M. (1999) 'Connectivity is King for VARs', *Computer Reseller News*, 831: 59.

Peppard J.W. (ed.) (1993) *IT Strategy for Business*, Pitman: London.

Proudlock M.J., Phelps B. and Gamble P.R. (1998) 'IS Decision-Making: a Study in Information-Intensive Firms', *Journal of Information Technology*, 13: 55–66.

Psoinos A., Kern T. and Smithson S. (2000) 'An Exploratory Study of Information Systems in Support of Employee Empowerment', *Journal of Information Technology*, 15(3), September: 211–230.

Quinn R.E. and McGrath M.R. (1985) 'The Transformation of Organisational Cultures: a Competing Values Perspective' in Frost P.J., Moore L.F., Louis M.R., Lundberg C.C. and Martin J. (eds) *Organisational Culture*, Sage: Newbury Park, CA, pp. 315–334.

Raymond L. (1990) 'Organisational Context and Information Systems Success: a Contingency Approach', *Journal of MIS*, 6(4), Spring: 5–20.

Raymond L., Pare G. and Bergeron F. (1995) 'Matching Information Technology and Organisational Structure: an Empirical Study with Implications for Performance', *European Journal of Information Systems*, 4: 3–16.

Reich B.H. and Benbasat I. (2000) 'Factors that Influence the Social Dimension of Alignment Between Business and Information Technology Objectives', *MIS Quarterly*, 24(1), March: 81–113.

Robey D. (1981) 'Computer Information Systems and Organisation Structure', *Communications of the ACM*, 24(10), October: 679–687.

Robey D., Smith L.A. and Vijayasarathy L.R. (1993) 'Perceptions of Conflict and Success in Information Systems Development Projects', *Journal of MIS*, 10(1), Summer: 123–139.

Ryker R. and Nath R. (1995) 'An Empirical Examination of the Impact of Computer Information Systems on Users', *Information and Management*, 29(4): 207–214.

Sahay S., Palit M. and Robey D. (1994) 'A Relativist Approach to Studying the Social Construction of Information Technology', *European Journal of Information Systems*, 3(4): 248–258.

Schein E.H. (1981) 'Does Japanese Management Style Have a Message for American Managers?', *Sloan Management Review*, 23: 55–68.

Schein E.H. (1985) *Organisational Culture and Leadership*, Jossey-Bass: San Francisco, CA.

Schein E.H. (1996) 'Culture: The Missing Concept in Organizational Studies', *Administrative Science Quarterly*, 41: 229–24.

Scholz C. (1987) 'Corporate Culture and Strategy – the Problem of Strategic Fit', *Long Range Planning*, 20(4): 78–87.

Selznick P. (1957) *Leadership and Administration*, Peterson: Evanston, IL.

Sillince J.A.A. and Mouakket S. (1998) 'Divisive and Integrative Political Strategies in the IS Adaptation Process: the MAC Initiative', *European Journal of Information Systems*, 7(1): 46–60.

Simons R. (1995) 'Control in an Age of Empowerment', *Harvard Business Review*, 73(2): 80–88.

Van Der Zee J.T.M. and De Jong B. (1999) 'Alignment is not Enough: Integrating Business and Information Technology Management with the Balanced Business Scorecard', *Journal of MIS*, 16(2), Fall: 137–156.

Veiga J.F., Floyd S. and Dechant K. (2001) 'Towards Modelling the Effects of National Culture on IT Implementation and Acceptance', *Journal of Information Technology*, 16(3), September: 145–158.

Venkatesh V. (1999) 'Creation of Favorable User Perceptions: Exploring the Role of Intrinsic Motivation', *MIS Quarterly*, 23(2), June: 239–260.

Wareham J., Neergard P. and Bjorn-Andersen N. (1997) 'Radical Organisational Transformation: Aligning IT, Organisation and Human Resources to Boost the Value of IT', in Galliers R., Carlsson S. and Loebbeckeet C. *et al.* (eds), *Proceedings of the Fifth European Conference on Information Systems*, ECIS: Cork, Ireland, pp. 1393–1406.

Watson R.T., Kelly G.G., Galliers R.D. and Brancheau J.C. (1997) 'Key Issues in Information Systems Management: an International Perspective', *Journal of MIS*, 13(4), Spring: 91–115.

Wetherbe J.C. and Whitehead C.J. (1977) 'A Contingency View of Managing the Data Processing Organisation', *MIS Quarterly*, 1(1), March: 19–25.

Whisler T.L. (1970) *The Impact of Computers on Organisations*, Praeger: New York.

Yadav S.B. (1985) 'Classifying An Organisation to Identify Its Information Requirements: A Comprehensive Framework', *Journal of MIS*, 11(1), Summer: 39–60.

Chapter 7

Information systems and organisational change

....

Learning objectives

After reading this chapter you should be able to:

- discuss the nature of organisational change;
- understand the forces that influence change;
- describe how IS can support organisational change, including business process re-engineering;
- describe the major organisational factors to consider when implementing an IS solution.

Introduction

The various elements of an organisation must work together to achieve corporate goals. The people, resources and management styles all need to coordinate to optimise efficiency and effectiveness. Critical issues arise that need careful management and these issues are frequently associated with change.

If the environment were free from uncertainty, organisations would not need to change. The reality is, however, that both the extent and rate of change are at present unprecedented and changes within and outwith organisations are relentless. Technological advances and the deregulation of banking and financial services are two examples of promoters of change.

Organisations which have identified the need to change have to decide how that change is going to come about and this will depend on which aspects of their business have been prioritised for change.

There are a number of reasons why change becomes necessary and these may shape the particular approach required. Both evolutionary change, characterised by continuous improvement over time, and revolutionary change, which involves organisational transformation, are discussed. Whatever the type of change or the motivating forces, some resistance will almost inevitably be encountered. The implications of change must be anticipated and appropriately managed.

Information systems and technology are frequently associated with organisational change. They may shape, support or hinder change.

What is organisational change?

The concept of the organisational life cycle provides a useful context in which to consider organisational change. There are four main stages of organisational development (Daft, 1995), which are:

1 The entrepreneurial stage, characterised by creative energy, the desire for survival, an informal structure and probably long working hours. Organisational growth and the need for leadership and control can frequently give rise to a crisis situation.
2 The collectivity stage. If the leadership crisis is overcome, the organisation develops goals, objectives, lines of control and authority that lead to job specialisation and areas of responsibility. As middle and line managers become more confident and competent, the need for autonomy and delegation arises. The question of the extent of supervision required from senior management may create problems.
3 The formalisation stage involves the emergence of formal procedures and control systems to ensure that everyone is working to achieve organisational objectives and what is best for the company as a whole. A crisis point can be reached when there is too much bureaucracy, different functions resent intrusion from other areas and innovation may be stifled.
4 The elaboration stage introduces teamwork and collaboration, with staff working in cross-functional task teams and some simplification of formal systems tending to occur. A crisis may be reached as the organisation becomes slow, complacent and unable to sustain its position in the marketplace.

Without some form of organisational revitalisation a company at this stage may well go into a decline.

Change may well be linked to organisational growth or decline. Change is also to do with surviving better in the environment and making sure organisational goals are the right ones. Both external and internal forces motivate change and create a situation where individuals and organisations are constantly in a state of flux and are constantly learning.

Organisations are born, change and die. They can be created by entrepreneurs, by legislation or by other organisations in the form of subsidiaries. The rate of organisational birth will be affected by the social environment and the characteristics of the founder.

Once created, organisations change. They adapt to their environment or are selected by the environment for survival. There are four basic principles that determine which organisations survive and which do not:

1 Whether change is intended and purposeful or occurring blindly and by accident.
2 Whether change enables an organisation to acquire resources from the environment.
3 Whether necessary skills and competencies are successfully retained and/or passed on to others. Such competencies are retained by organisational information flows and may become highly valuable or obsolete as a result of technological change.
4 Whether an organisation competes successfully with others for scarce resources and retains a strong position within its market niche.

Organisational change occurs as a result of environmental forces, by accident and as a result of rational planning. Some organisations then decline and die. The decline process often occurs in stages and these are shown in Figure 7.1. The first stage occurs when the organisation cannot see that it is beginning to decline. The second stage sees a recognition that change is needed but no action is taken. At the third stage actions are taken, but not the right ones. Stage four is crisis and stage five is dissolution or death.

Innovation represents change with a narrower focus, whereby maybe only a small part of the organisation is affected. Innovations are departures from state of the art practices or technologies, the latter often adopted at a faster rate.

Innovations are more or less radical. They may be planned through research and development, unplanned, when extra available or slack resources are used in an innovative way or imposed upon the organisation, such as technological innovation in an industry sector dictating to individual companies within that sector. An example might be Britannia Life (investment, fund management) installing the latest software package for trading on the Stock Market and prompting similar organisations to follow them as soon as possible.

What is to be changed?

Structure and culture

In the previous chapter organisational structure and culture were extensively discussed with regard to information systems. The concept of organisational 'fit' is very important and must be determined by strategic objectives if the company is to make successful progress in the right business direction. An organisation may be changed in a number of ways in terms of its structure:

- It needs to have an appropriate shape and physical design, which may involve changing the extent to which it is centralised/decentralised and the hierarchical levels, in terms of layers of management.
- It has to be in the right location. This may involve the creation of subsidiaries or independent business units in remote areas.
- It has to have the right type of ownership. It may benefit from privatisation or nationalisation. A privately owned company may need to become a public limited one.

Culture has to fit with structure. An atmosphere of informality, trust and absence of strict control works better in an organisation with a professional, motivated, innovative workforce. What is more, if radical performance improvement requires collaboration, teamwork and empowerment, strong departmental or functional loyalties may become an obstacle. If the focus is on customer and supplier relationships, a culture of stringent cost control will create conflicts. Organisational culture is most import-

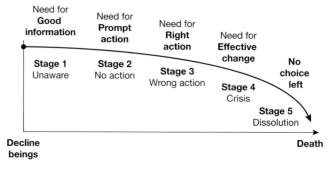

Figure 7.1 Organisational decline

Source: adapted from Weitzel and Jonsson (1989)

ant when implementing technological innovations, which may impact the very nature of work being done by imposing new behavioural requirements on users (Cabrera *et al.*, 2001). Aligning technology and culture is not an easy task and organisational effectiveness is a function of how well the social and technical systems are designed with respect to one another and the demands of the external market.

People

The balance within the workforce may need altering and redundancies may be necessary as a result. The skills-base may be inadequate and training of various types and at various levels of the organisation may be needed, particularly if new technology is to be introduced. The core workforce may have to shrink to reduce overhead costs and make way for contracting out to independent agencies or specialised consultancies. Location of workers has become increasingly flexible as a result of new communication technologies, resulting in teleworking and flexible hours of working. More in the way of networking may improve the quality of working life by allowing people to work from home and eliminating the need to face rush-hour traffic each day to travel into heavily populated metropolitan areas.

Processes

Business processes have internal or external customers and cross-organisational boundaries. Their change is discussed in some detail throughout this chapter in business process re-engineering. At this point it suffices to say that there are different business processes that may require change (see also Chapter 2, Figure 2.14). These are (Murdick and Munson, 1986):

Core processes, which are central to the functioning of the business and relate directly to external customers. They are usually the primary activities in the organisational value chain, e.g. sales, operations.

Support processes have internal customers and provide support for the core processes. They are usually the secondary activities in the organisational value chain, e.g. administration, finance.

Business network processes, which often extend beyond the organisational boundary to suppliers, customers and other stakeholders, e.g. outbound logistics.

Management processes, which are those used by an organisation to plan, organise and control resources and then make decisions, e.g. senior management review.

Technology

Information technology supports and facilitates change in a number of ways, such as ERP, which serve to integrate internal operations, and CRM, which serve to integrate the organisation and its customers, with the aim of increasing value for both. Two particular aspects of technology worth noting at this point are the following:

1 The potential of telecommunications technology to increase the scope of organisational and inter-organisational coordination and reduce the costs of that coordination.
2 The potential of shared information systems and databases to provide relevant information in a timely way to those who need it.

Reasons for organisational change

The reasons why organisations change emerge from both internal and external sources. The organisation may need to redefine its strategy, update plant and equipment or alter the balance of its workforce. Internal forces of change often relate to improving organisational effectiveness. External forces of change come from the environment in which the organisation exists, from the marketplace, the economy, legislation and government policies of the day.

Internal reasons for change

Organisations can be structured and restructured in different ways according to the decision-making and political processes within their own boundaries. As there is a reciprocal relationship between structure and strategy, a major task for senior managers is to determine the most appropriate organisational form for various situations.

If organisational effectiveness is to be improved to ensure future survival, *goals* need to be the right ones and need to be met. *Resources* have to be adequate and have to be distributed in the right way across the organisation. *Managers* and *staff* may be inadequately trained, demotivated and dissatisfied and lack cohesion. Lines of *communication* and *information flows* may be unsatisfactory or inappropriate. There may be contradictions and conflicts within and between the different elements of the organisation, such as strategic objectives, critical success factors, management style, degree of centralisation and information flows and networks.

Resources have to be adequate and have to be appropriately distributed across the organisation. Resources may decrease or increase and need to be reallocated, restricted or concentrated in certain business priority areas as part of a change process.

Technology may be introduced into the organisation. It may be an extension to what was already there or may be completely new. In either case, changes within the organisation will be triggered.

People within an organisation are themselves a stimulus for internal change. Redundancies require redeployment of tasks and responsibilities and skills shortages require training and staff development to be updated.

Priorities may need to be changed if, for example, organisational targets are not being achieved. Priority activities relate to critical success factors and organisational goals. The necessity to readjust internal priorities is a powerful force for change which will affect internal control mechanisms.

Problems of different types arise within organisations and these are often powerful motivators of change. Wastage costs may be seriously affecting profits, and information flows may be inadequate, resulting in inefficiencies and poor communication. Increasing customer dissatisfaction requires attention as does an unprofitable product range. Marks & Spencer have had to reconfigure their product range quite drastically on more than one occasion to realign the organisation with market demand.

The internal forces of change centre on the notion of 'fit'. Culture and structure must dovetail with management tasks and behaviour to produce a cohesive, integrated, cooperative whole. Mismatching elements, internal inefficiency and ineffectiveness will transgress the organisational boundary, creating negative external perceptions among customers, suppliers and stakeholders in general.

Internal change may start from a new business vision, translated into aims and objectives to ensure future success. An example is given in Figure 7.2.

External reasons for change

The external environment accounts for a great deal of organisational change, change which is imposed and which is more difficult, if not

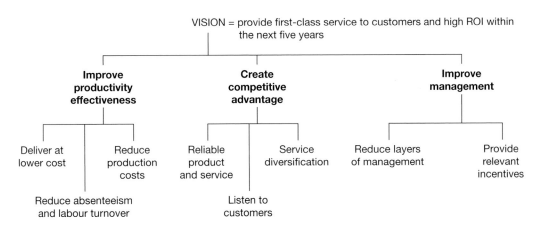

Figure 7.2 Developing a new business vision

impossible, to control. There may also be sequential changes that arise as a result of previous reasons for change.

The culture in different countries affects local operation of companies. Multinationals have to be aware of the necessity to take an entirely different business approach when establishing subsidiaries in the USA, Japan, China and Europe. Culture impacts significantly on local business behaviour/protocol and on strategies for the future.

Demographic trends are predictors of market opportunities which bring about change. The need to cater for an increasing ageing population is one factor and the location of organisations in growing or declining metropolitan areas is another. The greater sophistication of the requirements of the young upwardly mobile population has created opportunities for organisations to occupy select market niches.

Legislation in force is a powerful motivator for change. Organisations are having to tackle dramatic changes of various kinds in response to health and safety requirements and the Environmental Protection and Disability Discrimination Acts.

The political climate brings about the legislation affecting organisations, and political pressures will reduce or boost investment in different industry sectors. Reduction in public spending and increasing privatisation are both examples of powerful external forces of change.

The economy will shape the ways organisations operate in terms of confidence in times of boom and rationalisation in periods of recession. Interest rates and currency exchange fluctuations will dramatically alter organisational business policies.

Technological advances have created numerous opportunities for organisations which can capitalise on their use, but pose threats for those who lag behind, especially if the particular industry sector is heavily dependent on up-to-date technology, such as in the financial services sector.

Competition and increasing customer demands have generated very powerful forces of change. Customers are taking charge and their requirements must be met if organisations wish to stay in business in the longer term. Competition has intensified to the extent where companies must work both harder and smarter to stay ahead of the game.

Inter-organisational relationships create powerful synergies, particularly with the help of new communication technologies. Developing these relationships is an increasingly important factor in doing business in the longer term. Opportunities are presented to those who can respond well to the challenge, but necessary changes may give rise to increasing organisational complexity, unless well handled.

Public opinion will shape and prompt change, often with respect to issues of the day. For example, a perceived fall in educational standards provoked the introduction of the National Curriculum in the UK. Long working hours of junior doctors and the shortage of hospital beds have motivated public opinion to instigate change in the UK health care sector. The increasing importance of environmental issues has also provoked corporate responses to maintain favourable public perceptions.

Forces for and against change

Managing or even just coping with change is a complex problem for people and organisations (Steiner, 2001) and some researchers have looked at the introduction of new technology for answers to the problem (Jih and Owings, 1995; Levin, 1997; Makridakis, 1995; Onstad, 1995). Many see change as a threat because the outcome is less certain than leaving things as they are (Fox-Wolfgramm *et al.*, 1998; Greve, 1998) and suggestions have been made that the three main obstacles to change are cost, workload (Zaltman and Duncan, 1977) and legislation (Kotter and Schlesinger, 1979). Some see change programmes as one more thing to cope with when there are already insufficient hours to do what is deemed to be important (Kanter, 1995). Market conditions have also been cited as a barrier to change (Sachwald, 1998), but it is often more likely that they have forced organisations to change rather than actually preventing it. A

study by Hoag *et al.* (2002) has shown that, rather than cost, workload and legislation being the prime obstacles to change, it tends rather more to be cultural entrenchment created by a dysfunctional management which precludes organisations from experiencing positive change.

The introduction of computerised information systems can pose threats and give rise to resistance to change (Brown *et al.*, 2002). Concentration often focuses on technological changes and the need for training programmes to address skills and knowledge gaps. Such management and training programmes may overlook potential social changes and threats to groups or individuals in the organisation. Figure 7.3 shows some of the forces for change and some of the resistors pushing in the opposite direction.

Resistance to change can emerge for the following reasons:

- change threatens the status quo (Beer, 1980; Hannan and Freeman, 1988; Spector, 1989);
- interpersonal relationships change, with the result that social and informal groups are split up (O'Toole, 1995);
- the new information system may alter the balance of power between superiors and subordinates (Block, 1993);
- the information system may demand more coordinated action in a shorter time-frame;
- there arises a need to become more computer-literate and more capable of handling and understanding technical skills (Morris and Raben, 1995; O'Toole, 1995);
- there may be real or perceived threats to status or ego (Morris and Raben, 1995);
- automation may reduce job satisfaction or cause redundancy.

As with all change, the introduction of a new CBIS is likely to meet with some resistance. The nature and source of this resistance will depend

Forces for change	Forces resisting change
New technological opportunities	Fear of change
New skills	Complacency
Greater job satisfaction	Confidence in current skills
More responsibility	Threat to ego
Job made easier	Threat to status quo
Competitive advantage	Higher workload
Corporate survival	More demanding job

Figure 7.3 Forces for and against change
Source: adapted from Martin and Powell (1992)

very much on what has prompted the system's implementation. One factor which has a strong influence on the level of resistance is the source of the idea for the system. This 'trigger of change', as it is called by Skidmore and Wroe (1988), can be positive, negative or neutral.

Positive triggers are characterised by ownership by the users of the system. Having identified a problem with their own way of working, which lends itself to a computer-based solution, the users will happily accept such a solution. This may well be the case if the task or activity is tedious and/or repetitive. This ownership of the system leads to low resistance to its introduction, as users can foresee an improvement in their job satisfaction.

Negative triggers are characterised by lack of ownership, with the proposed system being imposed on the users. At best this can mean that the system is seen as unnecessary, and at worst detrimental to the users' job satisfaction or security. Such situations frequently lead to opposition to the system, either active defence against the perceived threat or passive lack of interest.

Neutral triggers are characterised by both a lack of ownership and a lack of threat. Typically, the

systems involved are required because of demands imposed from outside the organisation, such as new legislation. In this case, active resistance is likely to be low, but passive resistance may be a problem.

Whatever the cause, resistance to the implementation of a new computer system can usually be addressed by involving users in the process. The more that users can feel that they own the system, through involvement at all stages, from planning through development and beyond, the less likely resistance will be encountered. Similarly, the more security that users receive in terms of training, documentation and ongoing support, the safer they feel, and the more positively they will respond.

Managing organisational change

It is clear that the impetus for change comes from a number of sources, both within and outwith the organisation. More often than not, change will occur for a combination of reasons and it may then be difficult to decide where to begin and what the main priorities are. The questions which have to be answered are:

- What is to be changed?
- How is change to occur?

What is to be changed has been examined on pp. 198–199. We have now to address the management issues associated with change and how change is to occur, i.e. what types of change occur?

Change management has a cost. Changing aspects of the organisation, such as structure and culture, may result in additional training, redundancies, investment in new machinery and technology and reduced efficiency during the periods of change. Managing change well helps to bolster efficiency and keep the costs of change to a minimum.

Management

Given that there is no unique solution to tackling change, managers and developers need to be prepared to adapt every management technique and every potential use of IS/IT to match the culture of the organisation. Often those promoting new techniques and technologies fail to prepare managers and developers for the challenges and complications that lie ahead. The development of a new organic organisation to replace the old bureaucratic hierarchy may distort long-standing relationships between staff, now faced with much more impersonal networked CBIS. Not only are there the traditional organisational problems to deal with, but new problems have to be managed that may relate to the dedication and attention needed to make the new systems work, and to staff technical skills shortages. Management has to be ready to adapt to further innovation and modify original approaches as systems development and implementation progress.

Nowadays, the users are often the leaders and instigators of new IS and IT rather than the managers, who may be unwilling participants in the process of change. Management needs to help promote the right interactive impact of IS and IT among and between different elements of the organisation as a whole – by no means an inconsiderable feat! Rather than attempting to cloister IS and IT development and implementation within a specialist area of the business, it is the managing of information, knowledge and harmonious change that is important to the organisation of the twenty-first century.

A new management perspective needs to evolve, whereby people's roles, in terms of information processes, are better understood. If the IS and IT benefits are to be fully gained, 'hybrid' managers must be recognised and encouraged who possess good business and technical skills. Grasping the opportunities of managing information in new ways must go hand-in-hand with a thorough understanding of the way business is done or can be done more efficiently and effectively in the future.

Change management involves educating and training staff so that they can play a full and satisfying role in creating new working practices. Managers need to understand the relevant timing points for change, keep staff well informed and build on cultural strengths to be able to communicate more effectively the pros and cons of IS and IT implementation as an intricate part of the change process.

Three forces drive the organisations of today into new territory: customers, competition and change. The transition from an industrial to an information economy, increasing customer demand, constant changes in technology and phenomenal competitive pressures have all generated powerful forces of change. Change has become a constant factor of life, so the ability to cope with it is no longer optional. Managing the change process is often long and involved. It must be followed through to ensure effective outcomes. Change agents need to manage the process and these may be managers, specialists or external consultants.

People issues

People need to learn to work together more effectively, which may involve changing behaviour and attitudes and improving communication skills. It is often desirable to try and help people express their ideas and feelings more freely, as well as learn how to empathise more readily with others. Listening and conflict resolution skills may require improvement, and tolerance of individual differences may need to be enhanced. Insightful IS/IT leaders recognise that the greatest impediments to success are often related to people rather than to systems. What is not so clear, however, is exactly how to leverage human capital in support of business needs (Roepke *et al.*, 2000).

Teambuilding training is designed through high interaction to help members of a team learn to trust one another and develop interpersonal relationships. Such training has proven highly positive to date, particularly as it is often enjoyable and helps participants to appreciate the added advantages of interacting more readily and consistently with one another.

Planning and coordination

The change management process needs to be monitored and amended along the way to identify problems and clarify key issues for future planning and coordination. Survey feedback helps assess intra-organisational attitudes and perceptions on a range of relevant topics, such as decision-making practices, communication effectiveness, information availability, job satisfaction and coordination between business units or functions.

Managers need help to understand and act upon process events such as workflow, formal information management and relationships between staff, often aided by an external consultant. Managers need to make diagnoses on processes in need of improvement, so that problems can be solved without necessarily enlisting specialist help.

Structure

Structure of organisations may require modification. Structural components, such as complexity, formalisation and introducing more rules and procedures may have imposed too much control, while increased decentralisation may speed up the decision-making process. Structural design might need to change from a functional or product structure to a matrix design (see also Chapter 2). Jobs or work schedules may also need to be revised to improve motivation and increase skill flexibility.

Technology

Technological changes usually involve the introduction of new equipment, tools or operating methods by means of automation or computerisation. The need to compete more effectively or respond to industrial innovations are powerful forces for technological changes. Automatic mail sorters and the use of robots in manufacturing cars are examples of responses to the need for such change. Similarly, Electronic Data Interchange and bar-coding systems provide instant inventory and sales data for a variety of retailers, such as supermarkets and DIY stores. Managing change is also about stimulating creativity and innovation by developing novel approaches to tackling issues or unique solutions to problems. By taking a creative idea and turning it into a useful product, service or method of operation, a profitable outcome may result. The 3M Company managed change by being innovative in producing Post-it notes, Scotch-Guard protection for a variety of materials and nappies with an elasticated waist for better fit.

Types of organisational change (how change can occur)

Change comes about in a number of ways, but there are two main approaches to change, which are:

1 evolutionary change
2 revolutionary change

The approach adopted by an organisation will depend on a variety of factors, such as external pressures, industry sector and urgency of the need for change. Whatever the approach, change has to be planned and the consequences evaluated upfront so that staff are not faced with sudden unpleasant shocks. The consequences of change are more often than not a mix of positive and negative outcomes. The aim is to ensure that the positive outweighs the negative. Positive consequences of change may include increased profitability, productivity, flexibility and competitiveness in the marketplace, but they may be accompanied by staff redundancies and uncertainties as to their altered roles in the company. Consequences of change relate directly to reasons for change. It is generally better to be open and honest about change, rather than paint a rosy picture

that then ends in disappointments. Figure 7.4 illustrates the 'what' and 'how' of organisational change.

The scale of organisational change varies and this in turn will influence the approach needed. Large scale, radical change is risky but may lead to a high return. Change on a smaller scale may be possible over a longer time period, but competitive pressure may force the pace of change on no matter what scale. Organisations concentrate their first efforts where change is most needed, such as organisational structure, staffing, operations, product range, but the approach then adopted will be either evolutionary or revolutionary.

Evolutionary change

Evolutionary change, as its name suggests, refers to a change process that evolves over time, gradually rather than dramatically or radically. It may take the form of a series of projects carried out by task teams, followed by absorption of new work processes into everyday working life over a period of time.

An example of this type of change is total quality management, which is a process of continuous improvement over a number of years. The underlying principle is that a thousand

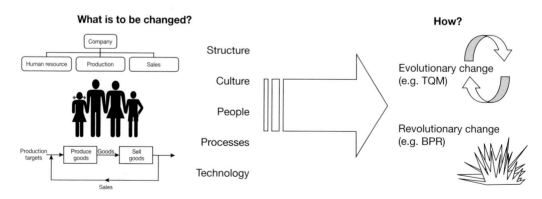

Figure 7.4 The what and the how of organisational change

small incremental steps in the improvement process are of greater value than one single quantum leap. The aim is to make total quality part of every activity in the organisation and to enlist commitment to getting things done right first time and taking on responsibility for one's own quality of work. Commitment is not something that can be gained quickly, nor does the habit of building quality into activities and tasks become ingrained over night! Change of this kind takes time and demands sustained effort to reach a successful outcome.

The impetus for evolutionary change, such as TQM, may be the need for greater efficiency and effectiveness, the desire for better productivity or the wish to change the corporate culture. Staff morale and motivation may need to be improved and absenteeism and labour turnover reduced. Changing corporate culture is neither quick nor easy. Service organisations, which have worked at it over time, have however seen considerable benefits, particularly in terms of more effective service delivery, enhanced customer satisfaction levels and good staff relations. Figure 7.5 provides a useful model for the various activities embraced by TQM. Some or all of them may be undertaken at different time intervals and in varying order of priority.

Revolutionary change

Unlike evolutionary change, revolutionary change is dramatic and intends to be achievable within a relatively restricted time interval. The

The Life Administration group of the Prudential Assurance Co. Ltd had a business plan in May 1989 that defined key business targets and activities to be undertaken over a three-year time frame (1990–1992). Extensive market research was carried out as part of the planning process. Two main conclusions were drawn as a result:

- Customers' requirements were defined, but performance could be improved.
- Life Administration's productivity needed to increase if its policy holders were to receive first-class returns on their investments. Market trends seemed to be indicating that current staffing levels could not be sustained in the future.

The decision was made to implement a Total Quality Management (TQM) programme, known as the Way of Life. Targets were set for staff numbers, cost and productivity. Efficiency and effectiveness became the key driving forces and a team of managers acted as facilitators to plan and support the initiative. These managers developed the Life Administration mission statement and the TQM programme, which consisted of the following elements:

- management involvement and commitment;
- measurement of staff perceptions;
- reward and recognition;
- transition from a traditional culture to a participative team-working culture.

Source: Oakland J.S. and
Porter L.J. (1994)

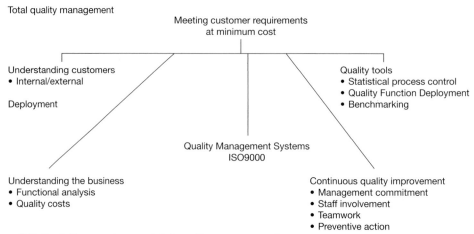

Figure 7.5 Evolutionary change: total quality management
Source: adapted from Munro-Faure and Munro-Faure (1993)

Dealing with change is not just confined to the private sector; indeed there are possibly more challenging environments in the public sector where profit is not the main aim. Gowrie Care, a not-for-profit care organisation providing a range of services to the public sector, is a good example of an organisation that is constantly dealing with change. The environment within which they operate is typified by constant change; from the short-term funding provided by local authorities to the service users they assist. The service users are people who can have mental health problems, drugs issues, or alcohol problems and typically have what can be described as 'chaotic lifestyles'. Designing and providing services for a sector of society that is usually forgotten is in itself a challenge. Change is constant. Gowrie have to deal (sometimes in partnership) with a number of government agencies; social work departments and health boards, all of whom have their own agenda and priorities. When asked to deliver a service the funding will be for a finite period and the design and implementation period could be very short. Gowrie's priority is to provide a high quality of care to the service user and this is something that has typified their approach from the start. One of the ways in which they achieve this is to provide constant training and supervision to their staff in conjunction with a superior level of remuneration in comparison to other care providers in what is traditionally a poorly paid job sector. The workforce is also trained in the organisation's ethos and culture, which centres on the provision of the best quality of care for the service users that they support which requires a high level of trust and commitment. The majority of staff find this approach works very well and there is a high level of staff retention. The organisation places a lot of emphasis on its recruitment function and sees this as a keystone of their success. This has led to a massive expansion of the organisation as local authorities have realised that Gowrie provides a higher quality of service and other voluntary organisations have also been keen to be part of their operation. This has lead to a number of mergers and takeovers which again have led to further changes in the organisation.

impetus for this type of change is often more imperative and frequently triggered by external forces that cannot be controlled, such as sharp competition and new legislation. Organisational response needs to be immediate and corporate survival may be in jeopardy if radical change is not undertaken. Table 7.1 contrasts some elements of continuous improvement and business process re-engineering (BPR), which is an example of revolutionary change.

Business process re-engineering

There is some debate as to whether BPR involves evolutionary or revolutionary change. Arguably the Japanese have only ever engaged in continuous incremental change rather than anything dramatic or radical. 'Kaizan' refers to many small steps along a journey to improvement and has been incorporated into the TQM concept and philosophy adopted by Western companies. The reality is that continuous improvement has been sustained over time by the Japanese, who have effectively redesigned their organisations to stay ahead of the field; their Western competitors, however, need to embark on something more drastic to catch up. Gradualist initiatives may be insufficient for contemporary survival and radical change is

now deemed the only route to realising the huge potential of computers and telecommunications to succeed in business. The Midland Bank, for example, having decided that their existing organisational design was inadequate for the purpose of offering good home-banking services, created First Direct. This radical redesign of the business entailed an independent entity able to articulate a vision and objectives specifically to tackle the way forward.

While definitions of BPR may vary, it typically has four critical characteristics:

1 It attempts to achieve dramatic improvements in performance.
2 It involves radical departure from existing practices.
3 It is usually enabled by information technology.
4 It is a deliberate and planned endeavour (Alter, 2002; Hammer, 1990; Venkatraman, 1991).

These four elements of BPR can be illustrated in the box on p. 210.

BPR involves a critical analysis and radical redesign of work-flows and business processes in order to improve performance dramatically where it matters most. Both the physical and

Table 7.1 Continuous improvement/BPR – evolutionary/revolutionary change

Element	Continuous improvement	BPR
Change	Incremental	Quantum leap
Focus	Current practice	Fresh start
Scope	Function by function	Cross-functional
Participation	Bottom-up	Top-down
Risk/rewards	Low/moderate	High
Type of change	Work design	Structure, culture
Role of IT	Non-essential	Key enabler

Source: adapted from Earl (1994: 11)

The deliberate plan to reengineer accounts payable at Ford came about upon the realisation that Mazda used only five accounts payable employees. The old process had the purchasing department authorise a purchase, send an invoice to accounts payable and the supplier. Inventory then sent a copy of the receiving document to accounts payable and the supplier's invoice was then matched to the purchase order and receiving document. The use of a shared database enabled all parties involved in the process to access the purchase order and any information on its status without the need to match documents. Ford reengineered the process, eliminating the time-consuming matching of documents, reduced its workforce by 75% and reaped dramatic cost savings.

(Source: adapted from Hammer, 1990)

informational aspects of business processes need to be considered, with particular regard to the information-processing activities. Re-engineering has provided a means for organisations to delineate their structure as they become more adaptable to the task environment (Dibrell and Miller, 2002). Huff (1992) sees the basic concept behind re-engineering as the reorganisation of tasks using IT to automate processes, while Hammer (1990) regards re-engineering as involving a change of mindset, challenging old assumptions and shedding the rules leading to organisational underperformance. Hammer and Champy (1993) suggested that an organisation should focus on larger objectives by embracing technology and recog-

nised that IT plays a critical role. IT staff act as catalysts in the re-engineering process, providing input as to how to use IT most effectively.

The assumption is that BPR improves competitive capability by combining radical operational changes, i.e. doing things more efficiently, with new strategies, i.e. more effective approaches. The aim of BPR is to transform the organisational resources of materials, labour and data into value-added outputs of products, services and information that are important to both internal and external customers. A process orientation replaces a functional orientation, whereby the current value and potential improvement of each business process are highlighted for consideration.

IBM Credit introduced a control desk to keep track of all requests. An administrator recorded completion of each stage and passed it on. The effect was twofold: overall request processing increased to an average of seven days, but the company could account for the whereabouts of requests in the system. The timing was the problem and the process needed a detailed examination followed by a major change. The original process had been designed to deal with difficult requests and each one had been treated as unique. It transpired, however, that many of the requests were straightforward and that databases and spreadsheets could be used by trained individuals. Consequently, the specialists were replaced by generalists who processed the requests from start to finish using a new computer system, with the average time of seven days being reduced to four hours.

Accounting systems at the National Savings Agency were computerised subsequent to the agency moving from being a government department to an executive agency responsible to the Treasury. The National Audit Office, the public spending watchdog, found errors in the accounts, which had culminated in a suspense account which should have been in credit appearing to show a deficit of £37m. Apparently, control systems were so poor that it was impossible to distinguish whether the string of mistakes had been made as a result of computer error, human error or fraud. The most likely probability was as a result of a computer malfunction. What is more, the absence of a clear trail from the individual customer transactions into the financial accounting systems meant that it was very difficult for management to establish the integrity of financial accounting systems information. The National Savings Agency had to issue strong reassurances to customers that their money was 100 per cent secure and that the system failure was being seriously and conscientiously addressed.

Source: *Financial Times*, 25 October 1996

BPR challenges established ways of operating and doing business. Managers must rethink objectives and activities; determine key business processes from the customers' viewpoint and then model new approaches to meet their needs. Specific aims may be cost reduction, quicker response, improved productivity or flexibility. Many processes may need to be redesigned from scratch, while others may need merely fine tuning. Processes that add no or insufficient value need to be eliminated. Outdated processes need to make way for innovative ones and multi-disciplinary task teams may be needed to breach functional barriers. Undertaking BPR involves potential risks and cannot be casually approached if it is to succeed. The seven stages to BPR success are detailed below:

1 confirm business vision and customer values
2 identify aims for each process
3 evaluate effectiveness of existing processes
4 set new performance standards and targets
5 redesign the business processes
6 implement the redesigned processes
7 evaluate process performance and refine processes

Three of the most common reasons for BPR failure are the following:

1 lack of senior management commitment
2 poor communication among those involved in BPR
3 poor implementation of the redesigned processes

These problems relate largely to inadequate understanding and poor management of organisational change. Both technological and human change have to be managed simultaneously: structures and policies have to fit with technological change and staff have to accept organisational change. Fear, anxiety and additional job responsibilities can all create problems, while the increasing use of IS/IT may arouse suspicions of staff monitoring and even workforce reductions. The preceding boxed example illustrates a failed BPR project. Table 7.2 illustrates these potential problems in a bit more detail.

It is clear from the table that problems come from a combination of organisational, technological and project management sources. Organisational change is complex and that

Table 7.2 Potential problems in BPR implementation

Problem type	Examples of problems
Management support	Lack of top management support for new values and beliefs Lack of senior management leadership Lack of BPR champion Lack of top management understanding of BPR
Technological competence	Lack of IT expertise Limited telecommunication infrastructure Limited database infrastructure Lack of IS participation and assistance in BPR
Process delineation	Scope of re-engineered process inappropriately defined Failure to identify process owners Difficulty in establishing performance improvement goals
Project planning	Lack of strategic vision Lack of appropriate planning Lack of alignment between corporate planning and IT planning
Change management	Failure to anticipate and plan for organisational resistance to change Absence of management systems to cultivate required values Failure to consider existing organisational culture Difficulty in gaining cross-functional cooperation Unreasonable expectations Failure to communicate reasons for change Lack of training and compensation for employees
Project management	Failure to assess project performance Too much emphasis on analysing the existing process Poor communication among re-engineering team members and with other organisational members The BPR effort takes too much time Lack of appropriate BPR methodology

complexity should not be underestimated. It is therefore essential that use of IS/IT to support organisational change should simplify and enable that change rather than complicating it.

The flip side of the coin is that BPR can be highly successful. A ground-breaking example of BPR in the NHS from the mid 1990s is illustrated in the boxed example, along with a more recent example.

Effecting change through process information

Organisations undertaking re-engineering programmes have often not realised the impor-tance of process information, having perhaps not given sufficient attention to ongoing process management or to the information needed. Over-emphasis on the creative side of process change can lead to insufficient focus on mea-surement and analysis and information about processes that contributes to managing and improving those processes (Davenport and Beers, 1995). Identification of the right sort of information – and not too much – is the first task in managing process information. An assessment of how each process fits in its wider organisational context is also essential to avoid disintegration and duplication of information. What is more, information selection is not a

The Leicester Royal Infirmary was a pioneering example of re-engineering in an NHS hospital. Five experimental schemes set up in 1992 by the local health authority to improve outpatient care, inspired the Leicester project, which began in June 1994. Separate projects had to be carried out in all 300 outpatient clinics, as it soon became apparent that no single template could be applied to different projects.

The number of patients waiting less than 30 minutes for treatment rose from 64 to 94 per cent by March 1995, a record which was sustained afterwards. The process of change was also used to improve and update medical procedures, which helped in the vital matter of gaining enthusiasm from nurses and doctors about the change process. One important finding was that no one had overall responsibility for individual patients because of rigid hierarchies and divisions between staff functions. Business managers were consequently transformed into 'patient process directors' and encouraged to work more closely with clinical directors on patient care. Practical suggestions for improvements were also supplied by patients who had previously complained, thereby gaining their involvement in re-engineering projects.

Patient improvements have been accompanied by benefits to the bottom line in the form of recurrent per annum savings of some £1m.

Source: *Financial Times*, 20 November 1996

A more recent health care example of process redesign has occurred in Dundee as part of the Joint Futures agenda. Dundee LHCC (Local Health Care Co-operative) and Social Services joined forces in a collaborative project to reduce waiting time for care among the over 65s. Without additional resources (in fact, with fewer resources!), access to the required service has been reduced tenfold by eliminating unnecessary repeat assessments in the interlinking service processes, with consequent huge improvements in patients' perceptions of the care service.

Source: Tayside Primary Care Trust, November, 2003

single event and should be frequently revisited to confirm fit as the business and process environment inevitably changes.

After the information selection process is completed, an organisation must decide how and to whom the information will be distributed or communicated. The best information will be wasted if it does not reach the appropriate people doing the jobs. Process information must also be systematically analysed, interpreted and acted upon if it is going to be of any real value. This is more likely to occur if information is effectively identified, collected and distributed, but these are not enough. There must be a context or framework for managing process information, in other words, a management process.

The effective gathering and distribution of process information will not in itself lead to business change. There are crucial underlying cultural issues such as an emphasis on the importance of information, the need for openness and sharing, a commitment to longer-term process management and recognition of the importance of people in process performance. Such challenges to a process information culture must be addressed by everyone, but, more especially, by senior managers who have the power to reward, ignore or censure behaviour. Without adequately addressing issues of organisational power, incentive and reward schemes and worker participation in process design, even the most meticulously designed processes and information support structures may become dysfunctional (Davenport and Beers, 1995).

Key CBIS opportunities for BPR and process innovation

In the past there has often been too great an inclination to look to information systems for the universal success formula to improve performance quality.

Organisations are not easily predicted and controlled, but contain closely intertwined elements, which are not equally affected by the introduction of new CBIS. While the ability to network and communicate may improve, there may be a lack of understanding as to which data should be collected and analysed. Rather than using IS/IT merely as a reporting mechanism and a basic communication tool, organisations must seek a framework for learning that is not too restrictive or detrimental.

Key elements of BPR

The main challenge of BPR is change management. Understanding the change management challenge has to precede the application of BPR. In order to tackle BPR implementation, it is important to understand certain elements of BPR that distinguish it from many other change projects:

- the theme of analysing business processes creates new complexities;
- there is no one proven methodology for BPR;
- the transformation of the organisation is a significant element;

- there is more often than not a link with technology.

This last point is of particular interest here. The IS/IT function should not lead BPR projects, but support them. BPR must be perceived and managed as a business project with ownership and impetus coming from outside the IS/IT function.

IT as a key element

What is important is the understanding and harnessing of IS/IT so that business processes can be redesigned in ways that would otherwise have not been feasible. Bearing in mind the potential for integrating IS and databases and for networking, Table 7.3 summarises the IT opportunities in terms of reducing costs.

The potential of IT for business change is achieved by viewing IT as an enabler of process innovation. Certain activities help identify key change enablers, which must then be analysed in terms of feasibility and constraints imposed

Table 7.3 IT opportunities in BPR

Aims	Processes
Reduce production costs	Automate tasks Eliminate repetitive activities More direct information flows
Reduce coordination costs	Integrate tasks Distribute and collect information Eliminate time and distance constraints
Reduce information costs	Monitor tasks Analyse information Provide decision support Retain expertise Model processes

Source: adapted from Earl (1994: 15)

by existing technology, activities such as the following:

- identify potential technological and human opportunities for process innovation;
- identify potential technological and human constraints;
- seek out opportunities with respect to specific processes;
- identify which constraints are acceptable.

Opportunities and constraints must be identified, along with their relevance to the process under consideration. Cost/benefit analysis and planning have to be undertaken and decisions must be made as to which constraints are acceptable and which need to be overcome.

The notion of IT as an enabler may well be more accurately represented as IS/IT helping to implement a process rather than enabling it. Suffice to say, IT can offer organisations considerable advantages in terms of providing innovative ways to improve existing processes and better design new processes. IT and other process change enablers all need to be considered as valuable tools for shaping processes, though it must be remembered that such tools can have a positive or negative effect on processes. IT may provide opportunities for and impose constraints on process design.

The potential impact of IT on process change has been summarised by Davenport (1993) under nine categories (see Table 7.4).

The *automational* benefit of IT lies in its ability to eliminate human labour and produce a more structured process. The use of robotics in manufacturing and automated call distributors in telephone-intensive services are examples of this benefit.

The *informational* impact of IT captures process performance information, which can then be analysed and used as the basis for making decisions (see also the *analytical* impact of IT). Computer-based tools are used extensively in a variety of chemical processes to optimise resource and energy consumption, while credit card companies benefit from rapid authorisation of large numbers of credit card purchases, thereby reducing corporate risk and maintaining customer confidence.

Sequential benefit is provided when processes can be carried out simultaneously or in parallel, thereby reducing process cycle times. It is often possible to design in parallel, components that

Table 7.4 The impact of IT on process innovation

Impact	Explanation
Automational	Eliminating human labour from a process
Informational	Capturing process information to aid understanding
Sequential	Changing process sequence or enabling parallel operations
Tracking	Closely monitoring process status and products
Analytical	Improving analysis of information and decision making
Geographical	Coordinating processes across distances
Integrative	Coordinating between tasks and processes
Intellectual	Capturing and distributing intellectual assets
Disintermediating	Eliminating intermediaries from a process

previously had to be designed in sequence. The design and development cycle for the Kodak 35mm camera was dramatically reduced as a result.

Tracking often implies bar-coding of items and scanning at different stages of the logistics and distribution chain. Federal Express have always tracked and monitored all their letters and parcels throughout the delivery process, so that a customer who has not received an item of mail can at least know where it is in the system.

Geographical benefits of IT enable processes to be connected globally. Worldwide electronic mail and teleconferencing enable more rapid availability and exchange of information, as well as cooperative decision-making.

The *integrative* impact of IT helps improve process performance where tasks are scattered across jobs and functions, making process management very difficult. Whole processes, such as patient care management and insurance policy underwriting can be managed better by using relational databases. Knowledge and experience of individuals is frequently lost unless formally captured and readily available.

The *intellectual* impact of IT can be seen in excellent service organisations, such as American Express Travel Related Services and British Airways, where extensive databases were built with customer service procedures and customer requirements easily accessible to staff.

Finally, *disintermediation* serves to 'cut out the middle man'. Intermediaries may slow down processes or make them less efficient in terms of passing on information quickly and effectively. Electronic trading of stocks and shares, for example, has not only cut lead times dramatically but has also saved a great deal of money.

Venkatraman (1994) maintains that the role of IT in organisations has evolved from a focus on efficiency (automation) to a focus on creating and maintaining flexible business networks, alliances and partnerships (see also Chapter 5 for inter-organisational IS and Chapter 8 for IS and competitive advantage). In his five-level framework, localised use and internal integration correspond to the lowest level at which IT impacts upon business functions. Business network redesign and business scope redefinition involve reconfiguring the scope and tasks of the business network that delivers the products and services (see Figure 7.6). It must, however, be remembered that, while higher levels of business transformation may bring greater benefits, they also entail risk and a higher degree of changes in organisational routines, such as logical structuring and lines of reporting. Each

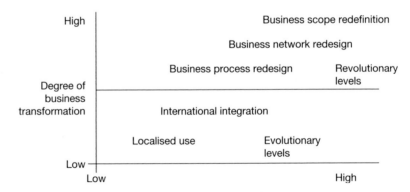

Figure 7.6 Five levels of IT-enabled business transformation
Source: adapted from Venkatraman (1994)

organisation needs to decide which level of transformation fits with potential costs and required effort to implement the necessary changes.

The five-level model of IT-induced reconfiguration charts the increasing use made of IT and provides a means of assessing current and future potential positions of organisations. The range and value of potential benefits are predicted to increase from each level to the next but only if accompanied by a greater degree of change in the way the business is operated (Brown, 1994).

The relationship between IT and BPR

It is important to recognise that IT-enabled transformation is more likely to succeed when everyone involved accepts that IT is not a magic bullet (Markus and Benjamin, 1997). Good ideas and good designs together are not enough and change management involves listening, understanding and giving people a chance to learn. Change management activity must be undertaken as an integral part of initiating, designing and building technology-enabled change. It is also essential to merge technological and process innovations in order to transform organisations, processes and relationships (Clark and Stoddard, 1996).

It is important to understand the recursive relationship between IT and BPR. Thinking about IT should stimulate thinking about BPR. IT needs consideration of how it supports new or redesigned business processes. Conversely, business processes and process improvements need consideration in terms of the capabilities IT can provide. This relationship is illustrated in Figure 7.7.

BPR and IT are not one and the same, nor are they inseparable. Re-engineering of business processes should take place before introducing technology. Applications of IT may well be cru-

cial to those redesigned processes but IS/IT architectures constructed to serve the organisation in the past may impose constraints on BPR. IS/IT infrastructure contributes to successful implementation of BPR, and organisations having developed a higher level of IS/IT infrastructure capability have been able to implement extensive changes to their business processes over relatively short time-frames (Broadbent *et al.*, 1999). This extends further to the mutually supportive nature of BPR and information architecture. A stable information architecture can support existing as well as improved business processes and reciprocally BPR provides a high-profile justification for the information architecture endeavour (Kettinger *et al.*, 1996).

BPR contains the three core elements of processes, IT and transformation, where IT is a key enabler rather than a necessity. IT can surmount time and distance constraints, contributing considerably to increased responsiveness and flexibility. Communication technologies increase the extent of collaboration, while shared information resources, such as relational databases, increase the extent of direct involvement by managers and users. BPR aims to optimise IT use and align more closely different IS to the value added or support processes they service.

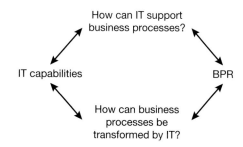

Figure 7.7 The recursive relationship between IS/IT and BPR

Source: adapted from Davenport and Short (1990)

BPR can help to dismantle organisational barriers, but new roles often need to be assumed by managers and staff (Markus and Benjamin, 1997). IS expertise is necessary to help coordinate technologies, processes and people. A process orientation demands an information management capability rather than just computer systems expertise.

It is also important not to allow expectations to soar. Many organisations have sought to optimise IT and gain competitive advantage, but have been disappointed, largely because technology by itself does not generate a sustainable market edge. The e-commerce platforms developed by British Airways a few years ago revolutionised the business of making travel arrangements and bookings. We have to bear in mind, however, that such technologies were developed in harmony with a whole corporate strategy for excellent service provision between internal customers and to external customers. Sustainable competitive advantage comes from a combination of IT, appropriate business processes, effective human interaction and the right strategic approach to implement the necessary changes (see Ross *et al.*, 1996).

BPR has to seek out opportunities actively to harness the power of IT in the redesigned processes. Configurations become possible that would otherwise not have been feasible. Remember though, that there is a reciprocal relationship between BPR and IT. While IT is a key enabler of BPR, it can also drive technological developments that open up the potential for redesign opportunities previously not considered.

Care is needed with any form of radical change and BPR is certainly no exception to this rule. Performance gains on the positive side must be balanced against potential organisational risk associated with implementing an all-or-nothing rather than an incremental approach to projects. Fuelled by the anticipa-

tion of enormous performance gains, radical altering of business processes can entail potential irreversibility of the changes, resistance to those changes and major problems with task ambiguity.

The extent of revolutionary change may preclude the simultaneous operation of old and new systems and thereby entail greater organisational risk. An all too radical approach, which is totally dissociated from traditional practices, may encounter higher levels of resistance to change among staff and increase the probability of suboptimal performance and system failure.

Crossing organisational boundaries also gives rise to a combination of risks and rewards. While significant benefits are to be gained by using IT to support processes that cross functional barriers, there is an accompanying increase in structural risk. Processes, such as new product development and outbound logistics, can be hugely enhanced by better information flows and reduced administrative redundancies. There are, however, potential risks associated with structural change within an organisation, such as increased structural complexity, which may be problematic to manage, and disturbed process ownerships, which may cause resentment and demotivation.

Ideally, organisations need to try and carry out IT-enabled change without exposure to excessive risk, while at the same time achieving the maximum possible benefit. Cross-functional BPR is associated with high risk and higher return, as opposed to intra-functional redesign projects. In the current environment of intense competitive and economic pressures, organisations capable of absorbing risk should perhaps try for the performance improvement potential offered by cross-functional BPR; risk-averse organisations and those able to avoid environmental pressures to some extent, such as regulated monopolies, should perhaps not be over enthusiastic about cross-functional BPR.

Table 7.5 Some implications of BPR

Level of strategy	BPR implications
Strategic use of IS	Cross functional/process systems IS strategic planning links with BPR
Strategic use of IT	Integrated systems Process analysis techniques Processes clarified Systems/BPR development methodologies
Strategic use of information	Broader view of project management Exploit project management skills in IS Exploit systems analysis skills of IS Exploit process knowledge of IS

Source: adapted from Earl (1994: 21)

Organisations must always bear in mind that there are a number of options when embarking upon IS/IT-enabled change and choose the option that provides the best fit strategically and operationally.

Relatively simple solutions to problems often provide the best examples of successful BPR.

Implications of IT use on BPR

BPR projects are strategic change projects and their consequences need to be built into strategic IS planning (see Chapter 8). Business change that aims to integrate technology into the more social organisational elements of people and the activities they perform is more likely to succeed than IT change per se.

The implications of BPR can be grouped against the three different information strategy levels (see Chapter 8) and these are summarised in Table 7.5. The three levels are IS (information systems) strategy, IT (information technology) strategy and IM (information management) strategy.

Chapter summary

It is important to understand change management and the difficulties associated with change. The process of changing and innovating is triggered by a variety of forces, both internal to the organisation and external in the surrounding environment.

The pressure to change may be more or less imperative, resulting in an evolutionary, continuous improvement approach or a more dramatic revolutionary approach to change. Business process re-engineering is an example of revolutionary change and has been discussed in some detail, with particular reference to the role of IS and IT in business change.

Change is frequently associated with technology and the implementation of CBIS. The potential risks and rewards of IS/IT-enabled change are also discussed, as are the problems associated with implementation. Change is frequently associated with innovation and the seeking of competitive advantage and these themes are taken further in Chapter 8.

Review questions

1 What is organisational change?
2 Which are the main reasons why organisations change?
3 In what ways can change come about?
4 Why is it important to be able to manage change?
5 Which aspects of organisations change?
6 How can these aspects that change be managed?
7 What are the main benefits of and obstacles to IT-enabled change?
8 What is Business Process Re-engineering?
9 What are the stages that lead to BPR success?
10 How can IS/IT support BPR?
11 What are the risks and benefits of IT-enabled BPR?
12 In what ways can IT impact upon process innovation?

Case study

Generale de Banque of Belgium

At the end of 1997 Generale de Banque was by far the largest bank in Belgium with a balance total of nearly 6,000 billion Belgian francs (approx. US$160 billion), more than 40 per cent higher than the nearest competitor. Although Generale de Banque's profit was also greatest, in relative terms it was less profitable than the Kredietbank because of a relatively high ratio of cost/return. One of the main objectives was, therefore, declared to be to decrease the cost ratio to 55 per cent (the same level as Kredietbank). The Generale de Banque had a three-level structure: the *Office* was the smallest entity comprising a number of local branches; the *Zone* coordinated a number of offices; the *Headquarters* in Brussels provided centralised decision-making. Important transactions mostly involved interactions between the three decision levels.

The BPR project

The new President of the Generale de Banque introduced the 'process' concept to the bank, which led to a number of 'process-oriented', IT-enabled, organisational change projects largely stimulated by his all-embracing systems plan. This plan defined the following three priority domains:

1 an international benchmarking study showed that credit processes were very labour-intensive;
2 the development of new/IT-based distribution channels, such as e-banking, was perceived as a priority;
3 this priority implied the need for further optimisation of products, processes and payment systems.

Andersen Consulting, the strategic partner of Generale de Banque in carrying out the systems plan, introduced *key performance indicators* as the starting point for each project. The objective of the corporate credits project was to decrease the cycle time of the credit processes by at least 25 per cent. However, dissatisfaction with the current performance was not the major driver, which was the strategic view concerning the new coordination and integration opportunities of IT. The other objectives were the limitation of credit risks through better risk-management, the increase of employee productivity and the improvement of the competencies of different participants in the credit processes. The President and two other members of the Management Committee (one responsible for new processes and information systems and one responsible for commercial credits) were the leaders of the systems plan and the re-engineering projects, authorising and motivating the overall engineering efforts (Hammer and Champy, 1993). The operational leader of the plan was assisted by three programme directors responsible for the different priority domains. The project team consisted of:

- a process manager
- a project leader IT
- a project leader of users
- the users – those directly involved in the process

The important role of the *process owner* (Hammer and Champy, 1993) was shared between the project leader of users and the process manager. The latter was more directly involved in the operations of the existing system, while the former had a thorough knowledge of the credit processes but not from an operational perspective. The process manager, as a non-operational member of the project team, would therefore potentially be able to redesign the operations more freely and with an unbiased view.

The old process and key problems

Traditionally, the process of granting corporate credits consisted of four phases:

1 the instruction phase performed by the account manager resulting in the credit file;
2 the analysis of the file by the credit analysts;
3 the decision taken by the authorised credit committee;
4 contracting: the juridical and administrative settlement.

Analysis of the existing process revealed several dysfunctions for specific phases and/or for all the phases, such as the following:

1 Inadequate document integration – the credit file was to a large extent a paper file which included:

- the credit application;
- a document with the formal decision;
- a copy of the client's other credit agreements;

- balance sheets;
- internal correspondence and exchange of letters with the client.

The different participants in the corporate credit process had some IT support but systems were merely functional and not integrated. People had their own separate systems that consisted primarily of simple databases, word-processing applications and email. Thus, the output of their work was in the form of paper-based documents. This paper file and the lack of information systems integration resulted in a time-consuming communication of data between the different parties involved. Each process participant also had their own version of the file, often with different data. As a consequence, decisions were often based on conflicting information.

2 Rework in the analysis phase – depending on the amount of the loan and the complexity of the file, it was sometimes analysed by three credit analysts at different levels. Each analyst would produce his or her own synthesis of and opinion on the document. For each level, the report was made by replicating and retyping data from previous credit reports, thereby entailing a rather complex process.

3 Inadequate functional integration – analysts had to cope with heterogeneous files often from different sectors. This sometimes resulted in conflicts between account managers and analysts when the latter appeared to have more expertise in a specific sector. The regional division also led to arbitrary regional differences in the analysis and evaluation of the credit files. Benchmarking with similar credit applications was simply not possible. This lack of functional integration also resulted in the account manager disagreeing with the analyst's decision in many cases. The reason for this was the greater commercial orientation of the account manager, who was a generalist rather than a specialist with a more thorough knowledge of credit policy and therefore considered each case with this policy and other similar applications in mind.

The re-engineering effort

The Bank's *Credit Charter* bound the BPR team members to a framework that governed the redesign of the existing functional organisation and old business rules. The two most important principles of the Charter were:

1 The principal division between instruction and analysis – the account manager's evaluation and decision has to be confirmed by the analyst (the principle of dual responsibility). This procedure increases cycle time but at the same time decreases the credit risk.
2 The connection of the decision authority with the person and not the function – in the organisation of Generale de Banque, functions are not primary but competencies are. A person taking over someone else's authority will not automatically be given the same authority without an assessment of his or her competence and experience.

Taking into account these Charter principles, the following redesigned corporate credit process was developed by the Bank:

- one single electronic file
- as much functional integration as possible

- reduction of analysis levels
- empowerment of the process participants

A central database was created to integrate all the documents and data into a *single electronic file*. This allowed the process participants to read and change the file simultaneously. It was also technically implemented through modern imaging techniques and a new integrated computer network. The potential and capacity of the technologies were first tested in a pilot project and production workflow management software was selected on the basis of a thorough market evaluation to integrate and coordinate workflow by connecting the already existing applications.

Functional integration and reduction of analysis levels were achieved through centralisation. In the old system, important credit files were analysed at three levels: the Office, the Zone and the Head-Quarters. In the re-engineered system, a file was assigned to an analyst at the Zone level, with all credit analysts centralized in the Zone, even those who had previously worked at the Head-quarters. The analysts now specialised by sector, evaluating all files for a sector, large, medium and small credit applications. As medium and small businesses tend to be more sensitive to new market trends and identify market signals much faster than large organisations, smaller credit applications needed shorter process workflows. Credit analysts now worked in a team, resulting in greater synergy and much more balanced evaluations and decisions. Case management teams of four or five were responsible for a sector or different sectors. More intensive formal and informal communication and interaction between the analysts, together with their sectorial specialisation, has increased the quality of decision-making.

Empowerment resulted in the relationship between the account manager and the credit analyst becoming more of a partnership. This was reinforced by an effective job rotation policy, whereby account managers had to be analysts for a certain period and vice versa. Although the final decision is taken by the authorised Credit Committee, it is for the most part a confirmation of the agreement between the account manager and the analyst, who are also responsible for the follow-up. The Credit Committees now had more time to concentrate on the evaluation of complex and high-risk applications, the commercial aspects, pricing credits and the general credit policy.

The effectiveness and benefits of the changes

The *cycle times* were substantially improved for all decision levels, most noticeably at the Zone level. A decision is made within four days of receipt of the application (depending on the size of the credit application). In the old system this took five to nine days. This decrease has been enabled by simplification of the process and electronic transfer of files. Further cycle time reduction could be effected once the Commission Bancaire accepts the electronic files and electronic signatures become legally acceptable.

Relations between the account managers and the credit analysts improved dramatically and differences of opinion decreased dramatically. The number of appeals lodged by account managers against negative opinions of credit analysts also decreased. A *productivity* gain of about 5 per cent was reported by account managers. This gain was converted into commercial time and eventually greater availability for clients. Productivity gains in the analysis phase resulted in a decrease in the headcount of 15 per cent (three full-time equivalents), with a reduced number of staff being able nevertheless to cope with a higher volume of work. An increased number of credit files are analysed and more time is spent gathering more relevant information to make a qualitatively better decision. These benefits were realised primarily because of the online access of all credit files and other credit information and the reuse of data in different output documents. The objective of a productivity gain of 25 per cent (six full-time equivalents) is therefore likely to be realisable in the future. Effective process time of an average credit file decreased by approximately one hour. There was no real gain for the decision-makers of the Credit Committee but redesigning of the process should produce a 30 per cent time gain in the future to be invested in more time for customers and for team coaching.

The quality of the delivered credit analysis reports improved, influenced by the new partnership between the account managers and the credits analysts, by the centralisation of the best analysts at the Zone level and the industry specialisation of the analysts. Moreover, the new workflow management software coordinated the new process such that the sub-processes were performed in the correct sequence and the most risky files were given priority. Time will reveal the positive effect of this better *risk management*.

Costs of the corporate credit project over its 18-month's lifetime were as follows:

- ten people were involved on a full-time basis;
- a training programme of three days for account managers, four days for analysts, two days for other credit workers and one day for decision-makers;
- additional hardware and software costing 20 million Belgian francs (approx. US$550,000) per Zone (100–150 users);
- additional hardware and software licenses for workstations amounting to 100,000 Belgian francs (approx. US$2,800).

Change management considerations

Although the human resources department had not been involved in the systems plan and the re-engineering projects, it turned out that this was essential. The transfer speed of the imaging information was too slow and more powerful systems had to be installed. For some users, this technology push was very difficult to digest, as one Zone Credit Director commented: 'For many years we have lived on bread and water (regarding the IT infrastructure) and now we get indigestion from what is installed and what is to come.'

Stakeholder and employee communication regarding the new process was effected in different ways. Besides continuous interaction between the project team and the different users, a very important event was a plenary meeting with *all* users at the different levels in a large conference hall. At this meeting, the Director General of the Zone explained the strategic importance and the objectives of the change project.

Changes in attitude within the processes were difficult to achieve, such as the change to reading, analysis, evaluation and synthesis directly from the screen instead of making use of printouts. This entailed more than simply expecting users to adopt new work methods, training and ongoing assistance being also required.

Centralisation and the switch to a written culture created a dramatic technological revolution for the decision-makers. They had problems adapting to the new style of making decisions on the basis of a written analyst's report rather than on the basis of an explanation given by the credit analyst in the Credit Committee. In the case of such fundamental changes there is a learning process involved and participants need to remain motivated, especially in the start-up phase of the project.

The top and operational level of the Bank were very enthusiastic about the project and supported it from the beginning. However, middle managers suffered from a decreased importance of their traditional role. The contracting phase was soon to be re-engineered as analysts and contracting employees no longer shared the same workplaces at the Office level, causing communication and coordination difficulties. Case management teams, consisting of analysts and contracting employees at the Zone level, needed to be integrated. This might, however be difficult, given that most of the contracting employees are part-time and have a lower level of education, making empowerment more difficult. They are also less mobile and less willing to commute every day to the Zone.

(Adapted from Van Grembergen W. and Van Belle J.L. (1999) 'Process Integration at the Generale de Banque of Belgium', *Journal of Strategic Information Systems*, 8(1), March: 63–81.)

Case questions

1 What were the aims and objectives of the BPR project?
2 How was the project carried out?
3 What benefits were achieved?
4 What problems were encountered?
5 What do you think Generale de Banque learned from the planning and carrying out of the project?

References and further reading

Alter S. (2002) Information Systems: Foundation of E-business, Prentice Hall: Upper Saddle River, NJ.

Baskerville R. and Smithson S. (1995) 'Information Technology and New Organisational Forms: Choosing Chaos over Panaceas', *European Journal of Information Systems*, 4(2): 66–73.

Beer M. (1980) *Organisation Change and Development: a Systems View*, Goodyear: Santa Monica, CA.

Block P. (1993) *Stewardship: Choosing Service Over Self-Interest*, Berrett-Koehler: San Francisco, CA.

Broadbent M., Weill P. and St Clair D. (1999) 'The Implications of Information Technology Infrastructure for Business Process Redesign', *MIS Quarterly*, 23(2), June: 159–182.

Brown S.A. (1994) 'Getting Value from an Integrated IS Strategy', *European Journal of Information Systems*, 3(2): 155–165.

Brown S.A., Massey A.P., Montoya-Weiss M.M. and Burkman J.R. (2002) 'Do I Really Have To? User Acceptance of Mandated Technology', *European Journal of Information Systems*, 11(4): 283–295.

Cabrera A., Cabrera E.F. and Barajas S. (2001) 'The Key Role of Organisational Culture in a Multi-system View of Technology-Driven Change', *International Journal of Information Management*, 21: 245–261.

Clark T.H. and Stoddard D.B. (1996) 'Interorganisational Business Process Redesign: Merging Technological and Process Innovation', *Journal of MIS*, 13(2), Fall: 9–28.

Clemons E.K., Thatcher M.E. and Row M.C. (1995) 'Identifying Sources of Reengineering Failures: a Study of the Behavioural Factors Contributing to Reengineering Risks', *Journal of MIS*, 12(2), Fall: 9–36.

Daft R. (1995) *Organisation Theory and Design*, 5th edn, West: St Paul, MN.

Daniels N.C. (1994) *Information Technology. The Management Challenge*, Addison-Wesley: Wokingham.

Davenport T.H. (1993) *Process Innovation: Reengineering Work Through Information Technology*, Harvard Business School Press: New York.

Davenport T.H. and Short J.E. (1990) 'The New Industrial Engineering: Information Technology and Business Process Redesign', *Sloan Management Review*, 31(4): 11–27.

Davenport T.H. and Stoddard D.B. (1994) 'Reengineering: Business Change of Mythic Proportions?' *MIS Quarterly*, June: 121–127.

Davenport T.H. and Beers M.C. (1995) 'Managing Information About Processes', *Journal of MIS*, 12(1), Summer: 57–80.

Dibrell C.C. and Miller T.R. (2002) 'Organisation Design: the Continuing Influence of Information Technology', *Management Decision*, 40(6): 620–627.

Earl, M.J. (1994) 'The New and the Old of Business Process Redesign', *Journal of Strategic Information Systems*, 3(1): 5–22.

Earl M.J., Sampler J.L. and Short J.E. (1995) 'Strategies for Business Process Reengineering: Evidence from Field Studies', *Journal of MIS*, 12(1), Summer: 31–56.

Edwards C. and Peppard J.W. (1994) 'Business Process Redesign: Hype, Hope or Hypocrisy?' *Journal of Information Technology*, 9: 251–266.

Fichman R.G. (2001) 'The Role of Aggregation in the Measurement of IT-related Organisational Innovation', *MIS Quarterly*, 25(4), December: 427–455.

Fiedler K.D., Grover V. and Teng J.T.C. (1994) 'Information Technology-Enabled Change: the Risks and Rewards of Business Process Redesign and Automation', *Journal of Information Technology*, 9: 267–275.

Fiedler K.D., Grover V. and Teng J.T.C. (1995) 'An Empirical Study of Information Technology Enabled Business Process Redesign and Corporate Competitive Strategy', *European Journal of Information Systems*, 4(1): 17–30.

Fox-Wolfgramm S.J., Boal K.B. and Hunt J.G. (1998) 'Organisational Adaptation to Institutional Change: a Comparative Study of First-Order Change in Prospector and Defender Banks', *Administrative Science Quarterly*, 43(1): 87–126.

Greve H.R. (1998) 'Performance, Aspirations and Risky Organisational Change', *Administrative Science Quarterly*, 43(1): 58–86.

Grover V., Jeong S.R., Kettinger W.J. and Teng J.T.C. (1995) 'The Implementation of Business Process Reengineering', *Journal of MIS*, 12(1), Summer: 109–144.

Hammer M. (1990) 'Reengineering Work: Don't Automate, Obliterate', *Harvard Business Review*, 68(4): 104–112.

Hammer M. and Champy J. (1993) 'Reengineering the Corporation', *Small Business Reports*, 18(11): 65–68.

Hannan M. and Freeman J. (1988) 'Structural Inertia and Organisational Change', in Cameron, K., Sutton R. and Whetton D. (eds), *Readings in Organisational Decline*, Ballinger: Cambridge, MA, pp. 75–94.

Hinton C.M. (2002) 'Towards a Pattern Language for Information-Centred Business Change', *International Journal of Information Management*, 22: 325–341.

Hoag B.G., Ritschard H.V. and Cooper C.L. (2002) 'Obstacles to Effective Organisational Change: the Underlying Reasons', *Leadership and Organisation Development Journal*, 23(1): 6–15.

Huff S.L. (1992) 'Reengineering the Business', *Business Quarterly*, 56(3): 38–42.

Jih W. and Owings P. (1995) 'From In Search of Excellence to Business Process Reengineering: the Role of Information Technology', *Information Strategy: The Executive's Journal*, 11(2): 6–19.

Kanter R.M. (1995) 'Managing the Human Side of Change', in Kolb D.A., Rubin I.M. and McIntyre J.M. (eds) *The Organisational Behaviour Reader*, 6th edn, Prentice-Hall: Englewood Cliffs, NJ.

Keen P.G.W. (1981) 'Information Systems and Organisational Change', *Communications of the ACM*, 24(1): 24–33.

Keen P.G.W. (1991) *Shaping the Future: Business Design Through Information Technology*, Harvard Business School Press: Boston, MA.

Kettinger W.J., Teng J.T.C. and Guha S. (1996) 'Information Architectural Design in Business Process Reengineering', *Journal of Information Technology*, 11(1), March: 27–37.

Kimberly J.R. and Miles R.H. (1980) *The Organisational Life Cycle: Issues in Creation, Transformation and Decline of Organisations*, Jossey-Bass: San Francisco, CA.

Kotter J.P. and Schlesinger L.A. (1979) 'Choosing Strategies for Change', *Harvard Business Review*, 57(2): 106–114.

Larsen T.J. (1993) 'Middle Managers' Contribution to Implemented Information Technology Innovation', *Journal of MIS*, 10(2), Fall: 155–176.

Levin M. (1997) 'Technology Transfer is Organisational Development: an Investigation into the Relationship between Technology Transfer and Organisational Change', *International Journal of Technology Management*, 14(2,3,4): 297–308.

McKeown I. and Philip G. (2003) 'Business Transformation, Information Technology and Competitive Strategies: Learning to Fly', *International Journal of Information Management*, 23: 3–24.

Macredie R.D. and Sandom C. (1999) 'IT-Enabled Change: Evaluating an Improvisational Perspective', *European Journal of Information Systems*, 8(4): 247–259.

227

Makridakis S. (1995) 'The Forthcoming Information Revolution: Its Impact on Society and Firms', *Futures*, 17(8): 799–821.

Manzoni J-F. and Angehrn A.A. (1997–1998) 'Understanding Organisational Dynamics of IT-enabled Change: a Multimedia Simulation Approach', *Journal of MIS*, 14(3), Winter: 109–140.

Martinsons M.G. (1995) 'Radical Process Innovation Using Information Technology: the Theory, the Practice and the Future of Reengineering', *International Journal of Information Management*, 15(4): 253–269.

Markus M.L. and Benjamin R.I. (1997) 'The Magic Bullet Theory in IT-enabled Transformation', *Sloan Management Review*, Winter: 55–68.

Martin C. and Powell P. (1992) *Information Systems. A Management Perspective*, McGraw Hill: Maidenhead.

Morris K. and Raben C. (1995) 'The Fundamentals of Change Management', in Nadler D., Shaw R. and Walton A. (eds) *Discontinuous Change: Leading Organisational Transformation*, Jossey-Bass: San Francisco, CA, pp. 47–65.

Munro-Faure L. and Munro-Faure M. (1993) *Implementing Total Quality Management*, Pitman: London.

Murdick R.G. and Munson J.C. (1986) *MIS Concepts and Design*, 2nd edn, Prentice-Hall International: Englewood Cliffs, NJ.

Oakland J.S. and Porter L.J. (1994) *Cases in TQM*, Butterworth Heinemann: Oxford.

Onstad K. (1995) 'Power from the People', *Canadian Business*, Technology Supplement, Fall: 74–84.

Orman L.V. (1998) 'A Model Management Approach to Business Process Reengineering', *Journal of MIS*, 15(1), Summer: 187–212.

O'Toole J. (1995) *Leading Change: Overcoming the Ideology of Comfort and the Tyranny of Custom*, Jossey-Bass: San Francisco, CA.

Peppard J.W. (ed.) (1993) *IT Strategy for Business*, Pitman: London.

Peppard J.W. and Rowland P. (1995) *The Essence of Business Process Reengineering*, Prentice-Hall International: Englewood Cliffs, NJ.

Roepke R., Agarwal R. and Ferratt T.W. (2000) 'Aligning the IT Human Resource with Business Vision: the Leadership Initiative at 3M', *MIS Quarterly*, 24(2): 327–353.

Ross J.W., Beath C.M. and Goodhue D.L. (1996) 'Developing Long-term Competitiveness Through IT Assets', *Sloan Management Review*, Fall: 31–42.

Sachwald F. (1998) 'Cooperative Agreements and the Theory of the Firm: Focusing on Barriers to Change', *Journal of Economic Behaviour and Organisation*, 35: 203–225.

Sampler J.L. and Short J.E. (1994) 'An Examination of Information Technology's Impact on the Value of Information and Expertise: Implications for Organisational Change', *Journal of MIS*, 11(2), Fall: 59–73.

Sarker S. and Lee A.S. (1999) 'IT-enabled Organisational Transformation: a Case Study of BPR Failure at Teleco', *Journal of Strategic Information Systems*, 8(1): 83–103.

Saxena K.B.C. and Aly A.M.M. (1995) 'Information Technology Support for Reengineering Public Administration: a Conceptual Framework', *International Journal of Information Management*, 15(4): 271–293.

Scott-Morton M.S. (ed.) (1991) *The Corporation of the 1990s. Information Technology and Organisational Transformation*, Oxford University Press: New York.

Senior B. (1997) *Organisational Change*, Pearson: Harlow.

Seidmann A. and Sundararajan A. (1997) 'Competing in Information-intensive Services: Analysing the Impact of Task Consolidation and Employee Empowerment', *Journal of MIS*, 14(2), Fall: 33–56.

Skidmore S. and Wroe B. (1988) *Introducing Systems Analysis*, Blackwell: Oxford.

Spector B. (1989) 'From Bogged Down to Fired Up: Inspiring Organisational Change', *Sloan Management Review*, 30(2): 32–46.

Steiner C. (2001) 'A Role for Individuality and Mystery in "Managing" Change', *Journal of Organisational Change*, 14(2): 150–167.

Stoddard D.B. and Jarvenpaa S.L. (1995) 'Business Process Redesign: Tactics for Managing Radical Change', *Journal of MIS*, 12(1), Summer: 81–107.

Tarn J.M. and Wen H.J. (2002) 'Exploring Organisational Expansion Modes and Their Associated Communication System Requirements: Consolidation and Complementation', *International Journal of Information Management*, 22: 3–26.

Tillquist J. (2000) 'Institutional Bridging: How Conceptions of IT-enabled Change Shape the Planning Process', *Journal of MIS*, 17(2), Fall: 115–152.

Venkatraman N. (1991) 'IT-Induced Business Reconfiguration', in Scott-Morton M. (ed.) *The Corporation of the 1990s: Information Technology and Organnization Transformation*, Oxford University Press: New York, pp. 122–158.

Venkatraman N. (1994) 'IT-enabled Business Transformation: From Automation to Business Scope Redefinition', *Sloan Management Review*, Winter: 73–87.

Weitzel W. and Jonsson E. (1989) 'Decline in Organisations: a Literature Integration and Extension', *Administrative Science Quarterly*, 34(1), March: 102.

Zaidifard D.R. (1998) 'Reframing the Behavioural Analysis of Reengineering: an Exploratory Case', *Journal of Information Technology*, 13(2), June: 127–138.

Zaltman G. and Duncan R. (1977) *Strategies for Planned Change*, Wiley: New York.

Chapter 8

Information systems and business strategy

••

Learning objectives

After reading this chapter you should be able to:

- describe the strategic use of IS by organisations;
- describe the potential IS support for sustainable competitive advantage;
- discuss different approaches to the strategic IS planning process;
- apply strategic IS analysis and planning models.

Introduction

Many organisations that have invested in IS in the past have found that IS expenditure did not produce value for money, nor did it help to achieve business objectives. Some companies have, on the other hand, gained significant competitive advantage from the strategic development and management of IS.

There is a tendency to consider IS/IT as an entity, rather than separating business information needs on the one hand and the fulfilment of these needs by means of technological and organisational solutions on the other. Although there will be an overall IS/IT strategy, there is a distinction to be made between IS strategy and IT strategy. IS strategy is business-based, oriented to demand rather than supply and focused on applications, whereas IT strategy is activity-based, oriented to supply rather than

demand and focused on technology. M.J. Earl (1989) makes this distinction quite clearly between the *what* of IS/IT, i.e. how to manage applications from the business point of view, and the *how*, i.e. how the applications are delivered in the form of technology to provide competitive advantage for the business.

In this chapter we need to begin by applying the following questions (*what? why? how?*) to IS strategy:

- *What* is IS strategy?
- *Why* is it important?
- *How* can it be achieved?

What is IS strategy?

The IS strategy gathers together the business aims of the organisation, the information requirements to support those aims and the development of computer systems relevant to providing that information. Strategic IS planning is concerned with developing systems to fit a vision of the role IS are to play in the organisation. If strategic planning is going to be effective, it should be closely aligned to business planning and should be a continuous process dovetailing with the business planning approach, time scales and outcomes.

What is IS management?

Strategic IS management involves the successful managing over time of all the inputs, processes and outputs from strategic IS planning. The data and information resource of the organisation must be managed so as to obtain the best potential business value. IS applications need to be managed in terms of fulfilling requirements of users and serving a useful business purpose in the longer term. IT introduction, development and replacement must be researched and managed to maximum benefit of the organisation. Finally, all IS/IT resources, their functions and administration have to be managed both individually and as they interrelate across the various business activities.

Why is a strategic approach to IS important?

If there is no coherent strategy for IS, technology is more likely to be incompatible and out of step with business needs. Senior management, IS/IT specialists and users will tend to lack a common understanding and direction. IS/IT productivity will remain sub-optimised, suffering from repetitive duplication of effort and inadequate advantage being gained from the information resource. Business objectives and needs may remain unfulfilled, with consequent lack of improvement in business performance and the loss of innovative opportunities. IS

strategy needs to be business-driven and totally integrated into the organisational strategy to provide long-term benefits. Most companies have been accustomed to a short-term tactical approach to IS implementation and it is difficult for them to develop a strategic approach from a position of considerable inexperience.

Effectiveness of IS use

There are a number of strategically important factors that affect the pace and effectiveness of IS progress (Ward and Peppard, 2002):

- the pressure on a particular industry sector or organisation to improve performance;
- the organisational capabilities to deploy and resource the right IS applications;
- the staff skills and ability to develop the appropriate applications;
- the organisational capabilities to evaluate IS costs, benefits and feasibility.

There is no doubt that problems abound as the complexity and criticality of the management decision-making process becomes more strategic. Where IS strategic management is concerned, it is vitally important to bring together the business and IS/IT managers to provide clarity and a fuller understanding of what is involved and how IS strategic planning can commence.

How can IS be used strategically?

If DP increases organisational efficiency, MIS improves managerial and organisational effectiveness. The use of IS does, however, have to be taken a step further towards SIS, the achievement of business objectives through optimised IS which can also respond to innovative competitive opportunities as they present themselves.

The government has outlined a strategic initiative for the electronic delivery of services direct to citizens and companies in the UK. The Government Direct Green Paper envisages online distribution of a range of services including vehicle licence renewal, benefit claims, tax return processing, Citizens Charter performance information and information for job-seekers. People would receive the information at home by means of a personal computer or television, or at public access points such as banks, shops or town halls in kiosks or at terminals. Electronic data interchange would make available business information on matters such as regulatory directives, taxation guidelines and export opportunities. Such accessibility of services and information is the sort of strategic use of IS/IT that is expected of the information age.

Source: Earl M.J. (1996) 'Viewpoint', *Financial Times*, 15 November 14

Strategic IS can be divided into *internal systems* that directly benefit the organisation and *external systems* that directly benefit the customers of the organisation. The four main types of strategic IS are:

1 Those that *improve the integration of internal processes*, i.e. enhancing the use of information in the organisational value chain. A new information-based approach to the roles played by people and departments needs to be fully understood in terms of the organisational implications if significant benefits are to be gained and sustained. Examples of such systems are computer integrated manufacturing, quality control systems and enterprise resource planning systems.

2 Those that *link the organisation to customers or suppliers*, organisational sales and marketing linked to customer distribution and supplier procurement. Just in Time production systems, for example, rely on technology-based systems to place emergency orders with suppliers for discrete batches of products that can then be delivered promptly.

3 Those that *enable the production and delivery of enhanced products or services* based on information. Examples of these systems can be found extensively in the financial services sector, where whole ranges of different types of financial service converge from insurance to managing share portfolios. In order to maximise the benefits from such systems, it is essential to have a thorough understanding of the industry products, particularly the extent to which they satisfy customer requirements.

4 Those that *provide information to executive management* to develop and implement strategy. Such systems would be DSS (decision support systems), EIS (executive information systems) and ES (Expert Systems) – see Chapter 5 – and provide summary or overview information from DP and MIS, tapping into external sources of information and providing some of the tools for seeking out competitive advantage.

Naturally other classifications of SIS are feasible, but no matter what they may be, it is important to consider the implications of the strategic use of IS and the ways in which traditional ways of doing business can be improved, often accompanied by significant structural changes to the organisation (see BPR – Chapter 7).

Success factors

As well as types of SIS, it is worthwhile to consider the main success factors that can help achieve an effective IS strategy. These factors are not meant to constitute an exhaustive list, but they do offer a useful framework for guidance.

Few examples of SIS display all the success factors, but may exhibit combinations of some of them. These factors may well conflict with traditional approaches to IS and tend to be more closely linked to business needs and innovation. Success factors according to Ward and Peppard (2002) include:

- An external rather than internal focus, looking to shareholders, stakeholders and the outside business world as a whole.
- Value additionality, as opposed to cost reduction, though cost reductions may ensue as a result of increased efficiency and effectiveness. The main aim is to do things better and provide better products or services.
- Sharing benefits with customers, suppliers and shareholders or stakeholders (e.g. the public as a whole, as a result of more environmentally friendly ways of operating).
- Understanding the customer, finding out particular needs and problems so that value can be added over time (e.g. allowing retailers to swap batches of goods which are overstocked with suppliers in exchange for batches of goods that they require, thereby solving a problem that was perhaps difficult to avoid in the first place).
- Innovation driven by business-needs rather than technology; business pull rather than technology push. IS should be seen as serving or enabling business needs or opportunities, rather than dictating how the business should develop. Failure is more likely to come about as a result of inadequate business vision and understanding rather than inadequate IS/IT.
- A step-by-step approach, building on what has gone before, developing applications by trial and error, not stopping at one success but always looking ahead to the next.

- Using the information gained from the systems to take the business forward. Market analysis and customer data are vital information sources capable of contributing to long-term business success.

After all, what is it that promotes business success and enhances long-term competitive advantage? The technology itself is the enabler to develop innovative systems and gather important information, but can easily be replicated by competitors. New information systems, using the technology, are more difficult to replicate, particularly if they change business relationships in an innovative and exclusive way. Above all, though, it is through the optimised use of the information gained from the systems to develop products, services and customer relationships that sustainable competitive advantage can be achieved.

What is strategic IS planning?

Strategic IS planning has been identified as the process of identifying a portfolio of computer-based applications that will assist in the execution of business plans and the realisation of business goals (Lederer and Sethi, 1996). Strategic IS planning is the process of formulating IS objectives, defining strategies and policies within the scope of these objectives and then developing detailed action plans to achieve them (Ang and Teo, 1997).

In the 1970s the main objectives of information systems planning were to improve communications between users and IS departments, to enhance senior management support for IS, to allocate resources for IS according to their relative contribution and to improve the IS department generally. More recently, the additional objectives have emerged of using IS to provide competitive advantage, developing an organisation-wide information architecture, sharing both data and IS across the organisation for maximum effectiveness (Lederer and Sethi, 1999) and bringing about significant change in the company's performance by fundamentally changing the way it does business (Ang and Teo, 1997).

Constructing an organisation-wide information architecture is unfortunately not a simple task and more often than not organisations have ended up developing fragmented systems that solved immediate problems in specific areas of the business but did not provide opportunities for future integration and organisational IS synergies. This approach has also tended to result in information redundancies and duplication as well as high costs. With these factors in mind,

the importance of implementation of IS plans cannot be overstated (Gottschalk, 1999).

As with any corporate-wide initiative, complexity is a major obstacle to progress and it is preferable to use methodologies and frameworks to aid the strategic planning process. Major issues that have to be tackled are the extent of IS impact on the organisation and knowing which applications contribute more or less to the overall business effort.

The evolution of IS planning

A useful framework in the form of an application portfolio helps map the progress an organisation is making in moving towards strategic use of IS. Figures 8.1 and 8.2 illustrate

Strategic	Turnaround
Applications critical for future success (e.g. links to suppliers)	Applications of potential future strategic importance (e.g. expert systems)
Factory	**Support**
Applications critical to sustaining existing business (e.g. computer aided design)	Applications to improve management and performance (e.g. word processing)

Figure 8.1 An application portfolio
Source: adapted from McFarlan (1984)

Strategic	High potential
• Credit balance for all customers • Websites dedicated to attracting elite athletes • Implementation of an MSc in Sports Studies	• Online bookings • Automated telephone bookings • Improved communications using related email between different sites and a bank of frequently asked questions
Key operational	**Support**
• Reliable information provision to and from users • Credit and debit control • Door control	• Membership tracking • Admissions • Word processing

Figure 8.2 An application portfolio for a university sports centre

McFarlan's (1984) application portfolio, Figure 8.2 being an example that a university sports centre might use.

The evolution of IS/IT planning can be demonstrated through a series of stages (see Figure 8.3), as follows:

Stage 1   Would involve early DP planning to build *support* systems to enhance management and organisational performance.

Stage 2   Would involve the establishment of *factory* systems to fulfill both operational (DP) and management support (MIS) needs. Priorities need to be agreed as to which systems take precedence. Examples of such systems would be order processing and sales analysis.

Stage 3   Is something of a watershed at the centre of the application portfolio to consider integration of existing systems with resource prioritisation for *factory* over *support* systems.

Stages 1 to 3 represent a progression from *efficiency*-driven systems towards integrated systems to increase *effectiveness*. They include various DP and MIS applications, but as yet there has been no evidence of strategic use of IS.

Stage 4   Represents the point at which users take an entrepreneurial role to innovate with information and IS in the search for new ways of achieving competitive advantage. Ideas can be tested which may later be turned to advantage, i.e. *turnaround* opportunities that may develop into future *strategic* applications.

Stage 5   May be a difficult one to reach, particularly if Stage 3 has been delayed and Stage 4 has been unproductive. The main task at this point is to evaluate the Stage 4 ideas along with opportunities presented by the *factory* and *support* infrastructure and link IS potential to the business strategy. Involvement of senior managers, line managers and IS specialists is essential to determine and deliver real *strategic* applications.

The evolution of IS planning is difficult to track and organisations frequently estimate their progress to be at a more advanced stage than it really is. In some functional areas of the organisation IS and business strategy may be more closely linked (e.g. finance, distribution) than in others (e.g. marketing) where there may be little or no obvious connection.

Towards sustainable competitive advantage?

Customers, suppliers and other stakeholders may be the driving force behind the organisation's need for different types of IS. Both internal and external forces will drive that need. There will also be the need for management to decide on which IS investments will be necessary to enable the implementation of the business strategy. In both cases the focus is on conducting *impact analysis* to understand the potential for IS in terms of the business strategy.

Although SIS have increased in profile, the majority of investment in IS will be in DP and MIS to support the business strategy. What is important, however, is that management never

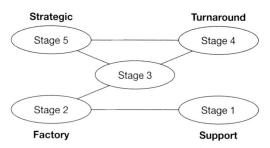

Figure 8.3 The evolution of IS planning in relation to the application portfolio
Source: adapted from Ward and Peppard (2002)

lose sight of the potential of information as a strategic resource and become accustomed to thinking of it as a routine part of the business planning process. IS need to be treated like marketing or purchasing or any other fundamental business function that has to be managed efficiently and effectively to ensure organisational survival.

The stages of impact analysis to achieve sustainable competitive advantage are as follows (see Figure 8.4):

- identify the potential impact of IS;
- evaluate IS implications in the business context prior to defining the strategy;
- change the organisation's competitive capability by developing IS-based business strategies.

IS can and should be considered an input to business strategy in terms of being able to change or shape that strategy or reveal new potential strategies. IS enables organisations to monitor their external environment (e.g. customers, suppliers, the public) and use this information to provide competitive advantage. IS have a more proactive role to play in future business strategy rather than the reactive one they have played in the past.

All organisations exist within an external environment shaped by the economic climate, politics, legislation in force and the rate of technological progress. These factors are changing with ever-increasing speed and must be care-

fully monitored when planning the business process. Organisations must also be mindful of their stakeholders (e.g. customers, suppliers, employees, the public as a whole) and pressure groups (e.g. the media, financial institutions, customers, employees) that influence them, creating opportunities and posing threats.

One crucial issue to be considered is that of long-term or sustainable competitive advantage. The capability to achieve such advantage through IS/IT assets derives from the management of a reusable technology base, a highly competent IS/IT human resource and a strong partnership between IS/IT management and business management (Ross *et al.*, 1996). Senior executives providing research data have focused on the better alignment of IS/IT products and services with an organisation's strategic objectives. They have also focused on the necessity to deliver solutions more quickly and provide high-quality, cost-effective support. Staff skills need to be able to build bridges between old and new systems. A valuable human resource asset will also assume responsibility for solving business problems. There needs to exist a well-defined technology infrastructure alongside a business partner ownership of and accountability for IS/IT projects. Furthermore, top management leadership has to be evident in the establishing of IS/IT priorities.

Feeny and Ives (1990) have provided a useful conceptual model in the form of a pillared framework for IS/IT-based sustainability of

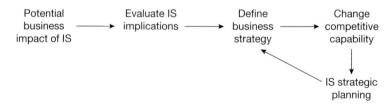

Figure 8.4 Achieving the required impact of IS

competitive advantage. The first and most obvious pillar involves analysis of the project development cycle to understand how long it is likely to be before a competitor can respond (termed the 'generic lead time'). The second pillar identifies the extent to which the project is protected by 'competitive asymmetry', involving the assessment of any handicaps that are likely to prevent a competitor attempting to respond to the challenge. In other words, which competitors will be able to respond and to what extent? The third pillar concentrates on supply chain analysis to consider the 'pre-emption potential' of the proposed application and the question of whether a response will be effective. The three pillars represent three fundamental questions:

1 How long will it take until competitors can put together the same application? (project life cycle analysis).
2 Who will be able to copy the application? (competitor analysis).
3 Once the competition has the application in place, will it do any good? (supply chain analysis).

The Merrill Lynch Cash Management Account (CMA) was successfully targeted at wealthy US individuals and stole the march on its competitors by means of pre-emption. Competitors eventually caught up to some extent but Merrill Lynch retained its customer base and five years after the introduction of CMA their nearest rival still only had 10 per cent of the number of accounts that Merrill Lynch had (Wiseman, 1985).

The first task of the business planning process is to set objectives, such as increasing profitability and market share. Second, it is necessary to evaluate the organisation's current strategy and understand organisational strengths and weaknesses in terms of resources, staff skills, finance, plant and machinery,

research and development potential. This situation analysis must then extend beyond the organisational boundaries to look at, for example, marketplace positioning and competition. Third, organisations need to decide upon future strategies, bearing in mind the degree of risk involved and the capability to achieve those strategies. Finally, the chosen feasible strategy/strategies have to be implemented.

Types of business strategy

According to Porter (1980) there are three fundamental strategies by which companies seek to derive a competitive advantage, which are low-cost leadership, differentiation and focus or niche market.

Some organisations try to increase their profit margins by maintaining lower costs than their competitors. Economies of scale in purchasing and marketing in an industry with set market prices will tend to increase sales volume and market share. Over time a low-cost leader will extend its competitive advantage.

Others seek to outwit competitors by distinguishing their products and services from others in the marketplace. The extent to which a differentiation strategy will succeed will depend on the availability of substitute products and services. Nowadays, many companies see the provision of excellent customer service, in addition to reduced prices, as a value-enhancing distinguisher in the marketplace, such as the supermarket chains Tesco, Morrisons and Asda. Redefining a mundane product or service by being innovative and creative is another approach by the differentiation strategist. Universities seeking to provide innovative e-learning opportunities are now able to differentiate themselves.

The competitive strategy of focus seeks to dominate in a niche market segment. A company may, for example, choose a luxury market niche, such as an insurance market providing expensive but highly effective products and services for very wealthy clients. A focus strategy may segment the market in a variety of ways: customer requirements, product and service characteristics, price, distribution channels or demographics, to name but a few.

IS to reduce costs

Automation is one of a number of ways in which IS can help the implementation of a low-cost leadership strategy. Automation reduces processing time, volume of labour needed and some rework. Automated equipment may, however, be expensive and staff training costs higher so that the necessary skills to operate the equipment are acquired.

Operational IS in manufacturing constitute the basis of statistical process control to help prevent huge failure costs in the production of defective items that either have to be reworked or scrapped. Reducing quality costs or the costs of non-conformance will increase profit margins often to quite a dramatic extent.

Just in Time (JIT) inventory reduces stock-holding costs by obtaining inventory in discrete batches just as it is needed. CBIS help to monitor complex and interdependent inventory and plan restocking logistics at the right time.

IS can help reduce structuring and overhead costs. Many organisations are becoming leaner, flatter structures as a result of improvements in communications and networking technologies.

IS to differentiate products and services

The operational IS performing the function of statistical quality control will also help an organisation to differentiate its products on the basis of quality and reliability. A reputation for defect-free products that can be relied upon

over time will enable a company to differentiate its reputation over that of its competitors. As Tom Peters said, when he spoke about the Maytag washing machine company gaining market share from GEC: 'Maytag has segmented its market by going for those people who like things that work!'

CAD/CAM (Computer Aided Design/Computer Aided Manufacturing) systems have helped companies adopt a differentiation strategy by maybe improving on the physical design of a product, but more importantly by improving service responsiveness. Bryan Upton, CEO of Richardson Steel, Sheffield, accounted for their competitive service advantage coming to some considerable extent from being able to produce a sample of a new knife or pair of scissors for a potential customer in a day rather than a week.

IS can help companies differentiate on customer service in a number of ways. More reliable delivery can be effected using bar-coding systems, such as those used by the Federal Express company to track all items of mail in the delivery process. Easier ordering can now be facilitated in a number of ways, such as via the Internet. More responsive and appropriate after-sales service is aided by a variety of telecommunications systems. Responding to changing customer needs in a flexible way is achieved by many airlines which now have systems capable of allowing more last-minute reservations and changes in travel plans by customers.

IS to focus on one market segment

Companies opting for a focus strategy can use IS to help identify potentially promising market segments and create new markets. Availability of online information has made it much easier to research new opportunities. Stores such as Marks & Spencer use the processed transactions from their existing customers to offer new services, for example, wine-tasting and financial services. Geographic IS can highlight locations with an underserved customer base worth focusing on.

New market segments can be created by customising products and services by means of IS. Products such as financial advice can be enhanced by providing more or better, more personalised, relevant information to the customer. Some estate agencies, for example, offer videos on CD-Rom disks of properties for sale. The videos allow customers to filter out properties of no interest in the comfort of an office rather than having to go through the lengthy process of visiting each property personally. Properties now posted on the Internet also allow rapid selection by potential buyers.

IS alliances

Aside the three basic generic business strategies of low-cost leadership, differentiation and focus, there is a competitive strategy of creating and maintaining inter-organisational alliances. New technologies have enabled stronger bonds to be established between allied organisations, bonds which are now harder and more costly to sever. What has historically been regarded as a risky strategy, in which alliances changed with consequent theft of knowledge and expertise, has become standard practice to gain sustainable competitive advantage.

Such strategic alliances frequently occur with customers and suppliers. Better, faster service with more feedback and direct communication will help lock-in customers who then purchase more over time, increasing sales and profits and reducing costs for the organisation.

Similarly, establishing a closer relationship with suppliers benefits both the organisation and its supplier. Simplified ordering and lower inventory costs for the company will promote more regular orders from a particular supplier. In both customer and supplier alliances advantages come from the closer working relationship itself as companies can estimate schedules, demand and potential problem areas more quickly and easily. Information sharing makes strategic alliances work. Inbound and outbound logistics are very closely linked to customer and supplier alliances. Getting products to the right people in the right place at the right time benefits all stakeholders in the process, thereby creating the proverbial 'win–win' situation.

Information leadership

Another strategic approach is that of increasing the value of a product or service by adding appropriate information into it. Comprehensive user manuals, good information on the care of products and inbuilt machine control systems are examples of this additional type of information. Products are now technologically more capable of collecting and processing information to improve the functioning of products. Driver airbags and more effective gauges predicting environmental conditions have improved the way cars function, and traffic predictor systems have made congestion control easier.

Information is now available as a commodity. Bar-code systems provide information on popular and less popular product lines. Customer information collected by transaction processing systems can be sold on to market research organisations or companies wishing to offer services to certain customer groupings.

The following boxed example illustrates competitive advantage from IS/IT in terms of both IS alliances and information leadership.

Strategic frameworks for IS planning

Michael Porter (1979; 1980; 1985) has produced two models of industry competition that

You are a police officer on the street, confronted by a suspected criminal. Using your video camera and a radio, you transmit a video image to your control room and a short time later receive confirmation of his identity. Similarly, police on patrol use portable data systems to check registrations and previous evidence as it is needed.

Computers in ambulances are linked to hospitals and medical centres so that information can be exchanged prior to a patient's arrival at the Accident and Emergency Unit. Ambulance personnel can receive expert advice on how to proceed with emergency patient treatment while hospital staff can obtain advance knowledge on the emergency case before the patient's arrival.

You are running a large city bus system. There has been an accident at a busy city intersection, so you can send data messages to terminals at bus stops warning waiting passengers of potential delays.

Source: *Financial Times*, 15 November 1996: 14

are of particular relevance to strategic alliances. The first model identifies five forces governing the nature of competition and the second relates to the value system as a whole in which value-adding partnerships can be formed.

The competitive forces model

The five forces that shape industrial competition are (see Figure 8.5):

1 the threat of new entrants
2 the threat of substitute products or services
3 the bargaining power of customers
4 the bargaining power of suppliers
5 competitive rivalry between organisations in the industry

Bargaining power of suppliers increases, for example, as soon as there are few suppliers manufacturing a certain product or product range. Customers will therefore tend to be prioritised for better service and delivery according to the price they are prepared to pay. Strategic alliances between customers will help lessen potential bargaining power, as well as making it harder for new companies and products to break into the existing market.

Figure 8.5 Porter's competitive forces model
Source: adapted from Porter (1979: 141)

Competitive forces analysis

Here the emphasis lies very much on identifying opportunities and threats from IS/IT. McFarlan (1984) poses five fundamental questions in the search for opportunity which can be directly matched with the five competitive forces identified by Porter (1979 and 1985), as illustrated in Table 8.1. McFarlan's questions are as follows:

- Can IS build barriers to entry? A successful barrier appeals to customers, ensures their loyalty and is difficult to replicate, such as electronic price quoting for salespeople.
- Can IS build-in switching costs? Electronic links to suppliers or customers and home banking systems can build-in such costs.
- Can IS change the balance of power in supplier relationships? Electronic inventory and Just in Time delivery systems and computer aided design (CAD) links between organisations can alter the balance of such power.
- Can IS generate new products? Products of higher quality, delivered more quickly, tailored to customers' needs at little extra cost create added value to products.
- Can IS change the basis of competition? Porter's generic strategies of *low cost, differentiation* and *niche* come into focus here.

Porter's generic strategies of low cost, differentiation and niche can also be related to the use of IS/IT as follows:

- A *low cost* strategy might be facilitated by IS/IT in order handling, cost recording and allocation or centralised supplies.
- A *differentiation* strategy might require IS/IT to help find out more about customer requirements or provide faster delivery when essential.
- A *niche/focus* strategy might necessitate IS/IT to identify target markets, link into customers' businesses directly or develop a unique information base for a certain selected market niche.

The value system model

The second model that motivates strategic alliances is that of the value system (see Figure 8.6) or industry value chain. The value system takes a step further the concept of the internal or organisational value chain (see Chapter 2) beyond the company boundary to upstream organisations, such as suppliers, who add value to products and services coming into the company, and downstream organisations, such as customers who repackage or rework products and services, thereby adding further value.

Analysing the internal value chain

The internal or organisational value chain refers to a system of generic interconnecting activities performed by a company to add value to

Table 8.1 Competitive forces analysis

Competitive forces – Porter (1985)	Search for opportunity – McFarlan (1984)
Threat of new entrants	Can IS build barriers to entry?
Bargaining power of buyers	Can IS build in switching costs?
Bargaining power of suppliers	Can IS change the balance of power in supplier relationships?
Threat of substitute products or services	Can IS generate new products or services?
Rivalry among competitors (generic strategies)	Can IS change the basis of competition?

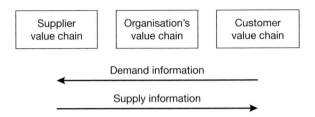

Figure 8.6 The value system
Source: adapted from Porter and Millar (1985: 151)

products or services. Such activities, referred to as primary activities, would include sales, marketing, production and distribution. These activities are supported by the secondary activities which are necessary, but do not clearly add value directly. These activities would include finance, personnel and administration (see Chapter 2 for more detail of the internal value chain).

An analysis of organisational structure and business activities often reveals some sort of mismatch. Existing systems may follow the organisational structure more closely than the value chain. Evaluation of strengths and weaknesses of existing systems and of information/IS requirements tends to necessitate matching systems to the value chain rather than to organisational structure. The type of questions that need to be asked include the following:

- What could IS/IT do to change business or industry parameters?
- What could IS/IT do for the organisation given its industry position?
- Which applications offer the most benefit to the organisation as it operates and is managed at present?
- Which applications could be of future value and what organisational changes would need to take place?

Analysing the value system

By examining a firm's value chain and the value system or industry value chain it is possible to analyse how effectively information flows along the organisation's primary activities and back and how effectively information is used by each activity. Activities need to be linked in order to minimise costs and maximise opportunities and support or secondary activities should serve the needs of the value-adding processes rather than hindering them.

Information flowing through the industry has to be analysed in order to assess its criticality to organisations in that industry and in what ways that information presents threats or opportunities according to its relative availability. For example, the supply of certain traded commodities, such as timber and cocoa, relies on the availability of accurate, up-to-date information.

Demand information from customers and supply information from suppliers flows in opposite directions. These flows must be integrated and serve each other's purpose and can therefore significantly impact upon an organisation's performance in the marketplace.

Once more, a questioning approach helps to highlight opportunities and threats from IS/IT as they vary over time and according to the status quo of the particular industry (see also Parsons (1983) and McFarlan (1984)):

- How could IS/IT affect the nature and value of products and services? Differentiated products offered by banks and financial services add value and help enhance customer loyalty.

- How could IS/IT change the pattern of demand for products and services, extend market share, provide innovative market segmentation or provide more distribution channels? Auction-based products that can be traded remotely via electronic means, such as the Dutch flower auctions, benefit from innovative distribution channels and enjoy broader access to international markets.
- How could IS/IT help to reach more customers or more appropriate customers and match products and services more directly to them? Hire-car companies are now making online interactive systems available to customers to find their best onward route.
- How could IS/IT alter the basis of costing and economics of production, establishing an optimum balance between customisation and standardisation? The innovative and much cheaper production of newspapers or the use of robots in flexible manufacturing are examples of the combination of low costs and customisation.

Wiseman's strategic thrusts

Rackoff *et al.* (1985) have produced a model that takes the competitive strategy work by Porter a step further. The strategic thrusts model provides a framework for a fuller identification of the strategic opportunities offered by IS. It suggests that all strategic moves or thrusts made by organisations are either offensive or defensive and fall into one of the following categories:

- differentiation of products or services;
- reducing value system costs or raising costs of rival companies;
- innovating with products or processes to change the nature of business within the industry;
- growth by vertical or horizontal integration or geographic expansion;
- making strategic alliances or agreements.

IS can be used to support or create the five strategic thrusts which can be aimed at the three strategic targets of suppliers, customers or competitors.

The Strategic Option Generator (see Figure 8.7) emerges by plotting the five strategic thrusts against the three potential targets.

The grid of the Strategic Option Generator can be filled in by asking a few questions:

- Are we targeting suppliers, customers or competitors?
- Which strategic thrust shall we use against the target?

Strategic thrust	Supplier	Customer	Competitor
Differentiation			
Low cost			
Innovation			
Growth			
Alliance			
	Strategic target		

Figure 8.7 The strategic option generator

- Is the strategic approach to be offensive or defensive?
- Which IS skills can be used, such as processing, storage, transmission?

IS can support or shape competitive thrusts and hence the organisation's strategy for sustainable competitive advantage. Senior management have to appreciate the potential of IS in order to create and evaluate different opportunities. The Strategic Option Generator helps to align IS to the chosen approach and decide on the impact of IS to effect the change in approach.

The planning process

The objective of making more effective use of IS/IT in business organisations has been around for some time. More recently, there has arisen an increasing awareness of IS/IT potential in contributing to competitive success both in the business and IS/IT communities. Strategic planning has consequently become a key activity in the search for value additionality, coupled with the need to improve return on investments by making the right decisions about which applications can produce the most benefits.

There are a number of examples of organisations which have gained competitive advantage by implementing CBIS (American Airlines, British Airways, Marriott Hotels, Thomsons, to name but a few) and, though successful companies may not have engaged in rigorous planning, there is still an element of risk that could escalate with little or no strategic planning. The impact of good planning often takes at least two or more years to be visible in the form of business practices and results, but the outcome of planning will generally improve as a consequence of a sound systems infrastructure, senior management commitment and early pilot successes with visible, high-impact applications.

Frameworks for planning

It is essential to understand the current role of IS in the organisation and how the IS function is perceived by the other business functions. By considering the application portfolio in terms of strategic, turnaround, factory and support systems (see Figure 8.1), a view can be taken as to how well the current and future business strategy is supported. Systems can also be evaluated from the perspective of their contribution to the efficiency, effectiveness or value added chain of the business.

The Sullivan (1985) matrix provides a useful tool to assess the current IS situation in terms of *infusion* and *diffusion*. Infusion represents the extent to which CBIS have been employed in the fundamental operations of the organisation and diffusion represents the extent to which CBIS have been extended out to the organisational end-users. The horizontal axis of the matrix indicates movement from centralised to departmental/personal use of CBIS, covering a wider range of business functions. The vertical axis represents incremental use of end-user computing and departmental systems. Hence, organisations moving into the top right-hand quadrant of the matrix (see Figure 8.8) would tend to have considerable awareness and experience of computer applications and be ready for strategic IS planning.

Other issues worthy of consideration when assessing the current IS role are the following:

- levels of user satisfaction with existing systems;
- the role and structure of IS in relation to the organisational structure;
- the extent of cooperation between IS and the other business functions;
- the level of integration between systems and across the different technologies;
- the level of executive responsibility for managing the IS function.

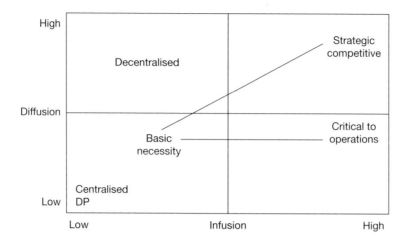

Figure 8.8 Based on the Sullivan matrix (Sullivan, 1985)
Source: Ward and Peppard (2002)

Scope and structure for IS planning

There is evidence to suggest that, rather than tackling IS planning from a corporate perspective in larger organisations, it is better to begin with the scope of the strategic business unit (SBU), as each SBU will tend to develop its own distinct IS strategy which can then be linked into the corporate strategy. Using the scope of the SBU may produce a more direct and immediate contribution from IS, though a centralised bureaucratic organisation may well benefit from a more centralised homogenous IS function.

Whether centralised or decentralised, IS functional structuring needs to fit the organisational structure (see Chapter 6). Vertically integrated organisations do tend to have the advantage that information flows more easily and more naturally vertically to and from customers and suppliers than horizontally across departments or functions. Primary systems to enhance the organisational value added chain rely to a great extent upon effective vertical linkages.

There is little in the way of evidence to support the achievement of a truly corporate IS

strategy in larger organisations. The corporation needs effectively to be a single coherent SBU in its own right, which in the current circumstances of increasing organisational complexity and diversification is rather improbable.

The way forward

Having decided that IS strategy is best determined at the business unit level unless the whole organisation is similar in terms of products, markets and operational approaches to strategy, there may still remain the need for an IS strategy to fulfil corporate information requirements, which support long-term planning and to pool consolidated information from the different business units.

In determining an approach to planning, both the structured and innovative or formal and informal approaches are best combined. On the one hand, consistency is necessary in the analysis of all the relevant elements of the business and, on the other, it is valuable to incorporate innovative ideas before and during the planning process in the effort to optimise the final strategic option selected. Business planning and analysis should combine with information analysis and innovative, creative thinking to provide the best solution.

Approaches to IS planning – an overview

Reasons for planning

It is essential to understand the underlying reasons which have prompted the need for planning. Reasons to date have included the following:

- to improve the utilisation of scarce resources, such as personnel, and to optimise prioritisation of those tasks that contribute the most to the organisational value added chain;
- to plan for the use of information as a competitive tool, as a more valued organisational resource;
- to integrate the use of information across the organisation to improve user access and to service the business as a whole, such as data and document storage;
- to integrate more efficiently and effectively the business and IS strategies to improve the overall contribution of IS to the business, such as supplier/customer electronic data interchange;
- to set up an IS infrastructure with an information architecture and tools to support that architecture, such as factory automation and communication networks;
- to undertake more cost/benefit analysis with regard to IS/IT investments.

There are several reasons for embarking upon strategic IS planning, though the priority has moved away from technology issues towards competitive use of IS, linking IS more closely with the business and the valuing of information as a corporate resource.

New Year's Day 1998 will see the opening of Malaysia's premier gateway, the K.L. International Airport at Sepang – an airport many in the industry believe will be the best gateway to the Asia-Pacific region.

KLIA is the first of a new generation of airports employing state-of-the-art technology and a Total Airport Management System (TAMS), which ensures maximum efficiency and safety. This unique high-tech airport located within a forest is symbolic of Malaysia's aspirations to preserve the past while reaching out for a dynamic future. Landing in the rainforest with its calm, lush greenery and beauty will uniquely combine with the atmosphere of a futuristic airport with its fully automatic baggage handling and track transit systems, multiple passenger service counters and highly effective road and rail links.

Furthermore, the airport is located in Malaysia's Silicon Valley, a strategic positioning to provide access to one of the fastest-growing economic zones in South East Asia and the newly emerging economies of Indochina.

KLIA's larger role, however, is to optimise Malaysia's rapid industrialisation and blueprint for further business and tourism development beyond the year 2000.

Source: Adapted from 'World Airports Survey',
Financial Times, 28 November 1996

External factors may well stimulate IS planning in response to threats or opportunities posed, such as new market opportunities created by IS/IT, new legislative pressures or the potential for improving productivity or customer service as a consequence of increased use of IS/IT.

The strategic planning for Malaysia's K.L. International Airport is a case in point.

Focus and objectives

Having established what are the reasons or impetus for strategic IS planning, it is very important to clarify the focus and objectives, which need to be achievable given the current situation and the available resources. Frequently there are pressures to be addressed or specific problems to be solved. If the main objective is to align IS and the business, the aims will probably be to develop an integrated IS architecture, stabilise the information resource and minimise maintenance.

Typical objectives would be:

- to ensure a more proactive, outward-looking approach for IS;
- to ensure the taking on of shared responsibilities by business and IS people in the organisation to develop a more strategic approach;
- to determine the right organisational structure to optimise the IS function;
- to identify staff skills necessary and achieve a balanced portfolio of them across the organisation;
- to identify current and future information requirements.

Finally, bearing in mind the fundamental systems concept of input–process–output, we need to consider what are the inputs and outputs of the planning process.

Inputs

The internal business environment has to be thoroughly understood so that the business IS needs can be determined. Business objectives, strategies and plans may exist at corporate, business unit and departmental or functional level and may be more or less formally documented. Key organisational activities and entities within them have to be examined to show interrelationships and information flows. Furthermore, the organisation as a whole needs to be evaluated in terms of structure, staff skills, culture and resources. Establishing the relationship between objectives, operational activities and information requirements across the organisation is crucial. With a deeper understanding of the internal business environment comes the determining of critical success factors (CSFs), which help prioritise what is important for the business to flourish and realise objectives.

The external business environment incorporates the forces acting upon the organisation, such as stakeholders and pressure groups, which influence the scope of strategic planning and the business strategy to be adopted. The external environment (politics, technological innovation, the government, the economy, customers and suppliers) has to be both analysed and understood to identify potential threats and opportunities.

The internal IS/IT environment involves analysing the current applications portfolio supporting operations, control, planning, and administration to assess value and contribution to the business. The IS/IT environment may also involve perceptions of cooperation between IS/IT and the business as a whole, decision-making and management responsibility, hardware/software assets, capital investment and expenditure and training.

247

The external IS/IT environment involves gauging technical trends and opportunities for innovation, concentrating upon novel or more cost-effective uses of existing technology. Competitor benchmarking is also useful to pick up ideas that may be implemented either in the current situation or sometime in the future.

Outputs

Outputs from the planning process may be hard deliverables, such as documents and plans of various kinds, or soft outputs, such as staff skills, commitment and awareness. The business IS strategy and the IS/IT management strategy are key outputs and must both be thoroughly understood by management and IS professionals alike. The IT strategy is a further output, involving the selection and implementation of the most appropriate and cost-effective technology (hardware, software, networks).

The business IS strategy needs to consider business demand for and deployment of IS/IT to achieve objectives. Applications can be represented, along with how they are to be developed and managed, within the *strategic, turn-around, factory, support* matrix in terms of their contribution to the current and potential business strategy. Strategy may well be determined at business unit level of the organisation and then linked to the corporate strategy, including infrastructure and application systems.

The management strategy helps to ensure consistency of policies across the organisation and coordination of individual business unit IS strategies which operate from a centralised IT supply function. The management strategy also addresses a number of common issues, such as the resources and responsibilities for IS/IT, defining the investment decision-making process, establishing policies for IS/IT sourcing

and accounting and the management of people issues, such as recruitment and training.

Models, tools, techniques, diagrams produced as a result of the planning process. Some of these are detailed in the next two sections.

In order to determine an IS strategy, the business has to be viewed as it is (current situation) and as it could be (future potential), either by achieving its predetermined objectives or if the direction of the business changes as a result of choice or pressures exerted.

Assessing the current situation

There are a number of useful techniques to assess the current situation, but care must be taken not to collect too much data. What is necessary is a sufficient and clear comprehension of the current business environment and information needs to develop feasible and realistic strategies. Documents need to be reviewed and a good deal of information can be gained from staff and their job descriptions.

Organisational modelling

This structured technique is designed to ensure a thorough understanding of the business and IS environment by means of documentation and interviewing of personnel. The model is made up of the following elements:

- the formal organisational operations as documented, such as plans, budgets, records;
- the people and physical assets of the organisation, including skills, training and financial assets;
- the informal organisation consisting of management styles, culture, attitudes, relationships;
- a review of the technology in use and available across the industry;

- the external environmental review in terms of competitors, industry standards, legislation, taxation;
- the internal driving forces ('the movers and shakers'), those with power and influence;
- the key operational processes that generate the products and services.

Such a model as this helps develop IS strategies that fit with organisational structure, values and culture. There are three fundamental reasons for using the organisational model (shown in Figure 8.9), which are:

1 To provide an effective filtering system so that the most suitable and implementable applications are considered for the future.
2 To aid the process of organisational change should this be necessary for the implementation of new IS.
3 To gather relevant, current data and information on the organisation to help ensure that the correct IS decisions are taken and that such decisions can be clearly justified.

Analysing and interpreting the business strategy

By analysing the data and information collected from organisational modelling, information needs can be defined, grouped and prioritised. Information needs then have to be matched with the current systems in place, which may be inadequate and require replacement or modification. Analysis of the business strategic framework makes it easier to reconcile disparate IS requirements across the organisation and their potential contribution to the business as a whole. The elements of the business strategy include the corporate mission, business objectives, CSFs, tactics and operational activities as well as different types of information required by different levels of the organisation.

There are three main reasons for interpreting the business strategy. First, to identify business activities and supporting information requirements, such as would be necessary in conducting market research prior to the launch of a new product. Second, to identify secondary business activities to measure and monitor performance, and third, to provide a framework for an information/IS strategy so that systems can be matched to the needs of the business.

CSF analysis

CSFs exist at a variety of business levels and help to focus attention on the key issues. They relate to areas of the business in which success

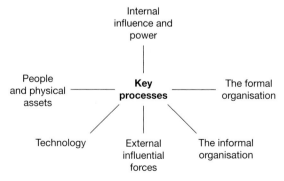

Figure 8.9 The organisational model
Source: Kotter (1978)

is crucial for competitive performance and where things must be done well in order for the business to flourish. CSFs should be determined once business objectives have been identified, as they are inevitably linked to one another. CSFs need to be identified against each objective and then consolidated across objectives to avoid duplication. Figure 8.10 shows this interrelation between CSFs and objectives, along with different levels of CSFs.

The relative importance of IS in achieving CSFs needs to be considered from the perspective of how they can contribute to, or how they prevent, their being achieved. Specific measures are associated with each CSF, such as company expenditure on advertising versus the industry average, and IS could potentially contribute to ensuring the accuracy and regularity of such measurement.

CSF analysis is an important element of the IS strategic planning process to enable management to assess the relative importance of IS opportunities to achieve business objectives and to determine executive information require-

ments to build business success. What is more, knowing which critical areas to manage helps enhance the chances of successful IS planning (Ang and Teo, 1997).

Information analysis

The main models for information resource management and systems development in the organisation produced during the planning process are entity-relationship models, activity decomposition diagrams and data flow diagrams, which are among the fundamental tools of system analysis.

Current portfolio evaluation

The current portfolio of systems in use and being developed represents the starting point or *where we are* before progressing to the future potential or *where we wish to go*. Evaluation of the current portfolio is designed to assess the extent of coverage and relative contribution of systems to business needs, establish unrealised potential in current systems and any necessary modifica-

Figure 8.10 CSFs and objectives
Source: adapted from Ward and Peppard (2002)

tions in order to breach any gaps between existing and desirable IS architecture.

It is also useful to evaluate current systems in terms of the *strategic, turnaround, factory* and *support* quadrants of the application portfolio, where the bottom quadrants may be well supplied with systems, but the upper quadrants significantly bereft. Systems may well exist that could fit into the *strategic* and *turnaround* quadrants, but have not had the opportunity to be developed.

Assessing future potential

Directing resources and actions towards the future is the next step in the IS planning process and the use of CSFs helps concentrate management attention on achievement in the future. As well as the use of various analytical techniques, a degree of creative thinking is required to assess *potential impact* of IS on the business. Assessing future potential is closely linked to seeking sustainable competitive advantage (see p.230).

Business portfolio analysis

IS/IT strategic analysis is best aligned to the strategic business unit with its distinct set of products and services, well-identified customers and competitors. The business unit is also the level at which Porter's generic strategic concepts best apply. Determining business units may not be easy, but logical units are needed to identify strategic IS opportunities and threats more definitively. Once identified, each business unit needs to be considered with a view to focusing IS/IT investment where it will best improve competitive performance, notwithstanding the need to create synergistic shared information resources and integrated systems.

In the emerging and growth stages of the industry and product life cycle, where demand is firstly unknown and then greater than supply,

effective IS/IT deployment could, for example, be aimed at enhancing the product, customer service, planning logistics and capacity development and at extending distribution channels. At the maturity and decline stages, when demand equals or is less than supply, however, IS/IT resources would be better applied, for example, to reducing costs, analysing margins, releasing capacity for alternative use and rationalising distribution channels.

Product portfolio analysis

Taking the Boston Consulting Group (BCG) matrix, it is possible to suggest strategic IS approaches for the different products in the portfolio (illustrated in Figures 8.11 and 8.12):

- With the '*wild cat*' product (low market share/high market growth) an innovative approach tends to be required with an IS strategy focused on product or process development or customer identification and segmentation.
- The '*star*' product (high market share/high market growth) requires a leadership approach to keep ahead of competitors and develop customer requirements. The IS focus needs to be oriented towards the customer, to achieving more than competitors and promoting business growth and innovation.
- The '*cash cow*' product (high market share/low market growth) requires cost-cutting and meeting customer requirements on a consistent basis. The IS strategy needs to concentrate on economy and capacity optimisation, focusing on control aspects rather than innovation.
- The '*dog*' product (low market share/low market growth) may require divestment with very little if any innovative IS, but rather more selective, well-justified investments to improve profitability and secure the customer base as well as possible.

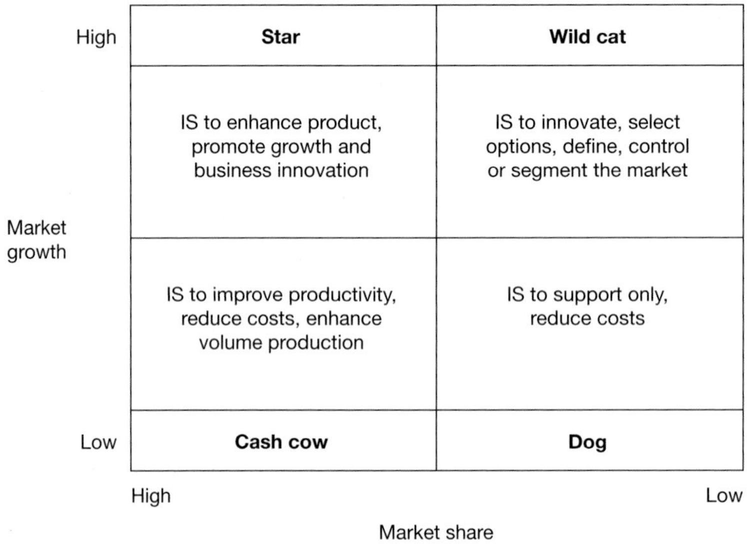

	Star	Wild cat
High	IS to enhance product, promote growth and business innovation	IS to innovate, select options, define, control or segment the market
Market growth	IS to improve productivity, reduce costs, enhance volume production	IS to support only, reduce costs
Low	**Cash cow**	**Dog**
	High	Low

Market share

Figure 8.11 IS strategic approach in the BCG product portfolio matrix
Source: adapted from Ward and Peppard (2002)

An organisation's business focus is likely to change from customers to products to customers as life cycle stages evolve and as requirements vary between improving market share or market growth. IS must change and flex with dynamic business requirements.

It is useful to combine the applications perspective with the business and industry position. From the organisational viewpoint there are a number of key issues to consider:

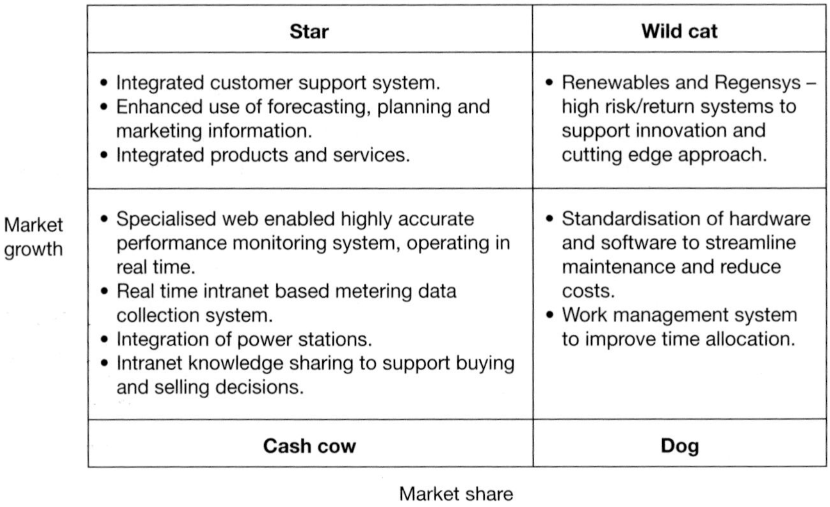

	Star	Wild cat
	• Integrated customer support system. • Enhanced use of forecasting, planning and marketing information. • Integrated products and services.	• Renewables and Regensys – high risk/return systems to support innovation and cutting edge approach.
Market growth	• Specialised web enabled highly accurate performance monitoring system, operating in real time. • Real time intranet based metering data collection system. • Integration of power stations. • Intranet knowledge sharing to support buying and selling decisions.	• Standardisation of hardware and software to streamline maintenance and reduce costs. • Work management system to improve time allocation.
	Cash cow	**Dog**

Market share

Figure 8.12 Example of a BCG matrix

- the roles of business units, their interrelationships and how they fit into the corporate whole;
- business unit product portfolios, profitability, productivity and resource demands;
- which competitive forces affect individual business units and the organisation as a whole;
- strengths and weaknesses so that actions can be prioritised.

From the industrial perspective the stage of maturity of the industry as a whole needs to be considered within which individual organisations have to compete with one another. The business strategy and objectives of the organisation must be viewed in the context of the business environment and potential IS impact for both the industry and the organisation has to be evaluated.

From the applications perspective, there are three potential phases for strategic development:

1 assessment of existing applications in terms of both present contribution to business performance and future potential contribution;
2 assessment of applications that will be required in the short- to medium-term to achieve business objectives;
3 assessment of potential applications which could be of value in the future, provided their implementation is feasible.

Consequently the organisation can begin to evaluate what it *might do*, what it *wishes to do* in response to its stakeholders' demands, what it *must do* in order to stay in business and what it is *able to do* with its resources and capabilities.

IS strategic management

Greg Parsons (1983) detailed six generic linking strategies for IS. Clearly there is no single solution to every organisation's problems with IS/IT. There are potential rewards from IS/IT in business terms, provided the right amount of time and effort is given to meet the challenge. This challenge tends to be dynamic and often complex, involving a mix of technical, organisational and strategic issues. One key issue is that of organisational *fit*, whereby IS needs are matched to the IS management framework. A linking strategy is needed to provide a framework to guide IS opportunity, develop IS resources and adopt new technologies. Such a strategy must be supported by consistent policies, practices and procedures.

Parsons' generic IS strategies

These six strategies provide a useful framework for consideration and are detailed below:

Centrally planned, which involves centralised responsibility for the IS strategy and its link to the main business strategy. By integrating business needs with an understanding of how IS can create or develop competitive advantage, a truly strategic approach and use of IS can be attained.

Leading edge involves using innovative technology development to create business opportunities. There is a large research and development component of potential applications, as yet unspecified and not requested by users.

Free market is governed by market forces and user preference. The internal IS function competes with external vendors for users who stipulate their own needs.

Monopoly provides an internal IS function as the sole source for users and this may exist centrally or as an information utility service. The aim is not to constrain users by offering them only a limited range of applications, but to satisfy their requirements at reasonable costs.

Scarce resource, on the other hand, does limit the use of IS, which as a scarce resource is allocated on a priority basis, possibly using ROI as a criterion for evaluation. IS applications are developed once the resources have clearly been defined up-front.

Necessary evil is not so much a strategy as such, but involves the use of IS only if no alternative is available, involving only those applications that are absolutely essential, such as payroll or accounting.

Organisations may use one, or more than one, of these strategies, which will fluctuate and develop over time. Care must be taken if mixing different strategies in case ambiguities arise and responsibilities become ill-defined. The fit between IS strategic impact on the organisation and the generic strategy is critical, as that strategy will identify opportunities and bring resources to develop them. Organisational and industry requirements for IS/IT will vary considerably from strategic dependence to administrative convenience, but in all cases

the linking strategy must *fit* the firm's needs for IS/IT. The best way of illustrating this *fit* is by superimposing the six generic linking strategies on to McFarlan's application portfolio, illustrating use of IS in the four quadrants of *strategic, turnaround, factory* and *support,* as shown in Figure 8.13.

Those linking strategies that are first choices (marked 1) are seen to provide the best fit. The strategic quadrant requires a centrally planned strategy; in the turnaround quadrant a leading edge strategy fits best; in the factory quadrant a monopoly strategy is optimum and in the support quadrant a scarce resource strategy will keep costs under control.

Parsons also suggests secondary strategies, which may work even if they are not ideal:

- *leading edge* could be used for strategic applications, but could prove to be both risky and expensive;
- *centrally planned* strategies could manage turnaround applications, but may slow the rate of innovation and inhibit progress with R&D;
- *scarce resource* strategies may work for factory systems, but may increase the potential for

Strategic	Turnaround
Centrally planned (1) Leading edge (2)	Leading edge (1) Free market (2) Centrally planned (2)
Monopoly (1) Scarce resource (2)	Scarce resource (1) Monopoly (2) Necessary evil (3)
Factory	**Support**

Figure 8.13 Generic strategies linked to the strategic importance of systems
Source: Parsons (1983)

systems failure from both the business and technical perspectives;

- *monopoly* strategies in the support quadrant may waste resources and *necessary evil* is always a last resort.

Mapping the evolution of IS/IT planning (see Figure 8.3 for stages of evolution of IS planning), the generic strategies would tend to begin with *scarce resource* in the *support* quadrant, moving on to *monopoly* strategy for *factory* applications. At the transition stage, before moving into the upper *turnaround* and *strategic* quadrants, a combination of *monopoly* and *scarce resources* would prevail, moving to *free market* or *leading edge* strategies in the *turnaround* quadrant and *centrally planned* or *leading edge* strategies in the *strategic* quadrant (see Figure 8.14).

Portfolio management

Once again, the Boston Consulting Group (BCG) matrix is a useful illustrative tool, as products and applications must be managed according to their contribution to the business throughout a life cycle. Applications and products will move around the matrix over time, according to positioning and variations in the

life cycle. Applications and products both require investment funding that can be justified and they need to be managed and allocated appropriate resources to match their contribution to the business. Maximising long-term profitability of products depends on successful management in each quadrant with an appropriate response to external market forces. Strategic IS application management can be considered from the same perspective. Figure 8.15 superimposes the BCG product matrix on McFarlan's application portfolio, indicating the most effective management for each quadrant.

Management styles and approaches

Management style should also change during the evolution of the product life cycle and the application portfolio.

- *Turnaround* applications, like wild cat products, tend to require an entrepreneurial management style, a free market approach that does not stick slavishly to established procedure.
- *Strategic* applications like star products, tend to require a developer type of management style, a central planner who nurtures and builds resources to achieve objectives.

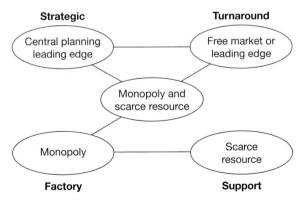

Figure 8.14 Portfolios, generic strategies and planning evolution
Source: adapted from Ward and Peppard (2002)

Products	Strategic Stars	Turnaround Wild cats
	Continuous innovation Vertical integration High value additionality	Process R&D Minimal integration Cost control
	Defensive innovation Effective utilisation of resources High quality	Rationalise Efficiency Maximise quality
Products	Cash cows Factory	Dogs Support

Figure 8.15 The business/products/systems portfolio matrix
Source: adapted from Ward and Peppard (2002)

A company in the defence aerospace industry had been performing very profitably when recession hit the manufacturing division in 1991. As airline components were becoming more sophisticated, there were fewer of them and they were lasting longer between failures. There was also a growing tendency in all industries to replace rather than repair electronic parts.

The repairs division talked of two strategies at middle management level: diversification into other forms of repair or building partnerships with the airlines based on outsourcing the whole maintenance operation. These strategies were debated by the 'old style' managers who could see times were changing and by 'new style' managers who had developed new ways of thinking based on the managerial challenges they had confronted.

The division was split across sites in the UK and the USA and these held differing views of the repairs process because of different customer bases, management styles and practices. The USA was generally regarded as more progressive with clear ideas of how to improve customer service by changing processes and introducing information systems. The UK staff regarded them as mavericks and funding was controlled from the UK.

In 1992 there was much anxiety and frustration at middle management level. A new IS/IT architecture was needed to provide integrated operations and financial systems and to promote standard working practices in the USA and UK divisions. Where were the strategic planning and management going to come from?

Source: Adapted from Wilcocks L. and Smith G. (1994)
'Case A', *Journal of SIS*, 4(3): 284–285

- *Factory* applications, like cash cow products, require a controlling, risk-averse management style with strict adherence to consistent standards. A controller is a monopolist who defends the status quo and operates within well-defined parameters.
- *Support* applications, like dog products, require a caretaker management approach, a problem solver and a scarce resourcer who strives to achieve as much as possible with as little as possible.

Requirements of IS strategic management

There are a number of key issues that are central to effective IS strategic management, including the positioning of IS resources and the required management structure to underpin IS responsibilities and the IS architecture.

The importance of 'organisational' fit cannot be over-emphasised. IS strategies and plans need to be in tune with business strategies and objectives, while the IS management culture should reflect the overall corporate culture. Critical IS activities must be monitored as they relate to business CSFs and the industry and organisational value chains to ensure maximum potential and benefit are being realised. Any new IS strategy has to take account of business risks, identify appropriate resources for implementation, set priorities and resolve conflicts, in other words be a viable proposition.

IS resources positioning

Resources for IS can be distributed in a number of ways. They may be centralised or decentralised to different business units, functions or geographical locations. Users may determine certain priorities with larger users having their own resources and smaller ones sharing a central resource. Sometimes there is a mix among different activities, with finance, for example, having a centralised resource and

R&D a decentralised resource. Sometimes IS resources are positioned according to resource type, such as networks and software data, which are centralised or distributed according to user needs and accessibility.

Organisations need to consider how to position their IS resources according to certain structural criteria. The company may or may not be geographically dispersed and have a broader or narrower range of business diversity. Complex and more widely spread organisations will need to think long and hard about how to position their IS resources, which will almost certainly be vital to their competitive success. There may be potential synergies to be capitalised on between business units, particularly with regard to information exchange, or there may well be financial implications associated with the resourcing and deployment of staff skills. Organisations will also position new IS according to the arrangement of the existing portfolio of applications, which may have been relatively recently implemented or have been in existence for some time.

IS management responsibilities

IS resources positioning in an organisation also relates to IS management responsibilities. There needs to be board-level responsibility for IS, but this may be spread among a number of directors, given the diffusion of systems throughout the whole organisation. It is often considered more effective to have one person at board level with responsibility for all or most aspects of organisational IS/IT.

IS managers may be based in each business unit and have more or less autonomy depending on responsibility distribution in the organisation. There may then be an IT manager with more centralised responsibility for the different business units. Some companies may have a Chief Information Officer (CIO) who has to operate through some sort of executive committee and has little in the way of real authority to get things done. Many such managers are business people with little or no technical experience. Conversely, IT directors may have more technical than management expertise. It is always difficult to achieve the right balance of business and technical skills in IS/IT management, but the majority of public and private sector organisations tend to establish steering groups, functional or business planning groups, application management groups, and service and technical management groups.

Good IS strategic management depends on the right kind of senior management commitment and involvement where it can be most helpful when combined with appropriate user contributions to determining strategy. Consistent control and policy decisions to develop and implement strategies over time are essential. Ideas from all organisational levels should be considered and the ability should exist to learn from and transfer experience across different parts of the organisation. All too often coordination of IS/IT management is insufficient across related functions and strategies end up being either not developed or not implemented.

Alignment between the business and IS/IT strategies

The alignment between business and IS strategies has been a critical issue in recent research but there are very few empirical studies that provide evidence to support the need for alignment and there is also little evidence about how the two interact (Sillince and Frost, 1995). However, it is widely agreed that for IS planning to be effective, there must be some coordination between business and IS planning. Business and IS activities must be coordinated for IS strategies to be aligned with business goals and activities. Furthermore, it is important to integrate business and technical issues to produce high-quality IT plans that focus on using IT strategically. Another dimension involves the 'reverse' flow of information from IS to business planning, a flow that illustrates the impact that IS resources can have on business strategies (Teo and King, 1999).

Henderson and Venkatraman (1992) developed a strategic alignment model in response to a rapidly changing business environment, a model that replaces a traditional functional linkage model of IS/IT planning with one that

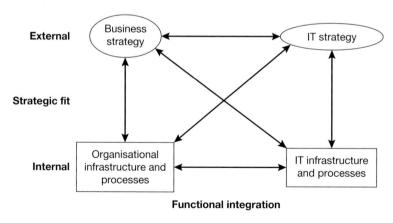

Figure 8.16 Strategic alignment model
Source: Henderson and Venkatraman (1992)

requires a highly integrated strategic management process (see Figure 8.16). The model is based on the relationship between strategic fit and functional integration, an interplay between business strategy and organisational infrastructure and processes. The IS/IT strategy involves, therefore, the following choices:

- scope of IS/IT in terms of range and typologies critical to the organisation;
- systemic competencies that enable the organisation to create or extend the business strategy;
- IS/IT governance in terms of ownership and management of the systems and technologies.

The model assumes a traditional, sequential approach to business strategy development, which may or may not be appropriate for all of today's businesses.

Alignment suggests a sequential process, whereby there is a leader–follower relationship that can create tensions in terms of how long the follow-up time is from the business decision to the IS/IT decision. This in turn can result in perceptions of inadequacy and lack of responsiveness, which in turn can have the potential knock-on effect of creating negative perceptions of IS/IT.

In practice it might prove more beneficial to consider the development of the business strategy and the IS/IT strategy as one and the same. The two need to be interconnected to enable IS/IT-related ideas to create business opportunities and business ideas to be generated from IS/IT ideas. With one strategy and one set of operational plans, activities are performed by all the functions together and impacts are evaluated at the same time. In this way, IS/IT forms part of a fully integrated organic structure.

Whether organisations decide to follow the more mechanistic, sequential model or a more flexible, closely integrated approach, there must be a definitive interlinking of the business and IS/IT strategies if maximum competitive advantage is to be achieved from systems and technologies.

Chapter summary

There is set to be an increasing use of IS for strategic purposes to provide sustainable competitive advantage as time progresses. It is therefore important to understand why and how SIS can be achieved. Issues of the business strategy have to be understood before the IS management strategy can be produced on the basis of information and IS requirements to achieve organisational objectives.

A number of frameworks exist to aid the process of strategic IS planning: competitive forces analysis, value system analysis and the strategic option generator. The inputs and outputs of the strategic planning process have been outlined. Companies must assess their current situation in some detail and estimate future potential, both from the business perspective and in terms of IS/IT existing and required.

Once the business and IS strategies have been defined, they must be managed. Parsons' generic IS strategies provide a definitive and useful framework for IS management in the business context. The importance of aligning business and IS strategies is briefly discussed, emphasising an integrated approach to achieve the best strategic results.

Review questions

1 Why is a strategic approach to IS important?
2 How can IS be used strategically?
3 Which are the three main business strategies and how can IS support them?
4 Explain how McFarlan analyses Porter's competitive forces. Why is this useful?
5 How can IS/IT be applied to the analysis of the value system model? How can this help organisations become more competitive?
6 What are Wiseman's Strategic Thrusts and why are they relevant?
7 Why do organisations need to undertake strategic IS planning?
8 Explain briefly the main elements of the strategic planning process
9 How can Parsons' generic IS strategies be mapped on to the application portfolio and why is this useful?
10 Which factors in terms of responsibilities and resources need to be considered in strategic IS management?
11 How can organisations achieve sustainable competitive advantage using IS/IT?
12 How important is it to align the business and IS strategies and why?

Case study

Towngas

Towngas was founded in 1862 and was the first privately run public utility in East Asia. In 1967 the company abandoned coal and switched to heavy oil as feedstock for its product – gas. In 1975 Towngas was invited to supply gas to the Ha Kwai Chung public housing estate in Kowloon and this represented the first venture into Government Housing Authority projects. From then on the company provided gas to all new housing estates within range of its supply network. In 1995 the company had fully operational joint ventures in Mainland China and by mid-1998 had its fourth such joint venture.

Towngas is a listed corporation whose main business includes the production and distribution of gas, the marketing of gas and appliances, and the supply of gas and related services. Today the company has about 2,100 staff to serve 1.3 million customers and is still investing in expanding supply capacity to meet future demand. The network coverage has reached 85 per cent of Hong Kong's homes.

Mission and objectives

Towngas's mission is: 'To provide our customers with a safe and reliable supply of gas and the friendly, competent and efficient service they expect.'

In order to fulfil the company's mission, the following objectives are to be achieved:

Safe and reliable supply of gas

- Ensure that the gas supply is available whenever the customer turns on the appliance;
- introduce a regular inspection programme of visits to customers to ensure gas safety and appliance efficiency;
- provide round-the-clock instant emergency maintenance to reduce injury and property damage;
- provide a virtual customer centre for convenient bill transactions on the web.

Friendly, competent and efficient service

- Provide direct phone contact with customer service officers, rather than interactive voice response messages;
- train customer service officers to provide assistance in English, Cantonese and Putonghua;
- provide seven maintenance appointment time-slots for customer convenience;
- modify the Towngas bill into a single-language, easy-to-read format and enable fast and convenient payment settlement.

Market segments and corporate culture

Gas and gas appliances are the major products of the company. The market segments and types of gas applications are shown in Figure 8.17 below.

Towngas offers many choices in gas appliances for the household so as to maximise residential gas consumption. The company also works closely with appliance manufacturers on product development. It has a well-established marketing programme targeted at increasing the use of gas applications in commercial and industrial processes from hotels and restaurants to bakeries and cold storage.

The organisational culture of Towngas is summarised by the shared values of:

- customer value – high quality and good service with short lead-time and low cost;
- customer focus – the customer is the company's first priority;
- sustained business growth – revenue growth, safety and reliability, costs, customer service, competition, business environment, organisational effectiveness, diversification, continuous improvement;
- leadership – at all levels of the organisation.

Strategic analysis

Towngas's industrial environment, current positioning, current strategic direction and future outlook are examined using Porter's five forces and generic business strategies.

The two major competitors of Towngas are liquefied petroleum gas (LPG) and electricity (CLP and Hong Kong Electric). The company has to persuade developers to let them lay pipes to new estates and industrial zones and it also has to keep its customers, while preventing them from switching to other fuels. Towngas has an advantage over LPG as not all buildings are suitable for

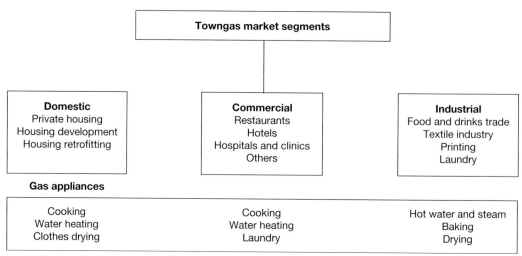

Figure 8.17 Market segments of Towngas

piped LPG and bottled LPG has raised issues over safety. While CLP Holdings and Hong Kong Electric strongly advocate the use of 'no flame' cooking to consumers, Chinese families still tend to prefer the use of traditional flame cooking methods.

Towngas manufactures its product using the raw material naphtha, which is supplied by a number of international oil companies, such as Shell and Caltex, and shipped directly to the gas production plants. There are also numerous manufacturers of gas appliances all over the world, such as in Japan, Australia, Italy and mainland China. What is more, property developers decide the primary type of fuel supply, with pipe installation and connections to the gas appliances occurring prior to occupancy of the properties.

In June 1998 natural gas supply was introduced into the Hong Kong retail market, thereby putting pressure on Towngas to open the existing distribution network to other companies. However, such companies would have to have enough technical know-how to cope with gas-related matters in the field and the initial high investment might not be warranted to enter an already almost saturated market. Moreover, Hong Kong does not require space-heating in winter and lacks large industrial users, most of which have moved to mainland China.

With the recent economic downturn in Hong Kong and the slowing of new building development, the growth rate of new customers was also lower. Towngas needed to determine a differentiation strategy to maintain steady growth. This strategy focused more sharply than ever on the importance of the customer and the necessity to provide more value than ever to the customer. Activities included visiting customers in residential estates to ensure the meeting of their expectations, and new product development aimed at the high end of the residential market. In the industrial and commercial sector the sales focus was on a total-solution approach for existing customers and an increasing range of specialised industries that had not previously used gas. In terms of societal impact, the company introduced an Elderly Concession Scheme for registered Towngas customers aged 60 or above living with other qualified elderly people in the self-care quarters of public housing estates. These seniors received a variety of concessions and discounts.

The company further pledged to use all economic means to minimise pollution and environmental waste. These initiatives created goodwill and enhanced the corporate image in the eyes of the customers.

Information systems analysis

The IT department of the company, headed by a Chief Information Officer (CIO), is responsible for systems development. The department is further divided into three service areas to accomplish the necessary business tasks:

1   the System Development Section, responsible for the business systems development projects;
2   the System Infrastructure Section, responsible for the design, implementation and support of computer systems, networking and infrastructure of the company;
3   the System Operation Section, responsible for the daily operations of the data centres and the administration of the computer systems.

Being aware of the importance of IS/IT as a strategic tool for business growth and the company-wide impact of computer systems, the CIO was appointed as a member of the Executive Committee of the company, the highest management authority. Better communication between the key IS/IT staff and the business was also established. The contribution of IS/IT to the business is depicted in Figure 8.18:

In the past Towngas employed a centralised computer system to handle daily operations on the following:

• account inquiry and maintenance, sales and after-sales service;
• consumption management and billing;
• materials management;
• financial and management accounting.

Strategic	High potential
• Consumption management	• Timely report on consumer and marketing information • New business system development • Design, implementation and support of the company IT product innovation
Key operational	**Support**
• Account inquiry and maintenance • Material management • Financial and management accounting	• Daily transactions

Figure 8.18 Application portfolio model of Towngas

These business transactions were processed by a VAX computer system, a file processing system storing various types of information, such as customer account information, material stock and appliance sales, in file format. Because of its programme-data dependence, it was often difficult to locate all the relevant programmes that were affected by changes in the file structures of any data. The system could not cope with the business requirements and created a heavy workload for the development of new applications.

Currently, a new IS system is being implemented and modified. The old VAX system is to be scrapped to cater for business changes in the industry and among competitors and to achieve the aim of making the company a consumer service rather than a gas product company.

IS strategic analysis

The Customer Information System (CIS) serves the following objectives:

- CIS supports marketing, sales and customer service functions in an integrated IS/IT environment to manage customer relations in a timely, efficient and effective way.
- CIS captures and consolidates relevant information for the formulation of marketing strategies in a highly competitive energy market.
- CIS assists exploration of new revenue generating sales services.
- CIS allows instant access to valuable customer and marketing information at site, office, customer centre or any workplace location to provide excellent customer service.

The CIS consists of the following modules:

- The consumption management sub-system – given the necessity to provide and integrate various related services to customers on a single system, this system should be able to supply convenient, friendly and prompt service. The system covers customer, account and premises creation and maintenance, capture and scheduling of meter reading, bill calculation, production and adjustment, payment and collections.
- The sales operation sub-system – the availability of sales operation data is essential to the formulation of sales plans and marketing programmes. The Transaction Processing and Executive Information System allow for flexible and efficient sales services. This system covers sales planning and promotion, daily sales operations and service contract management.
- The services order sub-system – maintenance is a major concern for customers. A manual system could not cater for the high demand on response time, maintenance quality and workmanship control. A computerised maintenance management system is necessary to keep up-to-date all the relevant records and requests. This sub-system covers the appointment-based services, including domestic maintenance, commercial and industrial maintenance, contract maintenance, domestic installation, emergency operations, riser maintenance and inspection and regular safety inspection.

Towngas began its quality journey in 1992 with the launch of the Superior Quality Service (SQS) programme. The company then obtained a number of ISO 9000 certifications for a number of its operations. In 1996 the company started the Continuing Transforming (CT) programme to catalyse a change in quality attitudes and behaviour within the company.

(Case adapted from coursework by Tony Brewerton (2001) MSc Information Systems Management, University of Stirling.)

Case questions

1 Summarise Towngas's strategic business position in terms of who their stakeholders are, the basic trends in their industry and any key uncertainties they need to be aware of.
2 Categorise the company's business strategies from the perspective of its products and services, the competitive environment and meeting their customers' needs and expectations in the domestic, industrial and commercial sectors.
3 Explain how the new IS system aligns with the business strategies for consumer service.
4 What do you consider to be the gap between Towngas's current and required use of IS?

References and further reading

Ang J. and Teo T.S.H. (1997) 'CSFs and Sources of Assistance and Expertise in Strategic IS Planning: a Singapore Perspective', *European Journal of Information Systems*, 6(3): 164–171.

Broadbent M. and Weill P. (1997) 'Management by Maxim: How Business and IT Managers Can Create IT Infrastructures', *Sloan Management Review*, Spring: 77–92.

Brown A. (1994) 'Getting Value from an Integrated IS Strategy', *European Journal of Information Systems*, 3(2): 155–165.

Cash J.I. and McLeod P.L. (1985) 'Managing the Introduction of Information Systems Technology in Strategically Dependent Companies', *Journal of MIS*, 1(4), Spring: 5–23.

Cragg P., King M. and Hussin H. (2002) 'IT Alignment and Firm Performance in Small Manufacturing Firms', *Journal of Strategic Information Systems*, 11(2), June: 109–132.

Curry A.C. and Stancich L. (2000) 'The Intranet – an Intrinsic Component of Strategic Information Management?', *International Journal of Information Management*, 20: 249–268.

Doyle J.R. (1991) 'Problems with Strategic Information Systems Frameworks', *European Journal of Information Systems*, 1(4): 273–280.

Earl M.J. (1989) *Management Strategies for Information Technology*, Prentice Hall: Englewood Cliffs, NJ.

Feeny D.F. and Ives B. (1990) 'In Search of Sustainability: Reaping Long-Term Advantage from Investments in Information Technology', *Journal of MIS*, 7(1), Summer: 27–46.

Flynn D.J. and Hepburn P.A. (1994) 'Strategic Planning for Information Systems – a Case Study of a UK Metropolitan Council', *European Journal of Information Systems*, 3(3): 207–217.

Galliers R.D. and Sutherland A.R. (1991) 'Information Systems Management and Strategy Formulation: The Stages of Growth Model Revisited', *Journal of Information Systems*, 1(2): 89–114.

Galliers R.D., Leidner D.E. and Baker B.S.H. (eds) (1999) *Strategic Information Management*, Butterworth-Heinemann: Oxford.

Gordon S.R. and Gordon J.R. (1996) *Information Systems. A Management Approach*, Dryden: Orlando, FL.

Gottschalk P. (1999) 'Strategic Information Systems Planning: the IT Strategy Implementation Matrix', *European Journal of Information Systems*, 8(2): 107–118.

Hackney R. and Little S. (1999) 'Opportunistic Strategy Formulation for IS/IT Planning', *European Journal of Information Systems*, 8(2): 119–126.

Hamilton D. (1999) 'Linking Strategic Information Systems Concepts to Practice: Systems Integration at the Portfolio Level', *Journal of Information Technology*, 14(1): 69–82.

Henderson J.C. and Venkatraman N. (1992) 'Strategic Alignment: A Model for Organizational Transformation through Information Technology', in Kocham T.A. and Useem M. (eds), *Transforming Organizations*, Oxford University Press: New York.

Ives B. and Learmonth G.P. (1984) 'The Information System as a Competitive Weapon', *Communications of the ACM*, 27(12): 1193–1201.

Johnston H.R. and Vitale M.R. (1988) 'Creating Competitive Advantage with Interorganisational Information Systems', *MIS Quarterly*, 12(4), June: 153–165.

Kearns G.S. and Lederer A.L. (2000) 'The Effect of Strategic Alignment on the Use of IS-Based Resources for Competitive Advantage', *Journal of Strategic Information Systems*, 9(4), December: 265–293.

Kettinger W., Grover V., Guha S. and Segars A.H. (1994) 'Strategic Information Systems Revisited: a Study in Sustainability and Performance', *MIS Quarterly*, March: 31–55.

King W.R. and Teo T.S.H. (1996) 'Key Dimensions of Facilitators and Inhibitors for the Strategic Use of Information Technology', *Journal of MIS*, 12(4), Spring: 35–53.

Kotter J.P. (1978) *Organisational Dynamics*, Addison Wesley: Reading, MA.

Kunnathur A.S. and Shi Z. (2001) 'An Investigation of the Strategic Information Systems Planning Success in Chinese Publicly Traded Firms', *International Journal of Information Management*, 21: 423–439.

Lederer A.L. and Sethi V. (1996) 'Key Prescriptions for Strategic Information Systems Planning', *Journal of MIS*, 13(1), Summer: 35–62.

Lederer A.L. and Sethi V. (1999) 'The Information Systems Planning Process', in Galliers R.D., Leidner D.E. and Baker B.S.H. (eds) *Strategic Information Management*, 2nd edn, Butterworth Heinemann: Oxford.

Lee G-G. and Bai R-J. (2003) 'Organisational Mechanisms for Successful IS/IT Strategic Planning in the Digital Era', *Management Decision*, 41(1): 32–42.

McFarlan F.W. (1984) 'Information Technology Changes the Way you Compete', *Harvard Business Review*, May–June: 93–103.

Mahmood M.A. and Mann G.J. (1993) 'Measuring the Organisational Impact of Information Technology Investment: an Exploratory Study', *Journal of MIS*, 10(1), Summer: 97–122.

Mason R.M. (1991) 'The Role of Metaphors in Strategic Information Systems Planning', *Journal of MIS*, 8(2), Fall: 11–30.

Min S.K., Suh E.H. and Kim S.Y. (1999) 'An Integrated Approach Toward Strategic Information Systems Planning', *Journal of Strategic Information Systems*, 8(4), December: 373–394.

Parsons G.L. (1983) 'Fitting Information Systems Technology to the Corporate Needs: the Linking Strategy', *Harvard Business School Teaching Note*, 9–183–176.

Peppard J. (1999) 'Information Management in the Global Enterprise: an Organising Framework', *European Journal of Information Systems*, 8(1): 77–94.

Peppard J. and Ward J.W. (1999) 'Mind the Gap: Diagnosing the Relationship Between the IT Organisation and the Rest of the Business', *Journal of Strategic Information Systems*, 8(1), March: 29–60.

Porter M.E. (1979) 'How Competitive Forces Shape Strategy', *Harvard Business Review*, 59(2), March–April: 137–145.

Porter M.E. (1980) *Competitive Strategy*, Free Press: New York.

Porter M.E. (1985) *Competitive Advantage*, Free Press: New York.

Porter M.E. and Millar V.E. (1985) 'How Information Gives You Competitive Advantage', *Harvard Business Review*, 63(4), July–August: 149–160.

Post G.V., Kagan A. and Lau K-N. (1995) 'A Modelling Approach to Evaluating Strategic Uses of Information Technology', *Journal of MIS*, 12(2), Fall: 161–187.

Rackoff N., Wiseman C. and Ulrich W.A. (1985) 'Information Systems for Competitive Advantage: Implementations of a Planning Process', *MIS Quarterly*, December: 285–295.

Robson W. (1997) *Strategic Management and Information Systems*, Pitman: London.

Rockart J., Earl M.J. and Ross J.W. (1996) 'Eight Imperatives for the New IT Organisation', *Sloan Management Review*, Fall: 43–55.

Roepke R., Agarwal R. and Ferratt T.W. (2000) 'Aligning the IT Human Resource with Business Vision: the Leadership Initiative at 3M', *MIS Quarterly*, 24(2): 327–353.

Ross J.W., Beath C.M. and Goodhue D.L. (1996) 'Developing Long-term Competitiveness through IT Assets', *Sloan Management Review*, Fall: 31–42.

Sabherwal R. and Tsoumpas P. (1993) 'The Development of Strategic Information Systems: Some Case Studies and Research Proposals', *European Journal of Information Systems*, 2(4): 240–259.

Salmela H. and Spil T.A.M. (2002) 'Dynamic and Emergent Information Systems Strategy Formulation and Implementation', *International Journal of Information Management*, 22: 441–460.

Segars A.H. and Grover V. (1998) 'Strategic Information Systems Planning Success: an Investigation of the Construct and Its Measurement', *MIS Quarterly*, June: 139–163.

Sillince J.A.A. and Frost C.E.B. (1995) 'Operational, Environmental and Managerial Factors in Non-alignment of Business Strategies and IS Strategies for the Police Service in England and Wales', *European Journal of Information Systems*, 4(2): 103–115.

Smaczny T. (2001) 'Is An Alignment Between Business and Information Technology the Appropriate Paradigm to Manage IT in Today's Organisations?', *Management Decision*, 39(10): 797–802.

Somogyi E.K. and Galliers R.D. (1987) *Towards Strategic Information Systems*, Abacus Press: Tunbridge Wells.

Sullivan C. (1985) 'Business Planning in the Information Age', *Sloan Management Review*, Winter: 3–12.

Szewcak E.J. (1988) 'Exploratory Results of a Factor Analysis of Strategic Information: Implications for Strategic Systems Planning', *Journal of MIS*, 5(2), Fall: 83–97.

Teo T.S.H. and King W.R. (1997) 'Integration Between Business Planning and Information Systems Planning: an Evolutionary–Contingency Perspective', *Journal of MIS*, 14(1), Summer: 185–214.

Teo T.S.H. and King W.R. (1999) 'An Empirical Study of the Impacts of Integrating Business Planning and Information Systems Planning', *European Journal of Information Systems*, 8(3): 200–210.

Teo T.S.H. and Ang J.S.K. (2001) 'An Examination of Major IS Planning Problems', *International Journal of Information Management*, 21: 457–470.

Ward J.W. and Peppard J. (2002) *Strategic Planning for Information Systems*, Wiley: Chichester.

Wiseman C. (1985) *Strategy and Computers: Information Systems as Competitive Weapons*, Dow Jones Irwin: Homewood, IL.

Zviran M. (1990) 'Relationships Between Organisational and Information Systems Objectives: Some Empirical Evidence', *Journal of MIS*, 7(1), Summer: 65–84.

Chapter 9

Overview case study EUROSELECT

Adapted from a case written by Angele Cavaye and Stefan Klein

···

The development of VEH during the 1980s

The story of Van Eerd Holdings (VEH) began in 1978 when Karel van Eerd took over the family business, a medium-sized grocery wholesaler serving small supermarkets in the area. VEH suppliers (grocery manufacturers) considered VEH to be small fry and hence not eligible for special discounts, while VEH's customers (small supermarkets) operated on low margins and were only interested in low-priced products. As VEH's competitive position was relatively weak, the decision was taken to integrate forward and extend the organization vertically by establishing independent retail outlets in the form of the Jumbo supermarket chain in the south of the Netherlands. This strategy meant that VEH was no longer solely dependent on wholesaling alone and could reap economies of scale in wholesaling with benefits for their own supermarkets and their customer supermarkets.

Industrial background

In the Netherlands 70 per cent of all food is sold through national chain stores with only 8 per cent of the Dutch food market serviced by small supermarkets and corner stores, usually family-owned. These shops often group themselves into small voluntary chains but they are constantly under threat from the large players. Trends in the European grocery industry in the 1980s led to greater competition, favouring large wholesalers, chains and producers. Internationalisation of supermarkets has further threatened the existence of small-scale regional wholesalers.

Industry structure

Take-overs and cooperation among producers have led to a decreasing number of producers of the same products. VEH went from dealing with 1,000 producers in the early 1980s to 400 in the late 1980s. Producers have taken over wholesalers, entailing further concentration in the European grocery industry, and the position of wholesalers has also been eroded by information technology enabling large producers and supermarkets to bypass the wholesaler. A few large international wholesalers increasingly dominate the market and have expanded by opening branches in other European countries.

Price differentiation

In spite of the existence of the single market, remarkable price differences are still evident among the different EU countries. This is the case for a large number of basic goods, even between identical products supplied by different national branches of the same producer. Different wage levels, national taxes and non-tariff trade barriers are some of the factors responsible for these price differences.

Increasing product range in supermarkets

Supermarkets steadily increase the number of products on the shelves. From some 9,000 products the average-sized supermarket has progressed to 14,000, much in the style of North American supermarkets. Consumers travel more than before or work in other European countries and expect to see international products available in their home supermarkets. Wholesalers and supermarkets wishing to remain competitive have to respond to these developments by offering a wider, more international range of products.

VEH in the late 1980s

In the late 1980s VEH presented itself as a conglomerate managing several enterprises at various stages of the grocery sector value chain. VEH supplied some 100 supermarkets as a wholesaler, owned a chain of 17 supermarkets and had stakes in various other small chains. VEH's customer-base consisted of relatively small, independent grocery outlets and supermarkets. Employing some 1,000 people, VEH's main asset was its wholesale business with a market share in the southern provinces of 10 per cent and of 1.5 per cent in the Netherlands as a whole. VEH turnover amounted to US$225m in 1990.

The VEH supermarket operation had consistently aimed not to be in direct competition with the existing customers of its wholesaling business. The Jumbo supermarkets became a chain of discount stores with a large range of products. It rapidly became clear, however, that the Jumbo supermarkets would not be able to compete in the discount market. As a wholesaler buying products from producers, VEH often paid a higher price than the one paid by consumers buying the same product from rival supermarkets. Individual products were sold in other supermarkets at a price 30 per cent to 40 per cent below the price at which the products were bought by the VEH wholesaling operation.

The business idea and strategic rationale

The management team of VEH felt that similar wholesalers in other European countries might be facing the same difficulty as themselves: stuck in a grocery logistics chain and in a segment where prices were not able to compete with product prices in larger and international grocery chains. The idea occurred to them that they might be able to cooperate with wholesalers in other countries within the EU to build an international network of independent wholesalers. Wholesalers in different European countries should be able to pool their knowledge of products and pricing in each market and thus obtain knowledge on international pricing and product availability. In this way, local wholesalers would jointly be able to leverage the same resources as existing large international wholesalers and supermarket chains.

VEH wanted not only to gain access to and buy products at competitive prices for their own Dutch customers but wished also to offer international wholesaling services to local wholesalers in other European countries. Local wholesalers in other countries would be sent internationally compared price lists and would be encouraged to order through VEH. By combining orders and then ordering in the country offering the product at the best price, VEH wholesaling should be able to achieve still further economies of scale and would receive extra income from a profit margin on all products ordered from the international price list. The rationale was that a product offered in country A at 30 per cent below the price of the same product in country B could still be offered to wholesalers in country B at 20 per cent below local prices, allowing for a 5 per cent margin for transport costs and a 5 per cent margin for profit.

This strategy of VEH was designed to achieve two objectives. First, VEH wished to gain access to lower prices for the same products through international cooperation and second, VEH envisioned the opportunity to increase the size of its market from the regional Dutch market to the EU market; this could be achieved by making the comparative pricing information available to other wholesalers internationally. The project was therefore named EUROSELECT to reflect this selection of products and prices from any country in the EU.

Making EUROSELECT happen

VEH made an effort to scan the European market to learn about business practices in other EU countries and to find out about trading and transport opportunities in each country. Specifically, VEH began to look for partners in other countries, considered which products to include in the project and thought of ways to compare product prices.

Network with partners

VEH set about finding similar wholesalers to themselves in other EU countries. These wholesalers did not have existing international connections and had a customer-base consisting of relatively small, independent grocery outlets and supermarkets. These wholesalers were potential partners in the EUROSELECT information-gathering network and would also be potentially in the international wholesaling component of EUROSELECT. One information-gathering partner was selected in each EU country, contracts with each partner were signed and other wholesalers were put on the list of potential clients. EUROSELECT opened an office in each EU country to facilitate contact with the partner and with clients in that country.

Product categorisation

As the total range of products offered in supermarkets is considerable, it would be too daunting a task to include all products straightaway. Hence, VEH had to decide on a category with which to start the EUROSELECT scheme. It was safest to start with non-perishable goods since transport might affect the shelf life of perishables. Faced with the choice of traditional versus non-traditional products, it was easier to start with traditional goods, given that every supermarket carries traditional goods.

Although the same product can usually be obtained in various countries, the quality (stronger or weaker blend) and quantity (larger and smaller sizes) of product tend to vary considerably among individual countries. Different common packaging sizes make even products of the same brand difficult to compare. Putting different sizes on the shelf also increases the complexity of labelling and warehouse management. Furthermore, the taste of brand products is often adjusted to local customs. All these issues create a range of practical problems and for EUROSELECT to be realised it would be necessary to categorise each product according to size and quality.

Product comparison

EUROSELECT would have to be able to compare data on products (identified by product, quality and size) with their associated prices from the various countries. The plan was to start with 4,000 different products. Considering the product differences in 12 different countries, those 4,000 products would translate into some 50,000 items to be compared. All the product prices would need to be translated into a common currency in order to enable comparison. It was decided to convert all prices to ECUs (European Currency Units) and to compare all prices daily.

Factors encouraging the *EUROSELECT* concept

The EUROSELECT business idea was novel and ambitious but in the early 1990s there were two factors which encouraged VEH to proceed with their plans. First, there was the pending internationalisation of Europe. The European Community was to become a single market from the beginning of 1993 and hence become the EU. EU plans indicated that every product sold in one EU country would be accepted for sale in any other country. Similarly, transport across national boundaries was to facilitate customs and taxation procedures. The vision of trans-Europe trading and moving grocery products across national boundaries fitted well with EU single market plans.

Second, VEH knew that there was technology available that in theory should enable the carrying out of their plans. Technological support would be essential to keep track of such a large number of items, translate local prices into a common currency, compare prices of similar products in different countries and provide continually-adjusted, up-to-date lists of products and prices. Such manipulation of data would require a technological solution. VEH did not know how to achieve it but knew that technology should be able to help them achieve their objectives.

The IT solution

It was clear from the onset of the business concept that the implementation of IT would be crucial, given the need for frequent transfer and processing of high volumes of data. These transfers and processing had to happen fast and at a low cost so as not to reduce profit margins and the potential for volume trading.

VEH approached consultants to help them develop and implement the IT components of EUROSELECT. The initial thought was that this was not going to be a very difficult task. VEH had no IT department and no IT experience to speak of. Therefore they were not interested in designing and developing a system of their own and intended to buy and customise an existing algorithm. However, VEH could not find a solid price comparison system to suit their needs. Large competitors had in-house systems but had no intention of sharing them with VEH. It was also not entirely clear whether those systems were truly capable of categorising and comparing thousands of products internationally.

For a short while VEH toyed with the idea of using software developed for stock markets since that is also a setting in which products and prices are compared. However, in stock markets homogeneity of products facilitates comparison of stock prices and currency rates, whereas in the grocery industry products are heterogeneous.

VEH even went to the USA in search of an existing algorithm. They found, however, that most grocery wholesalers operated on a regional basis; those that did operate nationally hardly leveraged prices across regions and those that tried to leverage price differences did so with the support of sophisticated systems. In all, VEH drew a blank and decided that they would have to develop their own bespoke system for EUROSELECT. The costs of developing a proprietary system were too high for a relatively small organization like VEH and there was no justification in reinventing existing and accepted norms. The decision was made, therefore, to design and develop a system with as many standard components as possible. When no standards were available, standard associations were consulted to ensure that codes and messages were designed in standard formats.

Development took place in cooperation with a large Dutch informatics and consultancy company (Volmac), the Dutch organization for EDI (electronic data interchange) in trade in industry (UAC-Transcom). Since VEH were already using BULL hardware, BULL became the hardware partner for the EURO-SELECT venture. EUROSELECT then presented an innovative way of using IT to facilitate trade among small and medium-sized enterprises across Europe as part of a bid for funding from the European Commission. The bid was successful and development of part of the system was funded as a European pilot project.

PRODEC – the backbone of EUROSELECT

The core application of EUROSELECT was an electronic price and product catalogue called PRODEC (Products European Community). Its functional scope comprised the following:

* the maintenance of a central catalogue (comparison and analysis of market information);
* the placing and controlling of orders;
* the coordination of delivery and payment procedures.

PRODEC was based on an Oracle relational database, and a Unix operating system was used

in conjunction with a minicomputer at head office and PCs in the national offices. The applications were developed with Oracle 4-GL/case tools. PRODEC became a mixture of standard and proprietary components. Standard Oracle software and standard tools were used to develop and implement PRODEC. The classification scheme and the comparison algorithm developed were proprietary VEH know-how.

Product categorisation and comparison

EUROSELECT had to develop a product classification system to enable comparison of products and prices from various countries. A framework for classification, allowing for up to 12 variations of each individual product in a database, was designed by VEH in the Netherlands.

Products were then coded according to EAN (European Article Number) standards. The VEH classification scheme, taking into account variations in a product's package size and quality, added various dimensions to the standard EAN product code.

Based on the product classification scheme a comparison algorithm matched comparable products and compared price and quality. The result was a list of 'lowest price buying suggestions' that was then checked by experienced EUROSELECT representatives in the central office.

EDI

EUROSELECT was built on the concept of electronic data interchange (EDI) with large amounts of information exchanged electronically among offices in the EU member countries. Standardised message formats were used to enable automatic transactions, even though a part of the data analysis was done manually.

Standardised messages

PRODEC had been designed to enable the exchange of product information between EUROSELECT offices. The standards used – in particular EDIFACT – were designed to provide flexibility and to facilitate future expansion to electronic ordering and invoice receiving from suppliers. PRODEC was the first operational system to employ the EDIFACT price catalogue message type (PRICAT) to maintain the central product database.

Telecommunication links

The information collected during the day was stored in a local database on a PC at each national EUROSELECT office. Every night the information was transmitted to the central database in the Netherlands. Initially the data was transmitted via dial-up lines using modems and public telephone links provided by national PTT's. Kermit (for the BULL) and GLINK (for the PCs) were used as communications software. As the quality of PTT services varied significantly across Europe, EUROSELECT intended to switch eventually to a VAN supplier.

Organisation

The framework and rules for product categorisation were designed by VEH in the Netherlands with actual categorisation of individual local products done by local employees in the different EU countries. Once PRODEC had been developed and the EDI links put in place with local offices, the system could start to work.

The local EUROSELECT offices gathered market information on price and product quality in cooperation with the national wholesale partner, which collected the data during their normal business activities. The local

EUROSELECT manager was responsible for verifying this information and assigning it to the appropriate product category.

The message flow

Two message flow cycles could be distinguished. The first cycle dealt with price and product information: the information was provided by the national partners, collected by the EUROSELECT national offices and transmitted to the central database at the EUROSELECT head office in the Netherlands. The transmitted data were collected and stored in a central database. The market information from throughout Europe was analysed and compared (calculating price/quality ratios), leading to buying suggestions. After final expert analysis by the central EUROSELECT manager, those suggestions were channelled back to the local offices, which made buying suggestions available to the national partners and other selected wholesalers.

Second, there was the order–invoice cycle. The local offices collected orders and fed them to the EUROSELECT head office. All the ordering was done via the EUROSELECT head office. Orders could be 'local orders' resulting from local selling opportunities, meaning both wholesaler and supplier were located in the same country. Orders could also be 'bulk orders' meaning that the EUROSELECT central office bundled orders from various national offices and placed them wherever the terms were most favourable. Orders were transmitted from the national partners to EUROSELECT, EUROSELECT placed the orders with the selected suppliers. The goods were delivered directly to the local wholesalers but EUROSELECT was the official business partner of the producers. Thus EUROSELECT received the invoices and billed their wholesaler clients in turn after having added their own profit margin.

Technical integration with the national partners

So far, direct electronic communication between EUROSELECT and its national wholesale partners had not been implemented. IT used by the partners was not always compatible with PRODEC and the internal data structures were not compatible with those used by EUROSELECT. In the future, EUROSELECT might move to electronic exchange of information with the national partners and with the client wholesalers but for the time being the information exchange was paper-based.

The reality of EUROSELECT in use

Several years have now passed since the implementation of EUROSELECT in 1992. The use of technology had enabled EUROSELECT to move from a vision to a working business concept but how well was it really working?

The EUROSELECT components

The technology

The technological solution was working very well. The local offices gathered prices and collected new products for categorisation. Every night updated information from the local offices in the various European countries was sent to the central office in the Netherlands. In the morning the central office updated currencies and made adjustments to the price lists, which were then returned to the local offices. The product database was continually expanded; the pricing comparison module was efficient and effective.

Managing the business component of the information network involved keeping prices adjusted for currency fluctuations and keeping customers informed of product/price offerings.

Adjustments to the currency module of the system took place daily with actual market rates being entered at the start of every working day. A forecasting model was used to indicate likely fluctuations in exchange rates so that price lists could label products with realistic price tags. EUROSELECT tried to guarantee product prices for a limited period of time. It did sometimes happen that unexpected and extreme currency fluctuations within the set time period made a price-product offering unprofitable. In that case, EUROSELECT informed its customers that the price was no longer valid.

The network of partners

EUROSELECT depended for its success on the commitment from its national partners in each EU country. It was therefore important that the relationship with the partners was well-managed. Partners for the information-gathering component of EUROSELECT were chosen with great care. In order to protect the partner from possible difficulties with producers in their own country, the identity of EUROSELECT partners was kept quiet. Partners benefited from the network in two ways. The up-to-date price-product comparisons enabled them to make the best-price buying decisions. Partners also received a percentage of the profit from the EUROSELECT wholesaling function.

At the same time as helping and rewarding partners, the management at EUROSELECT were aware of potential difficulties with partners. EUROSELECT insisted on loyalty and fairness from partners and ended a partner relationship if the partnership was not working out. This had happened at least once during the first three years of operating. One reason for not linking electronically with partners was that EUROSELECT did not wish to feel too obliged or tied into their partners. The Managing Director was concerned that too much interlinking would create partnerships

that were potentially difficult to break off if necessary and that such interlinking represented a
considerable investment in the relationship.

Transport

EUROSELECT had anticipated that transport
prices might make certain wholesaling deals
unprofitable but in fact transport prices had
dropped and with improvements in the road
network lorries had no longer been obliged to
wait for a long time at European borders.

Logistics for the EUROSELECT international wholesaling operation were organised
as effectively as possible. Orders were not collected and stored in a wholesale warehouse.
Instead, EUROSELECT organised for local
transport companies to collect orders from the
suppliers and those orders were then directly
delivered to relevant customers. Since orders
were usually large, there was little need for complicated ways of combining products from
various suppliers or combining orders for different customers.

The European single market?

In spite of the success of translating the business
concept into a working operation and the ability
to leverage price differences across the EU, the
management of EUROSELECT were still disappointed with the results of their business
venture. They were not able to supply products
as easily as they had envisaged; they were not
able to sell any product from anywhere in the
EU to any other country.

The potential EU market for EURO-
SELECT's business was much greater than had
been realised. The unexpected difficulty had
arisen that individual governments had been
reluctant to adjust national legislation according
to the spirit of EU agreements. The single-
market concept of the EU required harmonisation of national guidelines, which was in reality
still a long way off with national legislation
modifying or contradicting official EU legislation. National legislation was frequently more
restrictive than that of the EU, with consequent
limits to full exploitation of the single market.

For the grocery industry there were problems with labelling products in the language of
the country where it was to be sold and the only
solution was to label products in a number of
languages. There were also problems with
national laws requiring different declarations of
ingredients.

Restrictive legislation was often aimed at
protecting the home market. France has traditionally been one of the most difficult grocery
markets to enter, given its strict language legislation and additional restrictive demands for
certificates of guarantee from producers, limiting the sale of foreign goods in the French
market.

Reactions from competitive forces in the industry

The development of the EUROSELECT
operation was a competitive move. The information network enabled access to lower prices.
VEH had been able to increase their market
share from Dutch regional wholesalers and
supermarkets to such customers throughout
Europe. The type of customer had remained the
same; it was more a question of geographical
spread.

Reactions from suppliers

The grip of producers on the grocery wholesaling market had tightened. While ten years ago
VEH might have had 1,000 suppliers, that
number had now reduced to some 400 suppliers. Such concentration among the producers
made it difficult for wholesalers to obtain
market prices for products. Producers could
behave as oligopolies and force prices up.

EUROSELECT's objective was to thwart such behaviour from producers.

Most producers were comfortable with EUROSELECT's buying behaviour. A handful of producers had consciously tried to prevent EUROSELECT from buying their products in a country where the product price was lowest. In several cases producers had tried to restrict sale of their products in the VEH supermarkets only and it took a number of such cases to clarify that inclusion of such a restrictive clause in contracts with EUROSELECT was not permissible.

Still other producers' strategies made it unprofitable for EUROSELECT to buy outside the intended country of sale. Ferrero maintained the same marketing strategy in different countries with price fluctuations never in excess of 10 per cent. With such low price differences buying elsewhere was not advantageous, given that transport costs and exchange rates could easily erode potential profit margins.

Reactions from competitors

Competitors had tried to imitate EUROSELECT's information system but no attempt had been successful. The enthusiasm and commitment of VEH in developing an appropriate system was difficult to emulate.

Competitors had approached EURO-SELECT with offers to buy the product classification scheme and the comparison algorithm. Major competitors with more international wholesaling experience than VEH had to admit that they did not have a system to match PRODEC. Up till now offers to buy the system had been firmly rejected. The primary reason for developing the system had been to leverage information in order to be able to compete against the large chains that now wanted to buy the system. Selling the knowledge of the system would undermine the exact reason why the system had been set up in the first place!

Case questions

1 How are the roles of IS (structuring, communicating, coordinating) illustrated in this case?
2 To what extent was the PRODEC system a success and how was this success achieved?
3 What were the main inhibiting factors to the EUROSELECT venture?
4 How do you think the system could be further developed in the future to enhance its competitive potential?

Index